Donated by
Carl Lambrecht
to The Heartland Institute

CONTEMPORARY SOVIET SOCIETY

CONTEMPORARY SOVIET SOCIETY

SOCIOLOGICAL PERSPECTIVES

Edited by
Jerry G. Pankhurst
and Michael Paul Sacks

FOREWORD
by Walter D. Connor

PRAEGER SPECIAL STUDIES • PRAEGER SCIENTIFIC

Library of Congress Cataloging in Publication Data
Main entry under title:

Contemporary Soviet society.

   Includes bibliographies and index.
   1. Russia--Social conditions--1970-
I. Pankhurst, Jerry G. II. Sacks, Michael Paul.
HN527.C66   947.085'3   80-22324
ISBN 0-03-055916-2
ISBN 0-03-055911-1 (pbk.)

947.0853
C761
cop. 1

Published in 1980 by Praeger Publishers
CBS Educational and Professional Publishing
A Division of CBS, Inc.
521 Fifth Avenue, New York, New York 10017 U.S.A.

© 1980 by Praeger Publishers

All rights reserved

0123456789 145 987654321

Printed in the United States of America

to Alex Simirenko
1931-79

FOREWORD
Walter D. Connor

More than a half century separates us from the time when the USSR was recognized as a new, revolutionary nation; when outsiders, who were generally dependent on their own ideological persuasions and levels of knowledge (or, more accurately, levels of ignorance) about Soviet reality, regarded it either as a promising experiment, a new civilization or as a new and intensified despotism that was more menacing to Western values and security than any previous threat.

Discordant perceptions persist today — especially about the USSR's external purpose and direction, and about the relationship between its military capacities and its geopolitical intentions. But over the years, the Soviet system — state, economy, and society — has matured and our knowledge of its internal workings has grown immensely. While huge gaps remain, *terra incognita* is no longer an apt description of our perceptions of Soviet life and the essays in this volume demonstrate that fact. Their focus is on society, not as a residuum to be analyzed after the operations of the political system and the economy have been adequately mapped, but as the broad context in which political and economic activities take place, and of which they must take account. Their focus is on people, despite the fact that much power has been withdrawn from the larger society by a self-perpetuating and highly centralized political leadership that has state control over the economy in a non-market system.

Soviet society presents many facets simultaneously and they are all, to one degree or another, touched on by the authors whose contributions follow. It is an imperial society, in the sense that more nationalities fall under its single government than in any other contemporary state, and that the state is dominated by the one largest nationality among them: the Russians. While not precisely resembling other past empires, the USSR as an imperial society is strikingly anachronistic. The first World War destroyed the great contiguous land empires, the Ottoman and Austro-Hungarian, and dissolved them into their several constituent parts. It also "destroyed" the Russian Empire, but in special sense for virtually all the lands under the Tsar in 1914 were, ten years later, reconstituted as the Soviet Union. World War II set in train the processes that dissolved the great sea-borne empires: French, British, Dutch. For the USSR, however, it proved no graveyard but the occasion for re-incorporation of the three Baltic states and the extension of Soviet hegemony, if not legal incorporation, to the states of Eastern Europe. As an empire, it has developed as well as exploited its colonies: the peoples of the Baltic, the Ukraine, the Caucasus and Central Asia, as well as other smaller groups. It has accelerated the economic development of some backward areas, but restricted as well the development of areas more advanced than Russia itself. But in a century of ever more assertive nationalism, it has conceded little or nothing to the aspirations of its peoples in a political sense and thus faces problems — and perhaps opportunities — unique among the world's states today.

Soviet society is simultaneously an industrial and a developing society. This somewhat paradoxical quality means that the USSR is either the most backward of the industrialized or developed societies, or the most advanced of the backward societies, or both. Impressive achievements in the industrial sector, especially heavy industry and the military branches, coexist with a laggard rural-agricultural sector still absorbing a great deal of labor, and a service sector woefully underdeveloped outside the spheres of education and health care. The USSR has come a long way in economic and demographic terms from the peasant-agrarian Russia of the imperial period, but is still far from transiting the second industrial revolution of chemicals, plastics, and solid-state circuitry that has seen the advanced Western nations move to economies where more than half the employed are neither workers (material producers) nor peasants, but purvey services of various sorts.

As an industrial society, the USSR has lowered birth and death rates. As a developing one, it has done this unevenly and faces in Central Asia extraordinarily high fertility and its uncertain consequences. As an industrial society, it has brought the vast majority of females into the labor force, but as a developing society it has not thereby liberated them from a disproportionate share of the traditional female tasks. As an industrial society, it has produced a military establishment and weapons technology that confer it undoubted superpower status. As a developing society, it has little slack left in an economy perhaps two-thirds the size of the United States, and thus provides living standards far below those of Americans. It is thus an amalgam of a peculiar sort, impressively advanced on certain dimensions, appallingly backward on others.

It is an inegalitarian society, as are all societies, and does not give the lie to its own ideology, since as a socialist state it countenances contribution according to ability and reward according to work, rather than the need that should determine distribution in a communist future. But as the reader will learn the USSR has generated its material inequalities in a nonmarket economy; one where employment in organization plays an even more critical role in the stratifying process, since private resource and enterprise are effectively closed off; one where money income does not reveal the full span of inequality, since so many scarce goods are distributed bureaucratically as occupation-tied perquisites rather than as property purchased by those with money. Educational attainment is the major mode of access to jobs at a given level and in this too initial inequalities — in family background, finances, ability to forego the income from a job taken rather than a higher education pursued, in geographic location and quality of prior schooling — all play a role in the assortment process that determines who continues and who doesn't. Children of workers, peasants, and the white collar strata are proportionally represented in the elementary grades, but by university entrance a skewed pictured of underrepresentation of the first two and overrepresentation of the third group emerges. Thus Soviet society — against the backdrop of an ideological commitment to substantially greater equality in the seemingly ever-receding communist future — must grapple today with the question not of whether it is an equal society, but whether it is, in distributive terms, a just one. The reader will learn that these are, even in the muted phrases of Soviet public discourse, disputed questions.

The USSR is an ideological society, in a very explicit sense. "Marxism-Leninism," the state ideology, the legitimation of Communist Party rule, may not and indeed does not suffuse the everyday perceptions of the Soviet masses. But it need not. The inculcation — through formal education from its most elementary stages leading up through the university, through the media, etc. — of a materialist, rationalist world view of an essentially optimistic perspective that assures Soviet citizens the right decisions were made at past historic turning points, guides them with Communist ideology, and convinces them that they are living through the process of carrying out those decisions, aims less at fixing this frame in people's minds than at excluding all alternatives. This ideological character, as well as the USSR's heritage, at least as a radically totalitarian society from the late 1920s up to Stalin's death in 1953, leads to a definition of some phenomena as problems that are not so regarded in more open societies, and to different ways of dealing with phenomena defined as problems in other societies.

The reader will see that religious belief and participation — surely evidence of adherence to an alternative ideology — is regarded as a problem rather than a tolerated exercise of choice. The Soviet war against religion has been hot and cold and has emphasized certain religions as targets, while deemphasizing others, but it has never altered its ideological stance enough to reach a principled co-existence with religion. There seems little likelihood that the future will see it do so.

Crime and related forms of social deviance persist, indeed, flourish in the USSR. Their nature and form have assumed many of the general characteristics that confirm the Soviet Union's status as one more industrial society among many. But criminal behavior poses, in its persistence, a special problem for a regime whose ideology dictated that crime flows from exploitation and the ancillary characteristics of capitalist systems. It should wither away under the different objective conditions of socialism. The citation of the lag in consciousness — the delay between the change to socialist objective conditions and their accurate reflection in the consciousness and behavior of citizens who are still influenced by a capitalism they never lived in — fails to convince outside observers and Soviet citizens alike. At the bottom of Soviet society, criminogenic conditions are experienced by many citizens in ways not at all mechanically dissimilar to their counterparts under capitalist systems. The USSR, like other societies, gets the crime it deserves. That it can handle it more directly, harshly, and in a sometime-someplace more effective way than open societies reflects an authoritarian-totalitarian heritage, as much as any innovations born of a different assessment of the root causes of criminality.

No introductory comments can reflect the diversity of subject matter and approach evident in the following chapters, which are the products of a group of experienced professionals, who have dealt with many facets of Soviet society beyond those I have dealt with here, and from which the reader will profit.

ACKNOWLEDGMENTS

This book represents a collaborative effort with the cooperation of many people. The contributors deserve our deep gratitude for their fine essays. They graciously made special efforts to tailor their pieces to the purposes of this book. While Mark Field's contribution represents an extensive revision of an earlier paper, all other chapters were written originally for this volume. We are particularly indebted to Richard Dobson and Mark Field because their papers were solicited rather late.

The support for this volume from Praeger Publishers was very encouraging, and we have especially appreciated the interest and patience of former editor Mary Curtis and current editor Lynda Sharp.

Michael Sacks would like to express appreciation to his wife, Deborah, for her criticism and comments on many sections of the manuscript and, as always, for her support and encouragement throughout the project.

Many others have played a role in the completion of this endeavor, and though we cannot name them all here, they have our heartfelt gratitude.

While beginning work on this volume, one of the first people we turned to for aid and advice was Alex Simirenko. He had gone out of his way to be supportive of our earlier efforts and we respect his own research and ideas. Alex was immediately enthusiastic about this project and we looked forward to his planned contribution. It was with great sadness that we learned of his death in April 1979. His inspiration and friendship prompted our dedication.

Finally, it should be noted that the editing of this book was a joint effort to which the co-editors have contributed equally.

CONTENTS

FOREWORD
by Walter D. Connor   vi

ACKNOWLEDGMENTS   x

List of Tables   xvi

List of Figures   xviii

List of Abbreviations and Acronyms   xix

INTRODUCTION   1
       Michael Paul Sacks and Jerry G. Pankhurst

    Sociology and Soviet Area Studies   3
    Soviet Sociological Data   4
    References   9

1   THE ETHNIC DIMENSION OF THE SOVIET UNION, PART I   11
       Ralph S. Clem

    The Ethnic Composition of the Soviet Population   12
    The Formation of the Multiethnic Soviet State   13
       The Tsarist Legacy   13
       Ethnicity and Revolution   17
    Socioeconomic Development and Ethnicity
      in the USSR   21
       Soviet Nationality Policy   21
       Ethnic Groups and Development: The Reality   23
    References   30

2   **THE ETHNIC DIMENSION, PART II**   32

   Ralph S. Clem

   The Nature of Ethnic Group Relations   33
      The Ethnic Factor   34
      Ethnic Stratification   36
      Ethnicity, Federalism, and Territoriality   38
      Summary   40
   The Ethnic Situation in the USSR from a
      Comparative Perspective   41
      Ethnic Stratification Under the Tsars   41
      Ethnic Stratification and Development:
        The Soviet Experience   43
      Assimilation   47
   The Implications of Ethnicity for Contemporary
      and Future Soviet Society   53
      The Population Growth Dichotomy   53
      Ethnicity and Federalism   55
      Conclusions   57
   References   60

3   **POPULATION POLICY**   63

   David M. Heer

   Views of Marx and Engels on Population Policy   63
   History of Soviet Population Policy and
      Legislation from 1917 to the Present   64
      Legislation without Population Policy   66
      The Turn to Population Policy   68
   Three Current Issues in Soviet Population Policy   73
   Soviet Population Policy in Cross-National
      Perspective   80
   Difficulties in Studying Soviet Population Policy   82
   Prognosticating Future Shifts in Population Policy
      in the Soviet Union   83
   References   86

4   **SOCIALISM AND SOCIAL STRATIFICATION**   88

   Richard B. Dobson

   Comparisons with Western Countries   89

    Occupational Stratification   93
    Differences in Income and Standard of Living   97
    Attitudinal and Behavioral Correlates of
       Socioeconomic Status   102
    Occupational Mobility   106
    Conclusion   111
    References   112

5   **EDUCATION AND OPPORTUNITY**   **115**

    Richard B. Dobson

    Main Features of the Soviet Educational System   118
    Recent Research on Educational Attainment   120
    Access to Higher Education   127
    Equality of Opportunity and Educational Policy   131
    Conclusion   133
    References   135

6   **OBSERVATIONS ON RURAL LIFE IN SOVIET RUSSIA**   **138**

    Roy D. Laird and Ronald A. Francisco

    From Village to Collective Farm   140
    The Private Sector   144
    The State as Landlord   145
    Brigades and the *Zveno*   146
    The *Dvor*   147
    Advancement and Migration   150
    The Social and Political Orientation of
       the Soviet Peasantry   152
    References   154

7   **SOVIET SOCIETY AND COMMUNIST PARTY CONTROLS:
    A CASE OF "CONSTRICTED" DEVELOPMENT**   **156**

    Mark G. Field

    "Cult of the Personality," or "Cult of the Party"?   159
    Societal Evolution and Differentiation   161
    The Nature of Soviet Society   167
       Soviet Culture: National Communism   167

Political Structure: One-Party Rule
   or Monocracy   169
Economic Structure: Industrialism   170
The Question of Relative "Undifferentiation"   172
   The Limits of Cultural Differentiation   174
   The Limits of Economic Differentiation   176
   The Limits of Political Differentiation   178
Conclusions   178
References   180

8 RELIGION AND ATHEISM IN THE USSR   182

Jerry G. Pankhurst

Major Soviet Religious Groups   183
Soviet Atheism and Interest-Group Conflict   186
Options for Antireligious Policy   190
The Khrushchev Campaign and Its Effects   195
Current Religious Conditions   199
References   204

9 CRIME AND DELINQUENCY IN THE SOVIET UNION   208

Louise Shelley

Contemporary Soviet Criminology   209
The Soviet Theory of Crime   210
The Geography of Soviet Crime   214
Offenders and Their Offenses   217
The Sex of Offenders   219
Social Characteristics of Offenders   220
Patterns of Crime Commission   221
Political Crime   221
Recidivism   222
Conclusion   224
References   225

10 THE PLACE OF WOMEN   227

Michael Paul Sacks

Theoretical Perspectives   228
The Case of Soviet Russia   230

      Employment in Tsarist Russia   230
      Female Labor: Supply and Demand   231
The Consequences of Nonagrarian Employment   235
The Change in Beliefs About Women   240
Explaining the Continuity in Occupational
    Sex Differences   243
Conclusion   249
References   250

SUGGESTED READINGS   **254**

AUTHOR INDEX   **259**

SUBJECT INDEX   **261**

ABOUT THE EDITORS AND CONTRIBUTORS   **273**

LIST OF TABLES

Table		Page
1.1	Population of Major Soviet Ethnic Groups: 1959, 1970, and 1979	14
1.2	Level of Urbanization of Ethnic Units and Major Ethnic Groups, USSR: 1926, 1959, and 1970	24
1.3	Selected Socioeconomic and Demographic Characteristics of Major Soviet Ethnic Groups, 1970	29
3.1	Schedule of Payments to Mothers of Large Families and to Unmarried Mothers in the USSR	69
3.2	Index Numbers For Incidence of Abortions: Soviet Union, 1954-66	70
3.3	Relative size of 1947 and 1974 Child-Allowance Payments for Various Types of Families	73
3.4	Percentage of Population of Each Major Islamic Nationality Speaking Russian as Native or Second Language, 1970	80
4.1	Decile Ratios for Wages and Family per Capita Income (State Sector Only): USSR, Selected Year, 1928-75	99
4.2	Monthly Wages and Salaries for Selected Highly Paid Occupations: USSR, Early 1970s	100
4.3	Intergenerational Mobility in Kazan: Rates of Outflow	107
4.4	Intergenerational Mobility in Kazan: Rates of Inflow from the Manual Strata	108
5.1	Eighth Graders' Educational Plans, as Related to Father's Education and Own Grades: Syzran, 1968	122
5.2	Percentage of Eighth-Grade Pupils Continuing in the Ninth Grade, by Grade-Point Average and Parents' Occupational Status: Leningrad, 1968	123
5.3	Relationship of Graduating Seniors' College Plans to Family Income: USSR and United States	125
6.1	Urban and Rural Population of the USSR, 1913-79	141
6.2	Number and Size of Soviet Farms, 1940 and 1977	143
6.3	Percentage of *Sovkhoz* Households with Modern Amenities, 1975	148
6.4	Average Monthly Wages in 1978	151
8.1	Religious Organizations and Groups in Rostov Oblast, 1917 and 1972	202
9.1	Percentage Distribution of Convictions in the USSR, by Category of Offense, Circa 1960 and 1976	217
9.2	Rates of Recidivism for Murderers and Rapists, 1926-66	223

Table		Page
10.1	Employed Persons in the Russian Republic with a Higher and with a Secondary Education, by Sex: 1939, 1959, 1970	232
10.2	The Standardized Measure of Occupational Differentiation by Sex: 1939, 1959, 1970	246
10.3	The Educational Attainment of Men Compared with Women and of Russian Women Compared with Women of the Indigenous Nationality, by Republic: 1939, 1959, 1970	248

LIST OF FIGURES

Figure		Page
3.1	Birth and Death Rates in the Russian Empire and the Soviet Union, 1861-1977	65
4.1	"Factual" and "Ideal" Models of the Social Structure of the Rural Population, Krasnodar Region and Kalinin Province	96
5.1	Effect of Family Income on Plans for Higher Education, with Grades Controlled: Syzran, 1968	126
8.1	The "Hyperbolic Principle" of Church-State Relations in the USSR	193

LIST OF ABBREVIATIONS AND ACRONYMS

ASSR	Autonomous Soviet Socialist Republic
AUCECB	All-Union Council of Evangelical Christians-Baptists
CCECB	Council of Churches of Evangelical Christians and Baptists
CPSU	Communist Party of the Soviet Union
ECB	Evangelical Christians and Baptists
IREX	International Research and Exchanges Board
Komsomol	Young Communist League
MTS	machine-tractor station
MVD	Ministry of Internal Affairs
RSFSR	Russian Socialist Federated Soviet Republic
samizdat	self-published material circulated from hand to hand in the USSR; unofficial or underground literature
SSR	Soviet Socialist Republic
Ts.S.U.	Central Statistical Administration of the USSR Council of Ministers
Ts.S.U. RSFSR	Central Statistical Administration of the RSFSR Council of Ministers
USSR	Soviet Union; Union of Soviet Socialist Republics
VUZ	higher educational institution (plural: *VUZy*)

CONTEMPORARY SOVIET SOCIETY

INTRODUCTION
Michael Paul Sacks and Jerry G. Pankhurst

The Soviet Union (USSR) is an ideal social science laboratory. It is richly diverse in geographic regions, languages, cultures, religions, and population structure—in fact, its diversity extends to virtually all dimensions of social life. Furthermore, in this century the USSR has experienced extremely rapid social change. In this context the examination of a very wide range of social processes can be particularly enlightening.

One of the major purposes of this book is to inform a large audience about what kinds of sociological investigations can be done and are being done on Soviet society. The writers of the essays that follow are among a growing group of specialists who explore the USSR from a sociological orientation.

Its superpower status makes it an object of interest for many people, but there have long been major barriers hindering understanding of the USSR. The cultural differences from the West have often led Western observers to attribute all sorts of phenomena to the "inscrutability" of Russian or Soviet culture. Such a position has been fostered in part by the general lack of knowledge of the Russian language and, even more so, of the other languages of the Soviet peoples. In this regard, the support for language and cross-cultural studies provided by the National Defense Foreign Language fellowships and the International Research and Exchanges Board (IREX), among others, has encouraged some social scientists to develop a specialty in Soviet studies. In cooperation with the Social Science Research Council and the American Council of Learned Societies, IREX has sponsored many extended research visits to the USSR. These have provided social scientists with the firsthand experience that enriches their research and helps break down the barrier of the great distance separating the USSR from the United States and other Western countries, a barrier that supports the feeling that the Soviet Union is particularly strange.

In enlarging our knowledge and understanding of the Soviet Union, overcoming the barriers of distance, language, and cultural differences is easier than overcoming other barriers that are lodged solidly in our perceptions and thinking about the Soviet Union. The Soviet Union is a gigantic social experiment in progress, the largest sustained attempt to establish and develop Marxian socialism. While the diversity of Soviet society offers great potential for examining relationships between social variables, the fact that it is "someone else's" ongoing experiment has deterred in various ways the adequate analysis of this fascinating social system.

Marxist politics has been found unacceptable by the majority of Western social scientists, and because of their opposition to the revolutionary orientation in particular, they often have not examined the Soviet system without first judging it. Frequently the Communist party leadership has been seen as the Doctor Frankenstein of the Soviet experiment. Such a view was enhanced by the excesses of Stalinism, and is sustained by the current policy toward dissenters, the sometimes authoritarian prerogatives of centralized economic planning, and other factors.

While no one will claim that the Soviet Union is without blemish, and many will find significant inequities and injustices in the USSR, the development of an adequate sociology of the USSR demands that prejudgments be put aside and that the society be examined "as it is." This is particularly difficult when the prevailing world politics estranges the USSR from the West, as was the case in the "Cold War" of the 1940s, 1950s, and 1960s. While the debate over models of Soviet society (see, for instance Simirenko 1966a, 1971; Hough 1977; Breslauer 1978; Taubman 1974; and the essay by Field in this volume) cannot be fully addressed here, it reflects a self-consciousness about approaches to Soviet studies that is very healthy because it requires that our prejudgments be the object of consideration.

Another significant means of reducing bias is to examine the USSR in comparative perspective. Such an approach seeks not only to understand specific local or national conditions, but also to establish patterns that have some degree of universality (see, for example, Przeworski and Teune 1970). Precisely because the USSR is so culturally distinct and because it is socialist—that is, paradoxically, because of characteristics that have stood as barriers to our understanding—the Soviet Union is an important case to examine in a complete comparative sociology (compare Flerom 1969).

In comparative sociology, relationships found to exist in one setting must be examined in significantly different settings before they can be generally accepted. Although sociologists have largely given up on finding the "laws" of social life, they still seek to establish the relationships between such variables as age, sex, religion, economic status, education, occupation, criminal patterns, various aspects of urban and rural life, and myriad others. Thus, research on the Soviet Union can be very useful in clarifying the extent to which one can generalize about social processes from research on the United States or other societies. For this reason, the comparative approach is a subtheme within each of the essays in this book.

SOCIOLOGY AND SOVIET AREA STUDIES

Soviet area studies emerged as a distinct quasi discipline of teaching and research after World War II, and from the start sociologists have been involved in the effort to comprehend the Soviet Union. However, due to the variability of interests and activities among sociologists, they generally have not been as fully involved in Soviet studies as is desirable. Unfortunately, within some sociological circles, all area studies are decidedly deemphasized and even occasionally denigrated as atheoretical or amateurish. At least for Soviet area studies, this evaluation arises partly because a few sociologists tend to include in Soviet area studies all writings on the USSR, including many that are indeed amateurish. Also, research on the Soviet Union has not always had a clearly sound data base, a problem that is abating. Finally, too many scholars in the field of Soviet area studies have tended to treat the USSR as a unique case having nothing in common with other societies. This orientation is rapidly being altered, and some of the credit must be given to the increasing acceptance of the general methods and approaches of social science within the field of Soviet area studies.

Sociology has a problem similar to that of area studies. As more and more sociologists are realizing, the discipline of sociology is often in danger of being only a variety of "American studies," or at best "Western society studies," even though sociological theory claims much broader applicability. This assertion denies neither the importance of the contributions on Soviet society (or Third World societies) that sociologists have made in the past, nor the significance of social science research on the USSR done in allied disciplines. However, it does indicate that there is a need and a desire for more extensive use of Soviet studies and other area studies research in sociological discourse.

Given these problems of both sociology and Soviet area studies, it has become widely recognized that a greater involvement of sociologists in the study of the USSR would be helpful both to Soviet studies and to sociology—to Soviet studies because it would heighten awareness in areas that are of special concern for sociologists, and to sociology because it would broaden the comparative understandings of sociologists. Significant support for this viewpoint is indicated by the fact that encouragement for training of sociologists in Soviet studies is a high priority for IREX, for the National Defense Foreign Language fellowship program, and for other agencies and organizations. (Indeed, several of the contributors to this volume have benefited from support from such groups.)

A fundamental aim in compiling this volume has been to foster the integration of sociology and the study of the USSR. The more immediate stimulus was to provide a text for our students in classes on Soviet society and comparative sociology. The growing number of social scientists engaged in study of the USSR since 1970 or so has generated an impressive body of research. However, this material is widely scattered in various journals and other publications. Recent accounts of contemporary Soviet society by newspaper journalists have enjoyed considerable popularity, but they are unsatisfying in many respects. While journalistic accounts have their place, they often neglect to incorporate Western scholarship. They also tend to generalize solely on the basis of personal experience or of a limited circle of individuals, despite the availability of significant statistical data and empirical research from the USSR.

Each of the contributors to this volume has extensively studied primary sources from the Soviet Union. In addition to sociologists, two political scientists (Roy D. Laird and Ronald A. Francisco), a geographer (Ralph S. Clem), and a criminologist (Louise Shelley) are among them. Indeed, we feel that the research and theory in each chapter clearly transcend the parochial boundaries of any single social science discipline.

What has made the analysis in each essay possible is the proliferation of research in the USSR since the late 1950s, after a hiatus of more than two decades. The field of Soviet studies has come a long way since the years when Western scholars were almost entirely dependent on the data they culled from émigrés who left the USSR during and just after World War II (see Inkeles and Bauer 1959). While information from recent émigrés and the underground literature that comes out of the Soviet Union are currently valuable for many analytical purposes, a vast range of data is now also available from official sources.

The first Soviet statistical handbook since the late 1930s appeared in the spring of 1956, and later that year the chief of the Central Statistical Bureau of the USSR acknowledged the change in policy in his direct criticism of the past: "A majority of the State and department accounting and statistics were unnecessarily made secret or were put aside into materials not subject to press publication. And until recently, statistical data were not published" (cited in Feshbach 1972, p. 196). Particularly significant was the publication in the early 1960s of the results of the recently completed 1959 census along with results of the 1939 census that had not previously appeared.

SOVIET SOCIOLOGICAL DATA

It is instructive to look briefly at the processes underlying the emergence of modern sociology in the USSR, for this indicates some characteristics that must be taken into account when using the products of the Soviet sociological enterprise. During the Stalin years, the philosophy and ideology that were favored by the elite constituted the only legitimate "sociology." The post-Stalin emergence of Western-style sociology was related to four factors. The first two—the reinvigoration of the Marxist-Leninist vision, and change in the Soviet ideology—opened the possibility for the development of sociology, while the other two—the diffusion of ideas, and problems in the Soviet economy—gave a direction to the intellectual pursuits that were now possible.

First, the Marxist-Leninist vision provided a utopian ideal that allegedly could be achieved through altering social conditions. Lewis A. Coser (1965, p. 167) considered this utopian vision to have been lost under Stalin, when "understanding" in order to know how to direct change was replaced by the blindness of bureaucratic power. Although power was a rational instrument for social direction under Lenin and the early Bolsheviks, it became usurped by nonrationalists and bureaucrats. The vision reemerged after Stalin, however, to allow for development of scientific sociology. (See George Fischer's [1967] comments on "future orientation" among Soviet sociologists.)

The second factor allowing for the emergence of Soviet sociology after Stalin was change in the Soviet ideology. Under Stalin, every intellectual activity was measured against a single ideological norm, and variations from the norm were not permitted. After Stalin's death, the ideological restrictions were eased so that new variations of thinking were allowed. Karl Mannheim (1936, pp. 55-70) might describe this change as a move from a "general" to a "particular" ideology, where the general ideology is considered applicable in virtually all spheres of life and the particular ideology is applicable to a more delimited set of activities. Allen Kassof (1968, p. 44) has written that the true ideology of the 1960s was a matter of "a compulsive dream of beehive order projected on an entire society...." In a sense, then, content of social life was secondary to smooth operation within the bureaucratic state organization. In addition, there was less of an emphasis on the ideology as the sole source of truth. As the imputation of significant political content in ideas became more delimited in its range, more of the common concerns of sociology emerged from beneath the ideological umbrella to a place where they could be examined with greater detachment.

The third factor in the emergence of post-Stalin Soviet sociology—the diffusion of ideas—could provide some direction to scholarly pursuits only after the Marxist-Leninist vision was reenlivened and the ideology was made less restrictive. The diffusion of ideas affected developments because exposure to the sociological inquiry in other countries provided the Soviets with a model of detached, critical analysis conducted by specialized professionals (see Simirenko 1973). Such exposure was greatly enhanced by sending delegations to the congresses of the International Sociological Association (Fischer 1964; Kassof 1965; article by Labedz in Simirenko 1966a; Katz 1971; and Chapter 7, section "The Limits of Cultural Differentiation," in this volume). Of particular importance were the growing encounters with Polish sociologists (Bauman 1976), for Poland had a strong sociological tradition that became especially influential after the nation became part of the Communist bloc following WW II. The diffusion of ideas from these sources was also fostered by the return to the sociological tradition that had existed before the Stalin period. Indeed, the encounters may also have encouraged this return in the search for an appropriate Soviet model of the discipline.

Finally, the particular content to infuse the sociological form was mandated by the economic development of the USSR (see Lane 1970; Allen 1965). What emerged was largely a sociology of work and industry, and of topics concerning the development of the labor force. This, of course, directly reflected ideological priorities, but probably was also strongly related to the emerging economic problems of the USSR at the beginning of the 1960s. Planners were refocusing attention upon the motivation and skills of workers as a source of increased productivity, whereas earlier they had stressed the sheer accumulation of capital stock.

With the diffusion of ideas providing the form of sociology and the needs of the Soviet economy providing the major content, Soviet sociology grew quickly after about 1956 (Lane 1970; Simirenko 1976), and has become a very large enterprise.

Today there is an extensive and growing body of published data and empirical studies. There is evidence of enhanced exposure to Western social science literature and methodology, although the references in Soviet monographs and articles are frequently to outdated sources, and the training of researchers in quantitative analysis remains clearly inferior to that of their counterparts in the West. Also, as Mark Field shows in its broader context in Chapter 7 of this volume, trends in the discipline have not been consistent. Although Stalin's demise led to a distinct "thaw," so that the flow of ideas and the publishing and conduct of research increased greatly, cold spells have not been entirely eliminated. This is illustrated by the statistical handbook for the USSR. For the year 1955 it contained 263 pages; for 1973 the 880 pages were more densely packed with figures; but 1978 yielded only 631 pages. (See Chapter 3, section "Difficulties in Studying Soviet Population Policy," in this volume, for some of the subjects no longer included.)

Scholars studying Soviet society quickly learn that available sources are deficient in certain respects and that there is a special craft to using them. The empirical studies and statistics seem like scattered pieces of an intricate puzzle made more complex by the fact that only selected pieces are available. And of these, some are utterly useless, for they pertain to pictures that are based on ideology and have little correspondence to reality. But after sorting and arranging what can be found, we step back from the puzzle, squint, and attempt to describe what appear to be the true contours of the society. When asked for precision, for three-dimensional pictures (in color no less!), it is not surprising that our representations of contemporary Soviet life may differ somewhat.

Biases in Soviet monographs are blatant and usually consistent. Returning to the metaphor, it is as though the Soviet scholars know certain critical dimensions that are going to appear in the puzzle image they describe: in the distance is the utopia, but it is definitely within reach and the USSR is directly on the path to it. Capitalism is in dark colors and heading in an opposing direction; socialism emblazons the foreground. The primary theme is always this contrast between capitalism and socialism. The superiority of socialism is never in doubt.

Western scholars often will automatically discard the interpretations and repetitious discussion in Soviet sources and skip directly to the concrete findings. One first quickly thumbs through the pages of the monograph or article until the names of Marx, Engels, Lenin, and the current leader disappear from the footnotes at the bottom of the page. Then comes the cautious search for the pieces of the puzzle. Sometimes there is a casual mention of a figure conspicuously absent from the statistical handbook or the published census volumes. There are the extremely revealing discussions of policy and social problems in a specialized journal that never appear in periodicals aimed at a broader public (see Hough and Fainsod 1979, pp. 293-97). But even in the popular press there is the rich information that can be gained from letters to the editor and the responses by social scientists, legal and medical experts, and Communist party officials.

On the other hand, one is also confronted with strange tables percentaged in the wrong direction or failing to total 100 percent where they should. Instead of providing raw data, there are frequently only percentages, so that no corrections can be made. Often there is little or no discussion of sampling techniques or even of the sample size.

In spite of these problems, careful training in the social science disciplines and knowledge of how to utilize Soviet sources allow us to gather substantial data on a wide variety of subjects. The essays in this volume reveal how impressive the rewards can be.

Unquestionably, research methods and tools (including the use of computer technology) have aided Western social scientists in more fully exploiting scant or faulty data. Such ingenuity and sophistication may have revealed far more about the USSR than was intended by those responsible for deciding what should be published or withheld. Indeed, this may in part have resulted in the use of more stringent standards by Soviet censors (see Sacks, forthcoming).

An important skill for evaluating and interpreting Soviet publications is the ability to judge what kinds of findings are reasonable and how results might have been distorted by shortcomings in the way the subject was studied. This is where knowledge of social science as it has emerged in the West is exceedingly valuable. Research and theory can suggest not only what is most significant to look for and the questions that can contribute to the advancement of the general understanding of social processes, but also what findings are expected or are absurd or very improbable. Thus, we must maintain an informed skepticism. At the same time we must be careful to recognize what is unique and a challenge to prior knowledge and modes of explanation.

Unfortunately, it still remains common for Sovietologists to overemphasize the extent to which the Soviet Union is a distinct case or one that must be compared only with other Communist states. Such a view actually compliments Soviet scholars' stress upon the uniqueness of socialism. But, of course, the value judgments are reversed: much Western scholarship is strongly oriented to disclose the unfulfilled promises of the 1917 Revolution and the great distance from current Soviet society to any utopia. (Clem describes how this works in the study of ethnicity at the beginning of Chapter 2.) This, again, hinders recognition of the similarities between nations and the applicability of the same theories to both Communist and capitalist societies. (See the related exchange between Paul Hollander and Alex Simirenko, both sociologists: Simirenko 1974a, 1974b; Hollander 1974.) Furthermore, it is our view that only by taking a broader comparative perspective, well grounded in social science research and theory, is it possible to discern accurately the features of a society that are distinctly attributable to the political structure and ideology.

It is our hope that this book will stimulate the exchange of ideas and information. In the first place, a dialogue among teachers, scholars, and students should be fostered. The book has been organized as a reader-text for use in a broad range of classes, and suggested readings for each chapter have been included at the back of the book. Second, the dialogue between area specialists and sociologists should be encouraged by this book. Questions (and some criticisms) have been posed here that deserve the attention of a broad social science audience. Third, insofar as the book achieves some public attention—as we believe it should—it represents a communication between Soviet specialists and that general public. Given the political currents of the present time, there should be no doubt about the potential utility of such an exchange.

Finally, it is hoped that this book will be examined by Soviet social scientists. We have been frank about problems with Soviet social science here, and both covert and overt criticisms are found elsewhere in the book. While this has not been our primary aim, it is necessarily part of our dealing with Soviet research materials. As we learn a great deal from using these materials, we hope that Soviet readers will accept our evaluations as expressions of our interest in the development of world sociology (see the related remarks on criminology by Louise Shelley in Chapter 9, section "Contemporary Soviet Criminology," in this volume), and not as attempts to discredit their activities in a political or ideological way. Indeed, our strong criticisms of Western social science reflect the same interest in world sociology.

We believe that the essays below demonstrate the value of examining Soviet society in order to test hypotheses about social life. They provide the reader with an appreciation of the diversity of Soviet society, an insight into the processes that have sustained or given rise to this diversity, and an assessment of the potential directions of future change and conflict. While not a comprehensive treatment of Soviet society, the book reviews major institutions that are fundamental for understanding contemporary conditions. Not all of the authors agree completely with the editors' orientation to Soviet studies, but we feel that each has demonstrated the contribution that the sociological perspective can make to the field.

REFERENCES

Allen, Robert V. 1965. "Recent Soviet Literature in Sociology and Cultural Anthropology." *Quarterly Review of the Library of Congress* 22:246-58.

Bauman, Zygmunt. 1976. "East European and Soviet Social Science: A Case Study in Stimulus Diffusion." In *The Influence of East Europe and the Soviet West on the USSR*, edited by Roman Szporluk, pp. 91-116. New York: Praeger.

Breslauer, George W. 1978. *Five Images of the Soviet Future: A Critical Review and Synthesis*. Berkeley: Institute of International Studies, University of California.

Coser, Lewis A. 1965. *Men of Ideas*. New York: Free Press.

Feshbach, Murray. 1972. "Soviet Industrial Labor and Productivity Statistics." In *Soviet Economic Statistics*, edited by Vladimir G. Treml and John P. Hardt, pp. 195-228. Durham, N.C.: Duke University Press.

Fischer, George. 1964. *Science and Politics: The New Sociology in the Soviet Union*. Ithaca, N.Y.: Center for International Studies, Cornell University.

———. 1967. *Science and Ideology in Soviet Society*. New York: Atherton.

Fleron, Frederic J., Jr., ed. 1969. *Communist Studies and the Social Sciences: Essays on Methodology and Empirical Theory*. Chicago: Rand McNally.

Hollander, Paul. 1974. "The Persisting Limitations of and Obstacles to the 'Professionalization' of Politics in the Soviet Union: A Comment on Simirenko's 'Professionalization of Politics and Tension Management.'" *Sociological Quarterly* 15 (Winter):32-34.

Hough, Jerry F. 1977. *The Soviet Union and Social Science Theory*. Cambridge, Mass.: Harvard University Press.

Hough, Jerry F., and Merle Fainsod. 1979. *How Russia Is Ruled*. Rev. ed. Cambridge, Mass.: Harvard University Press.

Inkeles, Alex, and Raymond Bauer. 1959. *The Soviet Citizen: Daily Life in a Totalitarian Society*. Cambridge, Mass.: Harvard University Press.

Kassof, Allen. 1965. "American Sociology Through Soviet Eyes." *American Sociological Review* 30:114-21.

———. 1968. "Totalitarianism Without Terror." In *Liberalization in the USSR: Facade or Reality?* edited by D. Richard Little, pp. 37-46. Lexington, Mass.: D. C. Heath.

Katz, Zev. 1971. "Sociology in the Soviet Union." *Problems of Communism* 30:22-40.

Lane, David. 1970. "Ideology and Sociology in the USSR." *British Journal of Sociology* 21:43-51.

Mannheim, Karl. 1936. *Ideology and Utopia*. New York: Harcourt, Brace, and World.

Przeworski, Adam, and Henry Teune. 1970. *The Logic of Comparative Social Inquiry*. New York: Wiley-Interscience.

Sacks, Michael Paul. "Missing Female Occupational Categories in the Soviet Censuses." *Slavic Review*, forthcoming.

Simirenko, Alex. 1966a. "Models and Issues in the Analysis of Soviet Society." *Survey* (July): 3-17.

———. ed. 1966b. *Soviet Sociology: Historical Antecedents and Current Appraisals*. Chicago: Quadrangle.

———. 1971. "Models of Communist Societies: Towards a Therapogenic Model." *Newsletter on Comparative Studies of Communism* 5 (Nov.):25-39.

———. 1973. "Soviet and American Sociology in the Seventies." *Studies in Comparative Communism* 6:27-50.

———. 1974a. "Professionalization of Politics and Tension Management: The Case of the Soviet Union." *Sociological Quarterly* 15 (Winter):20-31.

———. 1974b. "Sociological Theory and the Communist Countries: A Rejoinder to Hollander." *Sociological Quarterly* 15 (Winter):35-37.

———. 1976. "Sociology in the Soviet Union: The State of the Discipline." Paper presented at the annual meeting of the Canadian Association of Slavists, Quebec City, June 1.

Taubman, William. 1974. "The Change to Change in Communist Systems: Modernization, Postmodernization, and Soviet Politics." In *Soviet Politics and Society in the 1970's,* edited by Henry W. Morton and Rudolf L. Tokes, pp. 369-94. New York: Free Press.

1

THE ETHNIC DIMENSION OF THE SOVIET UNION, PART I
Ralph S. Clem

    Without much doubt the most important feature of contemporary Soviet society is ethnicity.* The fundamental importance of ethnicity as a social and political force in the Soviet Union (USSR) derives first of all from the fact that the country is one of the world's most ethnically heterogeneous states, in terms of both the number of ethnic groups included in its population and the diversity among them. Further, the Soviet Union throughout its history has been in the throes of massive economic and social change and, at times, traumatic events, all of which have catapulted the ethnic issue to center stage. It is not ususual, therefore, that since World War II an ever-increasing interest in this vital ethnic dimension of the USSR has been evidenced, an interest inspired by the rise of the Soviet Union to the status of a major power in international affairs, by heightened consciousness among ethnic émigré communities in the West, by the transnational politicization of ethnicity in issues such as the

---

    *There is great confusion over, and many definitions of, the term "ethnic group" and its quality, "ethnicity." Not wanting to add to either the confusion or the number of definitions, in this essay what is employed is the definition of ethnic groups put forth by William Foltz (1974), with the understanding that there is no universally accepted usage and this is simply one among many (but, I believe, a good one). Foltz suggested that properties of an ethnic group would include shared physical characteristics, a common culture, linguistic affinity, and unique social-structural organization. Importantly, Foltz also warned against using these properties in presence-absence fashion; rather, he advocated a "clustering" approach and the avoidance of precisely defined interethnic boundaries. For a discussion of the problems of usage connected with terms such as "ethnicity," "nationalism," "nation-state," "tribe," and so on, see Walker Connor (1978).

emigration of Soviet Jews and the treatment of dissidents, and—perhaps most important—by the realization that problems stemming from multiethnicity in any setting are not as transitory as once believed, and must therefore command greater attention.

THE ETHNIC COMPOSITION OF THE SOVIET POPULATION

The Union of Soviet Socialist Republics ranks third among the countries of the world in population size (behind only the People's Republic of China and India); however, it is not the magnitude, but the ethnic heterogeneity of the Soviet population, that is of particular importance. The 1979 Soviet census listed about 100 different ethnic groups; and although many are quite small in numbers, at that time there were 22 groups with populations in excess of 1 million and another 29 groups larger than 100,000 persons (Table 1.1).

The cultural diversity among these ethnic groups (or, in Soviet parlance, nationalities) is remarkable, so much so that it is difficult to describe their attributes briefly. For illustrative purposes, we will consider in detail only those nationalities with over 1 million members.* Our description will focus on two key elements of ethnic culture: language and religion. It should be noted here that within language groups there are different degrees of mutual intelligibility among the individual tongues, and that religious affiliation refers to that belief historically associated with each ethnic group but says nothing about the strength of attachment to the various faiths (See Matthews 1951; Katz, Rogers, and Harned 1975; Goldhagen 1968; Aspaturian 1968).

By far the numerically largest of all the ethnic groups in the USSR is the Russians, who are slightly more than a majority of the population. Closely related to the Russians linguistically (all speak Slavic languages) are the Ukrainians (second in size and easily the largest minority) and the Belorussians (fourth in size). In terms of religious affiliation (See the paper by Pankhurst in this volume), Russians are Eastern Orthodox Christian, and Ukrainians and Belorussians divide between Orthodox and Catholic. After the three major Slavic nationalities, the largest bloc of ethnic groups is the Muslim peoples: the Uzbeks, Tatars, Kazakhs, Azeri, Turkmen, Kirgiz, Bashkirs, and Tadzhiks. With the exception of the Tadzhiks, who speak a

---

*The terminological chaos that reigns supreme in the field of ethnic studies is very much in evidence in the Soviet academic literature on the subject. The Soviet census enumerated people according to the "nationality" *(natsional'nost')* that they provided to the census taker. In the simplest meaning of this word, it is probably a good operational definition of "ethnic group," and the two terms are used interchangeably here. Also, enumeration of ethnic groups by self-identification, as is the practice in the Soviet census, is the preferred method of determining ethnic affiliation.

language related to Persian, the languages of these peoples are from the Turkic group.

Two other major Soviet nationalities, the Armenians and the Georgians, are both Christian peoples (of different rites) who speak distinctive languages. The three Baltic nationalities—the Estonians, Latvians, and Lithuanians—are generally regarded as the most "European" of the Soviet ethnic groups. Estonians and most Latvians adhere to the Lutheran denomination, while the Lithuanians and a minority of Latvians are Roman Catholics. Linguistically, Estonians speak a Finnic language and Latvians and Lithuanians, Baltic languages.

The Moldavians are akin to the Romanians (whose country adjoins the Soviet Union); they speak a dialect of Romanian and share the Orthodox faith. Of the remaining larger ethnic groups, the Mordvinians and the Chuvash are both religiously affiliated with the Orthodox Church but have different linguistic origins; Mordvinian is a Finnic tongue, while Chuvash is of the Turkic group. Finally, Soviet Jews, Germans, and Poles are foreign groups descended from immigrants or from people living in border territories annexed into the Soviet Union.

The foregoing is meant to demonstrate the range of cultural traits found among the Soviet nationalities. However, without going into additional detail, the point must be made that ethnic diversity is far more complex than this simple sketch illustrates. The host of smaller ethnic groups adds still more languages and religions to the mix. Also, and very important, there are wide variations among the nationalities of the USSR in terms of phenotype, or physical appearance. In other words, there are noticeable differences of skin and hair color, build, facial features, and so on.

Thus, within the Soviet population one finds ethnic groups as different as the Latvians and the Kirgiz; apart from their numbers, which are about equal, and the fact that each is the titular group of one of the fifteen republics of the Soviet Union, they have nothing in common. Whereas the Latvians, by any standard (language, religion, phenotype) would be considered "Europeans," the Kirgiz quite properly would be viewed by most people as typically "Middle Eastern."

Complicating the ethnic multiformity still further is, as we shall see later in this chapter, a considerable heterogeneity of socioeconomic characteristics.

THE FORMATION OF THE MULTIETHNIC SOVIET STATE

The Tsarist Legacy

An excellent question at this juncture is, How did peoples as dissimilar as the Latvians and the Kirgiz come to be in the same country? A key to understanding this situation is the fact that the Soviet Union, in territorial if not ideological terms, is the direct descendant of the empire of the tsars, an

TABLE 1.1
Population of Major Soviet Ethnic Groups: 1959, 1970, and 1979

Ethnic Group	Population (thous.) 1959	1970	1979	Average Annual Growth Rate (percent) 1959-70	1970-79	Percent of Total Soviet Population 1959	1970	1979
Russians	114,114	129,015	137,397	1.1	.7	54.65	53.37	52.42
Ukrainians	37,253	40,753	42,347	.8	.4	17.84	16.86	16.16
Uzbeks	6,015	9,125	12,456	3.9	3.4	2.88	3.80	4.75
Belorussians	7,913	9,052	9,463	1.2	.5	3.78	3.74	3.61
Kazakhs	3,622	5,299	6,556	3.5	2.4	1.73	2.19	2.50
Tatars	4,968	5,931	6,317	1.6	.7	2.38	2.45	2.41
Azeri	2,940	4,380	5,477	3.7	2.5	1.41	1.81	2.08
Armenians	2,787	3,559	4,151	2.2	1.7	1.33	1.47	1.58
Georgians	2,692	3,245	3,571	1.7	1.1	1.29	1.34	1.36
Moldavians	2,214	2,698	2,968	1.8	1.1	1.06	1.12	1.13
Tadzhiks	1,397	2,136	2,898	3.9	3.4	.67	.88	1.11
Lithuanians	2,326	2,665	2,851	1.2	.8	1.11	1.10	1.09
Turkmen	1,002	1,525	2,028	3.9	3.2	.48	.63	.77
Germans	1,620	1,846	1,936	1.2	.5	.78	.76	.74
Kirgiz	969	1,452	1,906	3.7	3.1	.46	.60	.73
Jews	2,268	2,151	1,811	-.5	-1.6	1.09	.89	.69
Chuvash	1,470	1,694	1,751	1.3	.4	.70	.70	.67
Latvians	1,400	1,430	1,439	.2	.1	.67	.59	.55
Bashkirs	989	1,240	1,371	2.1	1.1	.47	.51	.52
Mordvinians	1,285	1,263	1,192	-.2	-.6	.62	.52	.45
Poles	1,380	1,167	1,151	-1.3	-.1	.66	.48	.44
Estonians	989	1,007	1,020	.2	.1	.47	.42	.39
Chechens	419	613	756	3.5	3.4	.20	.25	.29
Udmurts	625	704	714	1.1	.2	.30	.29	.27

Group					
Mari	504	599	622	1.6	.4	.24	.25	.24
Ossetians	413	488	542	1.5	1.2	.20	.20	.21
Avars	270	396	483	3.5	2.2	.13	.16	.18
Komi[a]	431	475	478	.9	.1	.21	.20	.18
Koreans	314	358	389	1.2	.9	.15	.15	.15
Lezgins	223	324	383	3.5	1.9	.11	.13	.15
Bulgarians	324	351	361	.7	.3	.16	.15	.14
Buryats	253	315	353	2.0	1.3	.12	.13	.13
Greeks	309	337	344	.8	.2	.15	.14	.13
Yakuts	233[b]	296	328	2.2	1.1	.11	.12	.13
Kabardinians	204	280	322	2.9	1.6	.10	.12	.12
Karakalpaks	173	236	303	2.9	2.8	.08	.10	.12
Dargins	158	231	287	3.5	2.4	.08	.10	.11
Kumyks	135	189	228	3.1	2.1	.06	.08	.09
Uyghurs	95	173	211	5.6	2.2	.05	.07	.08
Gypsies	132	175	209	2.6	2.0	.06	.07	.08
Ingush	106	158	186	3.7	1.8	.05	.07	.07
Gagauz	124	157	173	2.2	1.1	.06	.06	.07
Hungarians	155	166	171	.6	.3	.07	.07	.07
Tuvinians	100	139	166	3.0	2.0	.05	.06	.06
Kalmyks	106	137	147	2.4	.8	.05	.06	.06
Karelians	167	146	138	-1.1	-.6	.08	.06	.05
Karachay	81	113	131	3.1	1.7	.04	.05	.05
Romanians	106	119	129	1.1	.9	.05	.05	.05
Kurds	59	89	116	3.8	3.0	.03	.04	.04
Adyge	80	100	109	2.0	1.0	.04	.04	.04
Laks	64	86	100	2.7	1.7	.03	.04	.04

[a]Figure includes Komi-Permyaki.
[b]The Yakut population was reported as 236,655 in the 1959 census.

Sources: Ts. S. U. 1973, pp. 9-11; 1980, pp. 23-26.

empire that grew by military conquest from a humble principality to a powerful state controlling one-sixth of the land surface of the world. During its expansionist phase, which lasted from the mid-16th century to the first decade of the 20th century, the tsarist Russian Empire acquired territories in Europe and in Asia that were the homelands of more than a score of major and countless smaller ethnic groups, all of which were ethnically distinct from the Russians. The initiation of the expansion of the Russian state is conventionally marked by the fall of the Tatar fortress at Kazan' to the army of Ivan IV (the Terrible) in 1552. After the defeat of the Tatars, the Russians gained lands in the Volga-Kama region and south to Astrakhan on the Caspian Sea, incorporating large numbers of non-Russians (Tatars, Mordvinians, Chuvash, Mari, and Udmurts) into the Muscovite state. (This historical summary is drawn principally from Allworth 1969; Donnelly 1968; Seton-Watson 1967.)

Following the conquest of the lands along the Volga, Russian military forces, traders, and adventurers secured the Urals region, and in the span of less than a century brought the vast Siberian territories and the ethnic groups of these areas into the imperial fold. During this period Bashkirs, Yakuts, Buryats, and many smaller groups known collectively as "Peoples of the North and Siberia" were added to the empire's population. During the middle and later 17th century, the Russian Empire also made territorial gains in the west, including part of the region known as Ukraine (east of the Dnepr River). In the early decades of the 18th century, Tsar Peter I (the Great), in a series of campaigns against the Swedes, obtained large areas along the eastern littoral of the Baltic Sea. Through these and later events (such as the partitions of Poland), still more non-Russian peoples, such as the Estonians, Latvians, Lithuanians, Ukrainians, Belorussians, and Jews fell under tsarist control. Also, Bessarabia (with its Romanian/Moldavian population) was taken from Turkish control in 1812.

In the early part of the 19th century, the Caucasus region and its array of ethnic groups was integrated into the empire; the conquest of the Caucasus, one of the most ethnically variegated areas of the world, added more than a dozen major non-Russian peoples to the long list of groups under imperial control, including Armenians, Georgians, Azeri, Ossetians, Kabardinians, Balkars, Chechens, Ingush, and many others. Finally, the Russian expansion into Kazakhstan and Central Asia through the 19th century annexed several large Islamic groups: the Kazakhs, Uzbeks, Tadzhiks, Turkmen, and Kirgiz.

One vital aspect of the multiethnic character of the Soviet Union is the ethnic geography of the country, a pattern that resulted from the tsarist method of territorial acquisition. The essential point in this regard is the geographic centrality of the Russian ethnic homeland and the peripheral location of most non-Russian groups. Whereas the majority of the ethnic Russian population is found in the interior, most non-Russians are concentrated in the borderlands, in their respective ethnic territories. These ethnic territories extend in a vast arc from the shores of the Baltic Sea in the northwest (Estonia, Latvia, and Lithuania), south along the western border of the Soviet Union (through Belorussia, Ukraine, and Moldavia), east across the Caucasus with its numerous nationalities (Armenians, Georgians, Azeri, and others), traversing Central Asia (and the areas inhabited by Turkmen, Uzbeks, Tadzhiks, and Kirgiz) and Kazakhstan, and finally across Asia and the homelands of such peoples as the Buryats, Tuvinians, Altays, and Khakas. Compounding this Russian/non-Russian center-periphery dichotomy are several irredentist situations — that is, situations in which members of the same ethnic group live on both sides of the border.

A number of reasons have been suggested to explain the large-scale expansionist moves by the Russian Empire, including economic, political, military, and religious rationales, plus such difficult-to-define motivations as "manifest destiny." Whatever the reasons, the result of these territorial annexations was the incorporation of a host of non-Russian nationalities (and the foregoing itemization is not exhaustive) into the tsarist, and originally ethnic Russian, state. In the words of Richard Pipes (1975), "...the processes of nation building and empire building are, in the case of Russia, hopelessly intertwined."

Ethnicity and Revolution

The imperial government desired social, economic, and political uniformity throughout the state, a uniformity based, of course, on the ethnic Russian norm (Raeff 1971). Until the assassination of Tsar Alexander II in 1881, the regime was largely content to leave the attainment of this uniformity to evolutionary means. However, following the accession to the throne of Alexander III, a period of reaction and repression was initiated, with the repression applied to the non-Russian ethnic groups, among others (Pipes 1968, pp. 1-49). This period of forced Russo-conformity, during which ethnic minority rights and limited autonomy were abrogated, coincided (unhappily for the ancien régime) with the rise of nationality consciousness resulting from the general social and economic development in the Russia Empire during the latter half of the 19th century. The growth of educated urban elites among the non-Russian ethnic groups, combined with the natural resistance to tsarist oppression, resulted in the heightening of nationalist emotions and contributed significantly to the collapse of the Russian Empire.

Responding to the increasing ethnic tensions in Russia, various political factions, among them the Marxist Social Democrats, began devoting serious attention to the nationality situation. During the first decade of the 20th century, most of the liberal political parties adopted platforms that embodied concessions to the nationalities of Russia, although the extent of these concessions varied widely. In 1903, for example, the Russia Social Democratic Labor party (later to become the Communist party) advocated several important points concerning the nationalities, including measures of regional autonomy, equality of all nationality groups, language and education rights, and the right of nationalities to self-determination (Pipes 1968, pp. 1-49).

The head of the Bolshevik faction of the Communist movement, V. I. Lenin, viewed ethnicity and nationalism, in the Marxist vein, as secondary to the class struggle (Low 1958, pp. 36-94). Emphasizing the economic benefits to be realized in large, centralized states, he was opposed in general to the fragmentation of existing states and to decentralized, federal political structures. Further, Lenin saw the amalgamation of ethnic groups as progressive (with the stipulation that forced measures be excluded), and he had little use for small ethnic groups that, he believed, could be assimilated into larger nationalities. As a shrewd judge of political realities, however, he began to realize the significance of the heightened ethnic sentiments in Russia, and saw in the various ethnic nationalist movements potential allies for the proletariat in the upcoming struggle with the tsarist regime.

In order to consolidate his alliance with the non-Russian nationalities, Lenin promulgated his policy of self-determination, which stated explicitly that all ethnic groups of the Russian Empire had the right to secede and form independent states. ". . . [W]e must inevitably reach the conclusion," he said, "that the self-determination of nations means the political separation of these nations from alien national bodies, and the formation of an independent national state" (1965, p. 397).

With regard to criticism from other Marxists that the policy of self-determination would result in historically retrogressive fragmentation, Lenin apparently believed that the nationalities would not secede and, in the event that they should try, sufficient qualifications were included in the principle to justify intervention to prevent secession. Self-determination was a right, Lenin stated, and to advocate the right did not mean the same as advocating self-determination itself. Recognizing the right of nations to self-determination would, according to Lenin, engender trust between the nationalities and the socialist movement, and reduce rather than promote the danger of secession. Further, Lenin maintained that the nationalities would not actually secede, because economic forces militated against fragmentation and the masses were aware of the fact. Thus, with the right to self-determination assured (removing ethnic oppression and animosities), economic considerations would promote consolidation into the larger proletarian state.

The revolution of February 1917 catapulted the nationality situation into a critical political and military problem. From the outset the provisional government was unwilling to take determined measures to placate unrest among the nationalities, beyond the removal of formal restrictions against various groups and the pronouncement of equality for all citizens regardless of their ethnic, religious, or racial background. As the internal order of the former Russian Empire disintegrated by degrees into chaos and finally civil war, those ethnic groups so inclined were presented with the opportunity for secession. Other groups that in the past had advocated only local autonomy found it necessary, in light of events, to adopt some form of self-rule in order to maintain order and to protect themselves from foreign military intervention or from the designs of neighboring ethnic groups. Civil unrest took on ethnic dimensions in non-Russian areas, particularly in the North Caucasus, Caucasus, and Central Asia, with indigenous groups taking up arms against Russian city dwellers, troops, and agricultural settlers. Many non-Russian nationalities saw in the fluctuating political-military situation the chance to regain lands or privileges that Russians had preempted during the period of tsarist rule (Pipes 1968, pp. 50-113).

The years 1917 and 1918 witnessed the secession from the Russian state of Lithuania, Latvia, Estonia, and Finland, together with the occupation of Poland by Germany and the annexation of Bessarabia (Moldavia) by Romania. In addition to these areas, large territories were controlled by counter-revolutionary military forces, notably in Siberia.

The slogan of self-determination had proved a disaster for Lenin and the Bolsheviks, intent on maintaining a large state territorially synonymous with the previous tsarist empire; and it became increasingly clear that the slogan needed theoretical and pragmatic qualification. Lenin, therefore, together with Josef Stalin (who was emerging as the principal Bolshevik spokesman on nationality problems), began to stress the qualifications built into the original, pre-Revolutionary concept of self-determination. Ethnic self-determination, Stalin wrote in early 1918, could not stand in the way of the development and interests of the proletariat.

> There are cases when the right of self-determination conflicts with another, a higher right—the right of the working class that has come to power to consolidate that power. In such cases—this must be said bluntly—the right of self-determination cannot and must not serve as an obstacle to the working class in exercising its right to dictatorship (Stalin 1946, p. 265).

With a theoretical justification in hand, the Bolsheviks moved rapidly to establish military and political power in the non-Russian areas. Secessionist regimes in Ukraine, Belorussia, the Caucasus, and Central Asia were defeated and their territories reincorporated into the Russian state through a combination of force of arms, treachery, and the granting of temporary concessions (Conquest 1967, pp. 21-49). The Bolsheviks found it expedient to conclude alliances with certain ethnic groups during the Civil War, particularly since the White forces held the minorities in contempt and virtually forced them into cooperation with the Reds. Following their consolidation of power, the vast majority of the pragmatic concessions granted to the nationalities were unilaterally abrogated by the Bolsheviks (Pipes 1968, pp. 161-68).

The force of nationalism had shown itself to be stronger than Lenin and the Bolsheviks had foreseen. More than a force to be exploited in the struggle for proletarian hegemony, ethnic nationalism proved to be a phenomenon that required some compromises, or at least the appearance of compromise. The federal concept of government increasingly began to suggest itself as the non-Russian areas were incorporated into the proletarian state, despite the previous outspoken animosity of Lenin and others for this decentralized form of government. Stalin justified the adoption of a federal state largely on grounds of expedience; in light of the outright secessions by some nationalities, federation was a step toward unity, a move toward a centralized state, and a sound tactic in the face of strong ethnic sentiments that the Bolsheviks had underestimated (Pipes 1968, pp. 242-93). Most important, however, was the fact that the decentralized state structure was more than balanced by a Communist party that was highly centralized and, in reality, in complete control of the state apparatus.*

The final result of the years of revolution, civil war, and ethnic nationalist insurrection was the creation, in 1922, of the Union of Soviet Socialist Republics. The Soviet Union is, in the political-administrative sense, a hierarchy of ethnic units, each of which represents one or more Soviet nationalities. Although there are exceptions to the rule, the status of a nationality's political unit is largely determined by population size.

At the highest level in the hierarchy are the 15 Soviet socialist republics or union republics, which together constitute the USSR. Each represents an ethnic group larger (in 1970) than 1 million.† Because one of the constitutional prerogatives of these republics is the right to secede from the union, several major nationalities (Tatars, Chuvash, Mordvinians, and Bashkirs) that otherwise might qualify for union republic status are relegated to the next lower level in the hierarchy — that of autonomous Soviet socialist republic — owing to the interior location of their homelands, where secession would be impracticable. Also, medium-size ethnic groups (those over 100,000 in number) are represented by autonomous republics, of which there are 16. There are two lower-level ethnic units, the eight autonomous oblasts and the ten national *okrugs,* which serve as political entities for the smaller nationalities, mainly those living in sparsely populated Siberia, the Far North, or mountainous areas. In some cases, ethnic groups have more than one representative ethnic unit because of problems of territorial contiguity. Likewise, many units represent two or more ethnic groups.

---

*In 1941 elements of the German army seized intact the records of the regional Communist party organization in the Soviet city of Smolensk. The archive, later captured by American forces and brought to the United States, reveals in detail how the party gained and perpetuated control of the state apparatus in Smolensk. (See Fainsod 1958, chs. 2, 3.)

†Because of its large size and the fact that it includes many subordinate ethnic units, the ethnic Russian Republic is officially termed the Russian Soviet Federated Socialist Republic.

Individually or collectively, virtually all Soviet ethnic groups enjoy official status in the federal system. Although the status of some nationality units has changed over the years, and some groups have had their titular units abolished altogether, the basic structure remains unchanged since Lenin's time.

SOCIOECONOMIC DEVELOPMENT AND ETHNICITY IN THE USSR

Soviet Nationality Policy

As a consequence of Lenin's political strategy and the use of military force, the territorial integrity of the tsarist state was ultimately maintained in the transition to Soviet power. Likewise, with only two exceptions (the Finns and the Poles), the large number and amazing assortment of non-Russian nationalities that had been incorporated into the Russian Empire over the centuries since the fall of Kazan' are currently included in the multiethnic Soviet Union.

Despite the fact that the USSR virtually replicates the former Russian Empire across the geographical and ethnic dimensions, the Soviet government obviously maintains that a qualitative difference exists between the two. Essentially, this difference can be summed up, according to Soviet theorists on ethnicity, by the simple fact that the "question of nationalities" or "nationality problems" in the USSR have been "solved" by the application of Marxist-Leninist nationality policy.

At the outset it should be understood that it is not possible to extract from Soviet government pronouncements or scholarship on the subject of ethnicity exactly what constitutes "Soviet nationality policy." To state, as is usually the case, that nationality policy aims at solving the nationality question is, of course, avoiding the issue and requires some explication of what constitutes the nationality question. It is possible, however, to discern at least one main theme implicit, and at times explicit, in Soviet theory and statements regarding problems associated with ethnicity: Soviet nationality policy is designed to remove the social and economic inequalities among the ethnic groups of the USSR, inequalities that developed during the tsarist period; the principal mechanism by which these inequalities are to be alleviated is economic development (Arutiunian 1972). This theme, which is crucial to the entire range of Soviet theory on society, has its roots in the writings of Karl Marx and found its implementation under Lenin.

It has been contended that Marx, who is the source of almost all aspects of Soviet social, economic, and political theory, provided precious little guidance pertaining to ethnic problems for his socialist successors. It is clear that societal relations based on ethnicity were not the central focus of Marx (or of Friedrich Engels); the Marxist theory of historical political-economic change is of course based on economic class conflict and its social correlates. It is equally clear, however, that Marx did not ignore ethnicity and its implications; rather he provided what he considered to be a viable solution to ethnic problems: the elimination of class conflict and economic exploitation of one group by another through the victory of the proletariat (Bloom 1967, pp. 1-32).* As Lenin stated, "Marx had no doubt as to the subordinate position of the national question as compared with the 'labour question.' But his theory is as far from ignoring national movements as heaven is from earth" (1965, p. 436).

The means by which the socioeconomic differences among nationalities were to be removed was the economic (in most cases, industrial) development of the non-Russian areas of the USSR. By promoting the economic growth of regions inhabited by non-Russians, it was assumed that eventually the indigenous population would be drawn into the development process. The centrally directed socialist economy was the key to this program, inasmuch as control over investment, technology, and manpower would enable the government to plan and implement the equalization directives. Vsevolod Holubnychy summarized this point nicely:

> Lenin saw the key to the solution of the national and colonial question under socialism in the economic, and therefore also social, cultural, and political equalization of all nationalities and races. He believed this solution to be possible only under socialism, because only a socialist government would be in a position to furnish the underprivileged and underdeveloped nationalities not only with legal, political, and social but—and most important of all—also with economic aid, that is with direct aid to their economic development, industrialization, technical modernization, education of native professional and leadership cadres, and the development of their culture in general (1968, p. 51).

The program of raising the level of development in the non-Russian areas of the USSR was officially promulgated in the early years of Soviet power, and has remained a central tenet of Communist party goals to this day. The 15th Party Congress (1927), for example, charged with initiating the First Five-Year Plan, stated that special attention would be paid to raising the level of development of all nationality regions, "liquidating their economic and cultural backwardness [otstalost'] . . ." (Rutgaizer 1968). If the cornerstone of the edifice of Soviet nationality policy is the elimination of the socioeconomic disparities among ethnic groups that were inherited from the tsarist regime, it

---

*Regarding the malleability of ethnicity, Solomon Bloom observes that in the opinion of Marx, "Nationality was not an indissoluble bond. The influence of social change and the more direct pressure of conquest, diplomacy, and state policy might or might not result, depending on the circumstances, in the nationalization or denationalization of populations" (1967, p. 21).

is clearly vital to any analysis of ethnic group relations in the USSR to assess the extent to which this goal has been attained.

Ethnic Groups and Development: The Reality

In this section two broad questions are addressed. First, have the various non-Russian ethnoterritories reached a level of development roughly comparable with that in the ethnic Russian regions? Two key factors must be understood here: most non-Russians live in their respective ethnic homelands or "ethnoterritories"; and as detailed earlier, these homelands are recognized as such in the constitution. Second, and most important, to what extent have non-Russians been integrated into modernized society, the development of their homelands notwithstanding? This latter point focuses directly upon the assumption implicit in Soviet nationality policy that the economic development of the non-Russian areas will lead to the socioeconomic advancement of the non-Russian peoples.

With regard to the first question, several Western scholars have investigated this topic, and the consensus is that the non-Russian areas continue to lag behind the European, mainly Russian, regions of the USSR in terms of economic and social-cultural development indexes. The degree to which economic development has manifested itself differentially in the geographical sense can be observed in data showing the level of urbanization (the percentage of the population of a given area living in cities) in the various ethnic units of the Soviet Union for years in which the government conducted censuses (Table 1.2). Especially for the Soviet Union, the level of urbanization is a good surrogate for "economic development," because in the USSR historically the level and rate of urbanization are linked both conceptually and empirically to industrialization, the principal mechanism whereby economic development has taken place (Lewis and Rowland 1969; Rodgers 1974). As a rule, therefore, the more industrialized a region, the higher its level of urbanization.

Urbanization is important as an indicator not only of economic development in the limited sense, but also of social and cultural development, because in the USSR urbanites enjoy appreciably higher living standards, better access to educational institutions, the media, services, superior health care, and so on. Hence, "urban" in the Soviet context not only connotes the extent to which industrialization (and economic development) has progressed, but also is indicative of broader change directly influencing the standard at which people live. The ideological raison d'être of the Soviet state stems from the dictatorship of the urban-industrial proletariat, and it should not be surprising that urbanites are a privileged group in comparison with their rural compatriots.

Two key points in this regard emerge from the figures in Table 1.2. First, although all ethnoterritories of the USSR have experienced economic

TABLE 1.2
Level of Urbanization of Ethnic Units and Major Ethnic Groups, USSR: 1926, 1959, and 1970

Ethnic Unit/Ethnic Group	Ethnic Unit Level (percent)			Ethnic Group Level (percent)		
	1926	1959	1970	1926	1959	1970
Russian Republic/Russians[a]	14.0	44.8	55.4	15.7	46.5	57.4
Ukrainian Republic/Ukrainians	13.0	33.5	42.7	6.8	28.8	37.9
Belorussian Republic/Belorussians	8.6	21.1	34.2	5.3	23.1	34.9
Lithuanian Republic/Lithuanians	11.8	24.4	36.4	7.6	21.6	33.5
Latvian Republic/Latvians	25.8	38.3	50.0	23.0	32.2	41.8
Estonian Republic/Estonians	23.2	39.0	51.4	21.1	32.5	43.6
Armenian Republic/Armenians	12.1	41.0	50.0	23.8	46.3	53.9
Azerbaydzhan Republic/Azeri	23.1	40.4	39.7	12.0	28.8	31.1
Georgian Republic/Georgians	15.5	34.4	39.5	7.1	28.8	36.0
Uzbek Republic/Uzbeks	17.2	28.5	32.2	13.8	17.5	20.7
Tadzhik Republic/Tadzhiks	7.4	20.5	24.5	11.5	13.7	17.7
Kirgiz Republic/Kirgiz	8.3	24.1	31.1	1.1	6.5	11.3
Turkmen Republic/Turkmen	7.3	29.7	31.9	.4	16.2	20.3
Kazakh Republic/Kazakhs	5.6	34.3	41.1	1.3	17.7	21.6
Moldavian Republic/Moldavians	8.5	15.2	22.9	5.8	8.0	13.9
Karelian ASSR/Karelians	6.5	34.3	44.6	1.5	16.8	10.0
Komi ASSR/Komi	0.0	41.0	43.8	1.3	18.7	24.0
Mari ASSR/Mari	0.0	18.9	32.8	.3	6.4	13.8
Mordvinian ASSR/Mordvinians	1.4	11.6	24.2	1.6	21.2	28.9
Chuvash ASSR/Chuvash	2.6	18.6	30.5	1.0	14.1	23.4
Tatar ASSR/Tatars	7.6	34.6	45.9	10.1	38.7	47.2
Dagestan ASSR/peoples of Dagestan[b]	7.3	26.8	29.5	2.7	15.0	20.4

Kabardinian-Balkar ASSR/					
Kabardinians and Balkars	0.0	27.7	44.2	.4	9.0	21.3
Kalmyk ASSR/Kalmyks	0.0	12.5	18.6	.7	11.5	19.1
Severo-Ossetian ASSR/Ossetians	29.8	49.8	56.8	6.0	29.3	44.1
Chechen-Ingush ASSR/					
Chechens and Ingush	16.9	36.8	38.5	1.0	7.8	19.9
Bashkir ASSR/Bashkirs	5.8	32.7	42.0	1.3	14.6	21.1
Udmurt ASSR/Udmurts	10.5	37.6	50.5	.6	15.8	26.1
Buryat ASSR/Buryats	11.6	26.0	33.1	.6	10.4	16.7
Tuva ASSR/Tuvinians	N.A.	20.0	22.4	N.A.	5.4	9.8
Yakut ASSR/Yakuts	0.0	15.3	25.0	0.0	5.2	9.1
Abkhaz ASSR/Abkhaz	10.7	27.1	34.8	2.6	20.0	25.6
Karakalpak ASSR/Karakalpaks	0.0	14.8	29.0	0.0	10.7	24.3
Russian areas/Russians	14.0	44.8	55.4	15.7	46.5	57.4
Non-Russian areas/non-Russians	11.8	31.1	39.1	9.8	26.9	33.9

N.A. = not available.

Note: Level of urbanization is standardized for all census years as the percentage of the population living in cities of 15,000 and over.

[a] The Russian Republic as used here excludes all autonomous republics subordinate to it.

[b] Peoples of Dagestan include Avars, Lezgins, Dargins, Kumyks, Laks, Tabasarans, Nogays, Rutuls, Tsakhurs, and Aguls.

Source: Clem 1975, pp. 249, 262.

development (as indicated by successively higher levels of urbanization), the Russian ethnoterritory continues to lead the homelands of the non-Russian ethnic groups. Second the Russian ethnoterritory urbanized at a higher rate than did the other ethnoterritories.

Beyond the data on urbanization, still other indexes of economic development point to the perpetuation of spatial inequalities. Leslie Dienes (1972) studied the economic geography of the USSR in the post-World War II period and found major interregional variations in such indicators of economic development as industrial employment, industrial output, fuel consumption, and national income. In general, his figures revealed a much higher level of development in the Russian ethnoterritory and a few non-Russian areas (notably the Baltic republics and the eastern Ukraine), with contrasting lower levels in remaining ethnoterritories (particularly in Moldavia, the western and southern Ukraine, Kazakhstan, and the Central Asian republics). Likewise, Allan Rodgers (1974, pp. 237-39) investigated regional trends in industrialization from 1940 to 1965 (by focusing on indexes of industrial employment) and determined that most non-Russian ethnoterritories were significantly behind Russian areas (exceptions again being the Baltic republics and the eastern Ukraine).

The overwhelming impression one obtains from these and other studies is that little headway has been made toward the goal of equalizing ethnoterritorial economic development. There are probably two reasons for this. First, the desire to maximize aggregate economic growth resulted in the allocation of scarce development capital to areas where return on investment would be greatest. Second, military-strategic considerations dictated the location of industry in interior, defensible regions (Koropeckyj 1965, ch. 6). The implementation of these higher-priority policies (higher-priority, that is, than the policy of ethnoterritorial equalization) meant that Russian areas were favored, not necessarily because they were "Russian," but because they fit the criteria for development better than did most non-Russian ethnoterritories. Iwan Koropeckyj, after examining regional economic trends in light of different government policies, concluded that ". . . these fluctuating developments throughout the postwar period certainly do not prove the continuous determination of Soviet planners to equalize the levels of economic development among fifteen national republics, although this objective and its alleged successes are constantly publicized in Soviet propaganda" (1972, p. 80).

The real importance of these spatial differences in the extent to which economic development has taken place in the USSR (as measured by urbanization and industrialization) lies in the fact that similar variations exist in standards of living among regions (ethnoterritories) of the country. The definitive work on this subject by Gertrude Schroeder (1973) established that even rough interregional equalization has yet to be attained in terms of most indexes of living standards. Hence, not only do substantial differentials continue to be evidenced in such critical areas as income, consumption, retail trade, and services; in many instances divergence, rather than convergence, in levels of social development is the rule. Broadly speaking, the same grouping of ethnoterritories is exhibited in the data relating to standards of living as in those indicative of economic development, with the Russian Republic and the Baltic republics on top and the four Central Asian republics, Moldavia, and Azerbaiydzhan on the bottom.

Peter Zwick (1976) found essentially the same patterns in his studies of socioeconomic development in the various republics. Although he noted a trend toward equalization for some indexes, the hierarchical rankings among republics remain very much in evidence. In fact, he perceived the emergence of "clusters" of republics according to their standing with regard to a wide range of variables (including measures of access to health and education services, housing space, retail trade, cultural facilities such as cinemas and libraries, and more). Generally, the Russian Republic and the Baltic republics were associated with high levels of socioeconomic development, while the Central Asian republics fared less well; the other ethnoterritories were grouped between these two extreme clusters. Zwick's conclusion from these studies is that ". . . no substantial reduction in the level of inequality among the Soviet republics occurred between 1940 and 1970, other than that which resulted from the amelioration of the most extreme discrepancies. . ." (1976, p. 521).

The link between economic development (as manifested principally in industrialization) and the standard of living in a given region is not necessarily direct and causal, since the state always has the option of transferring funds from one area to another to assist in the expansion of social and cultural services in economically lagging regions. Clearly, a significant effort has been made by the Soviet government to do just that; but, just as clearly, this effort has not yet succeeded in closing the gap among ethnoterritories in terms of the purely economic or the broader social and cultural aspects of development.

The second dimension of Soviet nationality policy as it applies to equalization among ethnic groups concerns the relative standing of the various ethnic groups (not their ethnoterritories) with regard to economic, social, and cultural development. As we shall see, the distinction between ethnoterritorial development and ethnic group development is an important one. If we look at the level of urbanization of ethnic groups (the percentage of the population of each ethnic group living in cities), as shown in Table 1.2, two facts are clear: with the exception of the Jews, the Russians are the most highly urbanized of all the Soviet ethnic groups; and the gap between the level of urbanization for Russians and that for the other groups (again excepting the Jews) has increased steadily over the decades. Whereas the Russian/non-Russian gap stood at 5.9 percent in 1926, by 1970 the differential had widened to 23.5. Remembering the significance of the urban variable as an indicator of economic and social change, this one index suggests that ethnic Russians have benefited from the development process to a disproportionately large degree in comparison with most non-Russians. In addition to the Russians, other nationalities that have urbanized to an appreciable extent are the Jews (the most highly urbanized ethnic group), the Latvians and Estonians, the Armenians, the Tatars, and the Ossetians.

Brian Silver (1974), an American scholar interested in Soviet nationality problems, studied the issue of socioeconomic equalization in considerably more detail and found a mixed record of accomplishment. On the one hand, significant progress has been made in the effort to raise the level of education for all ethnic groups and to eliminate major interethnic disparities in educational attainment, this progress being manifested in the fact that relatively little variation exists today among nationalities in the younger age groups. Yet the familiar ethnic hierarchical pattern is still in evidence in the education data (Table 1.3), with the Russians, Latvians, Jews, Armenians, Georgians, and Ossetians the only nationalities with above-average levels of schooling in the latest (1970) figures.

Another facet of socioeconomic advancement examined by Silver was the extent to which the various ethnic groups had been integrated into highly skilled sectors of the work force (the "specialist" occupations and scientific workers). Here he noted a considerably less sanguine picture with respect to equalization. Although there has been a slight trend toward equalization in these high-status occupations, there continue to be major discrepancies among ethnic groups (Table 1.3), and the expected ranking is once again evident. Thus, Russians, Latvians, Estonians, Georgians, Armenians, and Jews tend to dominate these professions. Based upon his analysis of these and other data, Silver concluded that ". . . although by almost every measure there has been substantial movement toward equalization of nationalities during the Soviet era, this movement is strongest for the least demanding indicator . . . , and especially for the youngest age cohorts. Once one compares the equalization of higher educational attainment and skilled manpower, . . . one observes significant remaining dispersion among nationalities" (1974, p. 1630).

To summarize this section, the massive economic growth and concomitant social change characteristic of Soviet history have had a differential impact in both the spatial sense and along ethnic lines. Thus, some regions of the country—and here it is important to keep in mind that in the Soviet context this means ethnoterritories—have experienced far greater economic development than other areas. The fact that social-cultural development (standards of living) closely follows the economic development pattern gives even more importance to this phenomenon. Lastly, these development disparities tend to be mirrored in ethnic group terms, with certain groups having attained relatively high levels of modernization and others lagging behind.

Given the historical and political background and socioeconomic reality of ethnicity in the USSR, it remains to place this vital dimension of Soviet society within the universal experience, a task undertaken in the following chapter.

TABLE 1.3
Selected Socioeconomic and Demographic Characteristics of Major Soviet Ethnic Groups, 1970

Ethnic Group	Educational Attainment[a]	Skilled Workers[b]	Child-Woman Ratio[c]
Russians	50.8	134.9	0.727
Ukrainians	47.6	108.3	0.691
Belorussians	43.8	102.8	0.759
Lithuanians	35.3	119.1	0.859
Latvians	48.8	140.9	0.675
Estonians	46.2	161.2	0.677
Armenians	51.8	132.4	1.203
Azeri	42.4	113.5	2.082
Georgians	57.8	148.8	0.933
Uzbeks	41.2	75.7	2.401
Tadzhiks	39.0	67.5	2.422
Kirgiz	40.0	84.0	2.445
Turkmen	43.0	79.9	2.384
Kazakhs	39.0	94.0	2.213
Moldavians	33.8	56.9	1.099
Karelians[d]	33.8	102.1	0.482
Komi	41.2	120.1	1.044
Mari	32.9	59.0	1.310
Mordvinians	32.2	61.7	1.015
Chuvash	42.4	82.1	1.154
Tatars	45.7	87.0	1.002
Kabardinians	41.7	91.3	1.584
Balkars	35.6	108.9	1.616
Kalmyks	29.8	92.0	1.741
Ossetians	48.5	147.8	1.032
Chechens	21.9	32.0	2.257
Ingush	25.2	44.2	2.265
Bashkirs	36.9	68.1	1.540
Udmurts	37.4	73.4	1.105
Buryats	42.7	156.5	1.563
Tuvinians	33.6	88.3	1.853
Yakuts	37.4	140.4	1.622
Abkhaz	43.3	105.8	NA
Karakalpaks	38.4	107.3	NA
Jews	77.3	402.6	NA
USSR average	48.3		

N.A. = not available.

[a] Percentage of the population, ten years and older, for each nationality having higher and secondary education (including incomplete secondary education).

[b] Number of "specialists" with higher and secondary education per 1,000 population aged 16 to 59 for each nationality.

[c] Number of children aged up to nine per woman aged 20 to 49 for each nationality.

[d] Data for Karelians and all nationalities listed below Karelians apply to those living in the main area of settlement of the group.

Sources: Ts. S. U. 1973, pp. 395-498; Lewis, Rowland, and Clem 1976, pp. 290, 337.

REFERENCES

Allworth, Edward, ed. 1967. *Central Asia: A Century of Russian Rule.* New York: Columbia University Press.
Arutiunian, Iu. V. 1972. "Izmenenie sotsial'noi struktury sovetskikh natsii." *Istoriia SSR* 4 (July-Aug.): 3-20.
Aspaturian, Vernon V. 1968. "The Non-Russian Nationalities." In *Prospects for Soviet Society,* edited by Allen Kassof, pp. 143-98. New York: Praeger.
Bloom, Solomon F. 1967. *The World of Nations: A Study of the National Implications in the Work of Karl Marx.* New York: AMS Press.
Clem. Ralph S. 1975. "The Changing Geography of Soviet Nationalities and Its Socioeconomic Correlates." Ph.D. dissertation, Columbia University.
Connor, Walker. 1978. "A Nation Is a Nation, Is a State, Is an Ethnic Group, Is a . . . ." *Ethnic and Racial Studies* 1, no. 4:377-400.
Conquest, Robert, ed. 1967. *Soviet Nationalities Policy in Practice.* New York: Praeger.
Dienes, Leslie. 1972. "Investment Priorities in Soviet Regions." *Annals of the Association of American Geographers* 62, no. 3:437-54.
Donnelly, Alton S. 1968. *The Russian Conquest of Bashkiria, 1552-1740.* New Haven: Yale University Press.
Fainsod, Merle. 1958. *Smolensk Under Soviet Rule.* New York: Vintage.
Foltz, William J. 1974. "Ethnicity, Status, and Conflict." In *Ethnicity and Nation-Building,* edited by Wendell Bell and Walter E. Freeman, pp. 103-17. Beverly Hills, Calif.: Sage.
Goldhagen, Erich, ed. 1968. *Ethnic Minorities in the Soviet Union.* New York: Praeger.
Holubnychy, Vsevolod. 1968. "Some Economic Aspects of Relations Among Soviet Republics." In *Ethnic Minorities in the Soviet Union,* edited by Erich Goldhagen, pp. 50-120. New York: Praeger.
Katz, Zev, Rosemarie Rogers, and Frederick Harned, eds. 1975. *Handbook of Major Soviet Nationalities.* New York: Free Press.
Koropeckyj, I. S. 1965. *Location Problems in Soviet Industry Before World War II.* Chapel Hill: University of North Carolina Press.
──────. 1972. "Equalization of Regional Development in Socialist Countries." *Economic Development and Cultural Change* 21, no. 1:68-86.
Lenin, V. I. 1965. "The Right of Nations to Self-Determination." In *Collected Works,* vol. xx, pp. 393-454. London: Lawrence and Wishart.
Lewis, Robert A., and Richard H. Rowland. 1969. "Urbanization in Russia and the USSR: 1897-1966." *Annals of the Association of American Geographers* 59, no. 4:776-96.
Lewis, Robert A., Richard H. Rowland, and Ralph S. Clem. 1976. *Nationality and Population Change in Russia and the USSR.* New York: Praeger.
Low, Alfred D. 1958. *Lenin on the Question of Nationality.* New York: Bookman.
Matthews, W. K. 1951. *Languages of the USSR.* New York: Russell and Russell.
Parker, W. H. 1969. *An Historical Geography of Russia.* Chicago: Aldine.
Pipes, Richard. 1968. *The Formation of the Soviet Union.* Rev. ed. New York: Atheneum.
──────. 1975. "Reflections on the Nationality Problems in the Soviet Union." In *Ethnicity: Theory and Experience,* edited by Nathan Glazer and Daniel P. Moynihan, pp. 453-65. Cambridge, Mass.: Harvard University Press.
Raeff, Marc. 1971. "Patterns of Russian Imperial Policy Toward the Nationalities." In *Soviet Nationality Problems,* edited by Edward A. Allworth, pp. 22-42. New York: Columbia University Press.
Rodgers, Allan. 1974. "The Locational Dynamics of Soviet Industry." *Annals of the Association of American Geographers* 64, no. 2:226-40.
Rutgaizer, V. 1968. "Torzhestvo leninskoi natsional'noi politiki v ekonomicheskom stroitel'stve." *Kommunist* 18:24-35.

Schroeder, Gertrude E. 1973. "Regional Differences in Incomes and Levels of Living in the USSR." In *The Soviet Economy in Regional Perspective,* edited by V. N. Bandera and Z. L. Melnyk, pp. 167-95. New York: Praeger.

Seton-Watson, Hugh M. 1967. *The Russian Empire, 1801-1917.* Oxford: Oxford University Press.

Silver, Brian. 1974. "Levels of Socio-Cultural Development Among Soviet Nationalities: A Partial Test of the Equalization Hypothesis." *American Political Science Review* 68, no.4:1618-37.

Stalin, J. V. 1946. "Zakliuchitel'noe slovo po dokladu o natsional'nykh momentakh v partiinom i gosudarstvennom stroitel'stve." In *Sochineniia,* vol. v, p. 265. Moscow: Gosudarstvennoe izdatel'stvo politicheskoi literatury.

Tsentral'noe statisticheskoe upravlenie pri sovete ministrov SSSR (Ts. S. U.). 1973. *Itogi vsesoyuznoi perepisi naseleniya 1970 goda,* vol. iv. Moscow: Statistika.

———. 1980. *Naselenie SSSR,* Moscow: Izdatel'stvo politicheskoi literatury.

Zwick, Peter. 1976. "Intrasystem Inequality and the Symmetry of Socioeconomic Development in the USSR." *Comparative Politics* 8 no. 4:501-24.

2

THE ETHNIC DIMENSION, PART II
Ralph S. Clem

In the spring of 1972, several thousand persons—mostly young workers and students—took part in rioting and street fighting in the Soviet Republic of Lithuania. This violent protest, reportedly precipitated by the self-immolation and death of a Lithuanian youth, reached such proportions that authorities were forced to summon army paratroops to assist local police in restoring order (*New York Times* 1972).

In 1978, in the Georgian Republic of the Soviet Union (USSR), an attempt by Communist party officials to change the constitutional status of the indigenous Georgian language brought scores of angry demonstrators into the streets of the republic's capital city, Tbilisi (Whitney 1978; *New York Times* 1978). Apparently taken aback by the vehemence of the crowd reaction, the government quickly reversed itself and reinserted in the constitution the clause that recognizes Georgian as the native language of the republic.

Throughout the 1970s, large numbers of Soviet Jews emigrated from the USSR amid considerable domestic hostility and with the active support of the Congress of the United States.

What are we to make of such incidents? It happens that there is a common link among these particular phenomena: ethnicity. That is, all resulted at least in part from the fact that members of a certain ethnic group were sufficiently motivated by what they perceived to be inequities in the multiethnic Soviet society and polity to challenge openly a regime not known for its receptiveness to such overt protest.

This century has witnessed in virtually every corner of the globe, the maturation of ethnicity as perhaps the most important force for political change. The increasing identification of individuals with their respective ethnic groups has led almost inexorably to demands for alterations in the political, social, and economic status quo in a long and varied list of situations. Thus, ethnic differences have been at the root of violent conflict in the Basque separatist movement in Spain, the Palestinian problem in the Middle East, the Eritrean secession struggle in Ethiopia, and the Nigerian civil war. There are also many countries where such grievances are being dealt with in earnest politically and, at least for the time being, peacefully: the new constitution in Belgium, decentralization of authority in Yugoslavia, political concessions made to minorities in Sri Lanka, and the crisis of the federal order in Canada are pertinent examples.

One important outgrowth of the analysis of the Soviet Union is the possibility of expanding our comprehension of ethnicity by integrating lessons learned from the Soviet case into the mainstream of thinking on the subject. In this sense the Soviet Union is very much a laboratory, and a good one at that; the range of ethnic groups, their cultural and socioeconomic characteristics, and the availability of voluminous data render the USSR a valuable testing ground for social scientific hypotheses.

It must also be said that there are many who insist or imply that Soviet society and its ethnic dimension in particular are unique, and hence cannot be understood by reference to other societies and concepts derived from them. Ironically, this insistence on uniqueness is agreed upon both by those in the West who are largely critical of the Soviet regime and its handling of ethnic group relations and by those in the USSR who attempt to make the case that in no other instance have ethnic groups flourished to the extent that they have since the advent of Soviet power. The apparent bases for this agreement are the belief (in the West) that the "totalitarian model" obviates the sort of social-ethnic processes characteristic of Western societies, and (in the USSR) that the dialectical shift to socialism places all aspects of society, including ethnicity, on a plane qualitatively different from those countries still in the capitalist epoch.

Here we will make an effort to stress similarities rather than distinctiveness, in the belief that there is no basis a priori for assuming that generalizations relating to ethnicity would not apply to the Soviet case. Only if no suitable concepts can be found of sufficient scope and utility with which ethnic processes in the Soviet Union can be explained should we accede to claims of uniqueness.

THE NATURE OF ETHNIC GROUP RELATIONS

It would certainly be presumptuous even to attempt the definitive summary of ethnic studies in such a brief format. Rather, and more realistically, our purpose here is to extract from the literature in this rapidly growing field some of the key concepts and generalizations that can then be utilized to shed some comparative light on ethnic processes in one specific case, the Soviet Union.

The Ethnic Factor

It was once widely thought that ethnic identity was a vestigial and retrograde quality, a primordial attachment that could be expected to vanish, or at least be reduced to insignificance, as the individual was integrated into the larger, modernizing society (Connor 1972). Further, it was assumed that ethnicity was dysfunctional in modern society because it stood in the path of "nation-building"; that is, attachments to subnational groups would sap the strength of the nation-state, which has conventionally been viewed as the medium for development (Enloe 1973). Thus, various development ideologies have explicitly advocated, or at least implicitly hoped for, an erosion of ethnic group attachments. The prevailing opinion historically was that modernization, broadly defined, would reduce the likelihood of ethnic conflict through its supposed homogenizing influences.

The process by which this erosion of ethnicity was supposed to take place is referred to as assimilation. Assimilation is said to have occurred when the individual abandons his or her original ethnic identity and assumes that of another group (usually the majority or dominant ethnic group in a given country) (Gordon 1964; Price 1969). Along the path to total assimilation, intermediate points might be passed, most importantly acculturation. Acculturation is usually thought of as the overt adoption of the culture, normally including the language, of the majority or dominant group, but with the retention of basic psychological identification with the original ethnic group (Gordon 1964, pp. 71, 81). In addition to language shift, another key indicator of ethnic assimilation is intermarriage (exogamy); the extent to which such marriages take place represents further "progress" along the assimilation continuum (Gordon 1964, p. 80; Bugelski 1961). Although some authorities on ethnicity allowed for a termination of assimilation at some point short of total assimilation (that is, at acculturation), or even for a reversal of the process, it would be fair to say that conventional wisdom—as epitomized by the "melting pot" notion—had it for quite some time that assimilation was unidirectional and inevitable.

The fact is that total assimilation has turned out to be very much the exception rather than the rule. Instead of a diminution of ethnic identification, we are witnessing a resurgence of ethnicity throughout the world, with a wide range of social and political consequences. Walker Connor (1972; 1973) convincingly demonstrates with a number of examples that modernization has led in most cases to heightened ethnic consciousness and from there to ethnic conflict; in his words: " . . . the accompaniments of economic development—increased social mobilization and communication—appear to have increased ethnic tensions, and to be conducive to separatist demands." (1972, p. 332).

Why is ethnicity now manifesting itself to such an extraordinary degree in the contemporary world? Daniel Bell (1975) suggests that several trends evident in recent decades are responsible. First, he notes a general increase in the power of political systems; " . . . the spread of political decision-making forces the organization of persons into communal and interest groups, defensively to protect their places and privileges, or advantageously to gain place and privilege." People increasingly rely on the ethnic group as a means of exerting influence on the political system, Bell posits, because other possible vehicles for group expression (the nation-state and class) have declined in importance. Further, the ethnic group has a particular appeal (and perhaps greater longevity) because it can be both an interest group and an affective tie (Bell 1975, p. 145; Glazer and Moynihan 1975; Van Dyke 1977).

Simultaneously with the expanded role of the state there has occurred a decline in the appeal of ideology, And this is critical because

> . . . societies undergoing rapid social change, or nation-building, or territorial or political expansion, can escape or postpone internal political difficulties—the fear of established groups for the loss of privilege, the demand of disadvantaged groups for the reallocation of privilege—by mobilizing the society against some "external" force, or some common ideological purpose (Bell 1975, p. 164).

Thus, as the attraction of ideology has faded, the state must face ethnic groups and their demands head-on, rather than deflecting the issues on the grounds of some higher national priority.

A concept that has been utilized frequently to explain the greater incidence of ethnic group conflict in modernizing states is relative deprivation, which relates socioeconomic status to the level of aspirations of individuals. Ted Gurr outlined the idea thus:

> Relative deprivation is defined as actors' perception of discrepancy between their value expectations and their value capabilities. Value expectations are the goods and conditions of life to which people believe they are rightfully entitled. Value capabilities are the goods and conditions they think they are capable of getting and keeping. The emphasis of the hypothesis is on the perception of deprivation; people may be subjectively deprived with reference to their expectations even though an objective observer might not judge them to be in want. (Gurr 1970, p. 24).

Gurr (1970, pp. 46–56) goes on to note three patterns of relative deprivation: decremental deprivation, where expectations (aspirations) are high but capabilities decline; aspirational deprivation, in which expectations rise but capabilities remain low; and progressive deprivation, typical of cases where both expectations and capabilities rise at first, but capabilities then stabilize while expectations continue to increase.

Rising expectations, according to Gurr (1970, pp. 92-254), are determined primarily by exposure to ideologies that hold out the promise of correcting what are perceived to be inequities in the status quo, with education playing an especially important role (compare Lerner 1958, ch. 2). Capabilities, on the other hand, depend largely on the ability of the system to satisfy the demands of individuals and groups, and the perception of the extent to which such performance is really possible. Thus, the gap between what people believe to be their due and the realization of these expectations will be, it is hypothesized, an important determinant of conflict. Clearly, in modernizing multiethnic societies, particularly those espousing an egalitarian or, beyond that, an affirmative-action philosophy, one might suppose that the potential for relative deprivation of all types would be great, because people will be promised certain rewards, and it will then be incumbent upon the state to deliver. It would also seem highly unlikely that the state could accommodate everybody.

Ethnic Stratification

Socioeconomic inequality among ethnic groups within countries seems to be a universal condition, and this universality suggests some underlying influence at work. One idea that has gained wide acceptance in this regard is ethnic stratification, the principal feature of which is the division of people into hierarchically ranked categories according to their ethnic origin (Shibutani and Kwan 1965). Systems of ethnic stratification have been formed historically by the establishment of political-military dominance by one group over another (or others), usually through territorial conquest but also, in some cases, by immigration (forced or voluntary) of lower-status groups. Typically, the dominant ethnic group imposes its culture and norms (including language) upon the minorities, and invokes social, political, and economic sanctions against them (Shibutani and Kwan 1965, pp. 139-250; Cole and Cole 1954, ch. 6). Ethnic groups are sterotyped according to their relative positions in the stratification system, with traits assigned to the various minority groups in keeping with their status. The dominant ethnic group perpetuates the notion of its own inordinately positive attributes, and sometimes will also assume the "burden" of paternalism vis-à-vis the minorities. Co-optation, whereby outstanding individuals from minority groups are allowed to "pass" into the dominant group, is a common feature of ethnically stratified societies, and serves to neutralize the most serious potential enemies of the system.

Problems arise in systems of ethnic stratification when the established order begins to break down, when the situation becomes, in military parlance, "fluid." Probably the most important change agent has been modernization. For once modernization begins in a multiethnic state, forces are unleashed that lead to a restructuring of the ethnic stratification system.

Not, mind you, that the system will vanish altogether; instead, it will realign in predictable fashion. Sanctions imposed earlier against minorities in education and employment will delay their entry into the expanding modernized sectors, once modernization is under way. Further, the dominant groups will have an inherent advantage over other groups in society because the modernized sector will be characterized by "social communication" channels open to the dominant group and entered only with difficulty by others.

As Karl Deutsch (1966, p. 102) noted, "In a competitive economy or culture, nationality [ethnicity] is an implied claim to privilege. It emphasizes group preferences and group peculiarities, and so tends to keep out all outside competitors." Likewise, Nathan Glazer and Daniel P. Moynihan stated:

> . . . as between different ethnic groups, which have made quite different selections from the universe of possibilities, the norms of one are likely to be quite different from those of another, such that individuals who are successful by the standards of their own group will be failures by those of the other. In a situation of mixed ethnic groups where one group is dominant, which is to say that its norms are seen as normal not just for it, but for others also, there follows an almost automatic consignment of other groups to inferior status (Glazer and Moynihan 1975, pp. 13-14).

Therefore, even though the once-rigid ethnic stratification system becomes more flexible as modernization ensues, and some members of minority groups attain higher-status positions in society, the rough outlines of the original ranking can be expected to endure. In a sense, then, the dominant group reserves for itself the majority of better jobs and favorable access to higher education, and generally controls the modernizing sectors of society.

One other common feature of ethnic stratification systems that we should note is the widespread occurrence of minority groups in multiethnic states that, although they are not in a dominant position, nevertheless manage to secure a relatively favorable status. Such "achiever groups" often ". . . discover that they are quite good at achieving the norms of the dominant group: even better than the group that laid down those 'laws'" (Glazer and Moynihan 1975, p.14). The Jews of Eastern Europe; the Armenians, Lebanese, and Greeks of the Mediterranean and Middle East; the Indians of East Africa; and the Chinese of Southeast Asia are obvious examples of achiever groups. It is difficult to explain this phenomenon, but it appears that these groups are characterized by a culture in which emphasis is placed on achievement and higher aspirations are encouraged (Strodtbeck, McDonald, and Rosen 1957; Rosen 1959; Hurvitz 1958). It also seems that such situations lead at some point to interethnic conflict over the position of these achiever groups relative to both the dominant group and other minorities, and they are frequently the target of hostility (Shibutani and Kwan 1965, pp. 168-98; Dotson and Dotson 1968).

If systems of ethnic stratification, with their typical hierarchical ranking of groups (either rigid or flexible), lead to interethnic socioeconomic inequalities, how do these inequalities translate into conflict? As noted above, ethnic groups now increasingly look to the state to redress their grievances, and this is understandable in light of the activist role that many governments have assumed lately in the realm of ethnic group relations. The change from "equal opportunity" to "affirmative action" in the United States is indicative of the extent to which the political system now takes a hand in things, and, as Daniel Bell noted, ". . . equality of result, or redistributive policies, essentially are zero-sum games, in which there are distinct losers and winners. And inevitably these conditions lead to more open political competition and conflict" (1975, p. 147). The invocation of ethnicity by one group as a means of attaining a more favorable position is likely, therefore, to provoke a similar reaction in defense from groups that are threatened—what William Foltz termed a "mirror-image" response.

An important facet of this issue is the manner in which ethnicity and socioeconomic status are related. If there is a high degree of ethnic stratification—that is, a strong relationship between ethnic group membership and status—one can expect more intense conflict. Foltz, paraphrasing, S. M. Lipset, stated that

> . . . stability depend[s] over the long run on the existence of secondary cleavages which cut across rather than reinforce, social cleavages like religion and ethnicity, and of the importance for the development of stable and legitimate government that it be allowed to confront and resolve major cleavage-producing issues sequentially, rather than being obliged to fight all the major battles not only at the same time, but over and over . . . (1974, pp. 107-08).

Similarly, Wendell Bell and Walter Freeman viewed the government's ability to satisfy ethnic demands for a reorientation of the stratification system as vital to the survival of the state; ". . . in a sense a state may never stop 'nation-building,' because ethnic, racial, class, and other cleavages may continually threaten the unity, legitimacy, and existence of the state . . ." (1974, p. 12).

Ethnicity, Federalism, and Territoriality

The ultimate gesture of the state to discontented ethnic groups—short of granting them full independence—is the conferring of some measure of formal recognition (autonomy or self-rule, for instance), usually within a federal political framework. Often this decentralization of power is viewed as a solution to political problems caused by ethnic unrest, the idea being that the dissenters will be satisfied with something less than complete ethnic-national sovereignty. Because of the recency of most such actions, it remains to be seen how successful the ethnic-federal solution will be over the long term. And, of course, as Cynthia Enloe (1973, ch. 4) has pointed out, there are a number of variables to be considered in any given case: the real power of federal units vis-à-vis the center, links with other institutions, and the ethnic composition of the territories.

A key issue that federalism evokes is one that is often overlooked in the study of ethnic group relations—territoriality. Except in cases where multi-ethnic states were formed through mixed immigration, the notion of an ethnic homeland is a powerful force in the political dynamic of most contemporary countries.* Perhaps the most important aspect of ethnoterritoriality that has emerged of late concerns the relative levels of economic development between areas of a country associated with ethnic minorities (the periphery) and the homeland of the dominant group (the core). Michael Hechter (1975) has discussed this situation under the rubric "internal colonialism," a concept in which it is hypothesized that the core will exploit the periphery (and, therefore, the dominant group will exploit the minorities) in much the same fashion as an imperial power will use colonies to its own advantage (Ragin 1977). Beyond the purely economic features of such an arrangement, Hechter suggested, internal colonialism also fosters an ethnic stratification system (a "cultural division of labor"). Finally, the workings of internal colonialism condition the temporal and spatial spread of modernization, with the core region experiencing early development and the periphery (because of its subordinate status) joining in later and to a lesser degree.

In some other instances, however, the territorial basis of ethnic animosity has involved groups whose ethnic homelands are relatively better off than other areas within the same country, such as the Basque provinces of Spain, or Croatia and Slovenia in Yugoslavia (Fisher 1966; Richardson 1975, pp. 57-77; Bertsch 1971). What we must propose here regarding this issue is, therefore, rather more complex than a simple economic disadvantage motive behind the issue of ethnoterritoriality, because the status of an ethnic group homeland area within a larger state entity (a relationship determined to a large extent by underlying economic-geographic factors) may be either relatively backward or relatively advanced. In the former, the basis for disenchantment on the part of an ethnic group would no doubt be perceived disadvantage vis-à-vis the national norm or in comparison with the socioeconomic conditions

---

*Even in countries of immigration, de facto ethnic areas may evolve through the workings of migration and residential segregation.

obtaining in more advanced regions. In the latter case (of relative advantage) ethnic conflict might result from hard feelings (probably not openly expressed) over having to slow progress in one's ethnoterritory to assist lagging regions. In both cases, it is clear that the economic interests of the ethnic group may not coincide with those of the state.*

Another aspect of ethnoterritoriality that can influence ethnic group relations in multiethnic states is the incidence of ethnic mixing—that is, the extent to which members of the various ethnic groups have migrated to areas outside their respective ethnic homelands. One feature of ethnic stratification systems is the penetration by members of the dominant group into the more advanced sectors of the society and economy of minority ethnic homelands (Meinig 1971; Horne 1978). In such cases, the dominant group uses its privileged position to secure the better jobs and the best agricultural lands, transplants its culture and language into the minority's homeland (usually in the cities, in particular), and takes control of the key institutions in the periphery. In cases where members of minority ethnic groups migrate to the dominant group's ethnoterritory, they can expect to occupy low-status jobs (unless they are "achievers"), to be subjected to residential segregation, and to encounter animosity ranging from condescension to hostility to outright violence.

Summary

Contrary to earlier expectations, ethnicity is not receding, but is becoming a more powerful factor in the society, politics, and economy of contemporary multiethnic states. This trend assumes even greater importance when one realizes that virtually all countries of the world are multiethnic to some degree. Thus, total assimilation to ethnic homogeneity is now a lost cause. About as far along the assimilation continuum as most groups have "progressed" is acculturation, where the adoption of a standard language and some intermarriage is the rule. Further, it is no longer certain that the assimilation process is unidirectional, since many groups once thought to be almost totally absorbed by the majority have "resurfaced." As ethnic groups have assumed the function of interest groups, we have witnessed the politicization of ethnicity, usually within multiethnic states but also in the transnational sense.

---

*In this regard, it is important to recognize explicitly that regional development is, over the short term, zero-sum. That is, assuming that capital and other normally scarce factors of production are finite, choices must be made as to where these resources are to be allocated. The difficulty arises at this allocation stage because not all locations possess economic-geographic qualities allowing for maximization of production or return on investment. Thus, states may be forced to trade off efficiency for equity to satisfy ethnic demands for homeland development.

The near-term goal of ethnic interest groups is the reallocation of the benefits to be derived by membership in the larger society, particularly when modernization opens up the possibility of changing the former rankings of ethnic stratification and when official rhetoric encourages people to seek an improved position. Most states can no longer divert attention from these issues because the nation-building ideology has lost credibility, and thus confrontation between ethnic groups and the government has become more open and more frequent. Finally, ethnic territorial issues are increasingly important, at least in part because of a tendency to recognize ethnic homelands officially as such. The task will now be to determine to what extent these very general ideas can be used to understand the ethnic situation in the Soviet Union.

THE ETHNIC SITUATION IN THE USSR FROM A COMPARATIVE PERSPECTIVE

Fitting the Soviet case under the universal rubric will of necessity be imperfect, if for no other reason than our lack of complete knowledge about ethnic group relations. At this point, however, we should state that, in light of generalizations in the field of ethnic studies, there are no great surprises when the ethnic scene in the Soviet Union is approached from the conceptual point of view.

In its most elemental form, Soviet society today can be viewed as an evolved system of ethnic stratification, with all of the features typically manifested by such societies, regardless of their professed ideology. An "evolved system of ethnic stratification" means that the original, rigid framework established over the centuries of tsarist rule has bent, but it most certainly has not broken. Tamotsu Shibutani and Kian Kwan (1975), who formulated the concept of ethnic stratification, were careful to say that ethnically stratified societies are adaptable to change; and it appears that in the case of the Soviet Union, this adaptation has been successful in maintaining the essence of the status quo.

Ethnic Stratification Under the Tsars

It is widely acknowledged that the tsarist regime pursued policies that discriminated against the many minorities that had been annexed into the Russian state through its territorial expansion; hence the well-known characterization of tsarist Russia as "prison of nations" (Pipes 1968, ch. 1). Actually, the relationships between the Russian state and the non-Russian nationalities were, as Marc Raeff (1971) noted, conditioned by the historical periods and circumstances under which the various ethnic groups were incorporated into the empire. In general, however, the overall impact of tsarist rule was the implementation and perpetuation of ethnic Russian hegemony in the imperial society and economy—or, in other words, the establishment of a Russian-dominated ethnic stratification system.

This must not be construed as a suggestion that all Russians within the tsarist state were better off in the material sense than all non-Russians; indeed, the conditions prevailing among Russian serfs were in most instances abominable. Rather, ethnic stratification meant simply that Russian culture, the Russian language, and Russian forms of economic, social, and political organization were in the ascendancy, and all non-Russians had to adapt to the Russian norm or be excluded from the larger society. To be a Russian in the tsarist empire, then, was an implied claim to privilege as a member of the dominant group, and provided one with the background necessary to attain higher status without necessarily guaranteeing success.

Other aspects of ethnic stratification were evident in the Russian Empire. For example, the practice of co-optation, whereby ruling elites from minority groups were induced to transfer their allegiance to the tsar and were rewarded for so doing, was commonplace. Also, Russian "cultural superiority" was frequently invoked as a rationale for conquest; the claim was made that over the long term the minorities would benefit from their association with their Russian conquerors. (See, for instance, Smirnov 1892.)

In the early years of Soviet rule, when such things could be discussed openly, a campaign was waged against the "Great Russian chauvinism" that had carried over from tsarist times (Conquest 1967, pp. 53-55). It was pointed out that historically non-Russians had been discouraged from membership in trade unions, and that they usually received less pay than Russians for similar work. Examples were cited (and denounced) wherein Russians had openly denigrated other nationalities as backward, lazy, incompetent, and the like. Illustrative of such attitudes is the following statement from a Soviet source of the period: "How can one hope to fulfill the industrial finance plan when Tatars have been put to work on lathes?" (Conquest 1957, p. 54).

Shibutani and Kwan (1965, pp. 82-115), in their exposition of ethnic stratification in general, suggested that such ethnic stereotypes are ". . . attributed to each [group and] are established in popular beliefs, and the symbols of identification in terms of which individuals are located in each type are also matters of convention." By stereotyping the Russian people as superior and the minorities as inferior, the ethnic stratification system dominated by Russians could be legitimated (at least in the eyes of those benefiting from the system). Such an arrangement would then be viewed as "natural" and "logical."

Although the Russians were clearly in command of the imperial government and thus most likely to benefit from tsarist rule, other nationalities within the empire, because of their cultural heritage, emerged as "achiever groups" (Glazer and Moynihan 1975) in the economic, social, and political sectors. Foremost among these ethnic groups were the Tatars (Pipes 1968;

Bennigsen and Lemercier-Quelquejay 1967), Armenians, Georgians (Pipes 1968), Latvians, Estonians (Dunn 1966; Seton-Watson 1967 pp. 414 ff.), and Jews (Ettinger 1970).

Ethnic Stratification and Development: The Soviet Experience

No less an authority on ethnic matters than V. I. Lenin viewed the pro-Russian bias of the tsarist ethnic stratification system as an anachronism, and a dangerous one at that. Referring to the evils of Great Russian chauvinism, Lenin wrote in 1919:

> Exceptional caution must be displayed by a nation [ethnic group] like the Great Russians, who earned the bitter hatred of all the other nations; we have only just learned how to remedy the situation, and then, not entirely (1965, p. 195).

Clearly, Lenin understood that the continued functioning of ethnic stratification would not help remedy the situation, and, as was indicated in the preceding essay, policies designed to break down the barriers of stratification were vital to the success of the Soviet regime.

Yet even a cursory look at the nationality situation in the USSR should convince one that the Russian ethnic group retains all the attributes of a dominant group controlling an ethnic stratification system. In terms of socio-economic development, in the preceding essay we have seen that the Russians have benefited to a greater extent (and in comparison with most Soviet nationalities, to a far greater extent) than the other ethnic groups of the USSR. Not only has the Russian ethnoterritory been developed economically to a higher level than the various non-Russian areas, but the Russian people today are characterized, on the average, by higher levels of urbanization (with all of its desirable aspects), education, and participation in higher-status occupations (such as specialists and scientific workers) than are the vast majority of non-Russian nationalities.

One major reason for this Russian advancement has been the imposition of the Russian language as a lingua franca upon the multiethnic Soviet populace, a feature of the ethnic stratification system that gives an inherent advantage to ethnic Russians. With Russian as the main language of science, higher education, and the economy, persons unfamiliar with it will suffer in the competition for the fruits of Soviet society. As recently as 1970, less than half (48.7 percent) of all non-Russians professed a fluent command of the Russian language; only about 3 percent of ethnic Russians claimed to be fluent in one of the non-Russian languages. (By 1979 these figures were, respectively, 62.2 percent and 3.5 percent.) Although there are pronounced differences in knowledge of the Russian language by age among non-Russians today (with younger age groups exhibiting much higher rates of Russian fluency than older persons), persistent socioeconomic development discrepancies in favor of the dominant group can be partially attributed to the fact that social communication channels historically were open to Russians by virtue of their language and largely closed to non-Russians because of their lack of Russian-language skills.

Ironically, many Western specialists on Soviet nationality issues have implied negative connotations concerning the spread of the Russian language among non-Russians, apparently in the belief that the adoption of Russian will facilitate the erosion of ethnic identity or facilitate assimilation (Guthier 1977). Without commenting on the merits of this argument, it seems clear that a knowledge of Russian (not necessarily as a substitute for the native language) is a virtual requirement for entrance into the advanced sectors of Soviet society, and the higher Russian fluency rates among younger non-Russians almost certainly presage further gains by the minorities in education and skilled employment.

The ethnic stratification system has had a major impact upon other aspects of the ethnic situation in the USSR. As was noted earlier, a feature of ethnically stratified societies in general is the penetration by members of the dominant ethnic group into minority-group homelands. Dominant-group status has greatly facilitated the geographical dispersal of Russians into non-Russian ethnoterritories (Lewis 1971). Historically, Russians have moved in large numbers throughout non-Russian ethnoterritories and have established a large presence (by 1979, about 24 million persons), mainly in urban centers, in these regions of the Soviet Union (Clem 1976). Thus, by 1979 Russians accounted for slightly less than one-fifth of the combined population of the non-Russian ethnoterritories and, more important, for over one-third of the urban population in these areas in 1970. (The latter figure is not yet available for 1979.) This dispersion has resulted from the more ready access enjoyed by Russians to jobs throughout the Soviet Union, in part because their language and culture are the universal ones, but also because their relatively early integration into the modernizing sectors equipped them with requisite skills.

For example, in a "classic" study of the ethnic composition of the work force in two large industrial enterprises in the Tadzhik Republic, the Soviet scholar V. I. Perevedentsev (1965) found that Russians had a distinct advantage over the indigenous Tadzhiks in the competition for jobs because the Russians possessed the necessary qualifications and because a knowledge of the Russian language was required for employment. Further, factory managers, according to Perevedentsev, were reluctant to initiate training programs for unqualified applicants (mainly, no doubt, Tadzhiks) because this would have involved diverting sorely needed funds from the production process.

According to V. V. Pokshishevskii, another Soviet scholar known for his work on population and ethnicity, the proliferation of Russians in non-Russian ethnoterritories was a "natural" result of the lack of skilled manpower in these areas. The in-migration of Russians is viewed in this way as providing a trained cadre that, in a fraternal vein, would assist the indigenous ethnic group in the attainment of higher levels of development. Although it is clearly the case that such development assistance was required in most instances, it is a little difficult to regard the more than one-third of the urban population in the non-Russian ethnoterritories who are ethnic Russians (some 17 million persons in 1970) as a "cadre." In fact, the favored position of the Russians in the ethnic hierarchy has allowed them to establish themselves in non-Russian areas, to secure a disproportionately large share of the better urban-industrial jobs, and to transplant their language and culture to these areas (especially in the cities). Over the long term, this can only have worked to the detriment of the minorities, who have in many cases found it difficult to gain entrance into the advanced sectors of the work force and, in the broader sense, into the cities of their own ethnoterritories.

This situation can be appreciated by comparing the level of urbanization in the various ethnoterritories with the level of urbanization of the ethnic groups themselves (Table 1.2); such a comparison reveals that in all save five cases, the non-Russian groups were characterized by a lower level of urbanization than their respective ethnoterritories, and in many instances the gap was appreciable; note also that this was not true of the Russians. There was almost a 20 percentage point gap between the level of urbanization for the Kirgiz Republic and the Kirgiz ethnic group, about a 5 percentage point spread between that for the Ukrainian Republic and Ukrainians, and so on. The differences here are attributable mainly to the presence of large Russian urban populations in the non-Russian ethnoterritories. The familiar characterization of cities in non-Russian areas (even the capital cities of non-Russian republics) as islands of Russian people, language, and culture is thus an apt one; in 1970 there were more Russians than Uzbeks in Tashkent (capital of the Uzbek Republic, and the largest city in Central Asia), about six times as many Russians as Kazakhs in Alma-Ata (capital of the Kazakh Republic), and about a third as many Russians as Ukrainians in Kiev (capital of the Ukrainian Republic).

Several studies have shown that the geographical spread of the Russians to non-Russian ethnoterritories was linked principally to economic development. In other words, those specific areas within the minority homelands that had experienced industrialization and urbanization were the locations sought by Russians (and in-migrants of certain other groups) (Clem 1973; 1975; 1976, ch. 4; Lewis, Rowland, and Clem 1976). It seems likely that such a pattern is the result of Russian dominance in the Soviet ethnic stratification system.

Beyond the tangible aspects of the ethnic stratification system—that is, beyond the issues of relative levels of socioeconomic development—other features of Soviet society point to the manner in which the Russian ethnic group has maintained its dominant status. One subtle means of legitimating the favored position of the dominant group is through the long-standing characterization of the Russians as the "leading nation" or, in a more banal vein, as the "big brother" to the formerly oppressed minorities (Conquest 1967, pp. 90-92). As was noted earlier, this sort of stereotype is common to ethnically stratified societies, and establishes a ranking of nationalities based on a quasi-moral argument. Hence the Russians not only are the "leading group" but also must assume the "white man's burden," a role in which they have—according to Soviet thinking—acquitted themselves admirably. The reverse of this "big brother" notion is, of course, that the other nationalities are childlike, and must be assisted along the path to socialist development. One hesitates to think of the consequences of using such phraseology in other parts of the contemporary world.

Another subtle feature of ethnic stratification in the USSR is the manner in which the political system is used to assure continued control by the dominant group. As Cynthia Enloe (1977) noted, in situations where a federal structure was employed to accommodate diverse ethnic groups, centralized institutions (such as political parties) could be utilized to crosscut the decentralized state apparatus. In the Soviet context, the highly centralized Communist party (CPSU) is used in this fashion to counter the centrifugal tendencies inherent in the federal form of state organization. Not only do ethnic Russians account for a disproportionately large share of CPSU members, but the party itself is a means by which Russian interests can be safeguarded in non-Russian ethnoterritories. Teresa Rakowska-Harmstone, in a detailed study of the power structure of the Tadzhik Republic, found a recurring pattern in which

> . . . a "representative aspect" . . . satisfied the requirements of nominal sovereignty of the minority nationalities, and a "control aspect," safeguarded the central political control of Moscow. . . . [Thus,] local nationals were required to occupy the highest hierarchical positions and all posts of representative character. Invariably, however, a local leader was either seconded by a Russian or backed by a Russian or Russians close to him in the hierarchy. The local leader satisfied the representative aspect of the pattern, and his Russian deputy provided the necessary control aspect (1970, p. 96).

John H. Miller (1977) investigated the ethnic composition of key CPSU posts in all non-Russian units of the Soviet federation and observed essentially the same pattern (albeit the non-Russians did not always occupy the highest party position. He concluded:

> . . . it is a matter of policy to have one Russian among the two top party officials in non-Russian areas. This can hardly be dictated—as it might once have been—by lack of non-Russian expertise, technical or ideological. If economic and ideological considerations are excluded, political cohesion of the Moscow-centred Union seems the most plausible reason for this policy (Miller 1977).

Systems of ethnic stratification typically include achiever groups, which, as was discussed earlier, are able to use the system to their own advantage (although the means by which they do this are not well understood). Achiever groups are very much a feature of the Soviet ethnic scene, as they were in the pre-Revolutionary era. Tatars, Armenians, Georgians, Latvians, Estonians, and Jews have, as groups, succeeded in attaining high levels of modernization (See Tables 1.2 and 1.3). It should be noted that in many cases they have outperformed the Russians—a reminder that, as Glazer and Moynihan suggested, the specialized minorities can beat the dominant group at their own game (compare Armstrong 1968).

Assimilation

Perhaps no other aspect of ethnicity in the USSR has received as much attention as the interesting and emotive subject of assimilation. There is a voluminous literature on the nature and extent of assimilation among Soviet nationalities, a literature emanating from both the USSR and the West. Needless to say, the content differs markedly between the two sources. Our purpose here will be to summarize the key elements of the conceptual and concrete facets of the process of assimilation as it applies to the USSR, and to assess the revelance of the Soviet case with regard to the general experience.

Although there are serious differences of opinion among Soviet authorities on certain features of assimilation, virtually all subscribe to a standard framework within which the process is to be acted out (Kozlov 1969). This conceptualization envisions the simultaneous occurrence of "two tendencies," one involving a "flourishing" (in Russian, *rastvet*) of ethnic awareness on the part of the various nationalities of the USSR, and the other involving a "drawing together" or rapprochement (*sblizheniye*) among the same groups.

A key to understanding this seemingly contradictory dualism is the premise that the advent of socialism imparted a new and distinctive character to the nature of ethnic-group relations. Once the juridical equality of all ethnic groups was established by the Soviet regime (to include language and cultural guarantees and ethnoterritorial political rights), it is contended, the nationalities could enjoy the full development of their respective cultures (along Marxist-Leninist lines), unfettered by the harsh Russian ethnocentric policies typical of the tsarist era. Hence it was that Stalin's famous dictum that the various cultures of the USSR were to be national (ethnic) in form and socialist in content came to be. At the same time, the overall development of the socialist state would eliminate the divisive socioeconomic and political inequalities and exploitation characteristic of the capitalist epoch, and would thereby facilitate the rapprochement among nationalities. Thus, whereas assimilation in the capitalist setting would be forced and based on economic and political exploitation (and therefore bad), assimilation under socialism would be natural and based on mutual trust (and therefore progressive).

Eventually, it is assumed, the rapprochement will lead to a "merging" (*sliyaniye*) or, in other words, to a total assimilation of all groups into a single identity. Even though the future identity is usually portrayed as the ethnically neutral "Soviet people," there is little doubt that the hoped-for merging will entail the assimilation of non-Russians into an essentially ethnic Russian norm.

Given this outlook, argument concerning assimilation centers not on the process itself, but on the timing of its stages and the desirability of attempting, through policy, to move ethnic groups slowly or quickly through the stages.

Apropos of this last point, assimilation as a social-psychological process can be viewed as being determined largely by two sets of factors: those that are linked to the maintenance of ethnic identity and are directly subject to manipulation through policy, and those policies that may influence ethnic identity in an indirect way but are not strictly assimilation policy questions (Silver 1972, ch. 2).

Probably the single most important element in the category of direct factors relating to the broader process of assimilation is that of language policy, particularly the respective role and status of the Russian and the non-Russian languages. The importance of this issue derives in part from the belief among many scholars (both in the West and in the USSR) that the increasingly widespread use of the Russian language by non-Russians is a harbinger of assimilation (Guthier 1977).

Specifically, the direct policy questions concerning the language issue are those having to do with the use of languages in the schools and in the media. With regard to language use in education, the principal consideration has always been the role to be played by the Russian language and, in the case of schools in non-Russian areas, by the respective native languages as either the medium of instruction or as subjects of instruction (Silver 1972, ch. 2). From the earliest years of Soviet rule the development of non-Russian language schools was a high priority, mainly in the ethnoterritories of the non-Russian nationalities. Over the ensuing decades, the network of such schools was expanded greatly, but the situation remains characterized by substantial variation in the extent to which non-Russian languages are in fact an integral part of the educational system.

First, the use of non-Russian languages as the medium of instruction varies considerably from group to group, but in general it can be said that instructional language rights are tied to the status of ethnoterritories in the Soviet federal hierarchy. That is, the larger nationalities with union republic status are accorded much more extensive native-language medium-of-instruction privileges in their ethnic homelands than are the smaller ethnic groups in the lower-level ethnoterritories (that is, autonomous republics, autonomous oblasts, and national *okrugs*). Typically, a union republic nationality can expect education in the native language in its own ethnoterritory through secondary school, and in most instances through higher education.

Lower-ranking nationalities, by contrast, may receive native-language instruction (as the medium of instruction) only in primary school. The Russian language assumes the role of medium of instruction in those cases where the use of the native language for that purpose is terminated after a certain level. Here, however, it is important to note that students may continue to study a non-Russian language as a subject once that language ceases to be the medium of instruction.

Another facet of this question is the choice available to parents as to the type of school (Russian or native-language medium of instruction) in which their children may be enrolled. In all non-Russian ethnoterritories, in addition to the native-language schools, there have existed schools in which Russian is the medium of instruction; parents of any nationality could send their children to either type of school. However, children were required to study—as a subject—the Russian language (in the native-language schools) or the non-Russian language of the relevant ethnoterritory (in the Russian-language schools).

In 1958 the Soviet government promulgated a set of educational reforms, one of which made the study of languages other than the medium of instruction voluntary rather than mandatory. Purportedly the reason for making such a change was to alleviate the load on students in non-Russian areas enrolled in foreign (non-Soviet) language courses, who technically would have been studying three languages in school (Russian, a non-Russian Soviet language, and a foreign language). The reform, however, led to an outpouring of hostility and resistance among several of the largest non-Russian ethnic groups, to the point that the political leadership in some republics was purged. This move was also seen by many in the West as a policy aimed at furthering assimilation or at least of facilitating the hypothesized "drawing together" (Bilinsky 1962).

The second direct policy question relating to language matters is that concerning the media. The Soviet government has direct control over the official media in terms not only of content but also of linguistic format. By making available, or by not making available, newspapers, journals, magazines, books, and radio and television programs in non-Russian languages, the regime can directly influence the degree to which languages are used in everyday life, and therefore the extent to which retention of these languages continues. For example, Roman Szporluk (1979), in an extensive study of native-language use in the media of the Ukrainian and Belorussian republics, found that Ukrainian was much more widely employed than was Belorussian in their respective ethnoterritories. He concluded ". . . that linguistic assimilation in West Belorussia was being promoted by the Belorussians' exposure to Russian in the press . . . [while] . . . on the other hand in West Ukraine the media, in so far as they had any effect on language maintenance, encouraged loyalty to Ukrainian." Again it is generally the case that the number and range of non-Russian native-language publications and broadcasts are a function of ethnoterritorial status.

In addition to the role of language policy, there are other influences on assimilation that are, or could be, directly manipulated by government policy. The ethnic basis of the Soviet federation, for instance, certainly reinforces ethnic identity in a number of ways. As Grey Hodnett (1967) has detailed, extensive debate regarding the role and continuance of the Soviet federation has taken place in academic circles in the USSR. Always implicit, and at times even explicit, in this long-standing discussion is the idea that a "de-ethnicization" of the political-administrative structure would facilitate an erosion of ethnic identity and a speeding up of the assimilation process (compare Enloe 1977.)

Government policies in the arts and in academia also have an impact on the perpetuation of ethnic awareness. If such policies are fostering the "flourishing" of non-Russian culture, the effect will no doubt be to slow the rate of assimilation. Last, the Soviet regime has chosen to label the population according to nationality. In the documents required of Soviet citizens, such as the internal passport, personnel records, and the like, nationality is a highly visible facet of everyday life, and ethnic labeling probably serves to perpetuate ethnic awareness (Silver 1972, p. 36).

Beyond those factors that through direct policy application can affect ethnic awareness and assimilation, there are several elements of the general societal ambience that are widely acknowledged to have an influence on ethnic identity and identity change, but are not subject to nationality policy per se. These factors are largely demographic and economic in nature, and include ethnic mixing through interregional migration and social mobilization—that is, urbanization, the attainment of a higher level of education, and exposure to mass communications.

Brian Silver (1974), in his study of ethnic identity in the USSR, concluded that urbanization and geographic mobility were strongly related to linguistic change, in that non-Russians living in cities and/or outside their respective ethnoterritory evinced much higher levels of adoption of the Russian language in lieu of their native tongues. He suggested that language shift may in some cases presage complete assimilation. Possible reasons for this phenomenon include exposure to Russians (who predominate in cities), the isolation from the reinforcing influences of the ethnic homeland (for those who migrate out), and the fact that in large measure the mobilized, ambitious individual is likely to be more amenable to the adoption of Russian as a means of facilitating social and economic advancement. Regional development and economic and education policies can, therefore, influence ethnic assimilation indirectly through the effects of such policies on migration, urbanization, and social mobilization, although in most cases it is likely that such effects are not intentional.

Given that direct and indirect policies have had an influence on assimilation, and assuming further that social and economic factors have acted as assimilating forces outside the scope of policy application, the key question is to what extent ethnic assimilation is actually taking place, or, in the historical sense, to what extent it has taken place. Unfortunately, it is almost impossible to answer this question definitively because of data limitations and the nature of assimilation itself.

Although the Soviet censuses provide relatively good data for ethnic groups and utilize the best method of enumerating ethnic groups (self-identification), when an individual becomes totally assimilated to a new ethnic identity and declares the new identity in the census, he or she is "lost" in the aggregate figures of the losing and gaining nationalities. That is, there is no means of tracking individuals to determine the extent to which assimilation is taking place. Therefore, assimilation must be inferred from aggregate trends, which is a risky procedure. Basically, this type of estimation involves an analysis of change in the population size of ethnic groups at the national or subnational level. If we know the size of some nationality at the beginning of a given period (usually a census date), and if we have some information concerning the components of population growth for that nationality (fertility, mortality, and—at the subnational level—migration), then we can make some judgments about the magnitude of assimilation by looking at the size of the same group at the end of the period in question.

The drawbacks to what appears to be a straightforward analysis are manifold, and at times defeat the purpose. First, information on the components of population change needed for growth estimation are not usually available. Second, much of Soviet history has been of such a traumatic nature as to preclude even gross estimation of change in the size of nationalities; war losses in particular were so large in western regions that assimilation trends are virtually impossible to detect.

Nevertheless, some general estimates of the extent to which assimilation has taken place historically have been made. One such study put the total number of non-Russians who from 1926 to 1970 assimilated to the Russian ethnic group at between 4 and 6 million persons (Lewis, Rowland, and Clem 1976, pp. 282-87). The vast majority of those assimilating, according to the same study, were Ukrainians, mainly those from rural areas with longstanding contact with the dominant Russian nationality. Other groups that, in smaller numbers, have apparently experienced a significant loss of population through assimilation to the Russian identity include Karelians, Belorussians, Mari, Udmurts, Chuvash, Poles, Germans, Jews, Mordvinians, and Finns. We can infer from this pattern of assimilation that the phenomenon is most prevalent among ethnic groups with a cultural and linguistic affinity to the Russians (such as Ukrainians and Belorussians) or among nationalities that have historically been mixed geographically with the larger Russian population (such as the Mari, Udmurts, and Chuvash).

To complete and summarize this section, we will make reference to one of the earliest works on ethnicity in the USSR, that by the American scholar Vernon Aspaturian (1968). Aspaturian conceptualizes the ethnic scene in the

Soviet Union as consisting of three related elements: Sovietization, Russianization, and Russification. According to his formulation, Sovietization involves the modernization and industrialization of the USSR along Marxist-Leninist lines, while Russianization entails the spread and institutionalization of the Russian language and culture as the national norm. Russification, on the other hand, is ". . . the process whereby non-Russians are transformed objectively and psychologically into Russians, and is more an individual process than a collective one. Thus while Sovietization is universal in its effects and Russianization almost so, Russification is more restricted" (Aspaturian 1968, p. 160). Importantly, Aspaturian also views Russianization as a necessary precursor to Russification, but states clearly that Russianization could ". . . be a terminal process as well . . ." (p. 160). Relating his terms to the general literature on ethnic studies, we could say that Russianization would be the equivalent of acculturation, while Russification equals total assimilation.

In Aspaturian's terms, it would seem fair to say that whereas significant Russianization has taken place in the USSR since the inception of the Soviet regime, comparatively little Russification has occurred. In other words, although many groups have experienced acculturation to a significant extent, assimilation has been a much more limited phenomenon. This assessment runs counter to much of the thinking on assimilation in the USSR in both the West and the Soviet Union itself. In my judgment, too much emphasis has been placed on linguistic affiliation and changes therein as evincing assimilation. Rather, if linguistic shifts are seen as manifesting acculturation, which is what the universal experience suggests, then it very well might be that Russianization will be the "terminal process" alluded to by Aspaturian.

One way of substantiating the contention that true assimilation remains a distant goal is to look at the extent of interethnic marriage in the USSR. If anything, the degree to which individuals marry those of their own nationality (endogamy) is an even more sensitive indicator of the retention of ethnic awareness than is language loyalty. Suffice it to say that among the non-Russian nationalities there is a remarkably high level of endogamy—that is, very few individuals marry outside of their respective ethnic group. In the definitive work on the subject, the Soviet scholar L. V. Chuiko (1975) presented data for 1969 showing that of the 14 non-Russian nationalities of union republic status, in no case did the percentage of individuals marrying endogamously drop below 81.7 percent. To an extent, as was pointed out by Wesley Fisher (1977), endogamy is a function of other demographic, social, and cultural factors; but even allowing for the fact that the ethnic composition of many areas remains relatively homogeneous (which reduces the odds of finding a marriage partner outside one's nationality), ". . . the strength of endogamy is quite impressive." (Also see Silver 1978.)

Ironically, the lack of progress toward the assimilation of non-Russians to the Russian ethnic norm is due in large measure to direct policies of the Soviet government, policies that have had the effect of strengthening non-

Russian ethnic identity rather than, as apparently intended, facilitating the hoped-for merger of nationalities. Unquestionably, the creation and proliferation of non-Russian language schools and language instruction, the encouragement of non-Russian cultural expression (even if restricted ideologically), the retention of the ethnically based federal political structure, and the ethnic labeling of individuals has reinforced ethnic identity and awareness to a far greater degree than other forces have eroded it. Thus, Brian Silver was led to conclude in this regard: ". . . the Soviet regime's claim to have promoted a 'flowering of national cultures' is in fact reflected in the persistence of ethnic identities of non-Russians" (1972, p. 10).

THE IMPLICATIONS OF ETHNICITY FOR CONTEMPORARY AND FUTURE SOVIET SOCIETY

The USSR is a country that, like many others will face some serious difficulties in coming years. Many of the problems that are confronting, and will confront, the Soviet leadership derive from the multiethnic character of the Soviet population and the fact that, although historically ethnicity has been "managed" at least successfully enough to prevent a breakdown of the system, the ethnic factor continues to be a critical one and may even be increasing in importance. Specifically, I should like to discuss here two potential problems relating to ethnicity and to suggest, in light of what is known about such problems in general, the implications of these and other trends for the Soviet polity and society.

The Population Growth Dichotomy

One of the most startling features of Soviet society today is the extraordinary variation among ethnic groups in terms of population growth rates. Differences in the rate of population growth result from contrasting levels of fertility—as evidenced by the child-woman ratios shown in Table 1.3—because mortality (the death rate) is uniformly low, and, of course, population growth (natural increase) is determined by the balance between births and deaths (Clem 1977).

Broadly speaking, the nationalities of the European USSR (the Baltic peoples, Belorussians, Ukrainians, and—importantly—the Russians) are characterized by low to very low fertility, while the ethnic groups of Central Asia (Uzbeks, Tadzhiks, Kirgiz, Turkmen, and Kazakhs) and certain ethnic groups of the Caucasus region (Azeri, Chechens, Ingush, and the peoples of Dagestan) are increasing in number at a phenomenal rate. Most of the smaller nationalities of the Volga and Ural regions (such as the Komi, Udmurts, Chuvash, Mordvinians, Tatars, and Bashkirs), plus two of the largest Caucasian groups (Armenians and Georgians), are intermediate in this regard.

In fact, natural increase among the Central Asians and a few other groups is equivalent to that found in developing countries, while the population growth rates in the European part of the USSR are about the same as those in developed countries.

Obviously, such natural increase differentials are resulting in a shift in the numerical balance among the various ethnic groups of the USSR, with the rapidly growing Central Asian and Caucasian nationalities gaining ground on the generally larger but slowly growing European groups. Many observers have attached particular importance to the erosion of the numerical-majority status of the Russians. Although population projections are inherently risky, it would seem safe to forecast that by the year 2000, the nationalities of the Caucasus and Central Asia will account for somewhere between one-quarter and one-third of the total Soviet population, whereas as recently as 1959 their share stood at just over 10 percent. The Russian share can be expected to decline further. In addition, since most Soviet nationalities remain concentrated geographically in their respective ethnoterritories, the spatial aspect of this situation involves a relative shift in the country's population toward the southern tier of republics. That is, the Caucasus and Central Asian regions are assuming a steadily larger share of the total Soviet population (Clem, 1980).

Fertility is probably one of the most difficult to explain aspects of any society. We can say with some confidence, however, that factors known to be associated in general with different levels of fertility are in operation in the Soviet Union, and go a long way toward explaining interethnic variations in the birth rate. It seems to be the case, for example, that higher levels of urbanization, the shift from agricultural to industrial and service occupations, higher education levels, and change in the status of women (particularly their employment outside the home and their attainment of schooling on a par with men) are elements associated with lower fertility. These factors are evidenced among the European ethnic groups to a far greater extent (as was noted earlier) than among the Central Asians and some of the Caucasian nationalities. Hence birth rates tend to be lower in the former and higher in the latter (Lewis, Rowland, and Clem, 1976, ch. 7). Ironically, therefore, the workings of the ethnic stratification system have, by retarding the socioeconomic development of minority groups, contributed to the present, potentially troublesome situation of dichotomous population growth.

The ramifications of differential ethnic population growth are wide-ranging. (See the essay by David Heer in this volume.) In the economic realm, the current variations in natural increase translate into future spatial disparities in the growth of the working-age population. It is projected that virtually all new increments to the labor force will be located in the Caucasus and Central Asia. Remembering that the Soviet economy is, by comparison with most Western countries, labor-intensive, economic planners must choose whether to locate new development projects in the southern tier, where workers will be available (but where other economic conditions are not so favorable), or in the European or Siberian parts of the country, where economic conditions are more favorable (but the labor-force situation is highly disadvantageous).

The issue takes on a social dimension when the question of migration is raised. One way of solving the economic efficiency/labor-force supply problem would be through migration from labor-surplus regions (the Caucasus and Central Asia) to locations where development would be optimal in terms of other economic criteria. It would be an understatement to say that there is considerable disagreement among scholars, both in the West and in the Soviet Union, regarding the likelihood and efficacy of such a migration (Lewis, Rowland, and Clem 1976, pp. 354-81). If appreciable migration from the South to the North and West does take place, the ethnic mixing that would result could lead to heightened tensions, as it has in most other settings. On the other hand, if there is no significant movement out of the labor-surplus areas of Central Asia and the Caucasus, the government will be hard-pressed to provide sufficient jobs in situ for the rapidly growing population, and discontent might arise because of perceived disadvantage. Also, the indigenous nationalities will in either case probably take an increasingly dimmer view of the large Russian presence in their ethnoterritories, a presence that no doubt has, to a large extent, foreclosed many opportunities for the local groups in their own homelands.

The political aspects of the changing ethnic balance are even more intangible, but clearly the regime will need to make some tough decisions in light of this phenomenon. Not only will the economic and social factors involved have to be weighed, but the decision-making process will of necessity include the impact of differential growth rates among the nationalities on the military (where ethnic Russians almost exclusively man the critical armored, motorized infantry, and strategic rocket forces, and aviation components) and on the Communist party itself (Azrael 1977). As the share of the total population accounted for by the non-European ethnic groups rises, the Soviet leadership will need to decide to what extent these nationalities should be further integrated into the power structure, a decision obviously fraught with serious implications.

Ethnicity and Federalism

The creation of the Union of Soviet Socialist Republics as a federation of ethnoterritories has been viewed as a clever solution to the problem of centrifugation inherent in multiethnic states, facilitating in this case the perpetuation of the territorial integrity of the former tsarist empire while allowing for the overt expression of ethnic political autonomy. Whether this federal ethnoterritorial state structure was established for pragmatic or ideological reasons (or some combination of the two), and regardless of whether the structure itself was (is) viewed theoretically as transitory, it seems increasingly to be the case that the various ethnic groups of the USSR see the arrangement as long-term if not permanent, assign importance to it, will resist attempts to alter it in the direction of fewer ethnic prerogatives, and are now making demands on the regime through the ethnoterritorial medium. It was stated above that the ethnoterritorial structure may serve to reinforce ethnic identity and thereby slow the rate of assimilation among the non-Russian minorities. Beyond this, it will be argued that what was once thought by many to be a fraud of sorts may in fact turn out to be a means by which ethnic group political and economic interests can be legitimated and a means by which these interests vis-à-vis the state can be protected.

By linking ethnic groups and their homelands to the very structure of the state, issues that might otherwise have been "regional" become "ethnic" instead. Hence, problems connected with the spatial allocation of capital investment for development translate directly into ethnic group issues, with some nationalities contending that their ethnoterritories are being shortchanged. In this specific regard, Leslie Dienes (1972) has pointed to arguments made by Ukrainian and Belorussian planners and economists against the continued high-priority status assigned to Siberian development. Their contention is that investment monies would be better spent in European parts of the country and that their own republics have been slighted by the emphasis given to Siberia by federal agencies.

In some cases the ethnoterritorial basis of the Soviet state has allowed the nationalities to express unhappiness about the social consequences of economic policies as they relate to ethnic issues. For example, evidence came to light that indigenous elites in the Baltic republics have argued for less economic growth in their ethnoterritories, because in the past rapid growth had produced a demand for labor that resulted in a large influx of Russians and other outsiders into the region, an influx that was generally viewed with disfavor (*New York Times* 1971; Gwertzman 1972). Although specific complaints voiced in these and other cases are different, the common theme among them is the lack of genuine ethnoterritorial authority. Thus, whether the issue involves the siphoning off of funds to develop other areas, changes in the local economy that are perceived not to be in the interest of the indigenous population, or the ethnosocial concomitants of economic policies, the arguments are framed mainly in ethnoterritorial terms.

Perhaps the most dramatic statement regarding the economic position of the non-Russian homelands is that of the noted Soviet Ukrainian dissident Ivan Dzyuba. In his important work *Internationalism or Russification?*, Dzyuba (1968) criticizes the net fiscal drain from Ukraine to the federal budget (through the turnover tax) on the ground that such transfers inhibit the development of the Ukrainian ethnoterritory. Even more important, however, he is sharply critical of the lack of local authority in the decision-making process. One gets the impression that it is not the actual transfer of funds out of the republic that is the issue, but the fact that the transfer is dictated by the federal government. Thus, he concludes: "These are verily 'sovereign' governments in the Republics . . . without even the right to intervene in the economy on their own territory!" (p. 106). Without the ethnoterritorial federal structure, the expression of such grievances would be moot.

Curiously, on the one hand the Soviet federal system has been thought of as a device whose manipulation will lead to the continued repression of minorities and to an erosion of ethnic identity among the non-Russians. On the other hand there are those who see the USSR as a country that will eventually be torn apart because of its multiethnicity and the tensions emanating from it. A third view is posited here: the ethnoterritorial nature of the Soviet federation may allow for an expansion of ethnic interests to more closely approximate the constitutional prerogatives of the nationalities. In other words, the minorities may be able to use the system to their own advantage. In this regard, Teresa Rakowska-Harmstone (1974), in an article devoted to the emerging ethnic problems confronting the Soviet leadership, concluded: "The nationality-based units of the federal political-administrative system have provided the minority elites with both the bases and the means for pursuing national-group interests."

Many changes are taking place in the contemporary world as political structures are altered to accommodate the desires of ethnic groups for more control over their own affairs. In the Soviet case, the changes necessary to allow an expanded role for the minorities are actually less dramatic than is typical of most multiethnic countries, because the basic constitutional structure already exists and can be adhered to more or less strictly, as circumstances dictate. Over the long term, the extent to which genuine "devolution" occurs in the Soviet political system may prove to be the key factor in the survival of the state itself.

Conclusions

In order to appreciate fully the implications of multiethnicity for Soviet society in coming years, one must relate the situation in the USSR to the general experience as summarized at the beginning of this chapter. By so doing, not only can one profit from the broader perspective and gain insights into the Soviet case, but the applicability to the Soviet case of so many aspects of the universal experience places the USSR and its ethnic dimension squarely in the general realm rather than in the unique category.

Daniel Bell's perceptive essay (1975) points to several key aspects of ethnicity in the contemporary world that are particularly relevant to the USSR. First, the politicization of ethnicity, wherein the proliferation of the power of the state forces people to rely on ethnic groups as a means of bringing pressure to bear upon the system, is clearly relevant to the Soviet situation. The "revolution from above" made it clear to all where the center of power is, establishing the state as the focus for any demands to be made by ethnic groups. As Glazer and Moynihan (1975, p.8) put it, in the Soviet Union the state is obviously "the direct arbiter of economic well-being." The overwhelming centrality of power in the USSR and the legitimating of ethnicity have crystallized Soviet society along ethnic lines, a crystallization that will no doubt continue so long as the leadership directly or indirectly sanctions ethnicity.

The ethnic group is the ideal vehicle for making demands on the state, as Bell (1975) noted, because it combines an interest group function with an affective tie. The Soviet state has done much to validate this approach, because it insists on labeling individuals ethnically and has in fact acted (perhaps not always consciously) to stimulate ethnic awareness. This is not to suggest that the Soviet regime actively espouses the notion that ethnic groups should function as interest groups. On the contrary, expressions of nationality self-interest are usually dealt with severely if those advocating the ethnic cause confront the system openly. Yet, one suspects that there is sufficient latitude in the system even today for subtle pressure and, of course, for political infighting. It would be a mistake, in my opinion, to view the Soviet political system as totally unresponsive to ethnic group desires, as long as those desires are expressed in terms considered to be within the limits of propriety and are not openly threatening to the regime.

Second, Bell pointed to the decline of ideology as contributing further to the salience of ethnicity. In fact, he singled out the Soviet Union as a country in which ideology has become largely a rhetorical exercise. At this writing, the Bolshevik Revolution is some 60 years in the past, and one suspects that to the average Soviet citizen today, the ideological fervor characteristic of the early decades of the Communist regime is difficult to understand at best. Other attempts to divert attention away from socioeconomic reality, such as the massive campaign to perpetuate the memory of the Great Patriotic War (World War II), are probably not much more effective than appeals to revolutionary zeal. Hence, it is unlikely that in the future ethnic group demands can be put off by appeals to a "higher purpose."

Third, societies that attempt to alleviate ethnic inequalities through "affirmative action" programs, Bell stated, run the risk of polarizing the populace along ethnic lines, as people seek advantage or attempt to maintain it through their respective ethnic groups. Although not much is known about the details of affirmative action-type programs in the USSR, the Soviet government apparently undertook some form of ethnic quotas in higher education in the 1960s. It is hypothesized here that at least some of the motivation for the rise of Jewish dissidence is a response to such policies; as an achiever group that had attained a relatively advantaged socioeconomic status in Soviet society, the Jews stand to lose the most from redistributive policies. Also, the recent rise in Russian ethnic consciousness, as manifested in the "neo-Slavophilism," appears to be in the category of a "mirror-image response."

That is, if non-Russian groups find it advantageous to resort to ethnicity as a "weapon" to obtain a larger share of the fruits of Soviet society, then the Russians may well resort to their own ethnicity to protect their favored position.

As William Foltz stated in this regard, ". . . if one party defines itself according to a particular trait [that is, ethnicity] and calls in allies at a particular level of identity, the other side will reciprocate by emphasizing [its] own distinctiveness in terms of the trait . . ." (1974, p. 105). Thus, ethnic conflict in the USSR is being exacerbated, as is true in many other settings, by redistributive policies that, for whatever reason, threaten the ethnic status quo.

Finally, I earlier took note of the concept of relative deprivation as being of considerable utility in understanding the rise in ethnic conflict in multiethnic societies. There is the potential in the Soviet case for relative deprivation in its various modes to play a vital role in ethnic-group relations. Specifically, it was pointed out that perhaps the greatest single achievement of the Soviet regime, with regard to the socioeconomic development of ethnic groups, was the dramatic increase in the level of education among virtually all nationalities; Ted Gurr (1970, pp. 92-254) suggested that education is the most powerful means by which aspirations are heightened.

In the case of the USSR, if sufficient opportunities are not available to satisfy the expectations generated by the attainment of education, relative deprivation of the aspirational or progressive type will no doubt be the result. Additionally, Gurr posited that the espousal of an equalization ideology, promising in effect to eliminate socioeconomic inequities, runs the risk of leading to relative deprivation if the promised equalization does not materialize. In this vein, Rakowska-Harmstone stated that "The failure of [Soviet] government policies to achieve the goal of equality may well have contributed to a resurgence and intensification of national [ethnic] feelings . . ." (1974, p. 9). Decremental deprivation, where expectations remain high (based on earlier privileged status or achievement) but capabilities decline because of redistributive policies, is also a major force in the contemporary Soviet Union, as is evidenced by Jewish dissidence and greater Russian ethnic awareness.

It is highly unrealistic to think that all parties will be satisfied by events and, in a sense, relative deprivation of some sort is inevitable in situations such as that in which the Soviet government finds itself. Simply put, in a multiethnic society such as the USSR, which was earlier characterized by a rigid ethnic stratification system, the catalytic effects of modernization and the equalization promise explicit in Soviet nationality policy have led to relative deprivation, and will continue to do so in the future. This does not mean that the Soviet experience with ethnicity has been better or worse than that of other societies. The point is that all societies must confront the same problems inherent in multiethnicity.

In 1967, on the occasion of the fiftieth anniversary of the founding of the USSR, and for years thereafter, a host of pronouncements concerning the manner in which the victory of socialism had provided the ideal solution to ethnic conflict emanated from the Soviet leadership. The tone of these remarks was self-congratulatory, and made explicit the contention that ethnic problems in the USSR have ceased to be a matter for serious concern. In fact, the Soviet Union is facing greater, not lesser, difficulties relating directly or indirectly to ethnicity. In this regard it is not unlike other multiethnic states, although its ethnic diversity may pose greater problems than is ordinarily the case. The lessons learned from the universal experience suggest strongly that ethnicity is an increasingly more contentious feature of the contemporary world, and the Soviet leaders can ignore this only at their peril.

REFERENCES

Armstrong, John A. 1968. "The Ethnic Scene in the Soviet Union: The View of the Dictatorship." In *Ethnic Minorities in the Soviet Union,* edited by Erich Goldhagen, pp. 3-49. New York: Praeger.

Aspaturian, Vernon V. 1968. "The Non-Russian Nationalities." In *Prospects for Soviet Society,* edited by Allen Kassof, pp. 143-98. New York: Praeger.

Azrael, Jeremy. 1977. "Emergent Nationality Problems in the USSR." Rand Corporation Report R-2172-AF. September.

Bell, Daniel. 1975. "Ethicity and Social Change." In *Ethnicity: Theory and Experience,* edited by Nathan Glazer and Daniel P. Moynihan, pp. 141-74. Cambridge, Mass.: Harvard University Press.

Bell, Wendell, and Walter E. Freeman. 1974. "Introduction." In *Ethnicity and Nation-Building,* edited by Wendell Bell and Walter E. Freeman, pp. 10-15. Beverly Hills, Calif.: Sage.

Bennigsen, Alexandre, and Chantel Lemercier-Quelquejay. 1967. *Islam in the Soviet Union.* London: Pall Mall Press.

Bertsch, Gary K. 1971. *Nation-Building in Yugoslavia: A Study of Political Integration and Attitudinal Consensus.* Beverly Hills, Calif.: Sage.

Bilinsky, Yaroslav. 1962. "The Soviet Education Laws of 1958-59 and Soviet Nationality Policy." *Soviet Studies* 14, no. 2:138-57.

Bugelski, B. R. 1961. "Assimilation Through Intermarriage." *Social Forces* 40, no. 2:148-53.

Chuiko, L. V. 1975. *Braki i razvody.* Moscow: Statistika.

Clem, Ralph S. 1973. "The Impact of Demographic and Socioeconomic Forces upon the Nationality Question in Central Asia." In *The Nationality Question in Soviet Central Asia,* edited by Edward Allworth, pp. 35-44. New York: Praeger.

―――. 1975. "The Integration of Ukrainians into Modernized Society in the Ukrainian SSR." In *The Soviet West: Interplay Between Nationality and Social Organization,* edited by Ralph S. Clem, pp. 60-70. New York: Praeger.

―――. 1976. "The Changing Geography of Soviet Nationalities and Its Socioeconomic Correlates: 1926-1970." Ph.D. dissertation, Columbia University.

―――. 1977. "Recent Demographic Trends Among Soviet Nationalities and Their Implications." In *Nationalism in the USSR and Eastern Europe,* edited by George W. Simmonds, pp. 37-44. Detroit: University of Detroit Press.

―――. 1980. "Regional Patterns of Population Change in the Soviet Union 1959-1979." *Geographical Review* 70, no. 2:137-56.

Cole, Stewart G., and Mildred Wiese Cole. 1954. *Minorities and the American Promise.* New York: Harper.

Connor, Walker. 1972. "Nation-Building or Nation-Destroying?" *World Politics* 24, no. 3:319-55.
———. 1973. "The Politics of Ethnonationalism." *Journal of International Affairs* 27, no. 1:1-21.
Conquest, Robert, ed. 1967. *Soviet Nationalities Policy in Practice.* New York: Praeger.
Deutsch, Karl W. 1966. *Nationalism and Social Communication.* 2d ed. Cambridge, Mass.: M.I.T. Press.
Dienes, Leslie. 1972. "Investment Priorities in Soviet Regions." *Annals of the Association of American Geographers* 62, no. 3:437-54.
Dotson, Floyd, and Lillian O. Dotson. 1968. *The Indian Minority of Zambia, Rhodesia, and Malawi.* New Haven: Yale University Press.
Dunn, Stephen P. 1966. *Cultural Processes in the Baltic Area Under Soviet Rule.* Research Series no. 11, Institute of International Studies. Berkeley: University of California.
Dzyuba, Ivan. 1968. *Internationalism or Russification?* 2d ed. London: Weidenfeld and Nicolson.
Enloe, Cynthia H. 1973. *Ethnic Conflict and Political Development.* Boston: Little, Brown.
———. 1977. "Internal Colonialism, Federalism, and Alternative State Development Strategies." *Publius* 7, no. 4:145-60.
Ettinger, S. 1970. "The Jews in Russia at the Outbreak of the Revolution." In *The Jews in Soviet Russia Since 1917,* edited by Lionel Kochan, pp. 14-28. London: Oxford University Press.
Fisher, Jack C. 1966. *Yugoslavia: A Multiethnic State.* San Francisco: Chandler.
Fisher, Wesley A. 1977. "Ethnic Consciousness and Intermarriage: Correlates of Endogamy Among the Major Soviet Nationalities." *Soviet Studies* 29, no. 3:395-408.
Foltz, William J. 1974. "Ethnicity, Status, and Conflict." In *Ethnicity and Nation-Building,* edited by Wendell Bell and Walter E. Freeman, pp. 103-17. Beverly Hills, Calif.: Sage.
Glazer, Nathan, and Daniel P. Moynihan. 1975. "Introduction." In *Ethnicity: Theory and Experience,* edited by Nathan Glazer and Daniel P. Moynihan, pp. 1-26. Cambridge, Mass.: Harvard University Press.
Gordon, Milton M. 1964. *Assimilation in American Life.* New York: Oxford University Press.
Gurr, Ted Robert. 1970. *Why Men Rebel.* Princeton: Princeton University Press.
Guthier, Steven L. 1977. "The Belorussians: National Identification and Assimilation, 1897-1970." *Soviet Studies* 29, nos. 1, 2:37-61, 270-83.
Gwertzman, Bernard. 1972. "Protest on Soviet Laid to Latvians." *New York Times,* Feb. 27, p. 11.
Hechter, Michael. 1975. *Internal Colonialism: The Celtic Fringe in British National Development, 1536-1966.* Berkeley: University of California Press.
Hodnett, Grey. 1967. "The Debate over Soviet Federalism." *Soviet Studies* 28, no. 4:458-81.
Horne, Alistair. 1978. *A Savage War of Peace: Algeria, 1954-1962.* New York: Viking Press.
Hurvitz, Nathan. 1958. "Sources of Middle Class Values of American Jews." *Social Forces* 37, no. 2:117-23.
Kozlov, V. I. 1969. *Dinamika chislennosti narodov: metodologiia issledovaniia i osnovnye faktory.* Moscow: Nauka.
Lenin, V. I. 1965. "Speech Closing the Debate on the Party Programme." In *Collected Works,* vol. xxix, pp. 186-96. London: Lawrence and Wishart.
Lerner, Daniel. 1958. *The Passing of Traditional Society: Modernizing the Middle East.* New York: Free Press.
Lewis, Robert A. 1971. "The Mixing of Russians and Soviet Nationalities and Its Demographic Impact." In *Soviet Nationality Problems,* edited by Edward Allworth, pp. 117-67. New York: Columbia University Press.
Lewis, Robert A., Richard H. Rowland, and Ralph S. Clem. 1976. *Nationality and Population Change in Russia and the USSR: An Evaluation of Census Data, 1897-1970.* New York: Praeger.
Meinig, D. W. 1971. *Southwest: Three Peoples in Geographical Change, 1600-1970.* New York: Oxford University Press.
Miller, John H. 1977. "Cadres Policy in Nationality Areas." *Soviet Studies* 29, no. 1:3-36.
New York Times. 1971. "Latvians Chided for Nationalism." *New York Times,* Mar. 21, p. 17.
———. 1972. "Two Hundred Lithuanians Reported Jailed." *New York Times,* June 14, p. 1.

_____. 1978. "Soviet Georgians Win in Language." *New York Times,* Apr. 18, p. 2.
Perevedentsev, V. I. 1965. "O vliianii ethicheskikh faktorov na territorial'noe pereraspredelenie naseleniia." *Izvestiia Akademii Nauk SSSR,* seriia geograficheskaia 4:31-39.
Pipes, Richard. 1968. *The Formation of the Soviet Union.* Rev. ed. New York: Atheneum.
Pokshishevskii, V. V. 1969. "Etnicheskie protsessy v gorodakh SSSR i nekotorye problemy ikh izucheniia." *Sovetskaia etnografiia* 5:3-30.
Price, Charles. 1969. "The Study of Assimilation." In *Migration,* edited by J. A. Jackson, pp. 181-237. Cambridge: Cambridge University Press.
Raeff, Marc. 1971. "Patterns of Russian Imperial Policy Toward the Nationalities." In *Soviet Nationality Problems,* edited by Edward Allworth, pp. 22-42. New York: Columbia University Press.
Ragin, Charles. 1977. "Class, Status, and 'Reactive Ethnic Cleavages': The Social Bases of Political Regionalism." *American Sociological Review* 42, no. 3:438-50.
Rakowska-Harmstone, Teresa. 1970. *Russia and Nationalism in Central Asia: The Case of Tadzhikistan.* Baltimore: Johns Hopkins University Press.
_____. 1974. "The Dialectics of Nationalism in the USSR." *Problems of Communism* 23, no. 3:1-22.
Richardson, Harry W. 1975. *Regional Development Policy and Planning in Spain.* Lexington, Mass.: D. C. Heath.
Rosen, Bernard C. 1959. "Race, Ethnicity, and the Achievement Syndrome." *American Sociological Review* 24, no. 1:47-60.
Seton-Watson, Hugh M. 1967. *The Russian Empire, 1801-1917.* London: Oxford University Press.
Shibutani, Tamotsu, and Kian M. Kwan. 1965. *Ethnic Stratification: A Comparative Approach.* New York: Macmillan.
Silver, Brian D. 1972. "Ethnic Identity Change Among Soviet Nationalities: A Statistical Analysis." Ph.D. dissertation, University of Wisconsin, Madison.
_____. 1974. "The Impact of Urbanization and Geographical Dispersion on the Linguistic Russification of Soviet Nationalities." *Demography* 11, no. 1:89-103.
_____. 1978. "Ethnic Intermarriage and Ethnic Consciousness Among Soviet Nationalities." *Soviet Studies* 30, no. 1:107-16.
Smirnov, I. 1892. "Obrusenie inorodtsev i zadachi obrusitel'noi politiki." *Istoricheskii vestnik* 47:752-65.
Strodtbeck, Fred L., Margaret R. McDonald, and Bernard C. Rosen. 1957. "Evaluation of Occupations: A Reflection of Jewish and Italian Mobility Differences." *American Sociological Review* 22, no. 5:546-53.
Szporluk, Roman. 1979. "West Ukraine and West Belorussia: Historical Tradition, Social Communication, and Linguistic Assimilation." *Soviet Studies* 31, no. 1:76-98.
Van Dyke, Vernon. 1977. "The Individual, the State, and Ethnic Communities in Political Theory." *World Politics* 29, no. 3:343-67.
Whitney, Craig R. 1978. "Soviet Georgians Take to Streets to Save Their Language." *New York Times,* Apr. 15, p. 3.

3

POPULATION POLICY
David M. Heer

VIEWS OF MARX AND ENGELS ON POPULATION POLICY

The Soviet state declares itself to be based upon Marxist principles. Accordingly, it will be fitting to begin this chapter with a summary of the views of Karl Marx and his collaborator Friedrich Engels on population. Much of what Marx had to say concerning this topic was a reaction to the views of the English economist Thomas Robert Malthus (1766-1834). In his *Essay on Population*, first published in 1798, Malthus (1959) advanced the viewpoint that population growth tends to outstrip increase in the means of production; the former grows at an exponential rate, whereas the latter increases only by a constant amount. Furthermore, Malthus believed that any short-term increase in wages would lead to a reduction in the death rate, hence to an acceleration of population growth, and thereby ensure the impossibility of any long-term increase in the wage level. In short, the existence of poverty was inescapable. In later years Malthus (1960) changed his views on the inevitability of an acceleration of population growth, given a short-term increase in the wage level. However, it was to Malthus' earlier opinions, not to his later views, that Marx (1959) devoted his attack, for if Malthus' original viewpoint was correct, then it followed that the advent of socialism could not abolish poverty. Therefore Marx argued that the "iron law of wages" was a feature only of the capitalist system and not of production systems in general. In particular he contended that the periodic crises of unemployment in capitalist societies were the result of overproduction and not of overpopulation.

Moreover, he believed that technological advance could most probably keep up with population growth (Petersen 1970; Meek 1971).

The most complete discussion of population policy from Marxian standpoint was contained in a letter by Engels (1971) to Karl Kautsky, written in 1881. After discounting the likelihood that under socialism population growth would ever outstrip the increase in the means of subsistence, he added:

> There is of course the abstract possibility that the number of people will become so great that limits will have to be set to their increase. But if at some stage communist society finds itself obliged to regulate the production of human beings, just as it has already come to regulate the production of things, it will be precisely this society, and this society alone, which can carry this out without difficulty (Engels 1971).

HISTORY OF SOVIET POPULATION POLICY AND LEGISLATION FROM 1917 TO THE PRESENT

Changes in the four components of population growth—mortality, fertility, immigration, and emigration—may all be influenced by government decrees and legislation. Some of the legislation affecting population size is intentionally designed to influence it. However, much of the legislation affecting population size has some other goal as its principal aim. Only the former can be called population policy; but one cannot neglect the latter, since its total effect on population size may be greater than that of the legislation consciously so designed. It is fair to say that in the early years of the Soviet regime, population policy was not a salient concern. On the other hand, a large number of decrees, designed to promote other ends, had a major impact on population growth.

In the Soviet Union (USSR), neither immigration nor emigation has played an important role in population growth. Accordingly, the population growth rate has been affected principally by changes in the death rate and in the birth rate. Figure 3.1 presents the birth and death rates in the Russian Empire and in the Soviet Union from 1861 to 1977. With the exception of sharp peaks in the death rate and nadirs in the birth rate associated with World War I, the collectivization campaign of the early 1930s, and World War II, the pattern shown is similar to the typical pattern of the demographic transition in which there is movement from an initial stage, marked by the presence of both a high death rate and a high birth rate, to an intermediate stage, characterized by an acceleration of the rate of natural increase induced by a sharp drop in the death rate but little drop in the birth rate, to a final stage, in which both the death rate and the birth rate are low. Disregarding the years of war and civil turmoil, it is also evident from Figure 3.1 that the demographic transition began in the tsarist period, which saw a substantial decline in the death rate and only a small decline in the birth rate. During the

FIGURE 3.1
Birth and Death Rates in the Russian Empire and the Soviet Union, 1861-1977

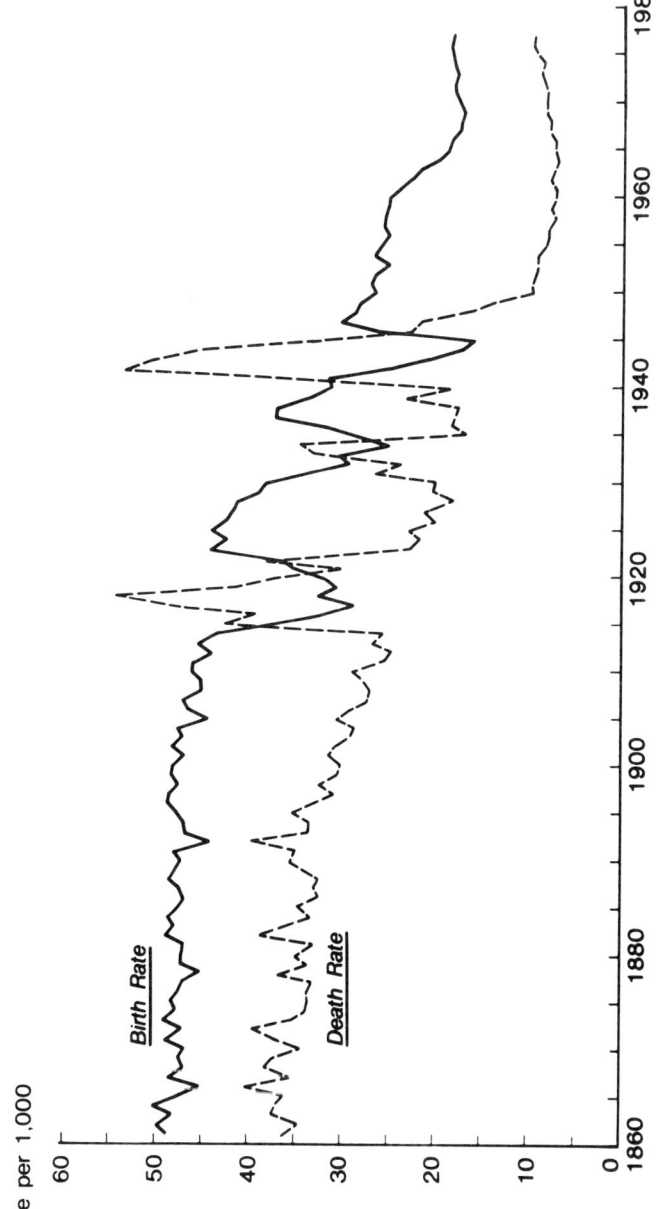

Sources: Biraben 1958; Ts.S.U. 1977, p. 69; *Vestnik statistiki* 1978, p. 86.

early years of Soviet rule, on the other hand, the birth rate began to decline precipitously. This rapid decline began during the period when the Soviet regime had no conscious population policy. However, there can be little doubt that this birth-rate decline played an important role in Stalin's decision in 1936 to take active measures to increase population growth by raising the birth rate.

Legislation Without Population Policy

Lenin displayed little interest in population policy. However, he did hold strong views on the status of women, and these views affected his position on specific issues that had repercussions for the Soviet birth rate. Lenin clearly agreed with Engels' assertion in 1884 (Marx and Engels 1934, p. 462) of the necessity to both establish legal equality between men and women and to draw women into "public industry" in order to overcome the "open or disguised domestic enslavement of women" within the family (see the essay by Michael Paul Sacks in this volume).

In accordance with Lenin's views concerning the position of women, the Soviet Union in 1920 became the first government in the world to legalize abortion. Following the legalization of abortion, the number of abortions relative to the number of births was at first small but then grew rapidly, particularly in the cities. In Moscow, for example, the ratio of abortions to births was 0.19 in 1921, 0.55 in 1926, and reached 2.71 in 1934 (Lorimer 1946, p. 127). By 1934 the impact of abortion was felt widely throughout the Soviet Union. The Soviet demographer Boris Urlanis (1963, p. 27) reports that in the Russian Republic in that year, there were 700,000 legal abortions and only 3 million births.

In his essay in this volume, Sacks shows that the Soviet government also took very seriously Lenin's ideas that women should participate equally with men in the labor force. The increased economic activity of females since the late 1920s was probably a major factor in the fertility decline in the Soviet Union. This was true even in rural areas, where the collectivization of agriculture was responsible for a very great intensification of female economic activity (Eason 1963, p. 47).

In addition to policies on the status of women, several other policies of the Soviet government, not directly designed to affect the Soviet birth rates, in fact had negative impact on it. One of these was the decision to promote rapid urbanization of the population in conjunction with the decision to promote rapid industrial growth. Since the birth rate in urban areas of the Soviet Union was considerably lower than that in rural areas, any net migration from rural to urban areas should have a negative effect on the Soviet birth rate as a whole. However, the effect of urbanization on the Soviet birth rate was less than might be expected, the birth rate in the rural areas of the Soviet Union declined much more rapidly than in the urban areas. This has mitigated the effect of increasing urbanization on the birth rate of the nation as a whole. We may make a rough estimate of what the birth rate in the Soviet Union in 1976 would have been, without any further urbanization since 1913, by multiplying the urban birth rate in 1976 by .18 (the proportion of the total population urban in 1913) and the rural birth rate in 1976 by .82 (the proportion of the total population rural in 1913) and summing the two products. The resulting birth rate for the entire nation in 1976 would be 19.7 per thousand, little different from the actual rate of 18.4. The calculation ignores the effect of differences in age-sex composition and of marital status on the birth rate of urban and rural areas. However, taking these facts into account probably would alter the results very little.

Another major policy decision that the Soviet regime made during the period of its industrialization drive, beginning with the First Five-Year Plan, was to allocate very little money for the construction of new urban housing. More funds would then be available for the construction of factories, new machinery, and other purposes the regime believed would increase production more than new housing would. During this period, the amount of urban housing space per capita declined. In 1926 there had been 8.21 square meters per capita; by January 1, 1940, there were only 6.67 square meters per capita (Heer 1968, p. 237). Since the rearing of children demands space, this change in the amount of available housing is likely to have had a negative effect on fertility. On the positive side, the Soviet regime may be credited with making substantial advances in three areas: health services, education, and social security.

The tremendous improvement in health services brought about by the Soviet regime, though not the only cause of the rapid decline of mortality in the USSR, has no doubt been a major factor. Because mortality decline most probably is highly influential in reducing fertility, the improvement of health services has no doubt been a major factor in the fall of the Soviet birth rate as well. Two indexes of the improvement of health services are the number of doctors and the number of hospital beds per 10,000 population. The first index increased from 1 in 1913 to 4 in 1928, to 7 in 1940, to 14 in 1950, and to 33.5 in 1976. For the same years the hospital beds per 10,000 were 13, 16, 40, 56, and 119 (Heer 1968, p. 222; Ts.S.U. 1977, pp. 626, 628).

Another impressive accomplishment of the Soviet regime has been a very marked increase in the level of educational attainment. Among males nine to 49 years of age, the percent literate increased from 40.3 percent in 1897 to 71.5 percent in 1926, to 93.5 percent in 1939, and to 99.3 percent in 1959. Among females of identical age and for the identical years, the corresponding percentages were 16.6, 42.7, 81.6, and 97.8 (Ts.S.U. 1962, p. 88). Data from nations throughout the world show that the level of educational attainment, particularly among females, is one of the strongest correlates of the level of fertility; as educational level advances, the birth rate declines. On a worldwide level, there are several reasons why educational advance provokes fertility decline. First there is an increased flow of information concerning birth control; second, a rise in the average age at marriage; and third, with respect to female educational advance, a shift in the balance between the desirability of work outside the home versus childbearing, since the higher the woman's educational attainment, the higher the wage she is likely to get for work outside the home. In the Soviet Union, advances in educational attainment probably reduced fertility by all three of these modes.

It may be supposed that a very important factor in the development of the small-family ideal may be the institutionalization of an impersonally organized social security system for the elderly. Such a system obviates the need to keep on bearing children until one has assurance that one's children (most probably one or more sons) will survive to support one in old age. Following the Bolshevik Revolution, a comprehensive government-sponsored system of social security was gradually developed for all wage and salary earners. Old-age pensions were first established for textile workers in 1927. All wage and salary employees were covered in 1937. Only in 1965 was a centralized pension system established for workers on collective farms under which the Soviet government assumed a partial responsibility. Currently, state employees have quite substantial old-age benefits, and there should be no motivation to have many children simply to support one in old age (Heer 1968, pp. 225-27).

The Turn to Population Policy

By 1935 the reduction of the birth rate from pre-Soviet levels had been very substantial. In 1913 the birth rate had been 45 per thousand; in 1935 it had declined to 28 per thousand. With the 1935 death rate at 16 per thousand, the rate of natural increase was only 12 per thousand (Biraben 1958). During 1935 the Soviet government began to question the wisdom of its policy of legal abortion in view of the declining birth rate. A new regulation issued in that year forbade the abortion of a first pregnancy. On June 27, 1936, abortion was prohibited except in cases where the health of the mother was in danger from certain specific diseases or where the child, if born, was likely to suffer from a hereditary defect (Lorimer 1946, p. 128).

The decision to raise the birth rate by prohibiting abortion was apparently taken out of fear of Nazi Germany. A low birth rate would mean insufficient soldiers some 20 years later.

The immediate effect of the 1936 prohibition of abortion was dramatic, especially in the cities. In the USSR as a whole, the 1937 birth rate was 20 percent higher than that of 1936. In Moscow the number of births in 1937 increased by 91.5 percent over the 1936 figure, in Leningrad by 68.7 percent, in Minsk by 38.5 percent, and in Baku by 39.4 percent (Urlanis 1963, p. 29).

The Soviet government also took its first steps in 1936 toward establishing a child allowance program. However, the program instituted in that year was of only minimal importance. According to the 1936 program, annual cash allowances were provided only for children of seventh birth order or higher until such children reached their fifth birthday (Heer and Bryden 1966).

The 45 million population loss during World War II is estimated at around 20 million deaths beyond what would have been expected in peacetime and a further deficit of 25 million persons, mainly in the form of births forgone (Urlanis 1971, pp. 284, 306). This provoked a marked change in the Soviet child allowance program. In 1944 this program was extended to provide a lump sum at birth for third and subsequent children, and for the fourth child and subsequent children, monthly payments from the first to the fifth birthday. Both types of payments increased sharply with the number of older living children. Unmarried mothers received, in addition, monthly sums for their first three children until they reached the age of twelve. However, in 1947, immediately after World War II, it was decreed that beginning January 1, 1948, all child allowance benefits would be cut in half. The 1948 schedule of payments is still in effect and is shown in Table 3.1. It should be made clear that a mother gets a separate payment for each of her eligible children. Thus, if she has five living children and her two youngest children are between one and four years old, she will receive a monthly payment of 6 rubles on behalf of her youngest child and 4 rubles on behalf of her second youngest (Heer and Bryden 1966).

TABLE 3.1
Schedule of Payments to Mothers of Large Families and to Unmarried Mothers in the USSR (in rubles)

	Lump Sum at Birth of Child	*Monthly on Behalf of Child*	*Period of Monthly Payments*
Mothers of large families			First to fifth birthday
Number of older living children			
2	20	—	
3	65	4	
4	85	6	
5	100	7	
6	125	10	
7	125	10	
8	175	12.5	
9	175	12.5	
10 or more	250	15	
Unmarried mothers			Birth to twelfth birthday
Number of living children			
1	—	5	
2	—	7.5	
3	—	10	

Source: Kal'yu and Morozov 1958, p. 333.

The incentive value of the child-allowance payments is most probably not a function of their absolute size, but of their magnitude relative to the average wage. Taking this into consideration, we must conclude that from 1944 to 1974, the official Soviet effort to encourage childbearing by financial subsidy was reduced drastically. For example, in 1944 the annual payment the year the fifth child was born and the fourth child was aged one to four equaled 50.5 percent of the average annual wage. In 1948 this percentage was reduced to 19.0 (following the 50 percent reduction in the amount of the payment and a considerable general inflation, which raised the average wage level), and it dropped to 11.2 percent in 1964 (Heer and Bryden 1966). By 1974 the value of the allowance was no more than 7.9 percent of the annual wage (Heer 1977).

The continual erosion in the relative value of family-allowance payments was not the only legislative action (or inaction) that had an antinatalist effect in the Soviet Union in the years following World War II. In 1955, after nearly 20 years of restrictive laws, the Soviet Union enacted a liberalized law under which abortions are performed on the request of the woman and in the absence of medical contraindications. This abortion law was of great importance in reducing the Soviet birth rate. From Soviet data on the ratio of abortions per thousand working women and per thousand nonworking women David Heer (1965) earlier estimated that in the late 1950s there must have been more abortions than live births in the Soviet Union. The East German demographer K. H. Mehlan (1966), came to a similar conclusion; he stated "on personal information and knowledge of the situation" that the ratio of abortions to live births may be assumed to be one to one. In 1969 official data on the percentage increase in the number of abortions since 1954 were published for the first time (Sadvokasova 1969). These data, presented in Table 3.2, include both legal and illegal abortions. They show clearly the substantial rise in the number of abortions immediately after legalization in 1955 and a gradual increase from that time until 1965.

TABLE 3.2
Index Numbers for Incidence of Abortions: Soviet Union, 1954-66

Year	Index Number	Year	Index Number
1954	100.0	1961	374.0
1955	130.9	1962	391.6
1956	238.0	1963	404.1
1957	268.9	1964	423.5
1958	308.7	1965	430.7
1959	322.3	1966	419.9
1960	354.5		

Note: Each figure in the table is the result of dividing the number of abortions, both legal and illegal, for the particular year by the number in 1954 and multiplying by 100.

Source: Sadvokasova 1969, p. 117.

The reasons given for legalizing abortion in 1955 were twofold. First, it was contended that there already was a large number of abortions being performed illegally, many of which were done outside hospitals and in unsanitary conditions. Second, the legalization of abortion was in congruence with Leninist doctrine that no woman should be forced to bear a child she did not want (Kal'yu and Morozov 1958, p. 333). Moreover, official Soviet statements concerning population policy enunciated at that time definitely contradict the hypothesis that Soviet population policy was intended to be antinatalist. The most explicit and authoritative pronatalist statement was made by Soviet leader Nikita Khrushchev in January 1955. He then declared:

> Bourgeois ideology invented many cannibalistic theories, among them the theory of over-population. Their concern is to cut down the birth rate, reduce the rate of population increase. It is quite different with us, comrades. If about 100 million people were added to our 200 million, even that would not be enough. Under socialism the raising of the birth rate is regarded not only as a means of providing greater labor power. The socialist state also looks at the matter from the viewpoint of the nation's future (*East Europe* 1959).

I have said that the relegalization of abortion in 1955 had a substantial effect in reducing the Soviet birth rate. However, paradoxically, the Soviet birth rate did not decline in the six years following 1955. The reason for this is that the trend in Soviet fertility was not well measured by the crude birth rate. In 1955, because of tremendous population losses during World War II, which struck particularly hard at men in uniform, the ratio of men to women in the reproductive age groups was still exceedingly low. This ratio rose constantly in each succeeding year. The fact that the birth rate did not rise after 1955 implies that the fertility of Soviet married women decreased substantially during the period from 1955 to 1961 and that this decrease in marital fertility was counteracted by the increased proportion of Soviet women who were married. Further evidence that the fertility of Soviet married women declined substantially after 1955 is obtained by examining figures concerning the trend in male fertility in the USSR. Estimates of the gross reproduction rate for Soviet males (the number of sons born per father at the age-specific rates of siring sons for a specific year) computed by the U.S. Bureau of the Census showed a reduction from 2.19 in 1955 to 1.84 in 1961, a decline of 16 percent (Brackett 1962, p. 546).

Concomitant with the decline in marital fertility was an apparent substantial increase in the proportion of urban women aged 16 to 54 who were employed. I have earlier estimated this proportion to have increased from about 61 percent in 1959 to 80 percent in 1970 (Heer 1977).

Moreover, beginning in the early 1960s, changes in age composition began to militate against the maintenance of a high birth rate. Specifically, the small number of births during World War II began to be reflected in a smaller number of women entering the chief childbearing ages. Whereas in 1961 the birth rate had been 23.8 per thousand, by 1965 it had declined to 18.5 and by 1970 to 17.5 per thousand. Changes in age and sex composition also contributed to an increase in the crude death rate, from 7.2 per thousand in 1961 to 8.2 per thousand in 1970. As a consequence of these changes in birth and death rates, the rate of natural increase, which had been 16.6 per thousand in 1961, sank to 11.1 per thousand in 1965 and declined again to 9.2 per thousand in 1970 (Heer 1972).

These trends set the stage for a new governmental effort to encourage childbearing. On November 1, 1974, the government put into effect a new program of income supplementation whereby families with a total per capita income (from all sources) of less than 50 rubles a month would receive a payment of 12 rubles per month for each child under age eight. This new program supplements rather than replaces the 1947 program that provides child-allowance payments to all families with given numbers of children, regardless of their income (*New York Times*, Sept. 28, 1974).

Introduction of the 1974 program followed repeated recommendations by Soviet demographers for increased government action to raise the birth rate. For example, Viktor Perevedentsev, a leading Soviet demographer, gave the following rationale for such action:

> Some thought should also be given to the international aspect. A country's position in the world, all other things being equal, is determined by the size of the population. In 1940 the USSR's share of the world population came to 8.6 percent, in 1960 to 7.2 percent. If we assume that the world population will grow 2 percent annually (as it has in recent years) and that the population of the USSR will grow 1 percent annually, then by the beginning of the 21st century the population of the USSR will constitute about 5 percent of the world population.
>
> Should we not weigh all the consequences of a decline in the birth rate? Is it not worthwhile to attempt to find some sort of golden mean between the interests of our "today" and our "tomorrow"? (1968, p. 11).

Table 3.3 illustrates the relative magnitudes of the old and new benefits for eight types of families. The first panel shows four families in which husband and wife earn incomes of 90 and 70 rubles per month, respectively; the second panel provides data for four families with identical numbers and ages of children, but with the husband and wife each earning 150 rubles a month—close to the current national average wage. As the table indicates, the 1974 allowance program provides benefits for families with as few as two children, provided the husband and wife do not each earn much above the minimum legal wage of 70 rubles; for families in which both husband and wife earn the average wage, the new program provides benefits only to those with more than four children.

TABLE 3.3
Relative Size of 1947 and 1974 Child-Allowance Payments for Various Types of Families

Family Income and Type of Allowance	Number of Children (and ages)			
	Two Children (aged 1 and 3)	Four Children (aged 1,3,5,8)	Six Children (aged 1,3,5,7, 9,11)	Ten Children (aged 1,3,5,7,9, 11,12,13,14)
Husband earns 90 rubles and wife earns 70 rubles				
Allowance under old program	—	4	13	25
Allowance under new program	24	36	48	48
Total allowance under both programs	24	40	61	73
Ratio of total allowance to allowance under old program	n.a.	10	4.7	2.92
Husband and wife each earn 150 rubles				
Allowance under old program	—	4	13	25
Allowance under new program	—	—	48	48
Total allowance under both programs	—	4	61	73
Ratio of total allowance to allowance under old program	n.a.	1	4.7	2.92

— = not eligible.
n.a. = not applicable.

Source: David M. Heer, "Three Issues in Soviet Population Policy," *Population and Development Review* 3, no. 5. (September 1977): 232. Used with the permission of the Population Council.

Another way of examining the relative importance of the old and new programs of child-allowance payments is to look at their relative cost in rubles. In 1975 total annual expenditures for the old program were 389 million rubles; for the new program they were 1.219 billion rubles. Thus total 1975 expenditures on the two programs combined were 1.608 billion rubles, more than four times the amount spent under the old program (Heer 1977).

THREE CURRENT ISSUES IN SOVIET POPULATION POLICY

I have already mentioned that the decline in the Soviet birth rate that took place after 1960 has been a matter of concern to Soviet demographers. The 1974 legislation on child-allowance payments reflected this anxiety. However, I have yet to mention a second trend in the Soviet Union that has also been troubling to Soviet demographers: the increasing proportion of total births and of total natural increase occurring in the five union republics of Central Asia and the Transcaucasus that are inhabited predominantly by persons of Islamic nationalities. The demographic processes in these five republics are now characteristic of those of a developing country in the second stage of the demographic transition—that is, falling death rates and continuing high birth rates produce an accelerated rate of population growth. In 1959 births in the Uzbek, Azerbaidzhan, Kirgiz, Tadzhik, and Turkmen republics constituted only 12.4 percent of all births in the USSR; by 1970 this proportion had risen to 19.5 percent. Moreover, the natural increase of population in these republics rose from 14.8 percent of the total natural increase in the Soviet Union in 1959 to 29.9 percent in 1970. By 1969-70 the net reproduction rate (the best measure of the intrinsic trend in natural increase, defined as the number of daughters born per woman, given the current age-specific fertility and mortality rates) in the USSR was 1.11. In the largely Islamic Transcaucasian Republic of Azerbaidzhan it was 2.1, and in the four Central Asian republics it was 2.5. By contrast, in the same year the net reproduction rate in the Russian Republic was only 0.92, in the Ukrainian Republic 0.94, and in the Latvian Republic 0.90 (Heer 1977). According to Viktor Perevedentsev (1973), "These five relatively less populous republics guarantee at the present time that the net reproduction rate for the country as a whole is greater than unity."

These two trends—the national fertility decline and the increasing dominance of fertility in Central Asia and the Transcaucasus—have given rise to a genuine debate among Soviet demographers as to proper policy for the Soviet government. The relevant issues may be formulated in three questions:

1. To what extent should the government extend child-allowance payments and other subsidies to mothers to encourage childbearing, even at the expense of such other social goals as the maintenance of the current proportion of women who work and the attainment by women of equal status with men?

2. To what extent should the government attempt to reduce the large and growing gap between the fertility of the Slavic and Baltic nationalities, compared with that of the Islamic nationalities in the Transcaucasus and Central Asia? Should government efforts be directed only at raising the fertility of the former nationalities, or at lowering the fertility of the latter as well?

3. Given the likelihood that a high rate of natural increase among the Islamic peoples will continue for some time, what measures, if any, should the government take to prevent the rapid population growth in Central Asia from having an adverse effect on local standards of living?

The following discussion of these three questions will be based both on an examination of the published writings of leading Soviet demographers and on my own interviews with many of them in January 1976.

Let us begin by considering the views of Soviet demographers on the need to increase the birth rate and on the value of financial subsidies to encourage childbearing. One school of thought is represented by Boris Urlanis and Viktor Perevedentsev, two of the best-known Soviet demographers, from the USSR Academy of Sciences, who have advocated additional government subsidies to mothers in order to raise the Soviet birth rate. A second view has been expressed by A. Ya. Kvasha of Moscow University, who questions the need to raise the birth rate but favors child allowances for other reasons. Still a third viewpoint has been voiced by V. P. Piskunov and Valentina S. Steshenko, a husband-and-wife team of demographers from the Academy of Sciences of the Ukrainian Republic, who oppose the provision of family allowances to encourage childbearing. Although our focus is on the differences in viewpoint among these individuals, it should be emphasized that none of them favors a repeal or modification of the 1955 legislation freely allowing abortion.

In a book published in 1974, Urlanis approved the legislation of that year with regard to child allowances for low-income families, but felt that it did not go far enough. In his own words:

> It is proper to consider the decisions of the 24th Congress of the Communist Party of the Soviet Union establishing the new allowances as a definite step in the direction of the perfection of demographic policy. Following these decisions, new decisions should follow which will guarantee the important and priceless element of the future productive forces of our nation—its population (1974, p. 306).

In Urlanis' view an additional type of child allowance was necessary:

> In our opinion subsidies granted at the birth of second and third children might play a large role in the matter of stimulation of the birth rate. It is generally well known that many married couples limit themselves to the birth of one child. Having one child is a widespread phenomenon.
>
> Meanwhile it is clear that having one child does not renew a generation. Therefore, it is especially important to stimulate the birth of second and third children (1974, pp. 294-95).

Uranis has also favored paid leave to working women with responsibility for taking care of small children. In his 1974 book he discussed the Hungarian policy of giving all working women a three-year leave after the birth of a child, with a payment of 600 forints a month in urban areas and 500 forints a month in rural areas. But the Hungarian policy falls short of maximizing the demographic effect, according to Urlanis, because it sets a fixed payment rather than an amount that would be a fixed proportion of the woman's wage. In my personal interview with him in 1976, Urlanis stated that he advocated a law that would grant a Soviet woman 60 percent of her former pay for one year if she stopped working after the birth of a child.

In the discussion of Soviet demographic policy in his 1974 book, Urlanis devoted considerable attention to the Soviet network of child-care establishments. Orthodox Marxian theory has held that, as socialism is gradually transformed into Communism, the family, like the state, will wither away and child-rearing responsibilities will be transferred from parents to public institutions. In contradistinction to this orthodox position, Urlanis stated:

> However, we consider that no social institution can be a substitute for maternal care and concern during the first period of the child's life. The very prominent authority on these matters, the American public figure Doctor B. Spock, states concerning this question: "The company of his mother grants the child tremendous satisfaction." "Affection," notes Spock, "has as much meaning for the emotional development of the child as milk for the physical" (1974, pp. 299-300).

Urlanis continued:

> [Despite] a high level of servicing of preschool establishments and despite the low cost of maintenance of children for the parents the birth rate in the greater part of the territory of the USSR is at a low level. This speaks for the fact that the provision of preschool establishments can be regarded more as a condition guaranteeing the possibility of the application of female labor than as a factor in the rise of the birth rate (1974, p. 301).

The views set forth by Viktor Perevedentsev are very similar to those of Urlanis. Noting the usefulness of the 1974 legislation on child allowances for the poor, he went on to elaborate further necessary measures:

> However, the great majority of Soviet demographers consider that in the current situation it is necessary to undertake even stronger measures. . . . In the opinion of specialists, one should establish one-time and monthly grants for children beginning with the second child, establish a yearly paid leave after each birth, develop thoroughly the network of kindergartens so that each family may, if it wishes, place its children in them.
> The possible measures of demographic policy are very numerous. One should, moreover, always consider the demographic aspects of measures which have chiefly another intention. Thus in the establishment of pensions it is proper to consider more fully than at present the number of children born and raised by the mother" (1975, p. 80).

More than any other demographer, A. Ya. Kvasha has been concerned with problems of defining optimum population size and growth rates. Expressing a viewpoint at variance with those of the majority of demographers, Kvasha (1970, pp. 40-47) questions the desirability of raising the Soviet birth rate. He states that the ideal level of the net reproduction rate for the USSR is between 1.0 and 1.2. The actual net reproduction rate in the Soviet Union in recent years has been about 1.1.

Despite his disagreement with Urlanis and Perevedentsev about the need to raise the birth rate, Kvasha (1974b, pp. 170-74) concurs with them on the value of child allowances for second and third children and of paid leaves for working mothers following the birth of children. Why he favors these measures while opposing a rise in the birth rate will be explained later.

The demographers V. P. Piskunov and Valentina S. Steshenko (1975) disagree strongly with the views of Urlanis, Perevedentsev, and Kvasha on the advisability of child allowances for second and third children and on the desirability of women with nursery-age children being given the means to stay at home. In a 1974 paper they first express doubts that the birth rate can easily be raised in socialist societies, and emphasize that a society has other goals than merely encouraging births. They then present their own "feminist" solution:

> Although voices have recently been heard contending that women's allegedly excessive activity in the economy is a factor in the decline of the birth rate to a most inauspicious level, the way to improve the present demographic situation lies not in reducing women's economic activity but in raising it further. . . . The task is gradually to create working conditions that will not require women to choose between children and jobs. . . . Only a rapid development of the area of service industries and education of the rising generation by society, along with simultaneous employment of all means of ideological and moral influence, can assure expanded reproduction of the families of people at the very highest professional levels. . . . Thus further development of free and subsidized goods and services and their adaptation to the needs of socio-demographic development is the principal path to solution of problems of population in developed socialist society (1975, pp. 53,54,56).

Let us now turn our attention to the second issue, the extent to which the Soviet government should attempt to reduce the large and growing fertility gap between the Islamic nationalities and the non-Islamic. More than any other Soviet demographer, A. Ya. Kvasha has devoted his attention to the disadvantages inherent in such a fertility gap:

> It is also doubtful whether one could consider optimum the type of reproduction of the population existing presently in the Central Asian Republics on account of the very great demographic investments: the rearing of a large number of children prevents the growth of the cultural level of the mothers who have many children, long interruptions in work limit the opportunity for participation in labor and social life (1970, p. 38).

In a later publication Kvasha discussed the adverse effects of the high birth rate in Central Asia on the qualitative composition of the USSR's population, and pointed out that an important feature of the qualitative composition was the ability to speak the language—Russian—"which is most widespread in a multilanguage nation" (1974a, p. 26).

Another drawback to the high population growth rate in Central Asia, as seen by Kvasha, is the fact that the rate of out-migration from that region is so low:

> The mechanization of agriculture also facilitates the liberation of a part of the labor force. There are even other reasons, of a social-cultural dimension, for the resettlement from country to city. In the republics of Central Asia these processes also go on but their intensity is slowed down by a series of difficulties of which we have already spoken above. This leads to a concentration in a number of regions of a large mass of labor force which it is hard to use in the areas of labor shortage (1974a, p. 29).

He sets forth his own policy goals as follows:

> It is necessary to stimulate by various measures the birth of first, second, and third children within the family; moreover of second more than of first, and third more than second. But, beginning with the fourth child, all measures of an encouraging nature should cease or as a minimum be considerably reduced. Such a system would encourage fertility in regions where it is low and further its reduction in areas where it is high (1974b, p. 140).

Among Soviet demographers only Perevedentsev (1973) appears to take the position that it is only necessary to increase the birth rate among the non-Islamic populations and not to lower it among the Islamic. His position is based on his belief that the fertility level in Central Asia will soon drop, and that it may drop so much that the net reproduction rate in the USSR as a whole may fall below unity.

What effect, if any, did the 1974 policy of allowances for children in low-income families have on the gap between the fertility of Islamic and non-Islamic populations? Unfortunately, since the Soviet government has released no information on the number of children receiving the new allowances by nationality, or even by republic, an exact answer to this question cannot be given. However, we can be reasonably sure that a much higher proportion of the families of Islamic background than of the families of European background are receiving the 1974 benefits. A nationwide survey of families of workers and employees conducted by V. A. Belova (1975, p. 136) provides some relevant data for 1969. Belova reported that among the Islamic populations the average number of expected children was 6.24, and 81.2 percent of families expected to have four or more children. By contrast, among the European nationalities the average number of expected children was 2.16, and only 6.0 percent expected four or more. In addition, because per capita income in the predominantly Islamic republics is only about half that of the USSR as a whole (in part because of very high fertility), more families in these republics will be eligible for the benefits for children in poor families ("The Development Gap" 1976). As was shown in Table 3.3, a family in which the earnings of both husband and wife were at the average level (each earning 150 rubles) would not be eligible for the new benefits, even with four children.

In assessing the impact of the 1974 allowances, it should be noted that benefits under the 1947 child-allowance program also went disproportionately to families of Islamic background (Heer and Bryden 1966); thus it is not certain whether the 1974 program helps reduce the fertility gap or serves to widen it further. Nevertheless, there can be little doubt that the kind of program advocated by Kvasha would be more effective in reducing the fertility gap than the policy adopted in 1974.

But the current very high rate of population growth in Central Asia (between 2 and 3 percent per year) is a fact, and it is unlikely that this high rate can be decelerated quickly. For this reason, the government of the USSR must decide to what extent, if any, it wishes to take positive action to prevent this rapid population growth from adversely affecting the local standard of living. A number of courses of positive action seem possible: stimulating the further industrialization of Central Asia and simultaneously encouraging a large-scale migration of the rural Islamic population to its cities; encouraging migration of the Islamic populations of Central Asia to other parts of the USSR, notably Siberia, where the shortage of labor is most acute; substantially enlarging the scope of agriculture in Central Asia by diverting waters from Siberian rivers to irrigate the Central Asian deserts; and providing financial subsidies of various kinds to the people of Central Asia so that their standard of living will not decrease relative to that of persons elsewhere in the USSR.

A major barrier to the migration of the rural Islamic population out of Central Asia or even to the Central Asian cities is their lack of fluency in the Russian language, as shown in Table 3.4. Lack of knowledge of Russian also partly explains the low enrollment of Central Asian nationalities in specialized technical institutes, where in most cases the language of instruction is Russian. The Soviet economist L. Chizhova (1975) has noted that a number of new enterprises in Central Asia and in Transcaucasia have had difficulty recruiting a sufficient number of skilled workers, and has called for an accelerated growth of enrollment of the native population in technical institutes. Another economist, R. Galetskaya (1975), has emphasized the language barrier as a major impediment to out-migration and has declared that the study of Russian should be mandatory in the USSR's national-language schools. However, such a policy of compulsory Russian study runs counter to the demands of many of the intelligentsia of the Islamic populations for limitation of the use of the Russian language rather than its spread (Katz 1975, p. 230; Hetmanek 1975, p. 257).

TABLE 3.4
Percentage of Population of Each Major Islamic Nationality Speaking Russian as Native or Second Language, 1970

Nationality	Total	Urban	Rural
Uzbek	15.0	36.3	7.9
Kazakh	43.5	61.1	37.0
Azerbaidzhan	17.9	34.9	6.7
Kirgiz	19.4	54.8	13.4
Tadzhik	16.0	34.4	9.6
Turkmen	16.2	34.5	8.0

Source: David M. Heer, "Three Issues in Soviet Population Policy," *Population and Development* 3, no. 5 (September 1977) :247. Used with the permission of the Population Council.

Although to my knowledge no Soviet academician explicitly advocates facilitating the out-migration of Central Asian nationalities to Siberia, the area with the greatest labor shortage, at least one Soviet economist, A. Dadashev (1974) has urged the establishment of "wage differentials to encourage a greater outflow of manpower from regions in which labor resources are in surplus and growing rapidly and to discourage outflow from regions in which labor resources are growing slowly." Such a policy, although no doubt helpful in the long run in guaranteeing Central Asia a living standard equal to that of the rest of the Soviet Union, would in the short run aggravate the differences in living standards between that region and Siberia.

SOVIET POPULATION POLICY IN CROSS-NATIONAL PERSPECTIVE

The formally pronatalist policy of the USSR is in strong contrast with the predominant thrust of population policy in the less-developed nations of the world. Among 130 developing nations, 33 have an official policy to reduce the rate of population growth. These 33 nations had a total population of 2.15 billion persons in 1975, a population equal to 54 percent of the world's total. Among the less-developed nations, an additional 31 countries with a total population of 454 million provided official support of family-planning activities for other than demographic reasons (Nortman and Hofstatter 1976). The policy of the USSR can be considered to fall into the category of nations supporting family-planning activities for other than demographic reasons.

This is because the USSR provides contraceptive and abortion services through its national health service. On the other hand, most of the developing nations that provide family-planning services for nondemographic reasons do not simultaneously attempt to increase the birth rate through child allowances.

Rather than compare the population policy in the USSR with that of the less-developed nations, it is more appropriate to compare the USSR policy with that in other developed nations. Here we find that Soviet policy, which provides both pronatalist financial incentive and free access to family-planning services, is duplicated by many other nations. Almost every European nation provides child allowances to all families with a minimum specified number of children. In fact, the United States is one of the very few developed nations that does not provide such payments. Bryden and Heer (1966) compared the magnitude of the Soviet child-allowance program relative to Soviet national income with that of the programs in a number of other nations relative to their national incomes. According to the results of that research, the value of the child-allowance payments relative to national income in the USSR in 1961 was less than that in eight other nations for which data were available. The payments were equal to 0.32 percent of the national income in the USSR (defined, according to Soviet usage, as net material product at market prices), whereas in the eight other nations the payments ranged from 0.39 percent of national income in West Germany to 4.76 percent in France.

How does the Soviet program compare with that of France, now that the USSR makes payments not only to all families with the specified minimum number of children but also to all children under age eight in poor families? In 1975 the total national income of the USSR (computed as net material product at market prices) was 363.3 billion rubles. The sum of the payments in 1975 under the old child-allowance program and under the new program for children in poor families (1.608 billion rubles for both) constituted only 0.4 percent of the national income (Ts. S.U. 1977, p. 485; *Vestnik statistiki* 1977, p. 96). This percentage can be compared with the latest figures on child-allowance payments as a percentage of total national income in France, where in 1974 the child allowance payments constituted 2.6 percent of the national income (Institut National 1976, pp. 607,689). Thus the expanded Soviet program, although providing much more in benefits than in years prior to 1974, is still quite small relative to the magnitude spent by France for this purpose. Moreover, since national income, under the Soviet definition, is somewhat smaller than it would be under a Western definition, the gap between the French child-allowance program and that of the USSR is even greater than stated in our comparison.

The child-allowance programs in the Soviet Union may also be compared with the Aid to Families with Dependent Children (AFDC) program in the United States. The AFDC program in each American state is administered separately, so requirements for admission are not uniform. However, with the exception that in some states children of unemployed fathers qualify, the payments are made only where the father is absent or permanently disabled. In 1975, among children receiving aid under the program, 87 percent had an absent father. The total number of children receiving AFDC payments in the United States in 1975 was 8.121 million. The $9.211 billion spent on the AFDC program in 1975 was equal to 0.8 percent of the national income in the United States (U. S. Bureau of the Census 1978b, p. 359). This figure is considerably larger than the 0.4 percent of national income spent for the combination of the 1947 and 1974 programs in the USSR. Moreover, when we consider that under Soviet definition the national income of the USSR is less than what it would be under Western definition, it is obvious that the Soviet expenditures on child allowances relative to national income are indeed small compared with AFDC payments relative to national income in the United States.

Nations have two major goals in setting a policy concerning an optimum population size or growth rate, and Soviet investments in pronatalist policies like child-allowance programs can be understood in terms of these. One goal is to maximize military power. A second goal is to maximize the level of living of the inhabitants. For some nations an attempt to influence the population growth rate will serve both of these goals. For others the attempt to attain one of these goals will militate against attaining the other. In general the population size that will maximize a nation's military power will be larger than the population size that will maximize the nation's level of living (Sauvy 1969).

At the present time the USSR is probably one of the nations for which the actual population is less than the one that maximizes military power, but more than the one that maximizes the average level of living. Moreover, the Soviet government currently appears to place greater emphasis on maximizing its military power than on maximizing its citizens' average consumption. Hence, the emphasis among most Soviet demographers on increasing the Soviet birth rate is not altogether surprising.

DIFFICULTIES IN STUDYING SOVIET POPULATION POLICY

At the present time the USSR publishes a large amount of demographic data on a regular basis. The situation today is very different from what it was prior to 1957. Until then the Soviet government had released no data either on the size of its population or on its birth and death rates since before World War II. In its latest statistical yearbook the Soviet Central Statistical Administration (Ts. S. U.) released estimates of population size for the Soviet Union as a whole, its local administrative units, and its cities; age-specific fertility rates for the USSR as a whole and urban and rural portions thereof, and for each union republic; and age-specific death rates for the USSR as a whole (Ts.S.U. 1977, pp. 39-74).

On the other hand, not all demographic data that are collected are published. For example, the annual number of abortions in the Soviet Union has never been released, despite the fact that a table showing the increase in number of abortions over the base year of 1954 has been published. Furthermore, the Soviet Union has never provided data on age-specific death rates for such local areas as republics or oblasts. Moreover, although the annual statistical yearbooks for many years published data on the infant mortality rate in the Soviet Union, this rate was not published for any year after 1974; age-specific death rates were last available for 1975-76, then were eliminated from subsequent yearbooks. The reason for this was most probably that the infant mortality rate had risen to a level that the Soviet government thought was unacceptably high. The infant mortality rate in the Soviet Union declined almost every year from 1950 to 1971, from 80.7 per thousand live births to 22.9. Then the rate rose each subsequent year, reaching 27.9 per thousand live births in 1974. The age-specific death rate for persons under five years of age was 8.2 per thousand persons for 1974-75 and 8.7 per thousand for 1975-76 (Ts.S.U. 1976, pp. 40, 43, 73). From this one might presume that the infant mortality rate has continued to rise (for a discussion of possible causes, see Dutton 1979).

With respect to the child-allowance program, the Soviet government has consistently published the number of women who received child allowances each year from the 1947 program, according to the number of children. There has also been consistent publication of the amount of money spent each year on that program. The Soviet government has also released, for each year from 1975 through 1977, the annual expenditures on allowances for children in poor families under the 1974 legislation.

Finally, it should be reiterated that the Soviet government has never published data on the ethnic distribution of its child-allowance payments under either the 1947 or the 1974 program. Given the published data on the much higher expected number of children among families of Islamic nationalities than among families of non-Islamic nationality, one can deduce that the awards go disproportionately to the former class of families. Nevertheless, there is still no way of determining the exact proportion of all payments made to families of Islamic nationalities.

PROGNOSTICATING FUTURE SHIFTS IN POPULATION POLICY IN THE SOVIET UNION

The thrust of legislation in the Soviet Union affecting the birth rate has sometimes been pronatalist and sometimes antinatalist. From 1917 to 1936 all legislation affecting the birth rate was antinatalist. Beginning in 1936, this direction was reversed. Abortion was prohibited and child allowances were introduced. Relative to the average wage, the child allowances were at their maximum in 1944, in the midst of World War II—a time when the Soviet Union had suffered gigantic losses not only from deaths in its existing population but also from births forgone. Beginning in 1947 and continuing through 1974, the thrust of Soviet legislation was again antinatalist; the monetary amounts of the child allowances were cut in half in 1947 and abortion was relegalized in 1955. Most recently, the 1974 legislation of allowances for children in low-income families has given a new pronatalist thrust to Soviet policy. Moreover, many Soviet demographers believe that additional measures should be taken to increase the Soviet birth rate.

Before venturing any comments on what future shifts to expect in Soviet population policy, it will be appropriate to look at the demographic position of the Soviet Union in comparative perspective. With a January 17, 1979, population of 262.4 million, the USSR ranked third in the world. Only China, with a population approximating 950 million, and India, with a population of 661 million, were larger. At the same time the population of the United States, which ranked fourth in size, was 220.3 million. In 1977 the birth rate in the USSR was 18.1 per thousand, the death rate was 9.6 per thousand, and the rate of natural increase was 8.5 per thousand. In the United States in that year the birth rate was 15.3 per thousand, the death rate 8.8, and the rate of natural increase 6.5. Because of substantial immigration from abroad, the growth rate of the United States was higher than the rate of natural increase—8.0 per thousand. Thus, in 1977 the rates of population growth in the United States and the USSR were quite similar. The rate of population growth in India was very much higher, approximately 20 per thousand, and that of China somewhat higher, perhaps around 14 per thousand. For the world as a whole, the rate of population growth was about 17 per thousand (*Vestnik statistiki* 1979, p. 67; 1978, p. 87; U.S. Bureau of the Census 1978a, pp. 5, 6; Population Reference Bureau 1979).

In the long run, if the USSR wished to maximize its power against its two chief adversaries, the United States and the People's Republic of China, it might plausibly advance toward this goal through an artificial stimulation of its birth rate. On the other hand, the short-run effects on military power of an attempt to raise the birth rate would be just the opposite. A rise in the birth rate might produce more soldiers, but only 18 to 20 years later. Meanwhile, the subsidies proposed by many Soviet demographers to raise the birth rate would have the immediate consequence of reducing the number of females in the labor force, and increasing the demand for housing and child-care facilities. In subsequent years there would be an increased demand for teachers and educational facilities. All of these factors would militate against large-scale military expenditures unless the consumption expenditures of the Soviet population were reduced by an amount equal to the direct and indirect costs of the additional births. Therefore, the Soviet government most probably has ambivalent feelings toward any further proposals to subsidize births.

Moreover, although the Soviet Union contains a very large proportion of all of the mineral and energy reserves of the world, these reserves are not unlimited. For example, even though currently the USSR is the world's largest producer of petroleum, the U.S. Central Intelligence Agency (1977) believes that Soviet petroleum production will begin to decline as early as the 1980s. The moral here is obvious: the population size that might provide a maximum level of military power today may be larger than the one that would provide the maximum level of military power a generation hence, when the USSR's reserves of materials and energy are less.

Moreover, the Soviet Union has always had difficulty producing enough food for its populace. In 1972 and in 1975 it was forced to import large quantities of grain from the United States. The present (early 1980) U.S. sanctions against the Soviet Union, as a result of its movement of troops into Afghanistan, are forcing the USSR to seek large-scale imports elsewhere, but they are unlikely to fully meet the nation's requirements. Can a nation that currently cannot always feed its own population expect to do better when its population is larger? Only persons with a very great faith in the future technological advance of Soviet agriculture can answer affirmatively.

In summary, in view of both the short-term negative consequences of efforts to raise the birth rate and the long-term prospects for the USSR with respect to the availability of natural resources, I find it difficult to believe that the Soviet government will take further steps to encourage the birth rate beyond what it has already done with its 1974 legislation.

Another major concern of Soviet demographers has been the gap between the rate of natural increase among the Islamic nationalities and the non-Islamic nationalities. Most Soviet demographers would like to see that gap diminish. Yet the 1974 legislation did little if anything to achieve this. If the Soviet Union wishes at least to maintain its birth rate at its current level, it will probably be easier to do so by keeping the existing fertility gap rather than attempting to raise the birth rate among nationalities that do not want many children and reducing it among the nationalities that do. Moreover, it is possible that the 1974 legislation was adopted not only for demographic reasons but also in response to pressure from the Islamic populations for financial help to reduce the burden of their large families. Given the continued existence of the Sino-Soviet conflict and the fact that most of the approximately 35 million Soviet persons of Islamic background live close to the Chinese border, the Soviet government may not have been able to risk the disaffection of this segment of its populace.

Finally, it is probable that most Soviet demographers would like to see an acceleration of the rate of population growth in Siberia and a deceleration of the rate of growth in Central Asia. One way of accomplishing this might be to make greater efforts to force the Central Asians to learn the Russian language and then encourage migration to Siberia by increasing the differential between the average wage paid in Siberia and that paid in Central Asia.

However, this policy would serve to antagonize the Islamic nationalities. Rather than risk their disaffection, I believe that the Soviet government will more likely decide to spend the large amounts of money necessary to divert the waters of the Irtysh and Ob rivers in Siberia to the arid areas of Central Asia, and thus greatly expand that region's agriculture base. Concurrently, I believe that the Soviet government will also decide to take further steps to promote large-scale industrialization in Central Asia rather than attempt as much industrialization in Siberia as might seem rational on other grounds.

REFERENCES

Belova, V. A. 1975. *Chislo detei v sem'e.* Moscow: Statistika.
Biraben, Jean-Noël. 1958. "Essai sur l'évolution démographique de l'U.R.S.S." *Population* 13 (June): 41-44.
Brackett, James W. 1962. "Demographic Trends and Population Policy in the Soviet Union." In U.S. Congress, *Dimensions of Soviet Economic Power,* pp. 542-54. Washington, D.C.: U.S. Government Printing Office.
Chizhova, L. 1975. "Methods of Analyzing the Available Manpower Supply of the Country's Regions." *Planovoye khozyaistvo* no. 3, pp. 50-54; translated in *Current Digest of the Soviet Press* 27, no. 34:7.
Dadashev, A. 1974. "On Increasing the Effectiveness of the Utilization of Labor Resources." *Voprosy ekonomiki* no. 4, pp. 119-23; translated in *Current Digest of the Soviet Press* 26, no. 34:4.
"The Development Gap Between the Union Republics Widens." 1976. *Radio Liberty Research,* RL363/76. July 20.
Dutton, John, Jr. 1979. "Changes in Soviet Mortality Patterns, 1959-77." *Population and Development Review* 5 (June): 267-91.
Eason, Warren W. 1963. "Labor Force." In *Economic Trends in the Soviet Union,* edited by Abram Bergson and Simon Kuznets. pp. 38-95. Cambridge, Mass.: Harvard University Press.
East Europe. 1959. Vol. 8, no. 7 (July): 32.
Engels, Friedrich. 1971. "Population and Communism (from Engels' letter to Kautsky of 1 February 1881)." In *Marx and Engels on the Population Bomb,* edited by Ronald L. Meek, pp. 119-21. Berkeley: Ramparts Press.
Galetskaya, R. 1975. "The Areas of Demographic Policy." *Voprosy ekonomiki* no. 8, pp. 149-52; translated in *Current Digest of the Soviet Press* 27, no. 45:15-16.
Heer, David M. 1965. "Abortion, Contraception, and Population Policy in the Soviet Union." *Soviet Studies* 17 (July):76-83.
_____. 1968. "The Demographic Transition in the Russian Empire and the Soviet Union." *Journal of Social History* 1 (Spring): 193-240.
_____. 1972. "Recent Developments in Soviet Population Policy." *Studies in Family Planning* 3 (Nov.): 257-64.
_____. 1977. "Three Issues in Soviet Population Policy." *Population and Development Review* 3 (Sept.): 229-52.
Heer, David M., and Judith G. Bryden. 1966. "Family Allowances and Fertility in the Soviet Union." *Soviet Studies* 28 (Oct.): 153-63.
Hetmanek, Allen. 1975. "Kirgizistan and the Kirgiz." In *Handbook of Major Soviet Nationalities,* edited by Zev Katz, Rosemarie Rogers, and Frederick Harned, pp. 238-61. New York: Free Press.
Institut National. 1976. *Annuaire statistique de la France.* Paris: Institut National de la Statistique et des Études Économiques.

Kal'yu, P. I., and N. N. Morozov, eds. 1958. *Postanovleniya KPSS i sovetskogo pravitel'stva ob okhrane zdorov'ya naroda.* Moscow: Medgiz.

Katz, Zev. 1975. "Kazakhstan and the Kazakhs." In *Handbook of Major Soviet Nationalities,* edited by Zev Katz, Rosemarie Rogers, and Frederick Harned, pp. 213-37. New York: Free Press.

Kvasha, A. Ya. 1970. "Concerning the Optimum Type of Population Reproduction in the USSR." In *Voprosy demografii,* edited by A. G. Volkov, pp. 33-47. Moscow: Statistika.

———. 1974a. *Problemy demograficheskogo optimuma.* Moscow: Izdatel'stvo Moskoskogo Universiteta.

———. 1974b. *Problemy ekonomiko-demograficheskogo razvitiya SSSR.* Moscow: Statistika.

Lorimer, Frank. 1946. *The Population of the Soviet Union: History and Prospects.* Geneva: League of Nations.

Malthus, Thomas R. 1959. *Population: The First Essay.* Ann Arbor: University of Michigan Press.

———. 1960. "A Summary View of the Principle of Population." In Thomas Malthus et al., *Three Essays on Population,* pp. 13-59. New York: Mentor.

Marx, Karl. 1959. "Critique of the Gotha Program." In *Marx and Engels: Basic Writings on Politics and Philosophy,* edited by Lewis S. Feuer, pp. 112-32. New York: Anchor Books.

Marx, Karl, and Friedrich Engels. 1934. *Correspondence, 1846-1895.* London: Lawrence and Wishart.

Meek, Ronald L., ed. 1971. *Marx and Engels on the Population Bomb.* Berkeley: Ramparts Press.

Mehlan, K. H. 1966. "Combatting Illegal Abortion in the Socialist Countries of Europe." *World Medical Journal* 13 (May-June):84-87.

Nortman, Dorothy, and Ellen Hofstatter. 1976. "Population and Family Planning Programs: A Factbook." *Reports on Population/Family Planning,* no. 2. 8th ed. New York: The Population Council.

Perevedentsev, Viktor. 1968. "Continuation of a Controversy." *Literaturnaya gazeta* no. 12 (Mar. 20):11.

———. 1973. "I Pay for the Responsibilities, I Give Loans." *Nash sovremennik* no. 7:142.

———. 1975. "Demography: Situation, Problems, Policy." *Zhurnalist* no. 6:80.

Petersen, William. 1970. *The Politics of Population.* Gloucester, Mass.: Peter Smith.

Piskunov, V. P., and V. S. Steshenko. 1975. "On the Demographic Policy of Socialist Society." In *Demograficheskaya politika,* edited by V. S. Steshenko and V. P. Piskunov. Moscow: Statistika, 1974. Translated in *Soviet Sociology* 13 (Spring): 42-59.

Population Reference Bureau. 1979. *1979 World Population Data Sheet.* Washington, D.C.: Population Reference Bureau.

Sadvokasova, E. A. 1969. *Sotsial'no-gigienicheskie aspekty regulirovaniya razmerov sem'i.* Moscow: Meditsina.

Sauvy, Alfred. 1969. *General Theory of Population.* New York: Basic Books.

Tsentral'noe Statisticheskoe Upravlenie SSSR pri Sovete Ministrov SSSR (Ts.S.U.). 1962. *Itogi vsesoiuznoi perepisi naseleniya 1959 goda: SSSR (svodnyi tom).* Moscow: Gosstatizdat.

———. 1973. *Itogi vsesoiuznoi perepisi naseleniya 1970 goda,* vol 4, *natsional'nyi sostav naseleniya SSSR.* Moscow: Statistika.

———. 1976. *Narodnoe khozyaistvo SSSR v 1975 g.* Moscow: Statistika.

———. 1977. *Narodnoe khozyaistvo SSSR za 60 let.* Moscow: Statistika.

Urlanis, Boris Ts. 1963. *Rozhdaemost' i prodolzhitel'nost zhizni v SSSR.* Moscow: Gosstatizdat.

———. 1971. *Wars and Population.* Moscow: Progress Publishers.

———. 1974. *Problemy dinamiki naseleniya SSSR.* Moscow: Nauka.

U.S. Bureau of the Census. 1978a. *Current Population Reports,* series P-20, no. 336. Washington, D.C.: U.S. Government Printing Office.

———. 1978b. *Statistical Abstracts of the United States.* Washington, D.C.: U.S. Government Printing Office.

U.S. Central Intelligence Agency. 1977. *Soviet Economic Problems and Prospects.* Washington, D.C.: Library of Congress.

Vestnik statistiki. 1977. No. 3.

———. 1978. No. 11.

———. 1979. No. 5.

4

SOCIALISM AND SOCIAL STRATIFICATION
Richard B. Dobson

Surely one of the most striking features of modern Soviet history is the degree to which the Communist regime has endeavored to shape the society's social structure and distribution of rewards. After seizing power in 1917, the Bolsheviks embarked on a social revolution of unprecedented proportions. Having quickly abolished the legal foundation of the traditional estate structure, the regime struck at the basis of capitalism by nationalizing banks, factories, and railroads. A decade later, abruptly ending the New Economic Policy (1921-28) that had permitted a modicum of private enterprise, it launched a "second revolution." To realize its ambitious First Five-Year Plan, the state pressed ahead with its program to industrialize the country at a breakneck pace. Meanwhile, "class war" raged in the countryside as soldiers expropriated land and livestock belonging to the more wealthy peasants (called kulaks), and all peasants were brought—often through coercion—within the collective farms.

In 1936, Stalin proclaimed the triumph of socialism in the USSR. According to the official interpretation faithfully ennunciated by party spokesmen since then, state and cooperative ownership of the means of production sharply distinguishes the Soviet "class structure" from that of capitalist societies. Finding theoretical support for this position in the works of Karl Marx, Friedrich Engels, and V. I. Lenin, Soviet ideologists take Lenin's definition of "social classes" as their keystone (cited in Blyakhman and Shkaratan 1977, pp. 145-46):

> Classes are large groups of people differing from each other by the place they occupy in a historically determined system of social production, by their relation (in most cases fixed and formulated by law) to the means of production, by their role in the social organization of labour, and, consequently, by the dimensions of the share of social wealth of which they dispose and the mode of acquiring it.

From this perspective, socialistic property relations have given rise to two "fraternal" classes—the working class, composed of industrial, agricultural, and other blue-collar workers employed in state enterprises, and the socialist peasantry made up of members of the collective farms. In addition, nonmanual employees (*sluzhashchie*) in state and public organizations, who are distinguished from state workers by their type of work, are seen as constituting a separate white-collar "stratum."

In line with the standard Soviet interpretation, the Communist party maintains this social order and directs its course of change in accordance with true "scientific knowledge" of social processes derived from Marxist-Leninist ideology. While socialist property relations are thought to preclude any conflict of interests among these three large groups, the party's policy avowedly ensures that differences among them are being constantly reduced. In contrast to capitalist societies, which continue to be torn by class conflict and to be subject to the many evils attendant to capitalism, Soviet society is viewed as having before it a vista of harmonious, continuous, and inevitable progress—movement ever closer to "communism," a social order in which all class distinctions will have been overcome, the state's coercive functions will have fallen away, and all workers will be rewarded according to their needs (see Amvrosov 1972, 1975; Chesnokov 1973; Glezerman 1973).

COMPARISONS WITH WESTERN COUNTRIES

By abolishing private ownership of the means of production, the Communist regime set the Soviet Union apart from Western countries, in which a small fraction of the population possesses the great bulk of private capital and its accompanying privileges. But concurrently, as the scope of state authority was expanded and elements of opposition were suppressed, an extraordinary degree of political power became concentrated in the hands of a small elite at the apex of the Communist party and the state. Taking account of the wide powers exercised by the political elite, the British sociologist John H. Goldthorpe argues that, resemblences notwithstanding, social stratification in the USSR is "genotypically" different from that in Western societies:

> ... in the West economic, and specifically market forces act as the crucial stratifying agency within society . . . [and] consequently, the *class* situation of individuals and groups, understood in terms of their economic

power and resources, tends to be the most important single determinant of their general life chances. . . . [In contrast,] stratification in Soviet society is subjected to *political* regulation; market forces are not permitted to have the primacy or the degree of autonomy in this respect that they have even in a "managed" capitalistic society (1956, pp. 655-56).

Making a similar point, the Polish émigré sociologist Zygmunt Bauman (1974) asserts that two principles of hierarchy—"officialdom" and "class"—coexist under socialism (cited in Connor 1979, pp. 104-05). The first reflects the ability of the political elite to manipulate the distribution of resources in society in accordance with its preferences. The second derives from the fact that labor, goods, and services are exchanged for money, so that in disposing of their incomes, individuals have differential life chances, as well as some autonomy in making choices.

The extent to which the distribution of rewards is subject to political regulation has consequences both for the determination of individuals' statuses and for the crystallization of social strata. Being able to set wage and salary rates across the board, state planners can manipulate earnings differentials among occupations and groups in accordance with policy objectives. Planners are, of course, subject to such constraints as the nature of the labor supply, workers' motivations, and so on; they have limited information at their disposal; and they confront value conflicts in choosing, for example, between "equality" and "efficiency." Yet, inasmuch as their decisions need not coincide with the outcomes in capitalist economies, the places of individuals and groups in the stratification orders may differ. Being contingent upon their performance, rather than based on institutionalized wealth or on skills that can be freely traded in a more open, competitive market, the privileges enjoyed by individuals in high-status positions (especially administrators and political officials) may be more precarious than those of their counterparts in the West. On the other hand, being assured of employment, Soviet workers may have a more secure position than workers in capitalist countries.

Also, the party's monopoly of power and the absence of institutionalized channels, such as competitive elections, for broad social groups to influence policy formation hinders their becoming conscious and politically relevant entities. Inasmuch as the party consciously attempts to prevent groups or classes from acquiring a corporate identity and from being able to articulate their interests, the USSR appears to be more of a "classless" society than Western countries do (Feldmesser 1960). Finally, in Soviet society, privilege is likely to derive from political power (that is, position of authority, especially in the party), whereas in a country like the United States, where wealth is an important asset in electoral contests, political power may flow from wealth (Hollander 1973, pp. 210-11).

Only rarely do Soviet sociologists address the problem of "power" and of inequalities associated with it. Yet, such problems were openly discussed in the one classic Communist work that sought to confront "bourgeois" sociology, Nikolai Bukharin's *Historical Materialism: A System of Sociology*. This book, first published in the Soviet Union in 1921, was a required party text during Lenin's lifetime. In it, Bukharin (1969, p. 309) dealt with the arguments of Robert Michels, who contended that socialism "assigns at least as much power to the administrators as would possession of their own private property," so that for Michels, socialism "seems to be nothing more than a substitution of one group of leaders for another."

Acknowledging the cogency of Michels' argument, Bukharin emphasized the importance of the social division resulting from "the differences between the work of those who command and those who obey, the differences expressed in the property relations" (p. 282). He insisted, however, that Michels made certain incorrect assumptions about the working class's inability to govern. During "the *transition period* from capitalism to socialism, *i.e.,* the period of the proletarian dictatorship," Bukharin foresaw conflicting tendencies:

> There will inevitably result a *tendency* to "degeneration," i.e., the excretion of a leading stratum in the form of a class-germ. This tendency will be retarded by two opposing tendencies; first by the *growth of the productive forces;* second, by the *abolition of the educational monopoly*. The increasing reproduction of technologists and of organizers in general, out of the working class itself, will undermine this possible new class alignment. The outcome of the struggle will depend on which tendencies turn out to be stronger (1969, pp. 310-11).

A decade and a half later, the exiled revolutionary leader Leon Trotsky published *The Revolution Betrayed,* an analysis of changes in Soviet society that was far more pessimistic than Bukharin's. The Soviet Union, Trotsky asserted, had witnessed the rise of a privileged ruling stratum "which does not engage directly in productive labor, but administers, orders, commands, pardons and punishes" (1965, p. 138). In Trotsky's judgment (pp. 52-60), the formation of this privileged stratum was caused by various determinants—above all, underdevelopment of the means of production and the resultant scarcity of goods and services. To stimulate workers' productivity and spur economic growth, the state relied on "bourgeois norms" and material incentives; under these circumstances, persons in commanding positions found it possible to expropriate a disproportionate share of the economic "surplus." As Trotsky saw it:

> The state assumed directly and from the very beginning a dual character: socialistic, insofar as it defends social property in the means of production; bourgeois, insofar as the distribution of life's goods is carried out with a capitalistic measure of value and all the consequences ensuing therefrom. . . . So long as even a modest "Ford" remains the privilege of a minority,

there survive all the relations and customs proper to a bourgeois society. And together with them, there remains the guardian of inequality, the state (1965, pp. 54, 57-58).

Though one would expect that recent Soviet sociological studies would shed some light on Bukharin's forecast (not to mention Trotsky's more heretical view), Soviet scholars have studiously avoided all research into the degree of privilege in the upper reaches of society and have seldom inquired into the degree of control that the "masses" purportedly exercise. The points made by Bukharin and Trotsky remain controversial.

Though differing importantly in political and economic structure, the Soviet Union and the developed capitalist countries of the West obviously share common features. As in other industrialized countries, forms of rational economic organization and technology shape the stratification order in the USSR by affecting the division of labor, the distribution of rewards, criteria for advancement, and many aspects of social relations. With the advance of industrialization, occupational specialization emerges as the key determinant of social stratification, because remuneration for work performed is the main institutionalized mechanism for the distribution of rewards. In all industrial societies, technical expertise is prized, and the educational system serves to train and select individuals for various positions in the work force.

Further parallels may be drawn between the USSR and the United States. Both countries were born of revolution—upheavals that differed in important respects, to be sure, but that marked a violent beginning of a "new order." The revolutionary creed in both countries gave strong emphasis to the ideal of equality among men—an ideal that, though imperfectly realized, has nonetheless left its imprint on institutions, attitudes, and behavior. Owing in part to their origins, the two countries appear to have less well-defined status groups with distinctive life-styles and less firmly established patterns of deference than do the more traditional West (or even East) European societies (Connor 1979, pp. 311-31). The stress on equality, together with the absence of well-established status groups, has meant, as the eminent Polish sociologist Stanislaw Ossowski (1963) observed, that the United States and the Soviet Union appear relatively "classless" in comparison with countries of the Old World.

This is not to say that these two societies are egalitarian; on the contrary, whether by income, prestige, power, or other valued resources, pronounced disparities between individuals and groups remain. Yet here, too, there are parallels. For, as Ossowski pointed out, the belief that differential rewards spur achievement and the ideology of "equality of opportunity" that helps to legitimize inequalities have a similar cast in the two nations:

> The Socialist principle "to each according to his merits" is in harmony with the tenets of the American Creed, which holds that each man is master of his fate, and that a man's status is fixed by an order of

merit. The Socialist principle allows of the conclusion that there are unlimited opportunities for social advancement and social demotion; this is similar to the American concept of "vertical social mobility." The arguments directed against *uravnilovka* [equalization or leveling of wages] coincide with the arguments put forward on the other side of the Atlantic by those who justify the necessity for economic inequalities in a democratic society (1963, p. 114).

Since the 1960s Soviet sociologists have used stratification schemes to analyze a wide variety of phenomena, including cultural demands, leisure-time activities, work satisfaction, participation in decision making, and chances for social mobility. In the remainder of this essay, we will explore various aspects of hierarchical differentiation in Soviet society, starting with occupational stratification and variations in income and standard of living. By reviewing this evidence, we will gain further insights into features of stratification distinctive to the USSR and those it shares with other countries, as well as delineate significant historical trends. Ethnic and sexual dimensions of social inequality will not be discussed, since these are treated elsewhere in this book.

OCCUPATIONAL STRATIFICATION

Though the tripartite distinction among working class, peasantry, and nonmanual workers still serves as the officially sanctioned interpretive scheme, empirically minded researchers have made conceptual refinements suitable for a more detailed study of social differentiation. Initially, however, many Soviet sociologists strongly attacked the notion—propagated, as they saw it, by "bourgeois ideologists" and "revisionists"—that socialist society is stratified by social groups along a hierarchy of income, power, prestige, or other valued attributes. As the prominent Soviet sociologist M. N. Rutkevich stated baldly in the early 1960s, "The concept of 'lower' and 'higher' social strata is fundamentally inapplicable to Soviet socialist society. The USSR does not have higher and lower classes and strata. . . . We reject the theory of 'social mobility' as anti-Marxist, as it is closely associated with the unscientific, arbitrary division of society into social 'strata'" (1964, p. 11).

More recently, Rutkevich and F. R. Filippov returned to this issue:

> The occupational hierarchy, of which Lipset and Bendix write [on the first page of *Social Mobility in Industrial Society*], exists in capitalist society, although in fact it is different than in their scheme, since in it there does not appear any place for such a decisive factor as ownership of the means of production. The extension of this schema to any "industrial society," i.e. modern society with a sufficiently high level of science, technology and production, is completely arbitrary. With the establishment of socialist social relations, the structure of evaluations of "prestige" changes fundamentally and the connection of these evaluations with capital disappears (1970, pp. 17-18; see also 1973).

Though arguing against the application of stratification schemes to socialist societies, Rutkevich and Filippov (1970, pp. 41-42) grant that "one may speak of vertical gradation . . . to the extent that there is still inequality according to the degree of the complexity of labor," since "more complicated labor demands higher qualifications and education of the worker and therefore is rewarded by society more highly in accordance with the principles of socialism." For this reason, one may refer to a worker's advancement from a job requiring less complicated labor to one requiring more as "interchange 'along the vertical,' i.e. as social promotion."

Other Soviet scholars state more forthrightly that under socialism, differentiation among social-occupational groups is more significant than under capitalism. Underlying this argument is the Marxist thesis that the decisive determinants of the class structure and the nature of social inequality under capitalism are relations to the means of production (notably, property ownership), the level of development of the productive forces, and the corresponding division of labor. With the establishment of socialism, not only is the exploitative "ruling class" done away with, not only does society cease to be divided into antagonistic classes, but property itself recedes in importance as a determinant of social status or class position. As the sociologist O. I. Shkaratan (1967, p. 30; see also 1973b) puts it, one of the distinctive features of the development of socialism is "the shift of previously secondary criteria to the foreground, as it were, and their transformation into the most characteristic marks of differentiation." "With the elimination of the class hierarchy," he explains (p. 5), "the remaining socioeconomic division of labor acquires direct and immediate . . . influence on the mechanism of intraclass structure."

Although Soviet investigations into stratification have generally lagged behind those in Eastern Europe, not to speak of the much older body of work in the West, they have gradually become more sophisticated in methodology and broader in scope. One of the more important studies is Iuri V. Arutiunian's *Social Structure of the Rural Population of the USSR,* published in 1971. Much of the rich empirical data contained in the book is derived from large-scale surveys carried out in the late 1960s in a number of regions of the Russian Republic—Kalinin and Moscow provinces, the Krasnodar Region, and the Tatar Autonomous Republic (see, in translation, Arutiunian 1973a,b,c).

While remaining faithful to key tenets of Marxism-Leninism, Arutiunian creatively adapts it to make it applicable to contemporary Soviet conditions. He points out that "role in the social organization of labor" (specified by Lenin as a class-forming factor) may be given various operational definitions, depending on whether one is interested in large or small units. In the former case, classes form the units of analysis; in the latter, sociooccupational groups do. When ranked according to skill level, prestige, or indexes of socioeconomic status, occupational groups form a stratification order (Arutiunian 1971, pp. 95-96, 353-55).

In the course of this survey, rural respondents were asked, "If you were starting your life at the beginning, what would you want to become?" Dividing the proportion of people preferring to be in one of the occupational groups by the proportion actually employed in it, Arutiunian assessed the relative prestige of the occupational groups, as well as the degree to which the respondents' aspirations had been realized. The results revealed the high prestige of skilled mental work and the quite low prestige of unskilled physical labor, which predominates in the countryside. Arutiunian (1971, p. 236) found, for instance, that ten times as many people wished to be in the higher-status intelligentsia positions than were actually employed in that group. Conversely, the number of people employed as unskilled workers was five times larger than the number desiring that status. These findings are represented graphically in the models of the "factual" and "ideal" social structure derived from the survey data (see Figure 4.1). When parents were polled on their aspirations for their children, there was a much greater discrepancy between the "ideal" and "factual" social structure.

A similar picture was obtained by V. N. Shubkin (1965; 1970), who did extensive research on the life plans of secondary school students in Novosibirsk Province during the 1960s. Several thousand graduating high school students were asked to rate 74 occupations on a ten-point scale in terms of their general "attractiveness." When average scores for individual occupations and types of occupations were computed, a general hierarchy of occupational groups emerged. All groups of respondents—male and female, urban and rural—assigned relatively high standing to scientific and engineering occupations, while assigning low standing to agricultural, sales, and service occupations. Workers' jobs in industry, construction, and transportation occupied intermediate positions (see also Yanowitch and Dodge 1969).

Realizing that "attractiveness" is only one criterion of social ranking, and not necessarily the best measure of social status, some other social scientists have carried out more refined, multidimensional analyses of people's perceptions of the occupational hierarchy. For instance, in a study conducted in Leningrad in 1965, V. V. Vodzinskaia (1973) divided 624 graduating students selected from five Leningrad secondary schools into two groups. The basic group containing 100 students was asked to rate 80 occupations on a ten-point scale according to four criteria—opportunity for creativity in the work, opportunities for "growth" (for increasing one's skills, improving oneself, and advancing occupationally), amount of earnings, and social prestige (the "authority" that the occupations possess in public opinion)—and to rate the occupations in terms of "attractiveness" according to their personal predilections. The remaining students were divided into five subgroups of equal size, each of which was instructed to evaluate the occupations according to one of the criteria. The rankings of occupations according to the various criteria were found to be very similar and highly intercorrelated. Notwithstanding certain variations by sex and place of residence, as in the Novosibirsk

FIGURE 4.1
"Factual" and "Ideal" Models of The Social Structure of
The Rural Population, Krasnodar Region and Kalinin Province

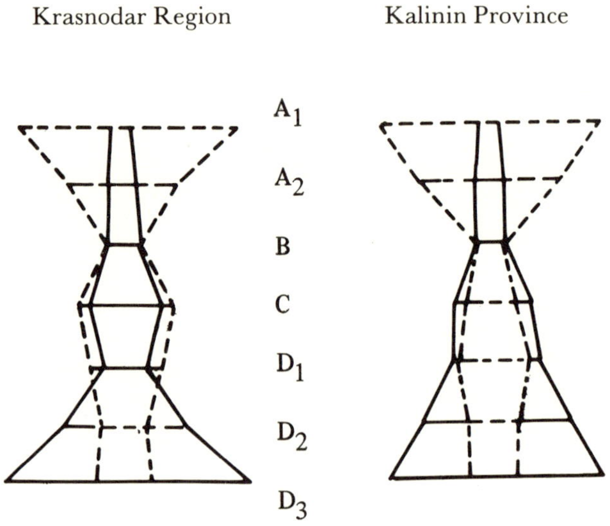

Krasnodar Region   Kalinin Province

A_1
A_2
B
C
D_1
D_2
D_3

A_1 Upper-echelon intelligentsia (top directors and specialists)
A_2 Lower-echelon intelligentsia
B   White-collar workers (*sluzhashchie*)
C   Equipment operators (*mekhanizatory*)
D_1 Skilled manual workers
D_2 Semiskilled manual workers
D_3 Unskilled manual workers

────── Actual social structure
— — — Ideal social structure

Source: Arutiunian 1971, p. 238.

study, the Leningrad students placed specialized occupations in science and engineering at the top, while relegating less-skilled jobs in agriculture, construction, and the services to the bottom of the heap.

There is considerable consensus among Soviet authorities that the generally low prestige of farm or manual work is a major cause of work dissatisfaction, labor turnover, and unemployment, especially among youth. After the Kiev Young Communist League asked 5,000 schoolchildren what they wanted to be, an article summarizing the results pointed up the problem posed by the widespread reluctance to enter manual jobs:

> Let us transport ourselves magically to a desert island where each of the pupils has become what he wanted to be. We find many designers, but only seven construction workers and one work superintendent. Every tenth person is a doctor, but there are only five nurses. Manufacturing is hopelessly bad, with only 80 factory workers. There are nearly 300 teachers and state security officials. There are hundreds of journalists and writers, but no printers to publish their work. We find one restaurant director, 23 cooks and no waiter—but with only seven livestock specialists, one tractor driver and one fisherman it is hard to feed all the scientists, actors and coaches at work on the island (Rushkis 1973, pp. 14, 27).

To what degree do Soviet evaluations of occupations coincide with prestige rankings in the United States and other Western countries? A study by Donald Treiman (1977) bears out the conclusion of earlier research by Alex Inkeles and Peter Rossi (1956) that the standing of occupations is very similar cross-nationally. Using Vodzinskaia's data, Treiman points out, however, that office workers in the Soviet Union (for example, bookkeepers) tend to receive considerably less prestige than is typical, while certain manual occupations (notably, coal miners) have a higher standing than would be expected. Such deviations from the general pattern appear to be the result of state policies, such as the payment of unusually high wages to workers in priority branches like coal mining, and to the extremely high proportion of females in the more poorly paid and less-skilled white-collar jobs (see Treiman 1977, pp. 144-48; Connor 1979, pp. 238-43, 264-66).

DIFFERENCES IN INCOME AND STANDARD OF LIVING

In the aftermath of the 1917 October Revolution, a general economic leveling occurred as large private holdings of land and capital were confiscated, and poor peasants were granted parcels of land to work. In industry, too, wage differentials were equalized under pressure from militant elements in the trade unions and the Communist party. Following the adoption of the New Economic Policy in 1921, differentiation once again increased: the more enterprising peasants were free to prosper and augment their holdings; traders and small shopkeepers were allowed to earn profits; and the wage scale in industry was widened. However, within the party the increased inequality was viewed as a temporary and undesirable expedient to be done away with as soon as possible (Inkeles and Bauer 1959, pp. 68-69). With the end of the New Economic Policy, many thought that the drive toward equality would be resumed.

Then, at the beginning of the 1930s, Josef Stalin signaled an abrupt turn in economic policy that had widespread ramifications within the social order. Addressing enterprise managers, he asked, "What is the cause of the heavy turnover of labour power?" His answer was simple:

> The cause is the wrong structure of wages, the wrong wage scales, the "Leftist" practice of wage equalization.... We cannot tolerate a situation where a rolling-mill hand in a steel mill earns no more than a sweeper.... Marx and Lenin said that the difference between skilled and unskilled labour would exist even under socialism, even after classes had been abolished; that only under communism would this difference disappear and that, consequently, even under socialism "wages" must be paid according to work performed and not according to needs (1931, pp. 25-26).

Following Stalin's campaign against vulgar "equalization," disparities in wages became quite large.

There are now ample data to warrant the conclusion that this trend has been reversed in the post-Stalin period. Not only have wage and salary differentials in industry been substantially reduced (Yanowitch 1963; 1977, p. 30) but, as Table 4.1 shows, lessened inequality is also evident in the distribution of wages among all persons employed in the state sector. In 1946 the wage exceeded by the best-paid 10 percent of the work force in the state sector was more than seven times greater than the wage exceeded by 90 percent. By 1970 the decile ratio had dropped to 3.2—less than half of what it had been in 1946. Janet Chapman (1979, p. 175) notes that this recent figure appears somewhat larger than the decile ratio for persons employed in the state sector in most East European countries in the early 1970s (3.1 in Yugoslavia, 3.0 in Poland, 2.5 in Czechoslovakia and Bulgaria, and 2.4 in Hungary); however, it is considerably lower than in the United States, where the comparable measure was 4.5 in 1972 for nonagricultural workers and salaried employees who worked full-time.

The data in Table 4.1 point also to a substantial reduction in the degree of inequality in family per capita income. Caution must be exercised in comparing these figures with data from Western countries. Because the Soviet figures are limited to the state sector and therefore exclude collective farm peasants, they undoubtedly underestimate the degree of income inequality in Soviet society. With this in mind, we may note that the decile ratio for family per capita income in the USSR (3.2 in 1970, peasants excluded) is only slightly lower than the comparable measure for nationally representative data from the United Kingdom (3.4 in 1969) and Sweden (3.6 in 1971), but much lower than in Canada (5.9 in 1968) and the United States (6.7 in 1968) (Wiles 1975, p. 35).

TABLE 4.1
Decile Ratios for Wages and Family per Capita Income (State Sector Only): USSR, Selected Years, 1928-75

Years	Wages	Family Per Capita Income
1928	3.8	—
1934	4.2	—
1946	7.2	—
1956	4.4	5.0
1966	3.2	3.7
1970	3.2	3.2
1975 (plan)	2.9	—

Note: The decile ratio is the wage (or amount of family per capita income) exceeded by 10 percent of the state workers and employees, divided by the wage (or amount of family income) exceeded by 90 percent. This measure is not equivalent to the ratio of the average wage of the best-paid 10 percent divided by the average wage of the worst-paid 10 percent. Calculations based on average wages show a greater spread between the upper and lower deciles than does the decile ratio: for instance, 8.1 in 1956 and 4.1 according to the 1975 plan (Yanowitch 1977, p. 25).

Sources: Wiles 1974, p. 25; Yanowitch 1977, p. 25.

In part, the movement toward greater equality appears to be a result of increased official recognition of the widespread incidence of poverty in the USSR. In the mid-1960s, Soviet economists estimated that the amount needed to maintain a minimal standard of living was approximately 50 rubles per person per month for an urban family of four. Families below this level as a rule suffer from "underprovision" (*maloobespechennost'*) of basic goods and services. By this standard, tens of millions of Soviet citizens, both in towns and in villages, were living below the poverty line in the 1960s (see Matthews 1972, pp. 81-90; McAuley 1979, pp. 16-20, 70-98).

A number of measures have helped to raise the standard of living of the poorest segments of the population. The lowest-paid occupations in the state sector have benefited from sizable raises in the minimum wage: between 1966 and 1971, the minimum wage was increased by 50 percent, to 60 rubles a month, and in the early 1970s it was raised further to 70 rubles (Hough 1977, p. 39; Yanowitch 1977, p. 27). Increases in pensions and in "public consumption funds" used to subsidize housing, health care, and education also have helped to reduce income differences among families.

Furthermore, the earnings of workers and collective farm peasants have been raised appreciably (Hough and Fainsod 1979, p. 266). From 1965 to 1976, the average wages of all workers and employees in the state sector rose by 57 percent. A lower-than-average rate of increase was experienced by such groups as employees in state and public bureaucracies (25 percent), engineering-technical personnel (39 percent), and agricultural specialists on state farms (32 percent). In contrast, the wages of industrial workers rose by 65 percent; of construction workers, by 71 percent; and of state farm workers, by 84 percent. The earnings of collective farmers rose at an even higher rate—86 percent. In the mid-1960s, collective farmers were also brought under a guaranteed minimum income system and made eligible for state pensions. Since the incomes of collective farm peasants have generally been so low, the rapid rise in their standard of living has been particularly significant.

TABLE 4.2
Monthly Wages and Salaries for Selected Highly Paid Occupations: USSR, Early 1970s

Occupation	Approximate Earnings (in rubles)[a]	
	Basic	Total
Marshal of the USSR	—	2,000
First secretary of the Union of Composers	800	1,400
Colonel	600	—
First secretary of party *obkom* (Tula oblast)	600	810
Well-known ballet dancer (all-union level)	500	900-1,200
Director of VUZ or research institute	500-700[b]	—
Manager of large industrial enterprise (more than 10,000 workers)	260-480[b]	350-655[b]
Professor or chief researcher	325-525	—
Editor of major newspaper (union republic level)	240	500-600
Associate professor (*dotsent*), assistant professor, or leading researcher	300-350	—

[a]Data derived by Matthews from published sources and interviews of Soviet-born individuals living in the West. Figures have been rounded to the nearest 5 rubles.

[b]The ranges reflect variations according to the type of institution or enterprise. For example, the basic rate for the director of a large enterprise in light industry would be 260 rubles per month, as against 480 for an enterprise of comparable size in the coal industry.

Source: Matthews 1978, pp. 23-24, 26-27.

However, the overall trend toward equalization of monetary rewards has not been carried so far as to preclude appreciable disparities among occupations. To illustrate this, Table 4.2 lists selected occupations that provide earnings well above the average. In the early 1970s the basic monthly rate was reported to be 800 rubles for the first secretary of the Union of Composers, 600 rubles for an army colonel or the first secretary of a provincial party executive committee, 500 to 700 rubles for the director of an institution of higher education (VUZ) or a research institute, and 260 to 480 rubles for the director of a huge industrial enterprise employing more than 10,000 workers.

In many cases, individuals in high-status positions may augment their earnings appreciably through bonuses, honoraria, or royalties, or by receiving extra pay for additional work or responsibilities. For instance, honoraria paid for performances by the most highly esteemed ballet dancers may push their actual earnings above the 1,000 ruble threshold. A professor who becomes head of a department (*kafedra*) typically receives a pay boost of 100 rubles per month, while one who is elected to the prestigious Academy of Sciences receives an additional 350 to 500 rubles a month (Matthews 1978, pp. 26-29).

The difficulties in securing accurate estimates of income variation are further compounded, as two leading Hungarian sociologists stress, by the fact that

> . . . differentiation according to hierarchical levels within socialist society does not appear merely in incomes. It has other forms too, which are frequently disguised and therefore most difficult to control. In the first place this concerns the goods and benefits which are generally considered socially desirable, but which are in short supply. Their distribution sometimes takes place in a preferential way and they become part of the privileges of certain strata of society, leading to considerable injustices (Hegedus and Markus 1972, p. 47).

A prime example is the distribution of housing, much of which is subsidized by the state and distributed administratively, rather than through the market. Though Soviet sociological surveys disclose only modest variations in size of living accommodations according to occupational status, it is clear that administrators, party officials, and persons in prestigious positions are most successful in acquiring higher-quality housing (Yanowitch 1977, pp. 40-43). They are more likely, that is, to live in new, well-constructed, separate (rather than communal) apartments equipped with modern amenities. According to Soviet legal statutes, moreover, "leading" workers and executives of state and party bodies, members of the Academy of Sciences, holders of advanced degrees or academic titles, persons who have received such honorific titles as "Hero of Socialist Labor" or "Honored Artist," members of creative and artistic unions, and military officers holding the rank of colonel or above are entitled to extra housing space (Matthews 1978, pp. 43-46; Connor 1979, pp. 277-87). Because of state subsidies, persons obtaining more or better-quality housing receive, in effect, "transfer payments" from the state.

Special privileges also extend to the pension system, health care, vacations, and access to goods and services (see Smith 1976; Matthews 1978).

The statute on pensions provides that special high retirement awards may be made to persons who have rendered exceptional service in the areas of revolutionary, governmental, social, and economic activity, and in the fields of culture, science, and technology. Retired military officers, university and academic personnel, and executives are among the categories that may receive pension awards far above the regular maximums. Other "fringe benefits" may accrue to top executives and others in high-status positions, who may be provided with automobiles, with payments for vacations taken for "a rest cure" (without a medical certificate or verification of treatment being needed), and with access to special shops and a closed trade network that provide high-quality goods and commodities not available in ordinary stores.

ATTITUDINAL AND BEHAVIORAL CORRELATES OF SOCIOECONOMIC STATUS

Investigations conducted by Soviet sociologists make it abundantly clear that social inequality linked to the occupational division of labor is not limited to income and living conditions—on the contrary, it often appears more pronounced in the sphere of cultural consumption. Reviewing data on the rural population, for instance, Arutiunian points to the "substantial differences" between socio-occupational groups in individuals' use of the means of cultural diffusion and communication:

> The most "democratic" is the radio, which is directed identically to the intelligentsia, employees, machine operators, and unskilled workers. The newspaper is somewhat more "discriminating"—it is to a great extent the property of rural intelligentsia. This is all the more true if one is referring to the female half of the population. The overwhelming majority of the rural intelligentsia as a whole regularly reads newspapers, [whereas] among unskilled workers less than half do. Books are especially "selective." While about half of those in the intelligentsia are in the habit of reading [literary works], among unskilled workers approximately 1/10 to 1/5 regularly read books (1971, p. 177).

Many such cultural variations appear to be linked more closely with individuals' educational attainment than with their occupational status or income level. In their major study of the nonwork activities of urban workers, to cite one instance, L. A. Gordon and E. V. Klopov (1972, pp. 110-12, 170-76, 277-340) observe that better-educated women are more apt to acquire such labor-saving devices as vacuum cleaners and washing machines, not simply because they earn more money than average women, but because they have higher cultural standards and more diverse interests, and thus "deemphasize" housework as a valued activity. Like their male counterparts, better-educated women tend to be more "active" in their cultural pursuits.

They spend less time watching television and more time reading newspapers and books, going to the theater and ballet, and engaging in study than the less-educated do.

The influence of an individual's social status extends also to patterns of interpersonal affiliation. Illustrative are Shkaratan's (1973a, pp. 290, 307) findings that persons in various hierarchically ordered strata tend to choose their marriage partners or their friends from the same or proximate social-occupational groups. Thus, among Leningrad workers surveyed, 60 to 70 percent of the friends of individuals in the three highest strata (organizers of production and personnel performing skilled or highly skilled mental work) are skilled nonmanual workers, whereas the great majority of the friends of those in the lower-ranking, less-skilled categories are of comparable status. The extreme cases are represented by highly skilled scientific and technical personnel and unskilled manual workers; these groups show the highest degree of "closure" in choice of friends.

Significant variations in attitudes toward one's work and life conditions are also connected with an individual's occupational status or educational attainment. As Arutiunian observes with respect to the rural population:

> The general regularity appears to be a growth of satisfaction with work connected with an increase in social status and skill level. As far as satisfaction with the cultural and life conditions of the countryside is concerned, it, on the contrary, is more inclined to decrease to the degree that skill level and education increase and the cultural demands of the population correspondingly grow.
>
> . . .
>
> The higher the socio-occupational status of a group, the more active is its social behavior and the greater is its inclination for mobility, both within the rural areas [through an increase in skill and occupational advancement] and outside of it [through migration to town] (1971, pp. 265, 267).

Another study disclosed that better-educated workers were more likely to cite the "interesting" nature of their specialty as a reason for having gone into a given line of work, whereas the less-educated more often alluded to high pay or fortuitous circumstances (Iovchuk and Kogan 1972, p. 138). The results of Soviet research indicate that, as in Western countries, men in occupations calling for higher skills want their work to be interesting, whereas those in lower-skill jobs tend to put much more stress on pay (see Zdravomyslov, Rozhin, and Yadov 1970). These findings appear to bear out Alex Inkeles' contention that in all modern societies a relation exists between the nature of an occupation and the part of it that leads to the most satisfaction.

In accordance with Communist ideology, authoritative spokesmen maintain that Soviet society is eliminating such difference by various measures designed to combine manual and mental work (see Amvrosov 1975; Blyakhman and Shkaratan 1977; Klopov, Shubkin, and Gordon 1977). Yet not a few Soviet sociologists continue to contradict those in their country who contend that economic growth and mechanization will provide a panacea for the high level of job dissatisfaction reported among unskilled workers. In the early 1970s, V. Churbanov reported that

> about 50% of our industrial workers perform unmechanical labor at present, and the proportion has declined only two or three percent during each of the last two five-year plans. In fact, in absolute terms the number of such workers is increasing. . . . [O]ne worker in three in our country works on an assembly line. Indeed, most of the laborers whose work is to be mechanized by 1975 (50% of all manual laborers) will then be performing even more limited tasks with even less intellectual content (1973, pp. 13-14).

Churbanov goes on to suggest that the problem of job dissatisfaction in the Soviet Union will worsen because educational attainment is increasing much more rapidly than the growth in the proportion of more interesting nonroutine jobs. As he puts it, the problem "would in fact be better formulated as 'educated youth and uninteresting work,'" a phenomenon not unknown in the United States:

> The higher a young person's educational level, the greater his need for interesting work. Yet most industrial work presently requires no more than a sixth to eighth grade education, and the scientific and technical revolution is not expected to keep pace with the spread of education in the next few years. The transition to universal secondary education, otherwise so desirable, will only exacerbate this problem (1973, p. 14).

Finally, available evidence indicates that in Soviet society, much as in Western countries, the incidence of participation in political or administrative affairs and the degree of power that individuals exercise are dependent on social status. For example, in the course of his study of the rural population, Arutiunian attempted to evaluate indirectly the degree to which workers exercise control over management. The purpose, according to Arutiunian, was to ascertain "the degree of a person's realization (though it be subjective) of his role as co-owner of this or that form of socialized property. Essentially, this is the subjective perception of the degree of the actual socialization of property" (1971, p. 106). When asked whether they exercised influence on the decisions made in their work collective, a high proportion of the respondents—the averages ranged from 51 to 57 percent in the three regions—answered that they lacked influence. No less important, the perceived degree of influence was clearly related to the respondent's social status. Only about one in ten of the persons in high-level administrative positions or in professional occupations felt that they were without influence, whereas six or seven out of ten of the rank-and-file workers and peasants experienced a sense of powerlessness (see Arutiunian 1971, p. 108; 1973b, pp. 111-14).

Whether or not Arutiunian's findings accurately reflect the relative concentration or dispersal of decision-making power, they point up the extent to which social status influences an individual's sense of being able to determine his life conditions. Numerous studies conducted in the West have shown that those who rank lower on the socioeconomic hierarchy have a greater sense of their own ineffectualness and impotence in determining political events. Such a sense of powerlessness is also reflected in their behavior—for instance, those of lower socio-occupational status are usually less likely to participate in elections. Though it has long been argued that such is not the case in the USSR, where workers are co-owners of the means of production and are given ample scope to participate in management, these findings suggest that the situation is not dissimilar.

Reviewing additional evidence on this issue, the American political scientist Jerry Hough observes:

> The more participation entails what westerners would instinctively define as "political" or "policy-oriented" participation, the greater the differentials in rates of participation by status of occupation tend to be. In some low policy-relevant activities such as the voluntary auxiliary police (*druzhinniki*), Soviet scholars privately report that workers are actually represented in greater number than their proportion in the population. . . . By contrast, only 11 percent of the articles and letters with suggestions for policy change or complaints about the work of individual administrators in *Pravda* and *Izvestiia* in December 1971 and six republican newspapers from December 1974 through February 1975 were [by] workers and foremen.
>
> . . .
>
> A disproportionately great number of white collar employees also participate in party and soviet sessions and committees. Thus, 24 percent of the deputies named to the 1970 Supreme Soviet were workers, but only 12 percent of the reported speakers in the committee (*postoiannye komissii*) sessions of that convocation (1970-1974) and only 6 percent of the speakers at the formal sessions of the Supreme Soviet themselves were workers.
>
> . . .
>
> Every piece of evidence suggests that peasant participation in policy-related activities is even lower than that of the workers. They very rarely write letters to newspapers (except *Sel'skaia zhizn'—Rural Life*), and they seldom are called upon to speak at sessions of the Supreme Soviet (Hough and Fainsod 1979, pp. 308-10).

Hough points out that "when American survey data are analyzed closely, education almost invariably is more strongly correlated with participation than is occupation, and it is very likely that such has also been the case in the Soviet Union in recent years" (Hough and Fainsod 1979, p. 311). Data on party membership that he has analyzed indicate that, as of 1970, the proportion of party members among persons of both sexes 30 years of age and older rises sharply with educational level: about one in twenty-five of the men and women with no more than eight years of schooling belong to the Communist party, as against one out of four individuals with high school degrees, more than one out of three of the college graduates, and one out of two of those with postgraduate degrees (Hough and Fainsod 1979, pp. 312, 344-47; see also Hough 1977, pp. 125-39).

Similarly, in a survey limited to urban workers in the Urals, M. T. Iovchuk and L. N. Kogan (1972, p. 178) found that the proportion participating to some degree in broadly defined "public activities" increased from one out of four of the workers with no more than four years of education to nearly three out of four of those with some higher education. One implication of these findings is that a better-educated work force is more "active" and demanding. Behind recent debates over workers' participation in enterprise management, the American economist Murray Yanowitch (1977, pp. 142-43) detects a concern on the part of industrial managers that new, more flexible methods be devised to accommodate the workers' demands.

OCCUPATIONAL MOBILITY

In the United States and other Western countries, sociologists have given much attention to patterns of occupational mobility—that is, to individuals' movement, either intra- or intergenerationally, from one occupational group to another. Such investigations not only depict processes of movement within the occupational structure; they also shed light on differences in the opportunities of individuals from various backgrounds and elucidate the factors determining manpower flows.

Earlier in this chapter, I cited a paper written in the early 1960s by the Soviet sociologist M. N. Rutkevich, who rejected the "theory of 'social mobility' as anti-Marxist." For some time Soviet scholars sought to maintain that the concepts of "upward" and "downward" mobility used in Western studies were inapplicable to their own society. As the discipline developed, however, Soviet sociologists gradually undertook research on the subject, while continuing to insist that there are qualitative differences in the nature of mobility in capitalist and socialist systems.

So far, their surveys have been limited to individuals in particular enterprises, branches of the economy, or regions, or to certain categories of students. Though the fact that no national surveys have been conducted makes it difficult to generalize the results and hazardous to draw cross-national comparisons, the studies have revealed some important patterns of mobility in the USSR (Dobson 1977). As would be expected, they show that a great deal of

TABLE 4.3
Intergenerational Mobility in Kazan: Rates of Outflow

	Occupational Status in 1967: Men and Women[a]					
		Skilled				
Status of Head of Household at Beginning of Respondent's Work Career	Managerial and Skilled Mental	Mainly Nonmanual	Mainly Manual	Low-Skill Manual and Nonmanual	Total (percent)	Row N[b]
Professional	72.0	5.7	20.4	1.9	100.0	211
Semiprofessional	50.3	12.5	30.1	7.1	100.0	352
Other white-collar	44.3	12.5	38.2	5.1	100.0	296
Blue-collar worker	15.5	13.7	58.1	12.7	100.0	1,564
Agricultural worker or peasant	9.3	10.6	59.0	21.1	100.0	1,306
Column N	823	447	1,942	517		3,729
No origins cited	54	35	152	45		286
Column total	877	482	2,094	562		4,015

[a] The nine groups shown in Table 4.4 have been collapsed into four categories here: the "Managerial and Skilled Mental" heading includes the first four groups; "Skilled, Mainly Nonmanual" includes the fifth and sixth groups; "Skilled, Mainly Manual," the seventh and eighth groups; and "Low-Skill, Manual and Nonmanual," the ninth group.

[b] Calculated from reported column totals and percents of inflow into occupational groups.

Source: Shkaratan 1970. p. 433.

intergenerational mobility has occurred and that most of the shifts have been in an "upward" direction—for instance, from unskilled agricultural work to more skilled industrial employment or from the working class into professional or semiprofessional jobs.

One of the more satisfactory sets of data on intergenerational mobility comes from a 1967 survey of the employed population of Kazan, a major city on the Volga River in southern Russia. As the "outflow rates" in Table 4.3 demonstrate, the parent's occupational status has considerable bearing on the occupational level that the respondent attained, much as in other countries. Individuals from the manual strata are most likely to be employed in skilled manual or low-skill occupations, whereas persons from nonmanual strata are more numerous in the skilled white-collar jobs. Clearly, these data show pronounced disparities in chances for entry into the more prestigious skilled mental and managerial jobs: seven out of ten of the professionals' offspring entered such positions, compared with about one out of six working-class

TABLE 4.4
Intergenerational Mobility in Kazan:
Rates of Inflow from the Manual Strata

Occupational Status of Respondent in 1967*	Origins (percent)		
	Agricultural Worker or Peasant	Nonfarm Blue-Collar Worker	Total from Manual Strata
Managerial personnel (93)	29.0	33.4	62.4
Highly skilled personnel in "creative professions" (43)	6.9	18.6	25.5
Highly skilled scientific and technical personnel (85)	9.4	24.8	34.2
Others performing skilled mental work (656)	12.7	27.7	40.4
Highly skilled, combining mental and manual work (30)	30.0	33.4	63.4
Skilled nonmanual, without specialized training (452)	28.7	45.3	74.0
Skilled manual (1,049)	39.3	40.6	79.9
Skilled manual, employed at machines (1,045)	34.3	46.2	80.5
Unskilled manual and low-skilled nonmanual (562)	49.1	35.3	84.4

*Men and women; Ns are in parentheses.
Source: Shkaratan 1970, p. 433.

children and fewer than one out of ten from farm backgrounds. Though overrepresented among the unskilled workers, a majority of the farm workers' offspring became skilled workers (59 percent). A comparable proportion of the nonfarm workers' children were skilled workers, but fewer occupied low-skill positions and more had moved into skilled white-collar or managerial jobs.

Table 4.4 casts data from the same survey in a different light by showing "inflow rates"—the percentage of members of the occupational groups who come from the manual strata. As we see, the proportion of respondents with working-class or peasant backgrounds is highest in the three lowest strata, where some eight out of ten come from such homes. In contrast, two out of five of the persons performing skilled mental work, one out of three of the highly skilled scientific and technical personnel, and one out of four of those in the "creative professions" come from the working class or peasantry. Note, however, that six out of ten of the managerial personnel (broadly defined to include shop heads, foremen, and similar positions) are from manual backgrounds.

Of course, the urban intelligentsia is highly differentiated according to specialization, skill level, prestige, income, and so on. Rutkevich and Filippov (1970, pp. 167-78) point out that the higher the category of specialists (in terms of skill level or prestige), the greater the degree of "self-reproduction" of workers performing mental labor: for example, among specialists in education surveyed in the late 1960s, two-thirds of the primary-school teachers and half of the secondary-school teachers in Nizhnii Tagil were children of workers and peasants, as compared to three out of ten of the faculty members at Kharkov State University (Rutkevich and Filippov 1970, p. 166; Yanowitch 1977, p. 113). Scientific and academic personnel with advanced academic degrees have an especially high rate of recruitment from the intelligentsia.

In contrast, administrative jobs and technical professions linked with "material production," such as engineering, draw more recruits from the manual strata, as a rule, than do traditional "liberal," "humanistic," or "research-oriented" occupations (Dobson 1977). The relatively high proportion of men from peasant and proletarian families in responsible administrative positions results, in part, from self-selection and the type of training called for. Such jobs evidently appear more attractive to men from the lower strata (see Titma 1973, pp. 215-17), and many administrators in industry and state agencies were trained initially as engineers. But it also reflects political concerns: especially in the 1920s and 1930s, workers and peasants were given preference in promotions because they were thought to be more politically reliable than the intelligentsia's offspring (see Feldmesser 1955; Azrael 1966; Bailes 1978).

Because advancement through the Communist party apparatus has provided a channel for upward mobility for workers' and peasants' offspring, there are significant differences in the composition of the political elites in the Soviet Union and the United States. Examining the social origins of high-level party officials and American senators and cabinet members, Zbigniew Brzezinski and Samuel Huntington (1964, pp. 134-40) found that members of the political elite in the United States are drawn predominantly from the middle and upper social strata. In contrast, the top Soviet political leaders have come overwhelmingly from proletarian or peasant backgrounds.

In explaining the causes of mobility, Soviet sociologists point to basic "structural" changes—for example, urbanization, the expansion of the skilled segment of the working class, the growth of the intelligentsia—that have proceeded at a rapid pace. From 1940 to 1974, the urban share of the total population rose from 33 to 60 percent (Amvrosov 1975, p. 47). The intelligentsia has grown much more rapidly: between 1940 and 1975, the number of skilled mental workers with a specialized secondary or higher education increased nearly tenfold—from 2.4 million to 22.8 million (Rutkevich 1977, p. 33; see also Gvishiani, Mikulinsky, and Kugel 1976, pp. 114-17).

However, one of the characteristics of "developed socialism" is a decrease in the rate of structural change, so that social strata tend to become more hereditary in composition. Despite the fact that tens of thousands of villagers continue to move to town, the proportion of workers from farm backgrounds is clearly declining in the younger groups; hence, more and more of the urban workers are workers' children (Rutkevich and Filippov 1970; Shkaratan 1970; Aitov 1976; Blyakhman and Shkaratan 1977). Expecting these trends to continue, L. A. Slesarev (1974, pp. 23-24) observes that workers' offspring are still likely to experience much intraclass mobility—that is, many will attain more skilled positions than their parents.

While the urban working class is increasingly replenishing itself with workers' children, the urban intelligentsia is drawing a growing share of its recruits from the nonmanual strata, especially the intelligentsia itself. Thus, in Sverdlovsk, L. I. Sennikova (1968, pp. 238-39) found that a fifth of the specialists over 40, a third between 30 and 39, and half under 30 were children of specialists. A study of 1,340 specialists in Syzran revealed a comparable trend (Gendel' 1971, p. 88): the proportion coming from white-collar strata increased from a quarter of those over 50 years of age to half of those under 30. (When only specialists with higher education are considered, the trend is more pronounced: the share from white-collar families reaches two-thirds in the youngest group.) Similarly, in studying the origins of members of the Union of Architects in Sverdlovsk, G. A. Nechaeva (1973, p. 220) found that the proportion coming from the working class and peasantry declined sharply with age from 58 percent of those over 50 to just 12 percent of those between 31 and 40.

What chances do workers have to move up into the intelligentsia in the course of their careers? The worker who becomes an engineer after years of evening study or who is promoted to plant manager after demonstrating initiative and administrative ability is a widely publicized and seemingly common case in the USSR. More than 70 percent of the managers of machine-building enterprises in Leningrad reportedly worked up to their present positions from the shop floor, and more than 50 percent of the managers of the country's largest industrial enterprises are said to have started out as workers (Blyakhman and Shkaratan 1977, pp. 186-87).

However, broader studies of intragenerational mobility show more modest chances for advancement. According to a 1970 survey of employed persons at Ufa that was carried out by N. A. Aitov (1976, p. 225), 88 percent of the respondents who were workers in 1950 were still workers 20 years later, about 3 percent had become white-collar workers, and 10 percent had entered the intelligentsia. Surveys of adult workers in Leningrad's machine-building industry revealed a great deal of career mobility from low-skill to more highly skilled workers' jobs, but much less movement out of the manual strata. The proportion who rose into skilled mental or managerial positions ranged from 13 to 18 percent for those who began their work career as agricultural workers or as unskilled or skilled urban workers, but rose to 47 percent for nonspecialist white-collar workers (Chulanov 1974, pp. 33-35). These findings suggest that upward mobility within the white-collar stratum is much more common than movement from blue-collar jobs into the more skilled or responsible nonmanual positions—a pattern characteristic of other industrial societies.

Like Aitov, Iu. G. Chulanov (1974, pp. 28-31) emphasizes that the workers' ability to complete further education is the decisive condition for advancement. His data show that workers who start out with more schooling are more likely to receive additional education and are likely to get more of it than those who entered the work force less well prepared. As specialized training has become increasingly important for promotion, and as workers compete for advancement with young technicians and engineers coming straight from school, it becomes less likely than in the past that workers can realistically expect to rise far in management unless they complete advanced education.

CONCLUSION

Despite the official insistence that the Soviet Union is moving ever closer to an egalitarian Communist society, it is clear that structured social inequality continues to be a salient characteristic of Soviet society. As in other industrial countries, occupational differentiation provides the main basis for the hierarchical differentiation evidenced in many aspects of social life—the existence of considerable consensus on positions of higher and lower prestige; inequalities in the distribution of income, goods, and services; the patterning of social contacts, aspirations, and satisfactions; the differentiation of distinctive life-styles; the incidence of participation in political affairs.

Owing to the extent of state control and to the concentration of decisionmaking power in the hands of a small elite at the apex of the Communist party, the distribution of rewards in society is more responsive to purposeful regulation than in Western nations. However, the political leaders have by no means consistently used such power to promote greater equality. When Stalin favored a widening of wage differentials as an incentive for individual achievement and stimulus for rapid economic growth, inequalities in income became quite pronounced. In the post-Stalin period, the leadership has substantially reduced wage and income disparities; in this respect (and certainly in the distribution of wealth) Soviet society now appears to be characterized by less inequality than most Western countries. Yet, in light of the Soviet experience, one wonders whether, in the words of the American sociologist Gerhard Lenski, "gains in *political* equality come at the expense of losses in *economic* equality—and vice versa" (1978, p. 380; compare Parkin 1971, pp. 180-84).

In this essay we have noted that the structure of inequality influences not only the direction that social mobility takes, but also the opportunities that members of various social groups have to attain desired positions. Like their counterparts in the West, persons born into the upper social strata are generally much more likely to move into the most prestigious and highly rewarded occupations than are peasants' or workers' offspring. Since the Soviet educational system serves both as a principal channel for upward mobility and as a means by which status and advantages are perpetuated intergenerationally, patterns of educational attainment will be examined in greater detail in the next essay.

REFERENCES

Aitov, N. A. 1976. "Sotsial'nye peremeshcheniia v SSSR." In *Problemy razvitiia sotsial'noi struktury obshchestva v Sovetskom Soiuze i Pol'she,* edited by V. Vesolovskii and M. N. Rutkevich, pp. 222-30. Moscow: Nauka.

Amvrosov, A. A. 1972. *Ot klassovoi differentsiatsii k sotsial'noi odnorodnosti obshchestva.* Moscow: Mysl'.

———. 1975. *Sotsial'naia struktura sovetskogo obshchestva.* Seriia "Razvitoi sotsializm." Moscow: Politizdat.

Arutiunian, Iu. V. 1971. *Sotsial'naia struktura sel'skogo naseleniia SSSR.* Moscow: Nauka.

———. 1973a. "Culture and the Social Psychology of the Soviet Rural Population." In Yanowitch and Fisher 1973, pp. 119-36.

———. 1973b. "The Distribution of Decision-Making among the Rural Population of the USSR." In Yanowitch and Fisher 1973, pp. 106-18.

———. 1973c. "Social Mobility in the Countryside." In Yanowitch and Fisher 1973, pp. 320-53.

Azrael, Jeremy. 1966. *Managerial Power and Soviet Politics.* Cambridge, Mass.: Harvard University Press.

Bailes, Kendall E. 1978. *Technology and Society under Lenin and Stalin: Origins of the Technical Intelligentsia, 1917-1941.* Princeton: Princeton University Press.

Bauman, Zygmunt. 1974. "Officialdom and Class: Bases of Inequality in Socialist Society." In *The Social Analysis of Class Structure,* edited by Frank Parkin. London: Tavistock.

Blyakhman, L., and O. Shkaratan. 1977. *Man at Work: The Scientific and Technological Revolution, the Soviet Working Class and Intelligentsia.* Moscow: Progress.

Brzezinski, Zbigniew, and Samuel P. Huntington. 1964. *Political Power: USA/USSR.* New York: Viking.

Bukharin, Nikolai. 1969. *Historical Materialism: A System of Sociology.* Ann Arbor: University of Michigan Press.

Chapman, Janet G. 1979. "Recent Trends in the Soviet Industrial Wage Structure." In *Industrial Labor in the U.S.S.R.,* edited by Arcadius Kahan and Blair Ruble, pp. 151-83. New York: Pergamon.

Chesnokov, D. I. 1973. *Istoricheskii materializm kak sotsiologiia Marksizma-Leninizma.* Moscow: Mysl'.
Chulanov, Iu. G. 1974. *Izmeneniia v sostave i v urovne tvorcheskoi aktivnosti rabochego klassa SSSR, 1959-1970 gg.* Leningrad: Leningrad State University Press.
Churbanov, V. 1973. "The Young Worker and Uninteresting Labor." *Molodoi kommunist* no. 6 (June 1972), pp. 64-71; abstracted in *Current Digest of the Soviet Press* 25, no. 2:13-14.
Connor, Walter D. 1979. *Socialism, Politics, and Equality: Hierarchy and Change in Eastern Europe and the USSR.* New York: Columbia University Press.
Dobson, Richard B. 1977. "Mobility and Stratification in the Soviet Union." *Annual Review of Sociology* 3:297-329.
Feldmesser, Robert A. 1955. "Aspects of Social Mobility in the Soviet Union." Ph.D. dissertation, Harvard University.
––––––. 1960. "Social Classes and Political Structure." In *The Transformation of Russian Society: Aspects of Social Change Since 1861,* edited by Cyril E. Black, pp. 235-52. Cambridge, Mass.: Harvard University Press.
Gendel', V. G. 1971. "Problemy sotsial'noi podvizhnosti molodezhi pri sotsializme." Cand. Sci. dissertation, Leningrad State University.
Glezerman, G. E. 1973. *Istoricheskii materializm i razvitie sotsialisticheskogo obshchestva.* 2d rev. ed. Moscow: Politizdat.
Goldthorpe, John H. 1966. "Social Stratification in Industrial Society." In *Class, Status, and Power,* edited by Reinhard Bendix and S. M. Lipset, 2d ed., pp. 648-59. New York: Free Press.
Gordon, L. A., and E. V. Klopov. 1972. *Chelovek posle raboty: sotsial'nye problemy byta i vnerabochego vremeni.* Moscow: Nauka.
Gvishiani, D. M., S. R. Mikulinsky, and S. A. Kugel, eds. 1976. *The Scientific Intelligentsia in the USSR (Structure and Dynamics of Personnel).* Moscow: Progress.
Hegedus, Andreas, and Maria Markus. 1972. "The Role of Values in the Long Range Planning of Distribution and Consumption." In *Hungarian Sociological Studies,* edited by Paul Halmos. Sociological Review Monograph 17. Keele: University of Keele.
Hollander, Paul. 1973. *Soviet and American Society: A Comparison.* New York: Oxford University Press.
Hough, Jerry F. 1977. *The Soviet Union and Social Science Theory.* Cambridge, Mass.: Harvard University Press.
Hough, Jerry F., and Merle Fainsod. 1979. *How the Soviet Union Is Governed.* Cambridge, Mass.: Harvard University Press.
Inkeles, Alex, and Raymond A. Bauer. 1959. *The Soviet Citizen: Daily Life in a Totalitarian Society.* Cambridge, Mass.: Harvard University Press.
Inkeles, Alex, and Peter H. Rossi. 1956. "National Comparisons of Occupational Prestige." *American Journal of Sociology* 61:329-39.
Iovchuka, M. T., and L. N. Kogan, eds. 1972. *Dukhovnyi mir sovetskogo rabochego: opyt konkretno-sotsiologicheskogo issledovaniia.* Moscow: Mysl'.
Klopov, E. V., V. N. Shubkin, and L. A. Gordon, eds. 1977. *Sotsial'noe razvitie rabochego klassa SSSR: rost chislennosti, kvalifikatsii, blagosostoianiia rabochikh v razvitom sotsialisticheskom obshchestve; istoriko-sotsiologicheskie ocherki.* Moscow: Nauka.
Lenski, Gerhard. 1978. "Marxist Experiments in Destratification: An Appraisal." *Social Forces* 57 (Dec.):364-83.
Lipset, Seymour Martin, and Richard B. Dobson. 1973. "Social Stratification and Sociology in the Soviet Union." *Survey* 12, no. 3 (Summer):114-85.
McAuley, Alastair. 1979. *Economic Welfare in the Soviet Union: Poverty, Living Standards, and Inequality.* Madison: University of Wisconsin Press.
Matthews, Mervin. 1972. *Class and Society in Soviet Russia.* New York: Walker.
––––––. 1978. *Privilege in the Soviet Union: A Study of Elite Life-Styles Under Communism.* London: George Allen and Unwin.

Nechaeva, G. A. 1973. "Formirovanie kadrov khudozhestvennoi intelligentsii na srednem urale (Po materialam Sverdlovskoi organizatsii Soiuza arkhitektorov SSSR)." In *Sotsial'nye problemy nauchno-tekhnicheskoi revoliutsii v usloviiakh stroitel'stva sotsializma*, edited by V. M. Semenov. Sbornik uchenykh trudov Sverdlovskogo iuridicheskogo instituta, vyp. 32, pp. 212-28.
Ossowski, Stanislaw. 1963. *Class Structure in the Social Consciousness*. New York: Free Press.
Parkin, Frank. 1971. *Class Inequality and Political Order: Social Stratification in Capitalist and Communist Societies*. New York: Praeger.
Rushkis, Val. 1973. "And Here We Are on the Island." *Komsomol'skaia pravda*, Sept. 21, 1972, p. 4, as abstracted in *Current Digest of the Soviet Press*, 25, no. 2:14, 27.
Rutkevich, M. N. 1964. "Elimination of Class Differences and the Place of Non-Manual Workers in the Social Structure of Soviet Society." *Soviet Sociology* 3, no. 2 (Fall):3-13.
———. 1977. *Intelligentsiia v razvitom sotsialisticheskom obshchestve*. Seriia "Razvitoi sotsializm." Moscow: Politizdat.
Rutkevich, M. N., and F. R. Filippov. 1970. *Sotsial'nye peremeshcheniia*. Moscow: Mysl'.
———. 1973. "Principles of the Marxist Approach to Social Structure and Social Mobility." In Yanowitch and Fisher 1973, pp. 229-40.
Sennikova, L. I. 1968. "Vysshee obrazovanie kak faktor sotsial'noi mobil'nosti." Cand. Sci. dissertation, Urals State University.
Shkaratan, O. I. 1967. "The Social Structure of the Soviet Working Class." *Voprosy filosofii* no. 1, pp. 28-39, translated in *Current Digest of the Soviet Press* 19, no. 12:3-8.
———. 1970. *Problemy sotsial'noi struktury rabochego klassa SSSR*. Moscow: Mysl'.
———. 1973a. "Social Ties and Social Mobility." In Yanowitch and Fisher 1973, pp. 289-319.
———. 1973b. "Sources of Social Differentiation of the Working Class in Soviet Society." In Yanowitch and Fisher 1973, pp. 10-21.
Shubkin, V. N. 1965. "Youth Starts out in Life." *Soviet Sociology* 4, no. 3 (Winter):3-15.
———. 1970. *Sotsiologicheskie opyty*. Moscow: Mysl'.
Slesarev, G. A. 1974. "Molodoe popolnenie rabochego klassa (problemy sotsial'noi orientatsii i sotsial'noi adaptatsii)." In *Vsesoiuznaia nauchnaia konferentsiia "Lenin i molodezh'," Tezisy dokladov i soobshchenii, Sektsiia 1: Sotsial'naia struktura razvitogo sotsialisticheskogo obshchestva i molodezh'*, edited by N. M. Blinov and G. A. Slesarev, pp. 15-28. Moscow: Institute of Sociological Research.
Smith, Hedrick. 1976. *The Russians*. New York: Quadrangle.
Stalin, J. (1931). "New Conditions—New Tasks in Economic Construction." In *A Documentary History of Communism*, edited by Robert V. Daniels, vol. 2, pp. 25-29. New York: Vintage Books, 1960.
Titma, M. Kh. 1973. "The Influence of Social Origins on the Occupational Values of Graduating Secondary-School Students." In Yanowitch and Fisher 1973, pp. 187-226.
Treiman, Donald J. 1977. *Occupational Prestige in Comparative Perspective*. New York: Academic Press.
Trotsky, Leon. 1965. *The Revolution Betrayed: What Is the Soviet Union and Where Is It Going?* New York: Merit.
Vodzinskaia, V. V. 1973. "Orientations Toward Occupations." In Yanowitch and Fisher 1973, pp. 153-86.
Wiles, Peter. 1974. *Distribution of Income: East and West*. New York: Elsevier.
———. 1975. "Recent Data on Soviet Income Distribution." *Survey* 21, no. 3 (Summer):28-41.
Yanowitch, Murray. 1963. "The Soviet Income Revolution." *Slavic Review* 22:683-97.
———. 1977. *Social and Economic Inequality in the USSR: Six Studies*. White Plains, N.Y.: Sharpe.
Yanowitch, Murray, and Norton Dodge. 1969. "The Social Evaluation of Occupations in the Soviet Union." *Slavic Review* 28:619-42.
Yanowitch, Murray, and Wesley A. Fisher, eds. and trans. 1973. *Social Stratification and Mobility in the USSR*, with a commentary by S. M. Lipset. White Plains, N.Y.: International Arts and Sciences Press.
Zdravomyslov, A. G., V. P. Rozhin, and V. A. Yadov. 1970. *Man and His Work*. White Plains, N.Y.: International Arts and Sciences Press.

5

EDUCATION AND OPPORTUNITY
Richard B. Dobson

After coming to power, the Bolshevik party set out to use education as a tool to reshape the social order—to provide the necessary ideological tempering, transmit the technical skills required for the building of a modern industrial economy, and obliterate distinctions between social groups and classes. Policies ensuring workers and peasants access to advanced schooling, in particular, were designed to bring talent to the top, to break the dominant classes' monopoly of privilege and "culture," and to create a new "socialist intelligentsia" devoted to the Soviet regime.

The drive to industrialize in the 1930s, coupled with a rapid expansion of the specialized secondary and higher educational institutions, made possible an extraordinary degree of upward mobility. Access to higher education was by no means afforded by merit alone—social and political considerations were no less important. Preparatory programs called "workers' faculties" (*rabfaki*) fed thousands of recruits from the working class into the higher schools. The graduates of the "proletarianized" *VUZy* (higher educational institutions) in turn swelled the ranks of the intelligentsia (see Feldmesser 1955; Tandler 1955; Bailes 1978; Fitzpatrick 1978, 1979).

Yet, as the regime pressed ahead with its ambitious plans to collectivize agriculture despite massive peasant opposition and to transform the Soviet Union into a modern industrialized country, steps of a less "revolutionary" nature were taken in education. In an about-face signaled by a series of decrees in the early 1930s, there was a return to more traditional methods of instruction in the primary and secondary schools. The Soviet school assumed an academic cast more like that of the pre-Revolution *gimnaziia* than of the labor school of the 1920s. The teacher's classroom authority was reaffirmed, discipline stressed, and grades restored. Once again uniforms resembling those of pre-Revolution days were required for boys and girls.

In the mid-1930s restrictions on the access of "alien social elements" to higher education were removed, academic standards were raised, and achievement tests were instituted in order to allow the selection of the best-qualified. The proportion of students classified as "workers" or "peasants" declined from 72 percent in 1932 to 56 percent in 1938. From that year until recently, figures on the class composition of students in higher education were not published. It is very likely that working-class and peasant representation declined further in subsequent years as a result of other changes. Not only were the workers' faculties phased out, but modest tuition fees were introduced in 1940 (and continued until 1956) for students in the upper grades of the secondary school and in universities and institutes (see DeWitt 1961; Fitzpatrick 1979).

In the meantime, while crushing real and imagined opposition within the society, the Stalinist dictatorship was concentrating information on political and social matters in its hands. In 1936 "pedology"—the social-psychological study of the learning process—was authoritatively denounced as a "bourgeois" pseudo science, and was suppressed. Independent research by social scientists was ruled out, and the valuable studies of the factors affecting educational performance that had begun in the 1920s ceased. The question of the extent to which differences in status affected educational opportunity, occupational attainment, and the distribution of rewards in society became shrouded in official secrecy. Certainly no Soviet sociological research explored this problem (Dobson 1977c, p. 256).

However, after World War II, American scholars at Harvard University launched a major research project. After interviewing a large number of Soviet-born displaced persons living in the West, these researchers found, not unexpectedly, that the educational level of the younger generation was appreciably higher than that of their parents, that a tremendous amount of upward mobility had occurred, and that most respondents viewed the state-supported educational system as one of the most positive features of Soviet society (see Inkeles and Bauer 1959, pp. 129-58). Yet the evidence also pointed clearly to the fact that de facto equality of educational opportunity had not been attained in the prewar period. As Alex Inkeles and Raymond Bauer (1959, p. 144) concluded:

> The explicit policy of the Soviet regime to favor with superior educational opportunities those in the laboring classes and to impede the opportunities of members of the "former exploiting classes" may have *inhibited* slightly the educational chances of this latter group. However, it did not offset

to an *appreciable* degree the tendency of the children of the upper classes to secure superior access to higher education.

In the Soviet Union itself, the issue of how privilege may be transmitted through the educational system was revived in the late 1950s. Expressing both practical and ideological concerns, Premier Nikita Khrushchev spoke bluntly about the shortcomings of the educational system that was to serve the building of Communism. As more and more young people went on not only to complete the mandatory seven years of schooling, but to graduate from secondary school, not every graduate could count on getting a higher education. The secondary school, which traditionally served as a springboard to higher education, was said to foster a disdainful attitude toward manual work. It was "divorced from life"—at variance both with the economy's needs for skilled workers and the values of the new Communist man.

Access to higher education had become restricted for those of lower status. Khrushchev disclosed that only 30 to 40 percent of the students in Moscow's higher educational institutions came from working-class or collective-farm families, although the latter constituted the great bulk of the population. Sometimes, he asserted, admission to *VUZy* was the result less of the student's motivation and ability than "a competition of parents," who would not only push their children along the path toward a high-status position, but also, by influencing or even bribing admissions officials, would pave their way (see Dobson 1977c, p. 255).

The antidote for these social ills, in Khrushchev's view, was a solid dose of labor training in secondary school, followed by practical work "in production." Regulations governing admission to universities and institutes were to be changed, as well. Recommendations of party, *Komsomol,* and union organizations were to weigh more heavily, and "production candidates" (those with a secondary education who had worked for at least two years) were to account for up to four-fifths of the entering classes. In this way youths would be taught to respect labor, and the work period would weed out the less motivated and less able, thus equalizing to some degree working-class and intelligentsia youths' chances for higher education (see DeWitt 1961).

The sweeping reforms carried out at the end of the 1950s gave rise to additional problems (see Rutkevich 1969a, pp. 1-27; 1969b). Although pupils learned trades in secondary school, and most college students acquired work experience, they regarded work in a factory, shop, or farm as an unfortunate detour from their main objectives—higher education, then work as a "specialist." In the course of working, trigonometry theorems and chemistry formulas were forgotten. Upon entering the higher school, many found themselves unprepared for serious study. An increasing number failed their courses and dropped out before graduating. The rate of attrition was particularly high among working-class and peasant youths.

Even before Khrushchev's removal from power, a reversal of the reforms began. In 1964, the eleventh year that had been added to the ten-year program in order to provide extra time for vocational training was dropped. In the following year, the regulations governing college admissions were changed so that secondary school graduates could apply right after graduation. Although some preference continued to be given to applicants with two or more years' work experience, a renewed stress was placed on academic performance in school and on the entrance examinations in determining who should be admitted.

Although neither Khrushchev's reforms nor their reversal solved the problems that he had publicized, other changes wrought under his leadership laid the ground for a fuller discussion and more able study of these problems. Having been broached and then openly debated at high levels, questions concerning privilege and the purpose of education in Soviet society became legitimate subjects of discussion for the leadership, the press, and even the larger, amorphous "public." Also, in the wake of de-Stalinization, sociology as an empirical science had been revived. Whereas previously it had been branded as a "bourgeois pseudo-science" antithetical to Marxism, now it came to be regarded as a method that as long as it remained firmly grounded in "dialectical materialism" and did not challenge official party ideology and policy, would be a useful tool for social engineering (Katz 1971).

MAIN FEATURES OF THE SOVIET EDUCATIONAL SYSTEM

Today all children—except those who are seriously handicapped or who pose severe disciplinary problems—are obliged to complete eight years of schooling within the general-education school. As a rule a child enters the first grade at the age of seven, often after having spent one or more years in a preschool. The eight years are broken down into three years of elementary schooling, followed by five years that form the first cycle of secondary education. The kind of departmentalized instruction that usually begins in the seventh grade in American schools starts in the fourth grade in most Soviet schools. The general-educational school is coeducational; and with minor exceptions, boys and girls are exposed to a common curriculum in which mathematics and science occupy a prominent place (see Jacoby 1974).

The largest share of the pupils who graduate from the eighth grade continue in the ninth grade of the general-education school, while most of the remainder go on to other types of educational institutions. Whereas the general-education school provides students with basic knowledge and skills, the other institutions are designed to prepare young people for specific vocations. Pupils who leave the regular school after the eighth grade may choose to go to work (while, in some cases, continuing their secondary education in evening school), to enroll in vocational-technical schools offering one-to-three-year courses for various skilled workers' occupations, or to compete for admission to specialized secondary institutions (most of which are called "technicums") that offer three-to-four-year courses for "semiprofessional" occupations (such as industrial technicians, nurses, elementary-school teachers). In short, a youngster may be able to receive a "complete secondary education" in a variety of ways—by graduating from the tenth grade of the general-education school (the most common way), by completing the course of general study in an evening school, or by graduating from a technicum. Since the late 1960s, moreover, a growing number of trade schools have been transformed into "secondary vocational-technical schools" that provide secondary education along with vocational training (see Swafford 1979).

Young people who graduate from secondary school have a similar array of options. Most enter the work force, though a portion of these continue their education on a part-time basis. Others enter trade schools, compete for admission to technicums designed for students who have completed their secondary schooling, or apply to higher educational institutions. College entrants are selected through competitions, and since the mid-1960s most have been recent graduates of the academically oriented general-education school. Those admitted embark on a course of study, usually lasting five years, that leads to a college degree, or *diplom,* in a given specialty (such as chemistry, philology, engineering).

The Soviet secondary education system is clearly more differentiated than the American high school, where students are commonly divided among college-preparatory and other programs within the same institution. It is also more selective. In the United States nearly four out of five young people graduate from high school, while in the USSR less than one out of two finishes the regular general-education school. However, the proportion doing so has risen appreciably since the early 1960s, and by the late 1970s the great majority were completing a secondary education through one of the programs outlined above (see Revenko 1973; Filippov 1976). On the other hand, the Soviet secondary system is less differentiated and less selective than those in most West European countries, where the more academically demanding secondary schools (such as the German *Gymnasium,* the French *lycée,* and the English grammar school) are sharply distinguished from the more practical short cycles (see Poignant 1973; Pellegrin 1974a,b; Husen 1975). In these countries relatively few children enter the select academic programs that prepare students for higher education.

The Soviet system of higher education differs from the American in a number of important respects. For one thing, all institutions are state-owned and -managed, being administered by the USSR Ministry of Higher and Specialized Secondary Education. The number of students accepted in various subjects is determined in consultation with the state planning agencies, so as to achieve a distribution of graduates that corresponds to the economy's expected manpower needs. As a result, there are many more openings in applied technical specialties like engineering than in the liberal arts. Soviet students pursue a course of study that is typically much more specialized from the outset than that of their American counterparts, and the great majority are enrolled in technical institutes, rather than universities.

The proportion of young people in the United States pursuing higher education (at either a two-year community college or a four-year institution) is much higher than in the USSR. Moreover, in recent years just over half of the Soviet students in higher education were full-time day students, while the others pursued their studies in the extensive evening or "extramural" (*zaochnye*) programs while working. Finally, no fees are charged for tuition in Soviet higher educational institutions (or for study in any of the other schools), and three-quarters of the full-time college students receive living stipends from the state.

RECENT RESEARCH ON EDUCATIONAL ATTAINMENT

The numerous studies conducted by Soviet sociologists since the early 1960s have shed new light on the educational attainment process (see Yanowitch and Dodge 1969; Markiewicz-Lagneau 1969; Lipset and Dobson 1973; Matthews 1976; Dobson 1976, 1977a,b,c, 1979; Yanowitch 1977; Jones 1978; Connor 1979; Dobson and Swafford 1980). First of all, they document the fact that children who grow up in higher-status families tend to achieve higher levels of academic performance in school. Studying schoolchildren in the town of Ufa, for example, L. G. Zemtsov (1971, pp. 106-07) found that one out of five of the children of industrial or agricultural workers received only "good" or "excellent" grades, as compared with about one out of three of the low-level white-collar workers' offspring and nearly one out of two of the children of professional and semiprofessional workers. Conversely, 13 to 18 percent of the parents in the manual occupational groups reported that their children had had to repeat a grade in school, as contrasted with 4 percent of the specialists.

M. N. Rutkevich and F. R. Filippov concluded that "An important precondition for young people's academic success in school and for their subsequent social advancement is the degree of their preparation for school, which is conditioned by the interaction of two factors: the parents' level of education and the children's attendance at preschool institutions" (1978, p. 81). The survey results presented (p. 82) revealed that a majority of the children whose mothers had no more than six years of schooling spent little or no time in kindergarten before starting school, in comparison with only a quarter of those whose mothers had at least graduated from secondary school. According to another study, children who reported that their parents had read to them when they were preschoolers were more likely to earn good grades than those who did not; and, not surprisingly, the intelligentsia's children more often stated that their parents had read stories to them than the workers' offspring did (Gendel' 1971, p. 257).

For these reasons, children of better-educated parents are much more likely to get off to a good start in school. When, in one inquiry, teachers were asked to evaluate the first graders' "level of preparation," it was evident that at that early stage readiness for schoolwork was appreciably linked with the mother's educational level: seven out of ten of the children whose mothers had not finished elementary school were thought to be "poorly prepared," whereas only one out of eight of those whose mothers had earned college degrees were so judged. Conversely, a much higher proportion of the college graduates' children were thought to be "well prepared" (Rutkevich and Filippov 1978, pp. 82-83).

Soviet sociologists who have studied differences in school performance generally attribute them to variations in the families' "cultural level." They argue that in comparison with the less-educated parents, the more highly educated ones may develop their children's cognitive abilities more fully, put greater stress on educational success, and instill this value in their offspring. Surveys conducted in Russia's Bashkir Autonomous Republic (cited in Dobson 1977c, p. 258) showed that in comparison with adults having four years of schooling or less, roughly three times as many of the college graduates made use of public libraries (90 percent) and six times as many had their own library at home (86 percent). Children from the culturally better-endowed families were more likely to get good grades in school and less likely to repeat grades because of poor performance. Enjoying a higher standard of living and less crowded living conditions, the intelligentsia may be more able to provide books for their children, hire tutors for them, or simply see to it that they have a quiet place to work (see Vasil'eva 1976, pp. 24-26). And as sociologist N. A. Aitov observes: "Clearly it is easier for an engineer, scholar, or teacher than for a cleaning woman or a worker with four years of schooling to monitor his children's study and help them in their work" (1968, p. 189).

Children from better-educated, more well-to-do, or higher-status families not only tend to get higher grades, but also are likely to have higher educational expectations than children from the lower strata. In analyzing data on eighth-grade pupils gathered in the town of Syzran in 1968, for instance, V. G. Gendel' (1971, p. 175) found that 47 percent of the pupils from specialists' families, 26 percent of the white-collar workers' children, and 16 percent of the workers' offspring intended to pursue a higher education after secondary school.

In Table 5.1 we see the relationship between father's education and the Syzran pupils' grades and plans. The percentage of eighth graders planning to graduate from the tenth grade and then attend college rises from 11 percent among those whose father had completed no more than six grades of schooling to 59 percent among those whose fathers had completed higher education. It is equally obvious that the pupils' choices are strongly associated with their academic achievement. Scarcely any of the students with low marks plan to pursue a higher education. Yet, among those with high grades, there are still pronounced differences in intentions according to the father's education. In short, much, but not all, of the influence of the father's educational level on the children's plans is mediated by the pupils' own performance.

TABLE 5.1
Eighth Graders' Educational Plans, as Related to Father's Education and Own Grades: Syzran, 1968

Father's Education	Percent Planning to Enter 9th Grade and Then Pursue a Higher Education			Percent with High Grades
	High Grades[a]	Low Grades[a]	All	
Higher	91 (22)	13 (15)	59 (37)	59
Incomplete higher or specialized secondary	75 (28)	4 (24)	42 (52)	54
Tenth grade	76 (41)	5 (43)	39 (84)	49
7-9 grades	54 (41)	3 (91)	19 (132)	31
5-6 grades	39 (23)	0 (57)	11 (80)	29
4 grades or less	42 (19)	2 (64)	11 (83)	23
Not indicated	(2)	(8)	(10)	
All	64 (176)	3 (302)	25[b] (478)	37 (478)

[a] Grades "5" (excellent) and "4" (good) are coded as "high grades"; grades "2" (unsatisfactory) and "3" (average), as "low grades."

[b] A higher proportion of the eighth graders plan to continue in the ninth grade of the general-education school (39 percent). Shown here are those who intend to enter the ninth grade and also plan to enroll in a higher educational institution after graduating from the tenth grade.

Source: Calculated from Gendel' 1971, p. 156, Table 3.

The way in which social origins and school performance combine in determining the likelihood of a child's entering the ninth grade of the general-education school is well demonstrated by data from a large sample of Leningrad schoolchildren in 1968 (see Table 5.2). The children's chances of entering the ninth grade increase as the parents' social status rises, while at every socio-occupational level the chances of those with high grades exceed those with lower grades.

TABLE 5.2
Percentage of Eighth-Grade Pupils Continuing in the Ninth Grade by Grade-Point Average and Parents' Occupational Status: Leningrad, 1968

	Grade Average[a]		
Parents' Status[b]	Under 3.5	3.5 and Over	All
Professionals	77	89	86
Semiprofessionals	50	80	70
Skilled workers	38	69	52
Low-skill personnel	19	41	25

[a]Grades are "1" (failing), "2" (unsatisfactory), "3" (average), "4" (good), and "5" (excellent).

[b]Students are classified according to the occupation of the parent with higher status.

Source: Vasil'eva 1976, pp. 50-51.

As a result of this selection process, the social composition of the ninth-grade class typically differs appreciably from that of the eighth grade. From the eighth to the ninth grade, according to this Leningrad study, the share of professionals' children grew by 46 percent, and that of semiprofessionals' offspring increased by 24 percent. But the proportion coming from skilled manual workers' families declined by 10 percent, while the share of children of semiskilled and unskilled manual and nonmanual personnel fell by 54 percent (Vasil'eva 1976, p. 51). In Leningrad and other towns, on the other hand, the great majority of the students enrolling in technicums and vocational-technical schools come from the working class (Rutkevich 1969a; Gendel' 1971; Vasil'eva 1976).

Though variations in the family's "cultural level" surely affect young people's academic performance and their distribution, there is evidence that financial considerations influence their decisions as well (see Dobson and Swafford 1980). In 1965, for instance, sociologists asked students in evening schools in Sverdlovsk why they had dropped out of the regular school (Tsukerman 1969, pp. 95-96). A quarter of the students—most of them children of low-skill workers and employees—alluded to family financial problems. Yet only one in twenty of the specialists' children gave this reason, in contrast with one out of three of the workers' children, nine-tenths of the pensioners' offspring, and all of the students without parents.

A more recent study of pupils enrolled in evening classes in Leningrad pointed to the same conclusion. When asked their reasons for having left school, one out of two of the respondents said that they found it necessary to help their families financially, one out of five stated they left because of poor grades, lack of interest in study, or conflicts with the teacher; and a comparable number cited a desire for independence. From this, S. G. Vershlovskii (1971, p. 51) concludes that financial considerations, linked with low family income, stand out most prominently in the minds of these part-time students. He notes, however, that the proportion mentioning financial difficulties declines with the respondents' age, reflecting, he believes, an actual improvement in the population's standard of living during the preceding decade.

Though children with low grades and low family status are more prone than the others to leave the general-education school before finishing the tenth grade, background factors continue to influence the academic performance and plans of those who graduate. The results of a 1973 study of nearly 10,000 Soviet tenth graders who were surveyed in six regions of the USSR show this quite clearly: one out of four of the collective farm workers' children, one out of three of the state workers' offspring, and seven out of ten of the children of white-collar workers expressed the intention of pursuing higher education after graduating (Mar'ianovskaia 1976, p. 173).

In the Soviet Union, as in the United States, it is the children from the more well-to-do or better-educated families who are most likely to plan to go to college. In Table 5.3 we see that the proportion of 1973 secondary school seniors planning to attend college rises from 23 percent of those from families with per capita monthly incomes of no more than 30 rubles to 44 percent of those from families in the 51-70 ruble bracket and 72 percent of those with incomes of 100 rubles or more. This pattern is quite similar to that obtaining in the United States: in 1974, 26 percent of the high school seniors with family incomes of less than $5,000 (annual) planned to attend college after graduation, as against 41 percent of the children from families earning $10,000-14,999 and 68 percent of those with family incomes of $25,000 or more. Comparable disparities are shown by the father's educational level in both countries.

The fact that children from the more affluent families tend to achieve higher levels of academic performance and that high grades are strongly associated with the likelihood of planning to attend college help to explain this association. Figure 5.1 shows the relationship between college plans and family income for eighth- and tenth-grade students in Syzran who earned high and low marks. Obviously, in both cohorts, students earning high grades were much more likely to plan to attend college. In fact, 84 percent of the tenth graders who were in the upper half of their class had college plans, while just 15 percent of those in the lower half did. Yet, even when level of academic performance is controlled, differences in educational expectations linked with family income persist—especially among the academically strong students.

In analyzing these data, V. G. Gendel' found that the strength of association between plans and grades was strongest for the most affluent and weakest for those coming from families in the poorest group. "As among the eighth graders," he observed (Gendel' 1971, p. 205), "as size of income increases its role as a hindrance decreases and the influence of academic

TABLE 5.3
Relationship of Graduating Seniors' College Plans to Family Income: USSR and United States

Soviet Tenth Graders, 1973[a]			American Twelfth Graders, 1974[b]			
					Percent Planning to Attend	
Monthly Family per Capita Income (rubles)	Distribution (percent)	Percent with College Plans	Annual Family Income	Distribution (Percent)	2- and 4-Yr. Colleges	4-Yr. Colleges
Over 100	9.0	72.2	$25,000 or more	8.4	67.6	53.5
71–100	26.2	61.2	$15,000–24,999	25.2	51.7	28.1
51–70	24.5	44.2	$10,000–14,999	26.9	41.3	21.7
31–50	26.2	32.9	$5,000–9,999	19.9	32.0	16.2
30 or less	11.2	22.7	Under $5,000	10.1	25.8	8.9
No info.	2.4	—	No info.	9.6	—	—
All	100.0	45.3	All	100.0	42.6	23.7

[a] Soviet tenth graders from six regions of the USSR (N = 9,915) who were surveyed in 1973 before graduation. Information on family income was provided by the students after consulting with their parents. "College plans" refers to the intention to pursue full-time study at an institution of higher education following graduation.

[b] Data from nationally representative sample of high school seniors who were surveyed in October 1974. Information on family income was provided by the students. Students "with college plans" are those who expressed a definite intention to pursue higher education at a two- or four-year institution sometime following high school graduation; students who said that they "may" do so are not included.

Sources: USSR—Mar'ianovskaia 1976, p. 178; Rutkevich and Filippov 1978, pp. 79, 100; United States—U.S. Bureau of the Census 1975, p. 12.

FIGURE 5.1
Effect of Family Income on Plans for Higher Education, with Grades Controlled: Syzran, 1968

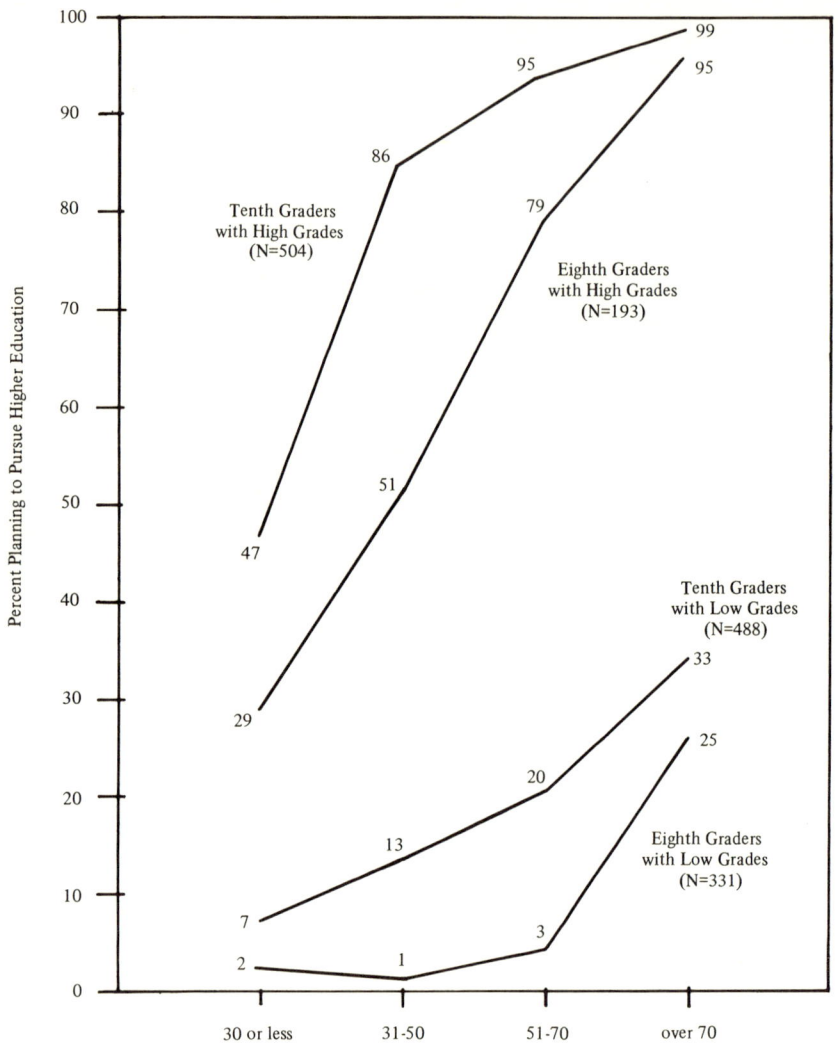

Source: Based on Gendel' 1971, pp. 157, 197.

performance [on the determination of plans] grows." In short, it is among the most well-to-do that the principle of "meritocratic" selection is best realized.

ACCESS TO HIGHER EDUCATION

Although children from higher-status families make up a disproportionately large share of the college applicants, they increase their share in the entering class because they are more successful in the entrance competition (see Liss 1973). With certain exceptions discussed below, admission to *VUZy* is determined primarily according to results on competitive examinations and, since 1972, secondary school grades. The admission criteria naturally affect the social composition of the students.

The results at Rostov State University in 1966 (a year of particularly intense competition) illustrate this selection process (Rubin and Kolesnikov 1968, p. 70; Isaiko 1969, p. 224). Whereas children of workers and nonspecialist white-collar workers made up 58 percent of the applicants, they accounted for 47 percent of the entering class. Children of collective farmers constituted 15 percent of the applicants, but less than 3 percent of those admitted. In contrast, specialists' children increased their representation from 27 to 50 percent. Altogether, children of nonmanual origin made up 75 percent of the first-year class.

Soviet scholars are aware of the "bias" in favor of applicants from higher-status families under the prevailing admission requirements. As sociologists M. N. Rutkevich and F. R. Filippov observe, there is a contradiction between commitments to equality and to the achievement of rapid economic and social development that will hasten the advent of "communism":

> Socialist society is interested in selecting those individuals who will yield maximum benefits in the future as skilled specialists. Competitive examinations for higher educational institutions, generally speaking, enable us to choose those who are best prepared to master a given specialty. But it is well known that the degree of preparation of an applicant depends not only on his natural abilities, but also on the material and cultural level of the family in which he was raised, on the quality of teaching in the secondary school that he attended, and on many other factors that promote the early development of abilities and the acquisition of greater knowledge by the time of the examination. . . . In ignoring the conditions under which applicants are trained, and in making judgments based only on the applicants' knowledge, admissions committees in effect sanction inequality of opportunity (1973, pp. 256-57).

Rutkevich and Filippov, however, argue that such selection is a "special form of socialist competititon" that has nothing in common with selection procedures in the West: "In capitalist countries, competition for admission to higher educational institutions does not exist in our sense of the word. Everything depends on the ability to pay for one's studies.... Competition in knowledge is replaced by the 'competition' of the purse" (1973, p. 257).

Though Rutkevich and Filippov minimize the importance of economic constraints, other Soviet sociologists who have looked into this question have found distinct differences among social groups in the degree to which parents can help their children financially. Though in recent years approximately three-quarters of the full-time college students received state stipends, and more than half lived in state-subsidized dormitories, most families still have had to contribute to their children's support. "It's no secret," Gendel' remarks, "that 'just on a stipend you can't get by' [*na odnu stipendiiu ne prozhivesh'*]" (1971, p. 114). In surveying day students at the Ufa Aviation Institute in 1965, N. A. Aitov (1968, p. 191) found that 83 percent of the children from white-collar workers' families, 70 percent of those from working-class households, and 32 percent of the peasants' offspring received financial support from home. Conversely, 47 percent of the students from peasant families, 38 percent of the working-class children, and 22 percent of the white-collar workers' offspring worked part-time in order to support themselves.

Surely the provision of scholarships helps many children from poor or middle-income families to pursue advanced education. Yet, as the figures cited above attest, the stipends alone are insufficient for the students' support—most must supplement their grants with money from home, or else work part-time.

In a later study, college applicants in Ufa were asked why they had not continued studying after secondary school (Khairullin 1972, pp. 79-80). The results once again showed that financial constraints were felt most keenly by children from the manual strata: 8 percent of the intelligentsia's offspring and 17 percent of the white-collar workers' children said that financial problems and family obligations had prevented them from pursuing a higher education; 33 percent of the working-class applicants and 39 percent of the peasants' children gave this response. Their reports on family income suggested that this assertion had some basis: whereas one out of ten of the applicants from the intelligentsia and about one out of four of the white-collar workers' offspring reported family per capita incomes of 30 rubles or less, the proportion rose to one-third among the working-class offspring and surpassed two-thirds among the peasants' children.

Furthermore, one reason that children from the upper strata are more successful in passing the entrance examinations is that their parents may use their income to provide special tutoring for them or to keep them off the labor market while preparing for the next year's exams. In 1969 the rector of Moscow University, in discussing the advantages that some had in gaining admission, pointed out that many children make use of the services of private coaches: in that year 85 percent of those admitted to the Faculty of Mechanics and Mathematics had received private instruction before taking the entrance examinations (cited in Voronitsyn 1970, pp. 42-43). A survey also was conducted in 1969 at one of the leading technical institutes in Moscow. "The results were shocking, though not unexpected," a teacher disclosed. "About 90 percent of the [successful] applicants, it turned out, had resorted to tutors" (Eppel' 1969). A more recent article in *Komsomol'skaia pravda* underscores the social implications of this common practice:

> "The contest of tutors"—do you remember how at first this sounded like a joke? But only at first. Just listen to your acquaintances, sit in on the entrance examinations for the higher schools, where the parents of secondary school graduates nervously await the results—it is a surprising fact that people are no longer ashamed of having tutors, they are proud of them. They call them by their titles and, among circles of friends, by the posts they hold. The costlier the tutor, the more prestige he has. This means that our system of free education, equally available to everyone and based on competition in knowledge, has been invaded by the ruble (Vasiltsova 1975, p. 7).

While enhancing the intelligentsia's children's chances of gaining entrance to college, the widespread use of tutors works to the disadvantage of rural youth. Writing to *Literaturnaia gazeta* in 1972, one village resident expressed outright resentment and indignation at these inequalities:

> What should we do, the villagers? Young men and women who grow up here also dream about one or another institute and also deserve to receive a higher education. Where are they to find coaches? We have no professors or Ph.D. candidates in our villages. Here it is difficult just to find good teachers. Who will prepare our children for entrance to the institute?
> Even without this [coaching], the village school is behind the city schools. Here the people often complain: the teacher is not as good, and the equipment is not the same, and the libraries do not compare at all with those in the city. The village children, especially those who live far away from the regional roads, are deprived of museums, theaters, lectures. Consequently their preparation is already worse. But in addition to all these other things, one must add "the competition of the purse . . ." (cited in Jacoby 1974, p. 140).

In fact, studies by Soviet sociologists leave little doubt that it is urban youth from well-to-do intelligentsia families who are the principal beneficiaries of private coaching. For instance, a survey of students at Gorky State University in 1967 revealed that 36 percent of the students from families in which the father had a higher education had made use of tutors in preparing for entrance examinations, compared with 17 percent of the children of fathers with a secondary education and just 3 percent of those whose fathers had an elementary education. One out of four students from nonmanual workers' families had had coaching, as opposed to one out of twenty of the workers' offspring and none of the peasants' children (Minkina, Sizova, and Terent'ev 1970, p. 23).

The advantages that children of the urban intelligentsia enjoy in securing admission to higher educational institutions does not stem only from a more affluent and cultured home environment that enables them to achieve better secondary-school records and to excel in examinations. Since the mid-1960s increasing numbers of specialized schools offering intensive training in science, language, or the arts have been established. The fact that most of these schools are concentrated in major cities near the colleges for which they prepare their students has meant that they are much more accessible to urban youth. In the early 1970s, for instance, the special physics-and-mathematics boarding school at Leningrad University, which recruits students through academic competitions (called "olympiads"), was the only school of its kind for a vast area containing 4,000 schools and embracing a population of some 22 million. Yet Leningrad city had no fewer than 57 special schools at that time—ten for mathematics, seven for physics, three for chemistry, and two for disciplines in the humanities, as well as 35 special foreign-language schools (Kossakovsky 1972, p. 16).

Because of the special training that such schools provide and the high representation of intelligentsia children in them, some have criticized them for "social elitism" contrary to the democratic principles of education in the USSR. "The selection of children for special schools is, more often than not, based not on their gifts, but on the ambition of some parents," observed G. Kulagin (1971, p. 20), director of a machine-construction combine in Leningrad. "Even if we were to admit that the general program in the mass schools retards the development of the really gifted child, this circumstance is much less detrimental to society than instilling from childhood the idea that a chosen person is set apart."

Parents vie with one another in trying to get their children enrolled in a university or institute, as well as in the special schools. As *Komsomol'skaia pravda* reported in 1970:

> Strange transformations occur in August and at the beginning of September. Reliable and respected engineers and teachers, intelligent people who have been through the war and the period of reconstruction, suddenly lose their human dignity and become pitiable supplicants, blocking the doorways of rectors' offices and ministries, bombarding prominent friends with telephone calls and imploring almost on their knees: "Get my daughter (or son) into an institute" (cited in Jacoby 1974, p. 141).

"No stone is left unturned," the writer observes, "from the exploitation of the names and the reputation of forebears to gambling with what are the most sacred values for us all" (cited in Jacoby 1974, p. 141).

Though cases of outright bribery presumably are rare, accounts in the Soviet press make it clear that such practices do occur. One report (Inovel 1976) detailed the activities of P. Gelbakhiani, the former rector of the Tbilisi Medical Institute, who was convicted of accepting hundreds of thousands of rubles in bribes in exchange for admitting children of well-to-do families to the institute. In the 1960s, Gelbakhiani had instituted a system by which favored applicants were virtually guaranteed admission: the examiners gave these applicants oral-exam question cards with the answers attached, corrected and completed their written examinations for them, let the applicants take the examinations home with them, or—if nothing else availed—arbitrarily raised their marks. In 1967, 170 of the 200 applicants who entered the institute's Therapeutic Division did so illegally. As a result of such corruption, the student body was saturated with children of wealthy and influential parents.

Like the intelligentsia, the Soviet system of higher education is differentiated according to social composition. Some institutions are much more accessible to children from the manual strata than are others. For example, a worker's or a peasant's child bent upon a teaching career would be more likely to enter a secondary teaching school than a pedagogical institute or prestigious Moscow State University, where working-class and collective-farm youth accounted for only a fifth of the enrolled day students in 1969-70 (Iurchenko 1971; Samoilova 1972, p. 129). Young people from the farm tend to be underrepresented in higher schools other than agricultural institutes, while white-collar workers' children account for well over half of the student bodies of medical institutes (Cheknev et al. 1971).

As in other countries, such differences in recruitment are no doubt related to the prestige of specialties and the perceived quality of given institutions. The relative standing of an institution appears to be based on such factors as the quality of its teaching staff and faculties. location, and so on (Filippov 1972, pp. 145-46). As a rule, institutions that are of higher prestige and better quality, are more academic as opposed to applied, and are located in major cities and scientific centers, draw a larger share of their students from the white-collar and intelligentsia strata.

EQUALITY OF OPPORTUNITY AND EDUCATIONAL POLICY

Given the ideological insistence upon egalitarianism and the superiority of socialism over capitalism, the pattern of inequality of educational opportunity continues to be a politically sensitive subject in the USSR. Regarding future trends and government policy, there have been divergent points of view. As M. N. Rutkevich stated: "The basic objective tendency consists in the social composition of those accepted by colleges [*VUZy*] steadily approaching the population's social composition, since the reduction in differences in material and cultural conditions leads to an equalization of the conditions for the preparation of the young recruits entering college'' (1967, p. 19). This "objective tendency" is being strengthened by policies designed to improve low-quality schools, especially in rural areas, and to achieve universal secondary education in the foreseeable future. As a result of the latter, not only will a greater share of the youth cohort have formal access to higher education, but children of successive generations will be less likely to suffer disadvantages because of their parents' low educational attainment.

In light of the persuasive evidence of the sociological studies, however, many leading policy makers and sociologists became convinced that the government should take positive measures to "regulate" the social composition of the student body. In 1969 the government adopted measures to establish at higher educational institutions preparatory divisions (reminiscent of the "workers' faculties" of an earlier period) for working youth, collective-farm youth, and demobilized servicemen. The heads of enterprises in which the young people have worked for at least a year decide, on the recommendations of party, *Komsomol,* and union organizations, who should be sent to these programs. "Auditors" who successfully complete a year's study are then enrolled in the regular first-year class. Between 1969-70 and 1973-74, the number entering college directly from the preparatory programs increased fourfold to 60,000 (Lisovskii and Dmitriev 1974, pp. 46-47).

It is difficult to ascertain to what degree these remedial measures have improved the chances of disadvantaged youth. According to some reports, the preparatory faculties are not doing effectively what they were designed to do—help the disadvantaged. Because of insufficient publicity, many workers are not aware of the opportunities open to them, and factory managers are reluctant to release able workers. In some higher schools, only half of the graduates of these programs get as far as the second or third year, and in the Russian Republic as a whole, just over a third of the first class that graduated from these divisions in 1970 reached the fifth year in the regular program (Maksimova and Ovchinnikova 1975, p. 12). On the average, one-third of the "production workers" have had a single year's work experience. Most of them are secondary-school graduates who have already tried to pass the entrance exams, and failed:

> For them, the most important thing is the opportunity to get into a higher school without taking the competitive examination (to be accepted as a student, it's enough to receive a three [average grade] on examinations taken following studies in a workers' faculty). So, instead of feeding mature and independent young people to the higher schools, as was intended, the workers' faculties send them youths who have served out a year in production (Maksimova and Ovchinnikova 1975, p. 12).

Since admission to the programs is determined by "social position," rather than origins, there is nothing to prevent privileged youth's entering through the back door, so to speak. Even worse, a sizable number gain admission with forged documents testifying to their exemplary (but fictitious) work career. In 1975, 17 percent of the students whose documents were checked in the Armenian Republic had presented fake work records and recommendations. In view of such practices, a correspondent for *Komsomol'skaia pravda* points out that "With the help of parental connections and forged documents, young idlers take the places in the preparatory divisions and workers' faculties which rightfully belong to young workers and collective farmers" (Sarkisian 1974). Thus, while preparatory programs have been established to achieve "affirmative action" on behalf of ostensibly disadvantaged youths, it is by no means clear that they are successfully accomplishing that objective.

CONCLUSION

Does the Soviet educational system provide greater equality of educational opportunity than Western countries, including the United States? The official position is an unequivocal "yes." As the Soviet Education Act of 1973 proclaims: "In our country, for the first time in the history of mankind, a genuinely democratic system of public education has been established" (Osnovy 1974, p. 93).

Soviet sociologists, too, affirm that the status-attainment process in socialist society is radically different from that in capitalist countries. For instance, N. A. Aitov writes:

> Under capitalism, the basic thing determining the position of man in society—capital—is transmitted through inheritance. Under socialism, that means—education—is not received as an inheritance; rather, each should attain it for himself. Under capitalism, [the gaining of] a "place in the sun" depends principally on the parents, and there it is easier to make one's way up the ladder of the social hierarchy for those whose father holds that ladder in his hands (1971, pp. 51-52).

In a similar vein, F. R. Filippov argues:

> The external resemblance of the school's and teacher's functions under capitalism and socialism cannot conceal the fundamentally different purpose of these functions, for in opposition to capitalism, the school in a socialist society solves the problem of the gradual overcoming of social-class differences in educational and cultural level and brings about a high degree of social mobility for youth who graduate from school (1967, p. 20).

These Soviet scholars are certainly correct in asserting that in Western countries, a student's social-economic background exerts considerable influence on his or her chances for educational and occupational attainment. Yet, the contrast between "socialist" and "capitalist" countries is overdrawn in two respects. On the one hand, it overlooks the significant variations among

Western countries in the absolute or relative chances that working-class or farm children have for enrolling in higher education (see Poignant 1973; Husen 1975; Levin 1976). On the other hand, the Soviet studies that we have reviewed demonstrate that the educational attainment process in the USSR is in many respects similar to that observed in most Western countries.

In the USSR, as elsewhere, a child's socioeconomic background, as measured by the parents' occupational status, their educational level, family income, and place of residence, has appreciable bearing on his or her eventual attainment. In analyzing data from a 1968 survey of eighth- and tenth-grade graduates in Syzran (Gendel' 1971), Michael Swafford and I (Dobson and Swafford 1980) estimate that perhaps as many as 75 out of 1,000 working-class children made the transition from the eighth grade to full-time study in institutions of higher education in two and a half years; the comparable proportion for children from the intelligentsia was at least four and a half times larger (325). As we note, these differences appear to be somewhat smaller than those obtaining in England and France in the 1960s, yet they are by no means negligible.

Such disparities in opportunity reflect the norms used for educational selection, as well as the structure of inequality in Soviet society. As long as the Soviet government gives priority to rapid economic growth over the long-range objective of social equality, it can be expected that this pattern will persist. Soviet scholars have stressed that like children in other lands, offspring of more highly educated parents are often exposed to an environment conducive to cognitive development. Being more likely to urge their children to pursue advanced education, while less often experiencing the constraints that low income imposes, intelligentsia parents can also use their resources effectively to further their children's careers.

Recent educational policies show contradictory tendencies at work. As the number of young people completing a secondary education rises, there is a tendency for the variance in individuals' educational levels to diminish; but whether this will result in greater equality of opportunity for postsecondary education remains in doubt. In order to channel more young people into the workers' trades where the manpower shortage has become acute, Soviet policy makers decided to upgrade and expand the vocational-technical schools. As long as working-class youth continue to be more likely to enroll in the trade schools, the continued use of differentiated programs after the eighth grade may serve to perpetuate social differences in opportunity. The regime's decision to establish "preparatory divisions" at *VUZy* for ostensibly disadvantaged youths underscores the seriousness of this problem, but whether they have succeeded in reducing differentials in opportunity has not yet been demonstrated.

REFERENCES

Aitov, N. A. 1968. "Sotsial'nye aspekty polucheniia obrazovaniia v SSSR." In *Sotsial'nye issledovaniia,* vyp. 2, pp. 187-96. Moscow: Nauka.
———. 1971. "Obrazovanie i sotsial'nye peremeshcheniia." In *Stroitel'stvo kommunizma i izmeneniia sotsial'noi struktury sovetskogo obshchestva,* vyp. 3, *Sotsial'naia struktura i problema obrazovaniia,* pp. 41-55. Moscow: Znanie.
Bailes, Kendall E. 1978. *Technology and Society under Lenin and Stalin: Origins of the Technical Intelligentsia, 1917-1941.* Princeton: Princeton University Press.
Cheknev, B. M., V. S. Nekhoroshev, and L. A. Blinov. 1971. "Pervye itogi raboty podgotovitel'nykh otdelenii meditsinskikh institutov Rossiiskoi federatsii." *Sovetskoe zdravookhranenie* no. 10: 41-45.
Connor, Walter D. 1979. *Socialism, Politics, and Equality: Hierarchy and Change in Eastern Europe and the USSR.* New York: Columbia University Press.
Dewitt, Nicholas. 1961. *Education and Professional Employment in the USSR.* Washington, D.C.: U.S. Government Printing Office.
Dobson, Richard B. 1976. "Education, Equality, and the Economy: Problems of Leningrad Youth." Introduction to Vasil'eva 1976, pp. vii-xxxi.
———. 1977a. "Educational Policies and Attainment." In *Women in Russia,* edited by Dorothy Atkinson, Alexander Dallin, and Gail Warshofsky Lapidus, pp. 267-92. Stanford: Stanford University Press.
———. 1977b. "Mobility and Stratification in the Soviet Union." *Annual Review of Sociology* 3: 297-329.
———. 1977c. "Social Status and Inequality of Access to Higher Education in the USSR." In *Power and Ideology in Education,* edited by Jerome Karabel and A. H. Halsey, pp. 254-75. New York: Oxford University Press.
———. 1979. "Class and Merit in the United States and the Soviet Union: A Comparative Study of the Determinants of Educational Expectations." Paper presented at the 74th annual meeting of the American Sociological Association, Boston, Aug. 27-31.
Dobson, Richard B., and Michael Swafford. 1980. "The Educational Attainment Process in the Soviet Union: A Case Study." *Comparative Education Review* 24 (June): 252-69.
Eppel', B. 1969. "O fakul'tativakh, repitatorakh i abiturientakh." *Uchitel'skaia gazeta* (May 13): 3.
Feldmesser, Robert A. 1955. "Aspects of Social Mobility in the Soviet Union." Ph.D. dissertation, Harvard University.
Filippov, F. R. 1967. "K voprosu o sotsial'noi roli sovetskoi shkoly." In *Sotsiologicheskie problemy narodnogo obrazovaniia.* Uchenye zapisiki Sverdlovskogo gosudarstvennogo pedagogicheskogo instituta, sb. 56, pp. 8-21.
———. 1972. "Sotsial'naia orientatsiia i sotsial'nye peremeshcheniia molodezhi." In *Molodezh' kak obshchestvennaia gruppa,* edited by Iu. E. Volkov, F. R. Filippov, and N. D. Bondarenko, pp. 141-47. Moscow: Academic Council of the USSR Academy of Sciences for the Study of the Complex Problem "Regularities in the Development of Social Relations and Cultural Life in Soviet Society" and the Higher Komsomol School.
———. 1976. *Vseobshchee srednee obrazovanie v SSSR (sotsiologicheskie problemy).* Moscow: Mysl'.
Fitzpatrick, Sheila, ed. 1978. *Cultural Revolution in Russia, 1928-1931.* Bloomington: Indiana University Press.
———. 1979. *Education and Social Mobility in the Soviet Union 1921-1934.* Cambridge: Cambridge University Press.
Gendel', V. G. 1971. "Problemy sotsial'noi podvizhnosti molodezhi pri sotsializme." Cand. Sci. dissertation, Leningrad State University.
Husen, Torsten. 1975. *Social Influences on Educational Attainment: Research Perspectives on Educational Equality.* Paris: OECD.
Inkeles, Alex, and Raymond A. Bauer. 1959. *The Soviet Citizen: Daily Life in a Totalitarian Society.* Cambridge Mass.: Harvard University Press.

Inovel, I. 1976. "Corruption, Favoritism, Bribery." *Zaria vostoka,* July 23, p. 3, abstracted in *Current Digest of the Soviet Press* 28, no. 38: 5.
Isaiko, A. V. 1969. "Nekotorye sotsial'nye problemy vysshego zaochnego i vechernego obrazovaniia." In *Effektivnost' podgotovki spetsialistov,* edited by Iu. Leonavichius. Kaunas: Kaunas Polytechnical Institute.
Iurchenko, A. K. 1971. "K voprosu ob izmenenii sotsial'nogo sostava sovetskogo studenchestva (na materialakh pedagogicheskikh institutov RSFSR)." In *Voprosy nauchnogo kommunizma: sbornik statei,* edited by V. F. Generalov, pp. 80-85. Moscow: Moscow State University Press.
Jacoby, Susan. 1974. *Inside Soviet Schools.* New York: Hill and Wang.
Jones, T. Anthony. 1978. "Modernization and Education in the U.S.S.R." *Social Forces* 57 (Dec.): 522-46.
Katz, Zev. 1971. "Sociology in the Soviet Union." *Problems of Communism* 20 (May-June): 22-40.
Khairullin, F. G. 1972. "Nekotorye sotsial'nye problemy formirovaniia studenchestva i adaptatsii studentov k vuzu." Cand. Sci. dissertation, Ufa Aviation Institute.
Kossakovsky, I. 1972. "There Is Such a School." *Izvestiia,* Mar. 23, p. 5, condensed in *Current Digest of the Soviet Press* 24, no. 12: 16-17.
Kulagin, G. 1971. "Problems and Judgments: The School of Labor." *Pravda,* June 19, p. 3, condensed in *Current Digest of the Soviet Press* 23, no. 24: 20.
Levin, Henry M. 1976. "Educational Opportunity and Social Inequality in Western Europe." *Social Problems* 24 (Dec.): 148-72.
Lipset, Seymour Martin, and Richard B. Dobson. 1973. "Social Stratification and Sociology in the Soviet Union." *Survey* 19 (Summer): 114-85.
Lisovskii, V. T., and A. V. Dmitriev. 1974. *Lichnost' studenta.* Leningrad: Leningrad State University Press.
Liss, L. F. 1973. "The Social Conditioning of Occupational Choice." In *Social Stratification and Mobility in the USSR,* edited by Murray Yanowitch and Wesley A. Fisher, pp. 275-88. White Plains, N.Y.: International Arts and Sciences Press.
Maksimova, E., and I. Ovchinnikova. 1975. "Whom Does the Workers' Faculty Need?" *Izvestiia,* Apr. 5, p. 5, condensed in *Current Digest of the Soviet Press* 27, no. 14: 12-13.
Mar'ianovskaia, I. S. 1976. "Orientatsiia vypusknikov srednikh shkol na vysshee obrazovanie." In *Obrazovanie i sotsial'naia struktura,* edited by F. R. Filippov, Iu. N. Kozyrev, and D. I. Ziuzin, pp. 171-79. Moscow: Institute of Sociological Research of the USSR Academy of Sciences.
Markiewicz-Lagneau, Janina. 1969. *Education, égalité, et socialisme: Théorie et pratique de la différenciation sociale en pays socialistes.* Paris: Anthropos.
Matthews, Mervin. 1976. "Educational Growth and the Social Structure in the USSR." In *Social Consequences of Modernization in Communist Societies,* edited by Mark G. Field, pp. 121-45. Baltimore: Johns Hopkins University Press.
Minkina, K. N., M. G. Sizova, and A. A. Terent'ev. 1970. "Sotsial'naia kharakteristika studentov-pervokursnikov universiteta." *Sotsiologiia i vysshaia shkola,* Uchenye zapiski Gorkovskogo universiteta, vyp. 100, no. 2: 20-29.
Osnovy. 1974. "Osnovy zakonodatel'stva soiuza SSR i soiuznykh respublik o narodnom obrazovanii." In *Narodnoe obrazovanie v SSSR: Sbornik dokumentov 1917-1973 gg.,* compiled by A. A. Abakumov, N. P. Kuzin, F. I. Puzyrev, and L. F. Litvinov, pp. 93-104. Moscow: Pedagogika.
Pellegrin, Jean-Pierre. 1974a. "Admission Policies in Post-Secondary Education." In *Towards Mass Higher Education: Issues and Dilemmas,* pp. 63-103. Paris: OECD.
―――. 1974b. "Quantitative Trends in Post-Secondary Education." In *Towards Mass Higher Education: Issues and Dilemmas.* Paris: OECD.
Poignant, Raymond. 1973. *Education in the Industrialized Countries.* Plan Europe 2000, published under the auspices of the European Cultural Foundation. Project 1: Educating Man for the 21st Century, Vol. 5. The Hague: Nijhoff.

Revenko, Tamara. 1973. *L'enseignement supérieur en l'Union soviétique.* Paris: OECD.
Rubin, B. G., and Iu. S. Kolesnikov. 1968. *Student glazami sotsiologa: Sotsial'nye problemy vosproizvodstva rabochei sily vysshei kvalifikatsii.* Rostov-on-the-Don: Rostov State University Press.
Rutkevich, M. N. 1967. "Sotsial'nye istochniki popolneniia sovetskoi intelligentsii." *Voprosy filosofii* no. 6: 15-23.
———, ed. 1969a. *The Career Plans of Youth,* edited and translated by Murray Yanowitch. White Plains, N.Y.: International Arts and Sciences Press.
———. 1969b. "Why a Student Does not Arrive at the 'Finish.' " In *Contemporary Soviet Education,* edited by Fred Ablin, pp. 151-60. White Plains, N.Y.: International Arts and Sciences Press.
Rutkevich, M. N., and F. R. Filippov. 1973. "Social Sources of Recruitment of the Intelligentsia." In *Social Stratification and Mobility in the USSR,* edited by Murray Yanowitch and Wesley A. Fisher, pp. 241-74. White Plains, N.Y.: International Arts and Sciences Press.
———, eds. 1978. *Vysshaia shkola kak faktor izmeneniia sotsial'noi struktury razvitogo sotsialisticheskogo obshchestva.* Moscow: Nauka.
Samoilova, E. S. 1972. "Sotsial'nye aspekty formirovaniia kontingentov sovetskikh studentov v period stroitel'stva kommunizma (1961-1971 gg.)." Cand. Sci. dissertation, Moscow State University.
Sarkisian, A. 1974. "V teni pod lipoi." *Komsomol'skaia pravda,* Sept. 11, p. 4.
Swafford, Michael. 1979. "The Socialization and Training of Soviet Industrial Workers." In *Industrial Labor in the USSR,* edited by Arcadius Kahan and Blair Ruble, pp. 19-41. New York: Pergamon.
Tandler, Fredrika M. 1955. "The Workers' Faculty (Rabfak) System in the Soviet Union." Ph.D. dissertation, Columbia University.
Tsukerman, V.S. 1969. "The Role of the School for Working Youth in the Career Plans of Youngsters." In Rutkevich 1969a, pp. 94-103.
U.S. Bureau of the Census. 1975. "College Plans of High School Seniors: October 1974." *Current Population Reports,* Series P-20, No. 284.
Vasil'eva, E. K. 1976. *The Young People of Leningrad: School and Work Options and Attitudes,* translated by Arlo Schultz and Andrew J. Smith, with an introduction by Richard B. Dobson. White Plains, N.Y.: International Arts and Sciences Press.
Vasiltsova, Z. 1975. "Tutor of Success?" *Komsomol'skaia pravda,* Jan. 17, p. 2, condensed in *Current Digest of the Soviet Press* 27, no. 4: 6-7.
Vershlovskii, S. G. 1971. "Znachenie uchebnogo opyta rabochei molodezhi." *Sovetskaia pedagogika* no. 11.
Voronitsyn, S. S. 1970. "Class Distinction in Soviet Higher Education." *Bulletin of the Institute for the Study of the USSR* [Munich] 70 (Nov.): 39-45.
Yanowitch, Murray. 1977. *Social and Economic Inequality in the USSR: Six Studies.* White Plains, N.Y.: Sharpe.
Yanowitch, Murray, and Norton Dodge. 1969. "Social Class and Education: Soviet Findings and Reactions." *Comparative Education Review* 12 (Oct.): 248-67.
Zemtsov, L. G. 1971. "Sotsial'nye problemy obshcheobrazovatel'noi shkoly v SSSR na sovremennom etape." Cand. Sci. dissertation, Ufa Aviation Institute.

6

OBSERVATIONS ON RURAL LIFE IN SOVIET RUSSIA
Roy D. Laird and Ronald A. Francisco

Unlike life in the cities, where most workers live in one place and must commute to work in another, farm life the world over combines the living place with the work setting. The Soviet collective farming system goes even further. Whereas British and American farmers engage in most of their political and social activities off the farm, usually in a nearby town, with the exception of their activity in the collective-farm markets, virtually all of the Soviet peasants' political, economic, and social activities are encompassed within the scope of the farm on which they live.

This is the basic fact that determines the character of life in the Soviet countryside. It is the will of the regime, and just one manifestation of the subordinate status of the Soviet peasantry. The countryside was, of course, an afterthought in the ideology that guided the Bolshevik Revolution. In the first decade of the new regime, Lenin continually underscored the superiority of industrial organization for all economic activity. Stalin's forced collectivization program carried this notion further and unleashed widespread violence against the rural population. Even today, Soviet peasants earn less, receive less formal education, enjoy fewer freedoms, and have much less mobility than their urban counterparts.

The authors are indebted to the University of Kansas for its generous assistance, which has made this study possible.

This history of disruption and persistent discrimination would seem, according to established Western theories, to foster active rebellion, political violence, and alienation. We know, for example, that the turmoil of revolution, collectivization, and modernization promotes "social mobilization." Karl Deutsch (1961) defines this as "the process in which major clusters of old social, economic, and psychological commitments are eroded or broken and people become available for new forms of socialization and behavior." Social mobilization, in turn, usually causes social and political instability and (not infrequently) insurrection, especially if the mobilization is rapid and is not compensated by concomitant growth in social institutions that manage its effects (Huntington 1968).

The 1979 Iranian revolution, for example, can be seen as an outcome of the shah's widespread and unpopular "white revolution" — including its coercive land reform and forced breaks with tradition, especially in the treatment and status of women. Similar fears are often expressed for social systems such as Saudi Arabia, where extremely rapid economic growth, sudden affluence, the erosion of traditional mores and life-styles, and the encroachment of Western materialism cause strains in the social fabric. One could argue that the Soviets avoided much social disorder by developing institutions to contain and control change. Indeed, as discussed below, the use of the machine-tractor stations as the key lever of control over the countryside, from the beginning of forced collectivization until their demise in 1958, probably explains why the turmoil and confusion that accompanied forced collectivization failed to precipitate a counterrevolution in the rural areas.

We also know that perceived relative deprivation often causes disaffection and political violence among individuals and groups (Gurr 1970; see also Ralph S. Clem, "The Ethnic Dimension, Part II," section "The Ethnic Factor," in this volume). Certainly, at the beginning of the 1980s the Soviet peasantry, with its poorer compensation, lesser mobility, and fewer privileges, *is* relatively deprived, and is aware of its status. Yet, since World War II we have seen no significant rural instability, no massive peasant uprisings, no peasants among the ranks of Soviet dissidents, and no large-scale efforts for peasant emigration. Indeed, there is considerable evidence of persistent and strong nationalism and patriotism in the countryside.

The passivity of the peasantry must be understood in terms of tradition and the enduring character of the peasant's relationship to the authority of his village and to the state. This can be appreciated by first looking at the present rural social organization in light of the heritage from the past.

FROM VILLAGE TO COLLECTIVE FARM*

Although the 1861 emancipation made the tsarist peasants politically free, economic realities dictated a minimal change in their lives prior to the 1917 Revolution. With few exceptions, the landlords still owned nearly all the land, even that small portion of the estates near the villages on which they had allowed their peasants to grow their own food. That land was to go to the peasants, but they had to pay for it. As a result, most were saddled with nearly impossible redemption payments and were limited to working at minimal wages for their former masters in a struggle to meet their new debt.

The villages were communes (although not as fully communal as some modern religious communities). The most important institution was the *mir*, whose major task was the administration of village activities. At its head was the *starosta* (village elder), and voting membership went to the head (only males counted) of each *dvor* (household). Sir John Maynard, has provided a vivid description of those institutions in their "nineteenth century form":

> [They acted] . . . . as an organ of village self-government: distributing among its members the customary peasant duties of repair of roads and bridges, escorting of holy icons and the like, forming by collection from all a reserve of corn for insurance against need, allotting his subsistence farm to the priest, managing communal field when there was one, organizing fire-fighting and protection against thieves, enforcing the patriarchal authority upon contumacious sons, and settling minor disputes among its members, it even made separation orders for quarrelsome spouses, regardless of the law, which gave the monopoly of divorce to the ecclesiastical courts — but the peasants were always half outside the law. It was the maid-of-all work for the miscellaneous demands of a busy administration, and we are not surprised that more tasks were soon laid upon it by the State (Maynard 1949, p. 24).

If a peasant (*muzhik*) from this past were to somehow be transported to the present, he would notice much change. But an extended stay would convince him that there was very familiar content in the often only superficially altered forms.

In the central village he would look for the church—the focal point of village life. Most are long since gone. For a time, however, some churches had been put to other purposes, such as the storage of grain. The center of activity

---

*Although the general outline of most of our considerations applies to all of the Soviet Union, our examples and the specifics of the analysis are taken from the European parts of the USSR and most fully from the comparison of the Great Russian tradition with the current Russian Republic. We cannot claim, in particular, that our analysis is completely applicable to the traditionally Islamic parts of the USSR, where the historic rural institutions differ from those of Russia proper, even though the current administrative forms are comparable with Russian ones.

has shifted to the building occupied by the chairman and his administrative staff, including agronomists, zootechnicians, veterinarians, accountants, and other specialists. Usually, as part of the administrative complex, there is the general meeting place, a huge auditorium where the workers periodically gather to vote on important farm matters put before them by the chairman and his assistants. But the *muzhik* would soon discover that the voting is only rubber-stamp legitimization of decisions already set in concrete by the administration.

The center of the village now has a paved road — a sign of the greater volume and efficiency of the geographic mobility that is a necessary concomitant of industrialization. Prior to the peasants' political emancipation in 1861, they were owned by the landlords, veritable rural slaves. Although present-day peasants migrate to the cities in large numbers, they are not issued the same internal passports as urban citizens, and their movement is more restricted.

Yet it is the vast movement of the population out of the countryside that is associated with the mechanization of farms (even though there is still much hand labor) and their aggregation into inordinately large units — indeed, the most striking contrast with the past. The former villages disappeared as the rural population after 1940 not only began to constitute a smaller proportion of the total population but also declined sharply in absolute numbers (see Table 6.1).

The major physical change in the farms came in the early 1950s. At the end of the 1940s the vast majority of the farms were *kolkhozy* (collective farms), which when first organized in the 1930s were based upon the existing villages and the several hundred hectares of surrounding fields that had belonged to the local landlord under the tsars. Much fewer in number but larger in size were the *sovkhozy* (state farms). These were usually based upon former crown lands, huge holdings once owned by the church, and some of the larger of the former estates. When the *sovkhozy* were first formed, the Soviet leaders stressed creating huge *sovkhoz* grain factories. Thus defunct churches could no longer be adequate storage facilities.

TABLE 6.1
Urban and Rural Population of the USSR, 1913-79 (millions)

Year	Total	Urban	Rural	Percent Rural
1913	159.2	28.5	130.7	82
1940	194.1	63.1	131.0	67
1959	208.8	100.0	108.8	48
1970	241.7	136.0	105.7	44
1979	262.4	163.6	98.8	38

Source: Ts.S.U. 1979, p. 7.

As suggested above, the machine-tractor stations (MTS) were vital to Stalin's success in achieving forced collectivization. Farm machines and implements were scarce in the early 1930s, and an economic justification for creating the MTS was to maximize the use of such scarce resources. The machines and tractors that did exist were taken by the state into a central place to serve several farms in the surrounding area. The move did make economic sense, but the major reason for forming the MTS had to be Stalin's realization that it provided a highly efficient instrument for control over both the peasants and their production. Proof of the pudding lies in the fact that the MTS seized the draft animals as well. The peasants were totally dependent upon the land for survival. Therefore, with the state fully in control of the means of cultivation, the peasants were left with no choice but to accept orders from the MTS officials.

As discussed below, the MTS dominated the countryside until 1958 (including playing a major role in collecting the grain for the state), when changes arising out of the amalgamations in the early 1950s meant that they were no longer needed as an instrument of control. Prior to 1950 very few farms had party units or party-member chairmen. By the end of that decade all had sizable party units, and all were headed by party members.

At the end of the 1940s, combining a Leninist and a traditional Russian conviction that what is huge is best (a sometimes admitted "gigantomania") with his own political maneuvering (that helped him become Stalin's agricultural boss and later head of the party), Nikita Khrushchev proposed a scheme for amalgamating neighboring *kolkhozy* into larger collectives. He promised the peasants that building *agrogorady* (rural cities) would bring all the superior advantages of urban life to the farms, for example, theaters, libraries, and clubs. Stalin bought the idea.

A few new structures were built. For a number of years the construction of new rural housing concentrated on multistory apartments, instead of the traditional individual peasant houses. However, no sooner was it clear that the amalgamation drive would be successful, than Krushchev must have had second thoughts about the enormous cost to the national economy of such a radical transformation of the countryside. The *agrogorady* remained a dream. Yet the relatively small collectives were reformed into huge new enterprises, mostly new *kolkhozy,* although in some instances assertedly "weaker collectives" were transformed overnight into *sovkhozy*. The enormity of the change is recorded in Table 6.2.

Although in theory the *kolkhoz* is still a "collective" institution (and its workers share the income according to their labor), while the *sovkhoz* is a state enterprise (and its workers are salaried employees), in practice little difference remains between the two. Since the late 1950s every *kolkhoz* has supported a sizable party unit, important for assuring outside control. On both types of farm the bulk of what is produced is determined by state-imposed purchase plans. *Kolkhozniki* incomes do remain below those of *sovkhoz* workers.

TABLE 6.2
Number and Size of Soviet Farms, 1940 and 1977

Type	Year	Number of Farms	Average Figures per Farm			
			Total Land (hectares)	Sown Area (hectares)	Number of Workers	Total Population*
Kolkhoz	1940	235,500	1,400	492	138	267
	1977	27,112	6,600	3,800	539	1,024
Sovkhozy	1940	4,200	12,200	2,800	429	815
	1977	20,066	17,800	5,600	578	1,098

*These are estimated figures. The Soviet yearbook shows the number of households on the *kolkhoz* but not the *sovkhozy*. Estimates are based on the number of workers for both kinds of farms and a statement by a Soviet scholar in 1970 that the average number of people in a *dvor* at that time was 3.3 in the countryside and 3.1 in the cities. Since families in recent decades have declined in size, the 1940 estimate is undoubtedly low and the 1977 estimate very probably is high.

Source: Ts.S.U. 1978, pp. 271-94.

However, the adoption of a crop insurance scheme and a guaranteed minimum wage in the 1960s has moved the *kolkhozniki* in the direction of the salaried *sovkhoz* workers.

From the onset of collectivization in the 1930s, Soviet commentators have made it clear that both the *kolkhoz* and the *sovkhoz* are acceptable socialist forms. However, little doubt has been left that the *sovkhoz* is superior, closer to the ultimate model that is to prevail under full Communism.

Although the *mir* fulfilled genuine needs of the villagers, the landlords and the state used it as their primary lever of control over the peasants. Today's *kolkhoz* serves the same function. The comrades' court — an institution found on all farms, in urban factories, and in apartment complexes of any size — illustrates the transference of function from old to new social forms. The courts are quasi-legal institutions composed of workers and/or peasants, established primarily to enforce production discipline. Thus, their primary concern is with drunkenness, tardiness, and other work-related violations, but they also may deal with neighborhood or family matters. Small fines may be levied or, at worst, dismissal from work can be recommended. However, the primary intent is to shame the deviant before friends and neighbors. A visitor from the past could well be reminded of the way the *mir* used to deal with deviant members of the commune, delving into matters that in most Western societies are deemed beyond the scope of legitimate public scrutiny.

THE PRIVATE SECTOR

In tsarist times, as noted earlier, the small household plots on which families grew their food were located adjacent to the village *dvor*. For a brief period after the 1917 Revolution, the fields formerly attached to large estates were divided among the peasants. However, Stalin again consolidated these lands through his program of forced collectivization. It quickly became apparent that the peasants would not accept fully communal arrangements. They slaughtered their own livestock rather than relinquish them to the collective, and this was on such a mass scale that it was not until the mid-1950s that the number of cattle equalled what it had been in 1930.

Stalin was compelled to respond by permitting private household plots (today no more than 0.5 hectare) on which a family could also keep a cow, a few pigs, goats, or sheep, and most of their poultry. However, all land in the Soviet Union is owned by the state, and the privately cultivated land is part of that allocated to the *kolkhoz* or *sovkhoz*. The right to use the private plots is vested in households, not individuals, and can be passed from one generation to the next. The amount of land is allocated according to the number of family members participating in the public sector of the farm.

If a *muzhik* from the past were to find the family home still standing, he might well discover that his descendants were still cultivating the same household plot, and deriving from it (and the private animals) most of their food and a substantial part of the family's livelihood. According to a Soviet economist, as of 1976 the average *kolkhoz* family devoted 68 percent of its working time to the collective fields (for which most receive a combination of wages and payment in kind, especially fodder for the private animals) and 32 percent of its time to the family private sector (*Ekonomika* 1978a, p. 79).

Most of the private cultivation is done by *kolkhoz* and *sovkhoz* peasants, although such activity is important to some urban citizens as well. According to one Soviet source, as of 1977, 0.9 percent of the average industrial worker's income came from private agricultural activity, and 26.3 percent of the average *kolkhoznik* family's income came from such pursuits (*Ekonomicheskie nauki* 1978). Here, again, as in tsarist times, although most of the time is spent working the landlord's fields, a substantial part of the income comes from private activity.

Only some 3 percent of the total sown land in the USSR is in private plots. However, such private activity in 1977 produced "59 percent of the potatoes grown in the country, 29 percent of the vegetables, 29 percent of the meat and milk, and 35 percent of the eggs" (*Moscow News* 1979).

THE STATE AS LANDLORD

Although all land has been nationalized, the *kolkhozy* are legally separate entities with their own administration and in possession of their land in perpetuity. In theory, important matters are decided by votes taken in general meetings of all active workers. And, in contrast with the former *mir,* women workers are guaranteed equal representation (although they are very rarely in positions of authority on the farm).

In practice, the control over *kolkhoz* affairs is clearly vested in the state — the new landlord. In the elections of *kolkhoz* chairmen (*sovkhoz* directors are appointed from above), a single candidate is put before the workers in the general meeting. This candidate is selected by the *obkom* (the regional party committee) from the *nomenklatura,* the party's appointments or nominations list. The selection of candidates according to the *nomenklatura* system occurs for all key posts at all levels in the USSR, and it assures that important decision makers are loyal to the party. As a result many, if not most, of those on the slate for *kolkhoz* chairman are outsiders, unknown to the constituents, but the record shows that nominees are rarely rejected. As noted above, one of the fruits of the amalgamations in the 1950s was to reduce the number of *kolkhozy* and increase their size so that each could have a party-member chairman and a primary party unit.

This pattern is repeated for all key posts on the farms. Thus, aside from the second most important person on the farm, the party secretary, who heads the farm's party unit and serves in that post only with higher outside approval, all other key members of the staff serve at the chairman's pleasure, despite the formal election procedures.

As was confirmed on numerous occasions by responses from farm leaders to our questions during a recent trip to the USSR, the average *kolkhoz* worker can hardly feel that he or she, along with several hundred fellow workers, is engaged in some kind of cooperative activity in which the ordinary worker helps run things. In practice they husband the livestock and cultivate the fields at the time and in the manner prescribed by the farm administration, much like past generations who worked the landlords' fields.

The huge Soviet farms demand strong leadership in order to operate efficiently. The concentration of authority that has a positive political function in the eyes of the state also has a distinct economic rationale in this context. Yet Professors Jan and Arthur Adams have observed, as we have, that this structure of control clearly transcends temporal boundaries:

> Like the *pomeshchiki* (landowners) of old the collective farm chairmen and state farm directors are in almost total social and organizational control over their farms and the people in them.
>
> . . . .
>
> Spying the director, the old muzhik halted abruptly, jerked off his hat and held it to his chest, bowing with the short repeated jerks of a humble peasant of imperial times.

The director *was* the farm (Adams and Adams 1977, pp. 31–63).

The Model Charter of 1935 (slightly revised in 1969), the "basic law" pertaining to *kolkhozy,* authorizes the chairman to enter peasants' homes, if this is required to assure women's participation in the economic and political activities of the collective. Since present-day chairmen clearly try to serve the *kolkhoz* as well as the state, our visitor from the past might see this role as somewhere between that of the old landlord's manager and of the former *starosta,* as it entails the duties of presiding over the *mir* and "distributing among its members the customary peasant duties . . . " (Maynard 1949).

BRIGADES AND THE *ZVENO*

Why collectivization? Certainly, given the history of the *mir,* such a way of life is more familiar to Soviet peasants than it would be to the traditionally independent U.S. or European farmers. For the most part, however, the answer lies in the demands of the Soviet leadership.

Stalin and his colleagues wanted political control over the countryside, and *kolkhozy* provided a means of governing the peasants. Both Marxist-Leninist ideology and practical economics (especially the leaders' felt need to extract the maximum capital from the countryside to subsidize industrial construction) demanded control over the peasants' "means of production." Lenin had preached, and his successors have accepted without question, that superior farming must follow the urban industrial pattern; and *kolkhozy* and *sovkhozy* provided the requisite large-scale base. Finally, when Stalin announced that the Soviet Union was building socialism in one state, he would have found himself in a ludicrous position if the majority of the population, who were peasants, were exempted from the superior way of life. Collective and state farms provided all of the answers. Yet today, the key phrase is that the "*kolkhozy* are schools of communism in the countryside."

Collectivity in work, for the most part, is a matter of being a member of a huge, permanent brigade, most of which count 100 or more workers. Almost from the beginning the doctrine has been that the large brigades are the superior organizational form. Obviously they answer the Marxian dictum that the "collective power of the masses" can achieve ends not possible by individuals. Volumes of words have been written on the superiority of the permanent large brigades. Nevertheless, there has been from time to time surprisingly vocal, often grass-roots, opposition to their superiority.

Starting even before World War II, arguments appeared in the press that the *zveno* (link or team) is better, resulting both in greater production and in labor savings. The genuinely "independent" *zveno* that is written about from time to time, exists on farms that, in essence, have been divided into several smaller farms with, for example, 200–300 hectares assigned to a half-dozen or so individuals, often members of the same family. Under such arrangements the *zveno* is wholly responsible for cultivating the crop, and the remuneration the members receive is determined largely by the success or failure of their efforts.

Repeatedly top theoreticians and officials have argued that the *zveno* represents a move away from communism, and that it encourages latent private-property instincts. Yet, every few years highly favorable reports on the success of *zveno* experiments appear in the press. Certainly, peasants working in a *zveno* are much more their own bosses than are their brigaded colleagues, and being one's own boss has always been one of the major attractions of farming in much of the world, at least where serfdom has not existed.

THE *DVOR*

In both the cities and the countryside, the extended family of three generations living in one *dvor* (household) has largely passed from the scene. Perhaps as late as World War II most peasant homes were mere huts with dirt floors. Even in 1960 we saw a few log homes on the outskirts of Moscow. Oil lamps served for lighting. Now, when one visits the countryside and the villages, the impression is that most floors have been covered with wood, tile, or cement. Electricity is almost everywhere, and nearly all homes seem to have grown TV antennas.

Statistical data bearing on the quality of rural life are far more readily available for Western societies than for the USSR. This is especially true of figures that throw unfavorable light on the Soviet system. Therefore, the material in Table 6.3 is particularly unusual in the relative backwardness of the farms it reveals.

TABLE 6.3
Percentage of *Sovkhoz* Households with Modern Amenities, 1975

Running water	20.2
Sewer connections	14.7
Central heating	18.8
Bath or shower	12.7
Electric lights	97.6
Gas	58.8
Hot water supply	4.5

Note: These data pertain to *sovkhoz* settlements. Not all of the members of the *kolkhoz* or *sovkhoz* live in one central village. Some farms encompass two or more settlements.

Source: Voprosy ekonomiki (1978).

One of Lenin's favorite dicta was that "Communism is the Soviet power plus the electrification of the whole country" (1943, pp. 247-48). In this formula he reflected a conviction that rural electrification would provide both urban amenities for the peasants and, especially, "a large-scale industrial basis" in agriculture, which would allow it to achieve urban industrial production standards. As can be seen from the data, the electrification goal has been virtually achieved, but the countryside has seen little improvement by way of supplying indoor water and central heating for the peasants' homes.

The following is Betty Laird's description of what must have been a better-than-average peasant home that she and one of the authors visited in 1970, in the highly successful (by Soviet standards) agricultural area near the city of Krasnodar.

> It was a neat little brick home measuring approximately 22 by 25 feet, not counting a narrow, enclosed porch. It had two tiny bedrooms, a kitchen and a living room. Its source of heat was a modified version of the traditional *pech* or stove built into the wall between the living room and the kitchen. The bedrooms were bright and pretty with pale blue, lacey bed and pillow covers. There were no closets. In the kitchen there was an extra bed, an apartment size refrigerator, and a table with a radio on it. There was no cupboard, sink, or visible source of water, although the house did have electricity. The living room contained a couch, dressing table, a

table, and a TV set. The lady of the house was especially fortunate in that she had a motorized washing machine which she kept on the porch next to a cabinet of some sort. In the mud yard there were several fruit trees, a few flowers, and a grape vine clinging to the trellis on the porch; the usual vegetable garden was behind the house. No toilet or bath house was visible, and water must have been carried by hand from a central source. This was home for a family of four (Laird and Laird 1979, pp. 17-18).

For a time (as noted earlier), especially under Khrushchev's leadership, efforts were made to persuade the peasants to abandon their private plots. These included speeches against working of private plots, the encouragement of farms to restrict plot usage, and economic sanctions, such as the restriction of the sale of private produce in the *kolkhoz* market. There was a parallel push to build multistory apartments on the farms whenever new housing was needed. Again, such actions included both speeches and articles favoring apartment life as well as economic moves that made it easier to build rural apartments and, conversely, most difficult to obtain materials for private homes. We have visited some of the apartments, as well as individual peasant homes, and agree with the observatons of the sometimes surprisingly outspoken Soviet social scientist Victor Perevedentsev:

> A completely equipped rural home standing on a garden site, adjoining an orchard — is an incomparably better living situation than an apartment in a multi-storied city building. It is no accident that old villages are wallowing in continuous gardens. A city apartment in the village is a bad thing. It is far from ideal even in the city. A confirmation of that is the mass movement of city dwellers to the dachas. A dacha is a second home, because a city apartment does not fulfill all the functions which a person demands from a full-valued dwelling place. It is amusing to have the situation get to a point where a rural inhabitant also needs a dacha. The rural home has always completely fulfilled the functions of a dacha also (1974, p. 141).

Perevedentsev notes that many of the upper floors in the rural buildings are empty. Peasants with private plots and animals are particularly reluctant to live in them, as the constant climbing of stairs obviously creates an added burden.

At present the campaign to move residents into multistory rural apartments has ceased in most areas. Indeed, Soviet farmers wanting to build private housing have been receiving both encouragement and material assistance from the state. This change is clearly tied to a reminder by Leonid Brezhnev that private agriculture remains important to the state, and that the peasants should be encouraged in their enterprise.

A final feature of the peasant household that should be mentioned here is the family shrine in the "icon corner." This is open evidence of religious faith. In a 1966 study of an allegedly representative agricultural area, only 7 percent of the homes of the skilled agricultural workers had icon corners, but they were found in 57 percent of the ordinary collective farmers' households — that is, the homes of the workers who do the manual labor on the farms (Arutiunian 1966). We have never been fully comfortable with arguments that the church is doomed in the USSR, or that there has been a significant revival of religion in recent years. Certainly not as large a percentage of the population attends the churches and openly embraces the Orthodox faith as was the case prior to the Revolution. However, and hardly surprising, according to studies by Soviet writers, religion remains important for most rural citizens.

ADVANCEMENT AND MIGRATION

As in almost every part of the world, farm youths in the Soviet Union receive less education than city youths. A desire for improved incomes and higher education, and a wish for the bright lights, theaters, and other urban excitements, are keys to the fact that a disproportionate number of the rural youths leave the villages for good. Few look forward to a life of manual labor.

Women constitute a majority of the rural population and do most of the work, including the heavy manual labor. In the total population women also considerably outnumber men. This imbalance is primarily a result of the enormous loss of males in battle during World War II. However, since the war the urge to go to the cities to better one's fortune has attracted more young males than females away from the farms. Thus, whereas the percentage of women in rural areas was 52.0 in 1959, it grew to 53.4 by 1979 (*Pravda* 1979). One probable explanation for this phenomenon lies in the military service required of all males. While in the service many rural youths live in, or at least travel to, the cities. After such experiences many men from the farms decide against returning to life in the country.

Farmers' sons and daughters in the United States tend to be taught to run the mechanized equipment as soon as their arms and legs are strong enough and long enough to manage the controls. In contrast, Soviet law does not permit youths under 19 to operate farm machinery without supervision (Dunn 1980). If we may stretch the concept a bit, such skills are reserved for a special class in the USSR.

The upper class on the farms is the administrators, for the most part an educated ruling elite. The bulk of the peasantry form a lower class, those who do the manual labor in the barns and fields. In between there is an important, respected, better-paid middle class, made up largely of peasants who have been trained as machine operators. Only they are allowed to operate the equipment. Apparently it is this group that has been subject to the greatest drain of manpower from the farms.

Given the relatively privileged position of machine operators on the farms, some surprising figures have been published on the extent of their migration to the cities in the Ukraine, a key agricultural republic. According to a Soviet article, every year 100,000 machine operators leave agriculture in that republic. As a result, only 10-12 percent of those trained for the tasks on the farms remain in agriculture. Therefore, although the fleet of tractors and combines increased by 38 percent from 1965 to the late 1970s, the number of trained operators working at their skills grew by only 18 percent, leaving many of the republics with fewer operators than pieces of equipment to be operated (Dunn 1980). Eighty percent of those who left were between 20 and 40 years old, and our guess is that most were still in their twenties (*Ekonomika* 1978b).

The Soviet farm population is aging, and the officials see that fact as a serious problem. Indeed, when we attended the 1970 International Conference of Agricultural Economists, which was hosted by the Soviets in the Belorussian capital of Minsk, our Soviet colleagues repeatedly spoke of two primary concerns. To paraphrase their questions: First, and less important, "Is there something of practical value in the use of the new econometric models in agriculture?" Second, and clearly more important, "What can be done to stop the drain of the best of the rural youth from the farms?"

TABLE 6.4
Average Monthly Wages in 1978 (rubles)

Overall (workers and employees)	160.0
Industrial workers	176.0
Agricultural workers and employees	143.0
Railway workers	172.5
Construction workers	195.3
Retail and public catering workers	125.0
Civil servants and managerial staff	144.0
Science and scientific services	169.0

Source: *Moscow News* 1979.

Even for that portion of the youth that wants to advance in the field of agriculture, an urban education is essential. Today, most of the key administrative posts on the farms are held by individuals who have had advanced or higher educational training. State agricultural workers' and employees' wages are lower than those in any other line of work, except catering (as shown in Table 6.4). *Kolkhoz* workers' wages are lowest of all — only some 106 rubles per month in 1978 (*Vestnik* 1978).

THE SOCIAL AND POLITICAL ORIENTATION OF THE SOVIET PEASANTRY

Given this degree of relative discrimination, deprivation, and regimentation, how can one explain the relative calm that has pervaded the Soviet countryside since World War II? The answer to this question is complex, and underscores the unique nature of many aspects of Soviet society.

First, the regime has understood from the outset that institutional controls are necessary to harness the centrifugal forces of social mobilization. Hence, there has always been a fairly stringent state control over rural activity, from the machine-tractor station era (in which peasants' means of production were confiscated by the state) to today's tightly controlled collective system with an average of 30 Communist party members in each collective. At the same time, however, authorities have consistently recognized the limits of control and coercion, and have introduced the minimum degree of flexibility necessary to avoid widespread insurrection. Stalin, for example, relented on the private-plot issue. Today, one of the most important "safety valves" is the ability of peasants to sell their private goods in *kolkhoz* markets.

The peasants' sale of private produce remains by far the major outpost of legal private entrepreneurship in the Soviet Union. As noted earlier, private agricultural activity provides most of the peasants' own food, a substantial part of a rural family's income, and a significant proportion of the nation's total food supply. The activity also provides them with other interesting activities, including extensive travel for at least some.

Especially in the early spring, peasants who live in the South and grow fruits and vegetables will purchase airplane tickets (relatively inexpensive) and fly with baskets of their precious produce to the northern cities still emerging from winter, which is always marked by shortages of fresh produce. Once there, the peasant entrepreneurs sell their produce in the *kolkhoz* markets (private peasant markets), often have a day or two on the town, and return home with a profit for the family. Of course, for the bulk of the peasants such market excursions are confined largely to a nearby town or city, but all fill a need that is more than just one of increasing the family accounts. Such excursions give the peasants a view of the outside world, a chance to meet city relatives and customers, and an opportunity to gossip.

Gossip and the exchange of tales are universal human practices, which must be even more important to Soviet citizens. All communications media in the USSR are tightly controlled as a state monopoly. Most negative news, which seems to dominate in the Western press — such as airplane crashes, political conflicts, or natural disasters — goes unreported in the Soviet press. In the summer of 1972 Moscow was under a continuing pall of smoke for several weeks. It was a hot, dry summer, and peat bogs near the city were burning uncontrolled; but never a story about the problem was printed in the papers. The *kolkhoz* markets are a key place where urban folk from different professions and different parts of the city meet, and where the peasant entrepreneurs join in the dialogue. Every kind of information is exchanged. From such a source we learned in 1970 of a widespread rumor that there was a cholera epidemic in one of the cities on the lower reaches of the Volga. The officials also must have heard the rumor, but no attempt was made to squelch it in the press. The saying "Where there is smoke there is fire" probably has a rural origin, and probably would have been the answer in the markets to any announcement by the officials that there was no epidemic along the Volga.

A second factor in the regime's strategy to retain loyalty and legitimacy in the countryside emphasizes the steady progress that has been achieved under socialism. This perspective is largely accepted by the peasantry. Hence, most Soviet peasants do not appear to perceive themselves as relatively deprived. Their reference group is not the skilled and higher-paid collective workers, or the urban industrial workers, but their own recollections of their past living standards and welfare. By this criterion, and only by this one, socialism has improved rural life, and the peasantry seems willing to exchange its loyalty for such progress.

Certainly, given the tight controls over all news media (which constantly point to the asserted shortcomings and failures of "capitalist" systems, including exploitation of the farmers), plus the relatively low levels of educational attainment by the peasants, there is little by way of information to lead the average rural worker to believe that some other system of farming might have resulted in even greater improvements in his living standards.

Yet a third group of reasons for the remarkable calm in the countryside has little to do with the regime or its policies. This set of factors might be termed the "mystical tie to the land." We have already pointed out the relatively high commitment to religion that remains among the peasantry. Yet there is an even stronger bond to the land and the tradition of "Mother Russia" or the Ukraine, and so forth. One sees this in the cryptic remarks of the exiled Aleksandr Solzhenitsyn and even in the romantic pining for the land in traditional Russian literature and folklore.

Yet this orientation is not entirely mystical and certainly is not irrational. Indeed, we may have been remiss in this portrait of village life, if we have left an impression that, given the alternative of urban life, there is no attraction to staying on the farm. Even in the United States there is growing recognition that the natural beauty of the rural landscape, the openness of the countryside, and the generally less hectic pace make rural living extremely attractive. This "quality of life" factor is even considered a form of supplementary compensation in some East European areas.

In spite of what Victor Perevedentsev's words, as cited above, imply, although many might rent a country *dacha* for a few days, for the most part only the elite of the elite own such retreats to which they can repair at will. Even for the fortunate few, professional demands keep most in their urban harnesses the bulk of the time. For the Soviet peasant's son or daughter to leave the village means a total break, for the USSR has nothing comparable with the U.S. suburban way of life.

On balance, the peasants' work is harder and the hours are longer, but for at least part of their time they have the satisfaction of being their own bosses. As noted above, this is an attraction that long has been important to people who choose farming as a way of life.

Thus, Soviet villages are not the hotbeds of insurrection that are generally produced by relative deprivation or of the social mobilization associated with rapid economic development and political change (see Gurr 1974). The regime has fostered institutions that control the rural population in a way that has direct parallels with the tsarist period. It has socialized the peasants to measure their life circumstances in terms of past impoverishment rather than relative to the clearly more advantaged strata in the present. This standard breeds pride and loyalty rather than discontent. And it has relied upon the ageless tradition of the peasant's spiritual marriage to the land to forge a loyal and largely contented countryside.

Finally, there is an old Russian proverb that probably is as applicable to the Soviet countryside today as it was in the centuries under the tsars. As quoted in Ivan Turgenev's *Fathers and Sons,* it says "A Russian peasant will get the better of God himself." As we have tried to stress in the preceding passages, with all the modernization that has occurred in the USSR, for the individual *muzhik* there is much continuity with the past. Our observations are that rural attitudes toward higher authority are little changed from what they were a century or two ago.

REFERENCES

Adams, Arthur E., and Jan Steckelberg Adams. 1977. *Agriculture in the USSR, Poland and Czechoslovakia: Men Versus Systems.* New York: Free Press.

Arutiunian, Iu. V. 1966. "Sotsial'naia struktura sel'skogo naseleniia." *Voprosy filosofii* 5:51-61.

Deutsch, Karl W. 1961. "Social Mobilization and Political Development." *American Political Science Review* 55 (Sept.): 493-514.

Dunn, Ethel. 1980. "Factors Affecting Social Mobility for Women in the Soviet Countryside." In *Agricultural Policies in the USSR and Eastern Europe,* edited by Ronald A. Francisco, Betty Laird, and Roy D. Laird, pp. 71-91. Boulder, Colo.: Westview.

Ekonomicheskie nauki. 1978. No. 7; 48-54.

Ekonomika sel'skogo khoziaistva. 1978a. No. 5: 79.

Ekonomika sel'skogo khoziaistva. 1978b. No. 6: 86-90.

Gurr, Ted Robert. 1970. *Why Men Rebel.* Princeton: Princeton University Press.

_____. 1974. "Persistence and Change in Political Systems, 1800-1971." *American Political Science Review* 68 (Dec.): 1482-1504.

Huntington, Samuel P. 1968. *Political Order in Changing Societies.* New Haven: Yale University Press.

Laird, Roy D., and Betty A. Laird. 1979. "The Peasantry Under Soviet Rule." In *The Peasantry of Eastern Europe,* vol. II, *20th Century Developments,* edited by Ivan Volgyes, pp. 15-24. New York: Pergamon.

Lenin, V. I. 1943. "Report Delivered at the Eighth All-Russian Congress of Soviets," Dec. 20, 1920. In *Selected Works,* vol. VIII, pp. 247-48. New York: International Publishers.
Maynard, Sir John. 1949. *Russia in Flux.* New York: Macmillan.
Moscow News. 1979. May 13-20, p. 2.
Perevedentsev, Victor. 1974. "Measuring Changes." *Nash sovremmenik* 3 (Mar.): 135-51.
Pravda. 1979. Apr. 22, p. 4.
Tsentral'noe Statisticheskoe Upravlenie (Ts.S.U.) 1978. *Narodnoe khoziaistvo SSSR v 1977.* Moscow: Statistika.
———. 1979. *Narodnoe khoziaistvo SSSR v 1978.* Moscow: Statistika.
Vestnik sel'skokhoziaistvennoi nauki. 1978. No. 6: 154.
Voprosy ekonomiki. 1978. No. 5: 78.

7

SOVIET SOCIETY AND COMMUNIST PARTY CONTROLS: A CASE OF "CONSTRICTED" DEVELOPMENT
Mark G. Field

There is a Soviet story—apocryphal perhaps, as most such stories usually are, and yet reflective of the realities of life—that a class of schoolchildren, while studying Russian history, came to Napoleon's retreat from Moscow. One of the pupils raised his hand and asked: "Comrade teacher, how could we ever defeat the French when we did not have a [Communist] party?" This naive question, coming from a child, makes good sense when viewed through the prism of contemporary Soviet society, and particularly in the light of the critical importance officially attributed to the existence and functions of the Communist party of the Soviet Union. Indeed, according to the Soviet definition, the party is the keystone of Soviet society, the alpha and omega, the cement that holds it together, the "organizer of victories," the essential structure, the indispensable ingredient in the march of the Soviet Union toward the goal of full Communism. At least this is what the party would like to have the world, including particularly the Soviet population, believe. In essence, this

---

This is a revised version of a paper originally published in Donald W. Treadgold, ed., *Soviet and Chinese Communism: Similarities and Differences* (Seattle: University of Washington Press, 1967). I thank the University of Washington Press for permission to use these materials. I want to express my gratitude to Professors Jerry F. Hough and Robert C. Tucker, who critically read this manuscript in its original form and provided many important suggestions. The paper also owes more than I can say to Professor Talcott Parsons and to the ideas expressed in his course on institutional structure and later in the *The Evolution of Societies* (1977). Needless to say, I alone bear the responsibility for the contents of this essay.

self-proclaimed role is a statement of "functionality": that the party is a "structure" that performs certain tasks or fulfills certain needs that are indispensable to the survival and the existence of the society in which it exists. And conversely, to use the null hypothesis, it is argued that the cessation of the performance of such tasks would have deleterious and dire consequences that would affect the fate of that society, its march toward the more perfect social order, and its ability to master the enviroment. And it may well be that, at least now, the party does most of what it claims to do. It has become such an integral part of practically every aspect of Soviet society and is so interdigitated with most social processes that its sudden elimination as a functioning organization might well throw Soviet society, at least temporarily, into serious disarray, since there are few alternative forces—or, more important, institutional mechanisms—that could take over the functions the party has arrogated to itself.

Indeed, in speculating on what might happen in the event of an anti-Communist revolt, Jerry Hough states:

> A post-Communist regime in Russia could not function without former party members serving in important administrative and even political posts, but undoubtedly there would be investigations and commissions to distinguish between "good" Communists and "bad" ones (Hough and Fainsod 1979, p. 568).

But, at least in my opinion, Russia would be more dependent on former party members than Germany was in the post-World War II period on former Nazi officials. The absence, of course, of any other "political" parties that might serve as "funtional equivalents" emphasizes the monopolistic nature of the party's role, and thereby differentiates it from "parties" as the term is commonly used in the West, particularly in pluralistic systems. It is precisely part of the party's modus operandi, derived from Lenin's definition of its role as the core of society, that alternative forces should not be allowed to rise and in any way threaten its hegemony. If they arise, they usually are either incorporated or co-opted into the structure of the party (as the intelligentsia was during the 1930s) or placed under strict party controls and supervision, as the armed forces are. It is the military, incidentally, and the organs of internal security, because of their organizational control of a large number of men and means of violence, and their possession of a relatively autonomous communications network that might be able to take over in the unlikely event that the party should cease functioning or falter. What is remarkable, particularly when compared with the experience of many other countries (particularly the developing ones) is the degree to which the Soviet regime (the party) has been able to hold the military at bay.

And yet it should be clear that the role and the position of the party cannot, in the nature of the case, remain static. For the very policies, programs, and purposes the party pursues alter, in the course of time, Soviet society; and the modus operandi of the party must, or should, change to keep up with the changes it helps to produce or promote. Seen in a developmental and evolutionary perspective, and given the inevitable ossification and petrifaction that accompany the oligarchic holding of power over a long period of time, and contrary to the image of itself that it wants to maintain and to perpetuate, the party may well be, at the present time and on balance, more of a source of retardation, conservatism, and stagnation than of dynamism, progress, and vision. Indeed, the further "modernization" of Soviet society may hinge perhaps not so much on what the party will actively do to promote the process of modernization as on its ability (or inability) to maintain what it feels is adequate control over the unfolding of that society, while at the same time divesting itself of enough day-to-day supervision over most sectors of society to permit these sectors to unfold without its direct supervision. This means the ability of the party to tolerate the further differentiation of Soviet society, the potential formation of interest groups (which have existed in a latent fashion for years), the articulation of group interests, and the maintenance of a legitimate role for itself that would continue to justify its retaining the ultimate power of making secular decisions and its privileges.

At the same time, if functions that are now performed by the party (in the political, economic, and cultural areas, for example) were to be replaced by fairly autonomous institutional mechanisms (democratic consultation, a market system, an independent judiciary, professional peer review, and so on), this would necessarily mean a degree of loss of control by the party, a situation that in itself must be anxiety-provoking. This loss of control would lead to two unacceptable consequences. First, the system might develop in directions deemed undesirable by the party, because it would lead to that anathema of Lenin and of the party, spontaneity. (Thus the people, given a choice, might "wrongly" opt for more consumer goods and better housing rather than for investments in heavy industry and the military.) Since, in the eyes of the party, there is not much evidence that the Soviet population is ruled by consciousness of what is eventually "best" for all (more investments in heavy industry and in national defense), a phasing down of controls, though it might increase efficiency to some degree, is seen as a slippery slope, a dangerous trade-off. Second, the replacement of current functions by other mechanisms and institutions would emphasize the resultant redundancy of the role of the party and affect its legitimacy, since it would become and appear increasingly functionless, and therefore parasitic. The party might thus become like so many aristocracies in the past, a privileged estate with no functional or social contractual justification nor reason for that privilege nor, for that matter, for its existence as a corporate group.

Functioning organizations, generally speaking, do not dissolve themselves when they see that the purpose for which they were created no longer exists. Usually they seek new goals, new functions, new mandates to perform in order to justify their existence. Thus the March of Dimes did not go out of business when a solution to the prevention of poliomyelitis was found: it shifted its organizational capabilities to other medical problems, such as birth defects. When ministers of religion see their congregations dwindle, they sometimes reinterpret their "pastoral" mission as including the type of nonspiritual "counseling" usually performed by social workers and to some degree, by psychiatrists and psychologists. It would, therefore, be patently absurd, even for a moment, to contemplate the idea that the party would deliberately rule itself out of existence if it perceived that its functions were no longer necessary. It is, however, possible to contemplate, at least in the longer perspective, a restriction and shifting of functions—let's say toward a general stewardship and oversight of Soviet society and toward keeping the faith alive through a guardianship of the ethos that is its official raison d'être, a secular equivalent to a return or retreat to the temple. But these are far-off speculations. At the conclusion of this essay I shall suggest how a Marxist interpretation of the workings of impersonal historical forces suggests a rather bleak future for the party.

At the same time the tantalizing possibility exists that when we speak of the Communist party of the Soviet Union, we may in fact (though not in theory) speak of the Communist parties, in the sense that it is difficult—indeed impossible—to conceive of the party as a monolith. Its many internal elements represent different social forces, interest groups, aspirations, sectors of the economy, conservative and reformist trends, and so on. Thus the competition for positions and priorities, for the commitment of resources—indeed, for policies and programs domestically and abroad—must constantly take place in the inner councils of the party. But these are not public debates; there are no appeals to constituencies; decisions are taken in executive sessions; and the outside world, including the Soviet population, is served the end product of these processes: the official party line.

"CULT OF THE PERSONALITY" OR "CULT OF THE PARTY"?

The expression "cult of the personality" with which Nikita Khrushchev and his successors chose to stigmatize Josef Stalin's rule was not entirely fortuitous. Neither was it quite accidental that Khrushchev, after his fall, also was accused of having created a small cult of his own personality.* And

---

*For example, a movie entitled "The Chairman" was held up because it portrayed a Khrushchev type. The essence of the type was that the chairman knew it all and trusted no one:

> Before us we have a chairman, a leader, who regards himself as a commander . . . in the sense that he knows only one way of dealing with subordinates, by command. It is no accident that he shouts so much . . . This is an essential part of his style of leadership. He is the leader who decides everything for all, he does everything for himself, he entrusts nothing to anyone. If he consults with an experienced peasant, it is only as if he were an obedient "apprentice," nothing more. (cited in the *New York Times*, Dec. 15, 1964, p. 12).

certainly, at the present writing (1979), the cult of Leonid Brezhnev's personality is alive and prospering in the Soviet Union, though his power is in no way exercised, insofar as all the evidence indicates, like that of Stalin or even Khrushchev. By 1976, as George Breslauer has pointed out:

> One could speak of a genuine personality cult, expressed in paeans of praise in newpapers, journals, and speeches of other leaders. By 1977 the general secretary [acquired] the titles of Marshal of the Soviet Union, supreme commander of the armed forces, and chairman of the Presidium of the Supreme Soviet (1978, pp. 15-16).

The word "cult" has, of course, a distinct religious flavor and conveys the impression of a religious type of activity: it denotes the uncritical worship of an individual leader who behaves as if he had divine wisdom and inspiration. Stalin was criticized, ostensibly, because he had cast himself in the role of an omnipotent and omniscient deity who could do no wrong. Implicit in the criticism, however, was another charge: that Stalin had arrogated to himself the role that rightfully belonged to the party, that he had reduced the party to a powerless instrument of his personal and unchecked rule, and that he had further degraded it by undermining its hegemony through other organizational instrumentalities such as the secret police (Brzezinski 1961). Khrushchev's aim, as expressed in his speech at the 20th Party Congress in 1956 and in his subsequent statements, was to restore what he termed "Leninism," but what might better be called the "cult of the party,"—that is, respect for and worship of that mystic entity and collectivity constituted by the party that, for lack of a better term, might be called the Communist living church or the body of Marxism.

And it is not inconceivable that Brezhnev' successor(s) might for a while peg his/their political appeals on a dismantling of the Brezhnev cult, and on again upholding the party as the supreme and unique entity that rules Soviet society. Or, by the same token, should Brezhnev's successor(s) be of the conservative, centralistic, and "hard-line" persuasion, it is not out of the question that he/they might evoke or resurrect at least part of the Stalinist style of leadership. Such a style might well appeal to those who feel uncomfortable with the lack of discipline, the relative liberalization, the decentralization, the "alien" orientation of certain intellectuals, the relatively mild ways in which dissidents are treated, and other aspects of "looseness" in the system.

The resemblance of the party to a secular church and to the role played by an organized and established church may serve as a possible model for an examination of the systemic nature of contemporary Communist society of the Soviet type. The use of the "church" or "religious" model is not, of course, new or particularly original. What is proposed here is an attempt to follow some of the consequences attendant on this kind of structural model and to advance the hypothesis that Soviet society, although it is in many respects and trappings an industrialized, mechanized, and urbanized social system, may lack certain of the characteristics possessed by other societies of that general type. Seen on an evolutionary scale, it may then fall somewhat short of being a fully modern social system in the terms that will be used and defined below.

No value judgment is implied in the term "modern" or "advanced," any more than such a judgment is implied in saying that a society is "primitive" or "preliterate." These are classificatory terms, and the criteria for their applicability are those of internal differentiation, complexity, and intergration, not whether one society is "better" or more conducive to "happiness" than another. The judgment, if any, is a functional one, and the ultimate test is an appraisal of the capacities of that social system to adapt and master its environment. By "environment" is meant here not only the domestic environments, but also the international one in which the Soviet Union, as a nation, competes with other nations. Indeed, were the Soviet Union to exist in a different world (without, say, a superpower like the United States, with which it must try to keep up and compete), the internal structure of Soviet society, and the very role and position of the party, might be vastly different.

SOCIETAL EVOLUTION AND DIFFERENTIATION

Talcott Parsons, in *The Evolution of Societies* (1977), holds that it is possible to trace the evolution (and transformation) of different societies from the relative simplicity of the primitive society to the intermediate level (such as ancient Egypt, the Mesopotamian empires, China, India, Israel, and Greece) to the modern societies, whose development was made possible in part by the Renaissance and the Reformation. While Parsons uses a three-stage analysis, other writers use more complicated schemes. The point at issue, however, is that it is possible to order types of societies on a scale of increased internal complexity and that "socio-cultural, like organic, evolution has proceeded by variation and differentiation from simple to progressively more complex forms." The most fundamental principle, as Parsons has outlined it, is that evolution consists of the improvement of the adaptive capacities of the relevant society or system, and that adaptation clearly implies the capacity to survive under conditions of the environment and in the ability to master that environment. This enables the system to cope with a range of different conditions and unexpected contingencies.

The development of the capacity to cope with and master the environment comes as a result of the internal differentiation and specialization of mechanisms of the organism, in essence a division of labor between specialized organs or structures. Thus, a relative lack of differentiation between the kinship and the economic systems (that is, a system in which economic activities are all carried out within a kinship arrangement, as is the case in primitive agricultural societies or the "family firm") is not as efficient an arrangement as one in which kinship and economic activities are carried out in distinct contexts, and in which recruitment for the different economic tasks can proceed on the basis of ability or achievement rather than particularistic and ascriptive ties of descent or marriage. By the same token, the governing of people in today's large-scale society is carried out more efficiently by a separate and differentiated governmental structure made up of individuals who work in that structure on a full-time basis than would be the case if every citizen had to participate (on a part-time basis) in making every decision and in administering the state, as was the case in the Greek polis.

The key concept is thus that of differentiation. S. N. Eisenstadt has stated that it is like complexity and specialization: "It describes the way through which the main social functions or the major institutional spheres . . . become disassociated from one another, attached to specialized collectivities, and organized in relatively autonomous symbolic and organizational frameworks within the confines of the same institutionalized system" (1964, p. 376).

Thus, the process of differentiation, which may be described as the gradual liberation of social processes from rigid kinship, tribal, or ascriptive bases, implies a fair amount of autonomy for the differentiated spheres and the development of criteria of action specific to these spheres; it also raises the important question of the integration of these different areas through a system of exchange of outputs. If this integration is missing, the process then becomes merely one of segmentation rather than of differentiation, and may lead to stagnation and breakdown. Differentiation, as Eisenstadt has pointed out, opens up new possibilities for development and creativity—whether they be in the area of technological development, or expansion of political, cultural, philosophical, religious, or personal powers and rights. Of course, this also poses the question of the delicate balance and interplay between social forces and the functional needs of the society. Indeed, differentiation, according to Eisenstadt, may lead to what he describes as "constricted" development, a situation in which one of the differentiated spheres will attempt to dominate the others coercively by restricting and regimenting their tendencies toward autonomy. More precisely:

> This probability is especially strong with respect to the political and religious (or value) spheres, because these spheres are especially prone to "totalistic" orientations that tend to negate the autonomy of other spheres. Religious and political élites may attempt to dominate other spheres, imposing rigid frameworks based on their own criteria. The aim of such policies is usually an effective de-differentiation of the social system, and they may result in rigidity and stagnation, or precipitate continual breakdowns of the system. These tendencies to de-differentiation are usually very closely related to the specific processes of change that may develop within any institutionalized system (Eisenstadt 1964, p. 381).

Indeed, it might be posited that modern society is characterized by the absence of an overarching and necessarily restrictive ideology or religion and of a coercive organization enforcing its tenets through which every human and institutional action is screened and evaluated, approved or disapproved. And it is further asserted that it is this absence, the general freedom from totalistic normative evaluation, that, in the final analysis, improves a society's adaptation and mastery of its environment. It is this ideal that Mao Tse-tung once expressed, but did not follow, of "letting one hundred flowers bloom."

Returning to the Soviet case, the basic ethos of that society, its fundamental weltanschauung, its normative base, is the body of ideas and theories generally known as Marxism or Marxism-Leninism. This theory constitutes an ideology and is not simply, as Marx would have claimed, an objective and scientific method of looking at, and understanding, man, society, and the historical process. It has reached the status of a faith—secular, to be sure, yet endowed, by virtue of its position and role in the Communist world, with the characteristics of religious beliefs, doctrine, and often dogma. As Robert V. Daniels (1962, pp. 349-50) has pointed out, the followers of the faith embrace the doctrine, not because it passes a particular test of metaphysical or historical truth, but because it conveys a sense of the exclusive possession of truth.

Émile Durkheim argued long ago that religion was not merely a superstructure reflecting material interests (as Marx asserted) but a fundamental matrix for the evolution of culture. Through a process of gradual differentiation, it was from this matrix that other elements of the culture emerged. In primitive society, thus, there seems to exist no sharp break between what is sacred and what is profane, nor is there a clear dichotomy between the "natural" and the "supernatural." In this type of social order, the society as a whole is the "church." It was only through a long process of differentiation that boundaries were established between the world of the sacred and the profane, and that there arose a lay culture relatively independent of religious criteria, injunctions, and sanctions. When it is possible, for instance, in the same society and culture, to worship in church and to teach freely that the earth is round and not the center of the universe, or that man did not descend from Adam and Eve, a process of differentiation has taken place. When, on the other hand, persons are burned at the stake; questioned by the Inquisition; strung up because they are witches; sent to jail, concentration camps, or insane asylums; expelled, exiled, shot, or tortured because they hold (and proclaim) views that are incompatible with the current theology or the state's or party's truth, then the process of differentiation is far from complete.

By the same token, at the societal level (in contrast with the cultural one) the process of differentiation from the church-society led, as in the case of Christianity, to the formation of a specialized, separate, corporate entity: the Church, staffed by full-time religious functionaries, organizationally quite distinct from other spheres, though its claim for competence has tended to be "totalistic." In the Soviet Union, the analog to that body would be the party.

It is contended here that Soviet culture and society have become differentiated, but perhaps incompletely so. At least, as seen on a comparative and evolutionary scale, that society falls short of other, more advanced, pluralistic social systems. The process of differentation is slowed by the "totalistic" nature of the value system and the orientation of the Communist party, the guardian of the Soviet weltanschauung.

Following this line of reasoning, it can be argued, for example, that in the Soviet Union *partiinost'* ("partyness") has often served as a criterion for the judgment of actions in most spheres of activity—that is, as a test of Communist morality, as well as a device to bludgeon nonconformers—and that it has hindered the development and the expression of autonomous or independent criteria of thought or action so that "secular" culture has not yet completely emancipated (or differentiated) itself from "ideology."*

Furthermore, if Marxism has become an official faith, then the Communist party is the guardian, the repository, a differentiated corporate embodiment of that faith; it has become a secular, or nonreligious, but "established," official, and unique church—regardless of whether party officials believe "sincerely" in its tenets. Indeed, there is no ground to assume a priori that the leaders of the Communist party are necessarily cynical manipulators of the doctrine, interested solely in power and nothing else:

> . . . the evidence, by and large indicates that they were really persuaded of their true orthodoxy, and that the flexibility of policy on which they insisted was enhanced rather than restricted by the aura of orthodoxy which reinterpretation could confer on each new twist and turn (Daniels 1962, pp. 32-33.

On the other hand, the question of belief, of acceptance, of internalization of the basic tenets of the ideology is a difficult one to document. The tendency in the West is to accept that most people in the Soviet Union, including particularly the members of the party, do not take the Marxist-Leninist ideology very seriously and that they are cynical about it; that it has become a kind of catechism that one must learn and formally repeat at certain times and at certain symbolic occasions; and that it certainly is not a guide to action. And yet the hold that certain aspects of the tenets exercise on the population cannot be gainsaid, since they have become part of the general Soviet culture, taught in schools and endlessly repeated. Indeed, some of the more famous dissidents, like P.G. Grigorenko *(The Grigorenko Papers* 1976)

---

*It might be argued that in the United States, "Americanism" has sometimes played a role similar to that of "partyness," although its application, and the implications of that application (except in moments of paranoid hysteria such as McCarthyism), are not of the same intensity as the more inclusive and universalistic Soviet term.

and Leonid Pliushch (*The Case* 1976), indict the regime precisely because they feel it has deviated from, and distorted, the basic principles on which it claims to base itself and from which it derives its legitimacy. In that sense they are fundamentalists; and fundamentalists may be dangerous because of their inability to compromise.

In addition, ideology and its symbolic linkage to the charismatic figure of Lenin provide the party with its claim to legitimacy, since this claim cannot be (to use Max Weber's terms) either of the traditional type, as in the case of monarchs and ruling houses, or of the rational-legal type, since it does not rest on the specific and limited mandate of an enfranchised electorate and an effective constitution.* The legitimacy of the party is thus of the "routinized charismatic" type. The party claims its right to exercise control and authority because it considers itself the only legitimate representative and interpreter of the ideology. If the party were to discover, or acknowledge, that its world view is based on "false premises" (an improbable event), it would logically have no choice but to dissolve itself. It is more likely, however, to assert time and again that the basic premises on which it rests are "true," in the sense that they rest on a materialistic interpretation of man, society, and history, and thus, by implication, that they are also "eternal." Interpretation of the doctrine, however, makes it possible for the party and its leaders to claim that their doctrine is not "dogma," but that it is broad and universal enough to provide answers to a variety of changing situations, and that these answers, while fitting the situation of the moment, are nevertheless faithful in spirit to the original doctrine—that is, to the "fundamental law" of Marxism. Furthermore, the party justifies its existence and its role in "functional" terms by claiming credit for all the achievements of the regime.

As the corporate body of the only true faith, the Communist party therefore cannot admit the legitmacy or the existence of other faiths or parties, and therefore rejects any idea of ideological or political pluralism. The position of the party is that the doctrine on which it rests must (and will) become universal—that is, embrace the whole of mankind—and its historical function is thus to help in the promotion of this inevitable march of history. The Soviet Union as such is the "resource base" on which the movement depends—that is, it provides the human and material underpinning for that movement—and the party is the agency responsible for the mobilization of these resources on Soviet soil. As such, the party as the proclaimed instrument of history has acquired a mystique of its own: its existence, its survival, and its perpetuation are the prerequisites and the guarantee for the actualization of the faith at home and in the world at large. This helps to explain the reluctance of such men as Leon Trotsky to attack or split the party even though they opposed its

---

*The fiction is maintained, of course, that party congresses are means to convey the wishes of the membership to the party.

leader. In other words, there may be bad "popes" who temporarily seize control of the party machinery, but this does not in any way bring into question the justifiability and "sanctity" of party supremacy.

We need not go, at this juncture, into the nature of the party as an organization of leadership within Soviet society, except to note its resemblance to an established church (it was more of a priesthood under Lenin), with a specific and differentiated membership, and to note (as others have on many occasions) that it does constitute, at least for its leading members, an interest group or, as Milovan Djilas puts it, a "new class." This class has at its disposal the major instruments of rule, such as the use of political power, the control of the means of production (which is the equivalent, under Soviet conditions, to their ownership), and the honorific goods (in terms of patterns of deference and prestige) that are associated with a privileged caste or an establishment. Status within the party hiearchy is not, of course, hereditary in the traditional sense, though it could be argued that the children of highly placed and influential party members enjoy certain privileges and opportunities for careers that other members of Soviet society (and particularly the nonparty majority) do not. This is simply to state that most party members have an interest in the perpetuation of the status quo—that is, the continuation of party controls over society—and therefore a vested interest in the maintenance of the system as now structured, regardless of whether they are sincere, believing Communists or not.

The party, by being the only source of "Communist morality," attempts to maintain not only a totalistic hold on Soviet society but also a diffuse, undifferentiated power of control and review. Its sphere of influence and competence in theory admits of no limitations, constitutional checks, nor boundaries; there are no "jurisdictions" over which it dares not trespass. The distinction, for example, between "private" and "public" interests does not hold. What a person is and what a person does at home, on the job, in public life, or in other areas is of legitimate concern to the party. The activity of a party secretary, according to Seweryn Bialer,

> . . . is restricted only by the territorial limits of his jurisdiction and by the decisions of the next secretary up the line; he may exercise his authority in any sphere, imposing his will on the economic administration, the educational system, the local governmental apparatus, etc., . . . [his] scope of professional interests and right of interference are virtually absolute and all embracing . . . he personifies the omnipotence of party apparatus within the society at large (1962, p. 259).

The party thus tends to operate in terms of a militant certainty and an absolutist outlook about objectively doubtful matters that is one, as Bertrand Russell pointed out, "from which, since the Renaissance, the world has been gradually emerging into that temper of constructive and fruitful skepticism which constitutes the scientific outlook" (1920, as cited in Djilas 1957, p. 127).

And it is this certainty that permits the party (or the leader) to say to one man, or to a group, "You are right" or "You are wrong"; it gives rise to that simple and classic dichotomy offered by the party: "Either you are with us, or you are against us"; it makes the principle of a "loyal opposition" an absurdity (the opposition, by definition, is treasonable and should be either in jail or six feet underground). In short, in its frequent inability or unwillingness to recognize that there may be shades of gray in the world, in its not having gone through the painful and sobering emancipation—embodied, for example, in the Reformation—that reminds man he is fallible and that there are very few absolutes in this life (on the importance of the religious tradition for this kind of perspective, see, for example, Overstreet and Overstreet 1964, p. 120), the party has tended to assume the cloak of infallibility, without fully realizing, or realizing too late, that the cloak can also serve as a blinder. Bertram Wolfe once suggested that not only was knowledge power, but that in the case of Stalin, Khrushchev, and the party in general, "power became knowledge"—that is, the position of the top leadership led to its being considered "infallible" in its pronouncements, whether they were on abstract art, music, genetics, the chemical industry, poetry, the frequency of the milking of cows, or the declaration of who was or was not an "enemy of the people." In some instances this "infallibility" has not been one of Soviet society's strong suits in solving the multitude of problems facing it.

THE NATURE OF SOVIET SOCIETY

It has been found convenient, for the sake of brevity, in surveying the plethora of theories of Soviet society, to regroup them into three main (though by no means exhaustive) clusters, the first one defining in general terms the "culture" of Soviet society, and the next two the "structure" of that society in terms of its political and econonic institutions. (I am, in essence, following and amplifying the analysis presented by Inkeles and Bauer 1959 and Moore 1954.)

Soviet Culture: National Communism

National Communism may be described as the search, on the part of a nation that has recently emerged as a major power on the world scene, for a national and cultural identity, and rests on the fusion of the doctrinal bases of the Communist movement and identification of the interests of that movement (which is, in essence, supranational) with the interests of the Russian nation. (For a description of this process for the United States, see Lipset 1963, pp. 61-98.) This fusion was born primarily out of the recognition, on the part of the Soviet leadership by the end of the 1920s, that no proletarian revolution (except for the short-lived episodes in Bavaria and Hungary) was in sight, and the resulting decision (primarily Stalin's) to build "socialism in one country."

From that point on, according to Stalin, Russia was to be considered as the bastion of the Communist movement and, as a corollary, anything that added to the strength of Russia as a nation (industrialization, for example) was good for that movement.

This kind of "reactive nationalism" (the expression is from Rostow 1960), which mobilized sentiments and emotions already established in the culture, was clearly expressed by Stalin (1940, pp. 165-66) himself in his famous and almost masochistic recital in 1931 of the past exploitation of Russia by foreigners, which mandated that industrialization must be pushed at all costs; it was intensified in the late 1930s and reached a climax during World War II and the postwar period until the death of Stalin. A strong component of this cultural orientation has been, and still is, to an important degree, its antagonism to the West, expressed both in terms of fear of Western intentions toward Russia and a feeling of inferiority toward the West, which comes out in the form of a compulsive assertion of the superiority of Russian culture and "priority" of the Russian inventive mind.

The regime, particularly under Stalin, had thus capitalized on these fears and insecurities by pursuing a policy of extreme cultural isolation and chauvinism, and by applying strong pressures on the intellectual community; any attempt at "objectivity" toward the West was branded as potentially (if not actually) subversive. Although the campaign for cultural isolation has receded from its high-water mark of the Stalin years, the regime has continued to look with diffidence and suspicion at the West or at anything "foreign" to the Soviet spirit. Even, and particularly, in periods of détente or rapprochement with the West, the fear of contamination by "alien" ideas, by Western music or abstract art, for example, remains. Although the decrease of that xenophobia since the 1950s can be interpreted as a result of a greater sense of national self-confidence as well as of the recognition (for instrumental reasons) of the need for freer communication with the West, the Soviet Union still remains a closed or limited-access society.

At the same time, strange as it may seem, strong Russian chauvinism has reappeared in the Soviet Union. Both among some intellectuals and among workers it is of a type that is so extreme as to undermine many aspects of the Communist doctrine, which is then seen as a foreign, non-Russian import. As such, this takes up the theme of the Slavophiles of the 19th century, who believed in the special nature and mission of Russia and of the Russian people, who rejected the legalistic and industrial West, who sought a solution to social and other problems in the Russian soul and particularly among the "uncorrupted" peasantry. Strongly tied to the Eastern Orthodox Church, this doctrine or idea has been expressed, to the surprise of many Westerners, by such a well-known (and expelled) dissident as Alexander Solzhenitsyn.

In summary, then, a very important component of contemporary Soviet society, operating at the cultural level, is that amalgam between the doctrinal bases of Communism and Russian nationalism described here. It remains to be seen to what degree Great Russian chauvinism can be maintained in the light of demographic changes that are tilting the ethnic balance toward the Central Asian Muslim population that has, hitherto, been treated more as a colonial people than as an equal part of Soviet society.

Political Structure: One-Party Rule or Monocracy

It is difficult, at the present historical juncture, to give a simple and precise formulation of the Soviet political structure. It is perhaps easier, at least for Westerners, to state what it is not: it is not a constitutional system with checks and balances of the democratic type, nor is it a parliamentary system. The holders of power are not elected by a constituency from whom they might claim legitimacy, nor do they depend on votes of confidence given to a party (or a coalition of parties) to govern as long as they are able to obtain such votes. Indeed, the idea of several parties, each representing an aggregation of interests, and each vying for power or a role in the government, is rejected out of hand. This is sometimes justified by stating that antagonistic interest groups do not exist.

Earlier, and particularly under Stalin, the expressions of totalitarianism and dictatorship, in the sense of personal and absolute rules, were probably appropriate and on the whole relatively accurate and unambiguous, though often oversimplified. Now some aspects of these definitions may no longer be valid. And yet a basic, if not central, feature of that political structure has remained the same under Lenin, Stalin, Khrushchev, and Brezhnev: the concept that the role of the polity (in this case the party, acting directly or through the soviets) is to decide, to lead, and to govern according to its own lights. The function of that polity, then, is not primarily to reflect the wishes or the aspirations of the population at large, nor to satisfy the wishes of that population or of groups of the population (united into parties, as is the case in the West). Rather, it is to make secular decisions that affect the entire society, and then proceed to realize or implement these decisions. To this end. the party uses a combination of coercion and persuasion, and is committed to the mobilization of human and material resources to accomplish its goals and programs.

In earlier days the leadership (or leader) manipulated Soviet society (and until recently societies in which Communist regimes were subservient to the Soviet Union) in any way it saw fit. It destroyed and created social classes; it arrested, jailed, tortured, shot, expelled, exiled, or declared "unpersons" those it suspected of disloyalty; it controlled what was said over the radio, printed in the press, seen on television, expressed in the classroom, depicted in novels, sculpted in marble or painted on canvas. It decided to invest in *sputniks* and *luniks* rather than housing and flush toilets. It, and it alone, determined what was the correct party line and decided who (or what nation) was anti-party or un-Marxist. Absolute power and control over the population was its first concern, and its unwillingness to compromise and to liberalize the system reflected its fear of the dissatisfaction of the masses and its conviction that government from above by a small, self-selected elite should not perish from the face of the earth.

It may be noted that in today's perspective, and from what we know of Soviet society since Stalin died, the above description reads more like a caricature or some "ideal type" than a reflection of the reality under the Soviet regime today. Indeed, in the last few years we have seen a variety of models that modulate, if not modify and transform, the relatively undifferentiated picture of totalitarianism. Some have defined it as the administered society, totalitarianism without terror; others, as monistic rational tutelage, or as a variation of the bureaucratic model, the Soviet system being held as a kind of large-scale corporation. Still others talk about a society that is essentially pluralistic, with various interest groups that are articulated or arbitrated by the regime—the party (Kassof 1964)—or as a society based on nonideological consensus arising from post-Revolutionary consensus. (These different models have been reviewed and summarized by Lowenthal 1976. I am grateful to him for a concise formulation of these different models or hypotheses.) Whatever the relevance of these models, Soviet society remains a variant, or a modification, of the totalitarian model, and any understanding of that society must consider the nature of this type of system.

Economic Structure: Industrialism

Industrialism may be described as the form of the economic structure of a society as it is affected by the use of a specific type of production. This mode of production, the industrial plant or firm, is an important element of any modernization process, and immeasurably increases the national product of a society; it is characterized (regardless of its ownership form) by the concentrated employment of large numbers of workers and employees. This mode of production is usually operated by a professional management, divorced from ownership in the legal sense (but not in the sense of control and use) almost as much as the workers and employees are, and in its operations it applies technology and scientific advances. This is in sharp contrast with agricultural production or the family firm of early capitalism, with its fusion of ownership and management, its more or less paternalistic attitude toward its workers, the particularistic and ascriptive mode of selecting personnel, and the limited scope of its operations because of constraints on available capital for expansion and on managerial skill for administration, supervision, and research.

In a society of this type, the individual's primary ties with family, church, village, and small community are weakened and replaced by affiliation with larger reference groups, such as trade unions, professional organizations, employee or worker groups, class, the firm, the party, and the nation itself, as focuses of personal loyalty and emotional commitment.

Industrialization brings, in addition, a whole spectrum of consequences resulting from large urban concentrations of population, the development of mass culture, and the gradual replacement of traditionalism, religious orientation, and family-(or kinship-) centered values and solidarities by new attitudes and commitments consisting of a sort of secular morality. This morality tends to emphasize the importance of occupation and, to some extent, the "consumption" ethics of the city rather than the "production" ethics of the countryside, rooted in the soil and stressing physical toil. It also brings in its wake many "social problems" characterisitc of urban life almost everywhere, resulting from a loosening of family and community controls. They include crime, juvenile delinquency, family disorganization, alcoholism, and social deviance in general (see, for example, Connor 1972).

Occupation, and particularly occupational achievement (including employment in the political sphere), tend to become the central determinants of an individual's life chances and of the society's pattern of social stratification. In this respect Soviet class structure resembles to a considerable degree that of Western industrial societies. An increasingly important role is played by specialists, and particularly by professionals on whose activities the functioning of a modern society to a large extent depends. The rehabilitation of the intelligentsia in the Soviet Union during the 1930s, in connection with the program of industrialization, provided dramatic notice that, in spite of ideological exaltation, manual laborers had become relatively unimportant when compared with specialists not engaged in physical labor. It also brought to light the uneasy relationship between specialists as a social force on whom the regime has to rely for operations of the system, but whom the regime also tends to distrust politically because of the power inherent in their activities and because the critical faculties inherent in their work cannot always be limited to that work. And here increasingly the problem has been how the party maintains control over those whose effectiveness and contribution are enhanced by lack of control—that is, by independence.

In general, the physical sciences have been granted significantly more leeway than the humanities. Thus specialists and professionals have in the 1960s and 1970s been considerably emancipated from party supervision, so that, for instance, it is now possible to be "wrong" or to express reservations and criticism in professional matters without incurring the risk of being punished. And failures of a technical nature are no longer, as far as one can judge, seen as the result of "wrecking" or "sabotage" activities for which people have to be penalized. Given the paralyzing effect of the former situation, one can see the degree to which decrease of party supervision, at least in this specific sphere of activities, redounds to the advantage of Soviet society.

As for the social sciences, sociology, in particular, has led a precarious existence since its official reestablishment after Stalin died. Social science is a double-edged weapon: it provides otherwise unobtainable insights into social processes of all types, yet it also constitutes social (and political) criticism that the party is reluctant to allow.

With the development of classes and class consciousness, Soviet society has not escaped such phenomena as the attempt by the upper or middle class to monopolize certain privileges and advantages and to pass these on to their children. The two essays by Richard Dobson in this volume demonstrate that in the Soviet Union, as is often true in American society, it does make a difference where one starts off in life.

Industrialism thus leads to important and largely irreversible structural changes in the society. Some commentators have argued, for example, that the excesses of the Stalin era were the results of the tremendous strains attendant on the rapid takeoff of a backward agricultural country into becoming a mighty industrial power. These pressures, regrettable as they were, found their justification in the Soviet military actions against Germany during World War II and in the contribution they made to the Allied cause and freedom. Now that industrialization has been achieved and the wounds of the war have been healed, certain consequences are bound to occur—indeed, according to some writers, are happening under our very eyes.

For example, the increased rationality and education needed to operate an industrial and technological society, it is felt, cannot be limited to a narrow field, but will eventually alter the entire nature of Soviet society. Or, expressed slightly differently, the economic system always places a constraint upon the political system. As the functions performed by the educated members of the middle class (the intelligentsia) become more strategic, the regime will find it impossible to ignore their demands for greater freedom.

In summary, then, it may be said that it is the combination and the interpenetration of these three major elements (national Communism in the culture, one-party rule in politics, and industrialism in economics) that may account for many aspects of contemporary Soviet society.

THE QUESTION OF RELATIVE "UNDIFFERENTIATION"

The party has taken it upon itself to shape the culture, to govern the society, and to manage the economy. It has done so because its leadership, starting with Lenin, has been imbued with the conviction that nothing less than "total" control in these spheres would permit it to remain in power and to accomplish its foreordained historical mission.

It may be argued, furthermore, that in the past the party (and Stalin) played a critical and "objectively" necessary role in the development of some aspects of Soviet society. It would be difficult, for example, to conceive of the rapid industrialization of Soviet society after 1928 without the existence of the party and of a Stalin (or some similar organization or man) that would, through control of the three spheres mentioned earlier, effect such a rapid mobilization of human, material, financial, and emotional resources in the pursuit of that goal, particularly under conditions in which it was not felt desirable, nor perhaps possible, for the Soviet Union to borrow large amounts of capital from abroad. Indeed, it is a result of the decision taken by the party to industrialize under forced draft and to engage in a process of primitive capital accumulation that the main contours of Soviet Russia emerged. It can also be suggested that because of the diffuse power with which the party is endowed, it can intervene like a flying squad or a benevolent monarch at almost any point in Soviet society and unravel knotty problems caused, for example, by bureaucratic conflicts or breakdowns in supplies (see, for example, Cocks 1978). But these often tend to be particularistic interventions that need to be activated for the specific problem rather than universal regulative mechanisms of the type more available in pluralistic societies, such as an independent judiciary, the political franchise, or market mechanisms. There is no doubt, as Jerry Hough (1965, 1969) has pointed out many times, that the party plays a significant role in many aspects of Soviet political and economic life and has helped resolve "several important problems inherent in very large organizations." Hough argues, and quite soundly, that the role of the party is functional, particularly at the lower administrative levels, in "getting things done," and that if there were no party, some other agency would have to perform these tasks. In contrast, according to Milovan Djilas, the party has become a parasite on society. While this is a politically inspired hyperbole, the party *has* become, as suggested earlier, in many respects a conservative, if not a reactionary, force in Soviet society. At least, at the present moment (1979) "Brezhnev and his colleagues are devoted to the status quo" (Shipler 1979). Perhaps in the 21st century, when the party will have passed into history, some schoolboy will query his teacher on how it was possible for Russia to win the war against Hitlerite Germany *in spite* of the existence of the Communist party!

It is precisely the party's reluctance to relinquish controls that may slow down further differentiation and modernization. This reluctance leads to the kind of social structure noted earlier, which Allen Kassof (1964) has called the "administered society," or what others have called "totalitarianism without terror" or "without coercion." This implies that one central authority plans and administers all social, cultural, political, and economic processes, and mutual adjustments between the demands of these different spheres and the supply (conceived in a broad form) continue to be "administered" rather than allowed to find their own level. This may lead to a situation in which "rational" planning and administering border on the irrational, uneconomical, and dysfunctional.

One imaginary illustration, from the realm of economic planning but perhaps of broader significance, is the well-known case of the pile of potatoes that must be fitted into a sack, so that the maximum amount of potatoes and the minimum amount of waste space occur. The "scientific," "rational," "planned," "administered" way to go about it would be to give each potato a different ordinal number; to draw profiles for each potato (let's say six to eight profiles per potato); to translate these profiles into codable items and, with the use of a computer, to determine precisely how each potato is to fit with the others so as to keep the waste space to the irreducible minimum. This is perfectly feasible; it may entail the work of a team of mathematicians and may cost several hundreds or thousands of dollars, but it can be done. The other solution simply consists of dumping the potatoes into the sack and shaking hard, letting each potato adjust to its neighbor in a "spontaneous" manner. The difference between the two solutions, in terms of waste space, is not likely to be greater than 5 or 10 percent, or perhaps a bit more. But the overall cost of the entire operation is likely to be considerably less, although it would deprive the team (read party) of employment and involvement in fitting the potatoes to each other.

It may be said, furthermore, that in comparison with the situation that obtained at the time of Stalin's death, there has been, relatively speaking, a substantial amount of "loosening" or "thawing" in Soviet society toward decentralization and cautious attempts at some degree of differentiation, coupled with an increased awareness by the party of the demands of different social groups for increased recognition and a larger share of goods and services.

The Limits of Cultural Differentiation

One of these groups is undoubtedly the professionals, who need a fair amount of autonomy to pursue their activities at a high level of performance. Since these activities are, in many instances, of critical importance to the regime in the pursuit of its domestic and foreign policies, it is perhaps in the cultural area that the process of differentiation has been carried furthest, though unevenly. It is now possible, as we have seen, for scientists in the physical sciences to publicly espouse principles and theories that were placed on the ideological index only a few years ago for being of foreign, Western origins (cybernetics, for example). In the so-called life sciences—in biology and genetics, for instance—the vicissitudes of Trofim Lysenko's career indicate how gradual this process has been, and how deeply rooted was the idea that science must conform to ideological orthodoxy, rather than to scientific criteria of evidence. Lysenkoism was admittedly an extreme case, and yet it does illustrate the result of ideological controls over inquiry, the sanctions and punishments meted out to those who did not conform or recant their "mistakes," and the "price" paid by the discipline itself in lost time and advances. Almost 12 years elapsed between the death of Stalin and Lysenko's removal as director of the Institute of Genetics. (See Joravsky 1970 for an account of the "Lysenko affair.")

In clinical medicine, to take another example, the Central Committee of the party refused, in the 1960s and presumably ever since, to intervene in the case of a cancer cure that had been judged worthless by the Academy of Medical Sciences and prohibited by an order of the Health Ministry. The Central Committee declared that it "does not consider it possible to take upon itself the role of arbiter in approving methods of medical treatment" (*Pravda*, Aug. 1, 1962, p. 2). In an earlier period the Central Committee and "comrade Stalin personally" would not have been so reluctant to take a stand.

Generally speaking, the development of the Soviet sociological establishment has been marked by crises, internal conflicts, changes in leadership and directions, and redefinitions of the mission of sociology (see Fischer 1961). These reflect, in all probability, the ambivalence the party feels toward a discipline that can uncover important insights into the actual workings of society but that, at the same time, can easily become, or be interpreted as, social criticism of contemporary conditions: it thus has a potentially "subversive" role that must be constantly and carefully monitored lest it get out of hand. Contacts and cooperation with sociologists from the West have been accepted, in principle, but the history of the last few years indicates that this is a thorny question for ideologues, one fraught with potential problems and pitfalls.

The question is particularly acute at international sociological congresses held outside the Soviet Union, where the kind of control exercised by the regime at home cannot be duplicated. Thus international sociological congresses are seen as arenas of battle between socialist and bourgeois sociologists. Indeed, delegations come well organized and well led; assignments are made to their members to attend specific sessions, to show the Marxist flag, to refute and defeat "bourgeois" views; invited sociologists whose names appear on the program may be denied exit visas at the last moment, and replaced by unknown persons. (For a remarkable insight into what goes on in the wings during such congresses, the reader is referred to "Cultural Détente at Scientific Congresses: The Secret Report of the Czech Sociologists" 1977.) Thus, the further differentiation of sociology and its autonomy from the political system, and hence its greater ability to contribute to sociological theory and knowledge, will undoubtedly be a long and probably not unilinear process.

The uneasy relationship between the regime and artists and writers, and more specifically the poets (with their Russian tradition of social protest), may also serve as an illustration of the congenital difficulty the party has in letting the muses sing without a party-appointed conductor. Although the demands and the straitjacket of "socialist realism" have been toned down, the artist and the writer still remain under surveillance; and those who exhibit too much independence are likely to find themselves invited to visit the local unit of the KGB, or sent to the hinterland to gather materials at the grass roots, or facing deportation. Few, however, are likely to lose their lives or their freedom, as was the case earlier. But jobs, appointments, and promotions often are affected by party determination. Thus, as David K. Shipler reports:

> A Jewish expert on American literature discovered when he applied for a teaching job at an institute that he was to appear not before an academic board but a party committee . . . he was asked if he had ever tried to change his citizenship—a euphemism for emigrating to Israel. He replied indignantly that the question, obviously about his intentions rather than his past, had no relevance. He did not get the job (1979, p. E3).

At the same time, one cannot discount the impact of the generalized knowledge of what is acceptable and what is not acceptable to the party in the realm of art and literature. As a Soviet émigré once put it, the Soviet Union is the country of perfect understanding in these matters: this "precensorship" thus cannot be held to promote innovation, daring, or the breaking of new ground in the cultural or artistic realms.

More recently, starting in the early 1960s, the regime has added two more instruments of control over intellectuals: the threat of their being brought up on criminal charges of anti-Soviet propaganda or of libeling of Soviet reality, and the more ominous one of their being certified as mentally irresponsible or incompetent, and thus being placed in mental hospitals for indefinite periods of time. (This writer is in the process of completing a manuscript on the use of psychiatry to "medicalize" dissidence in the Soviet Union; details on the practice can be gathered from, among others, Bloch and Reddaway 1977; Field 1972; Medvedev and Medvedev 1971.)

It might, finally, be interesting to speculate on what would take place if the party were to remove most or all of its strictures on cultural life. It may be conjectured, on the basis of what has happened since Stalin's death, that Soviet culture would only benefit through such a step. On balance, in cultural life the party impoverishes rather than enriches, constricts rather than promotes.

The Limits of Economic Differentiation

As in cultural life, one might argue that the Soviet economic system has reached a level of development and complexity that requires further differentiation from the party in order to acquire flexibility. In addition to the relative decentralization of many economic decisions, this might mean the introduction of market type mechanisms permitting an automatic or spontaneous adjustment of supply and demand, and rationality in terms of actual costs and customer demand, while keeping the economy responsive to the needs and the interests of the nation as a whole. The Soviets have recognized the necessity, for example, to calculate interest in the use of capital for national economic decisions. But there are two elements that prevent, or at least slow, such a development. One is the ideological impact of economic policy and decisions, and centers on the potential ideological erosion attendant on the introduction of devices that have been associated with "capitalism" or declared ideologically unacceptable. In other words, the party ideologues are saying,

"What does it matter if we become economically more efficient, if this is purchased at the price of compromising our basic value commitments?" The other element is the loss of party functions and power that would follow the further differentiation of the economic life from party controls.

Actually, the relationship between the party and the economy, particularly the industrial sector, is more complicated than stated above. There is every evidence that the Soviet economic system is not working well, and this in spite of various reforms that have been proposed and implemented since Stalin died. The reason, I would gather, is that a sophisticated economy of the advanced industrial type needs a fair amount of autonomy and flexibility to perform its tasks, and to maintain flexibility under changing demands and circumstances.

One might argue, as some have, that the provision of this autonomy—this differentiation and separation from the political power represented by the party—would, as seems to be borne out by the experiences of the West, increase the efficiency and the productivity of the Soviet economy in its industrial sector, and would thus eventually place at the disposal of the party greater aggregate resources with which to pursue its aims. But the provision of this kind of autonomy would mean, in the eyes of the party, the increased power of managers and, eventually, a situation in which the hold and the control of the party over industrial production might be jeopardized. The problem has been well formulated by Robert W. Campbell in the following terms:

> The difficult ambiguity with the present problem is whether the party aspires to power as an end in itself or as an instrumental value to be used in the furtherance of still higher objectives—perhaps national, ideological, altruistic. In the first case, Party people would be very bearish—more interested in defending their fortress than in the extension of power through enlarged commitments. . . . In the second the Party would be more willing to make adaptations that would enable power to be diffused but expanded, in the aggregate, to permit better fulfillment of the Party's ultimate goals (1978, p. 36).

There is, of course, no absolute nor definitive answer to the above question. But the weight of the evidence seems to suggest that this concern about the erosion of its own power has kept the party firmly in control of all phases of the econmic system. This has contributed powerfully to retard the development of the economy, particularly when compared with the economies of the West and of Japan, with which it must necessarily compare itself and with which it competes on the world arena.

By the same token, the state of agriculture, which is perennially in a crisis situation, might well improve if the peasants were given more latitude, particularly with respect to the private plots. But the private plots smell of private property, of the bourgeois spirit, of that "worm of private ownership" in the means of production that the party has sworn to extirpate from the consciousness of its people. Thus greater control by the peasants over the productive activities, though it might mean more food and feed (and decreased reliance on foreign purchases), would also imply the power of the peasantry to dictate its terms to the party, to enforce its will against the party's wishes, to charge prices commensurate with its efforts and supply and demand—to exercise, in short, power and blackmail that the party would not countenance any more than it would from industrial managers, blue-collar workers, or the military. Instead of giving the peasant economic independence, the regime has chosen to increase the peasantry's range of social benefits and bring them more or less in line with those of the urban population.

On balance, the fusion of economic and party functions may, at the present level of maturation, constrict the further development of the Soviet economy.

The Limits of Political Differentiation

It is in the realm of politics and power that the least differentiation has taken place. The soviets, local governing councils, have continued to remain the political instrument of the party—ruled, controlled, managed by the party—and have not been allowed to be what they claim: the representatives of the people. Nor has the concept of the polity, with citizens given an effective franchise and responsibility for the choice of those who govern them, been allowed to take root in Communist society. The unanimous elections are not expressions of popular suffrage, but contrived symbolic manifestations of the kind of organic (monolithic) unity that the party claims for the society it rules. By claiming to embody the "will of the people," the party has effectively deprived the people of this will. By claiming that it speaks for the interests of all groups in Soviet society, the party has deprived these groups of the ability to articulate, in public, these interests (they may, of course, be articulated within the bureaucratic structure of the party; see, for example, Skillings 1969). It thus has eliminated and constricted public debates, and the possible enrichments, in terms of a variety of solutions, that might arise from such debates.

CONCLUSIONS

There is no indication that the party is prepared to "wither away" or to give up substantial portions of its power in controlling most aspects of the society it inhabits. There is evidence, however, that since 1953 some differentiation has taken place, although very cautiously and probably with mental reservations on the part of the party. It is possible that, with time, the professionals, the specialists, the managers—in short, the members of the intelligentsia—will constitute an ever-increasing and potentially more powerful pressure group in Soviet society, and that the party will have to grant them more autonomy.

It is also possible that the regime will grant more latitude to the operation of economic forces, particularly if it can convince itself that this would be a prerequisite for the maintenance of the Soviet posture in the world, and would not lead to erosion of the party's power. There is no shred of evidence, of course, that the regime will ever allow a "loyal opposition" or a second party to develop.

Thus the party that, in earlier phases of Soviet history, was an element of strength in the mobilization of societal resources for specific goals may now (on balance) be a source of structural rigidity, and may account for the disappointment of those Westerners who have gone to the Soviet Union expecting to find the "wave of the future."

The "archaic" nature of Soviet society may be due to the philosophy and the modus operandi of a party leadership that believes in the total centralization of control and that, in the process of trying to enforce this control, tends to stifle initiative and inventiveness that would add immeasurably to the power and efficiency of Soviet society. This is not to deny the possibility that in many instances, as was mentioned earlier, the party is playing the role of "expediter." Furthermore, there is no doubt that the party is playing an important role in the articulation of interest groups, and of arbiter among them (but of course not a neutral arbiter, since it has vested interest in the outcomes of interest group conflicts). The party has done a fairly good job of surviving and keeping itself in power; it has been able, when necessary, to adjust its structure in order to admit into its ranks those members of society who are most important in reaching the goals it has defined. It has been to some degree responsive to the demands of professionals, industrial workers, and (lately) peasants. But these responses are necessarily in terms of party interests, party ideology, and party power.

It may, then, be possible to entertain the hypothesis that the party now may contrive to retard and constrict the society it inhabits and helped to develop, since further differentiation, decentralization, and democratization could be secured only at the cost of ideological erosion and power concessions, a price it is extremely reluctant to pay. Some in the West, and in certain countries of Eastern Europe, have even commented on the good fortune of having the Communist party at the helm in the Soviet Union, since that party substantially decreases the might and the power of the Soviet Union. Imagine, they say, what the situation would be if that country were run efficiently and if its potentials, now frozen by the conservative style of its party leadership, were unlocked by a new system or a new regime! To echo in a radically altered form the classical statement of a latter-day American cultural hero, what is good for the Communist party may not necessarily be good for Soviet society toward the end of the 20th century.

To recast the hypothesis presented in this essay in a Marxist perspective: the party objectively and historically was, on balance, a progressive and liberating force when compared with tsarism; it led to the mobilization of resources, both human and material, to industrialize, urbanize, mechanize, educate, and otherwise propel Russia to a higher stage than reached before; it has by now accomplished its historic task, and unless it is willing or able to radically altering its modus operandi it may become increasingly redundant, superfluous, and dysfunctional to the society it inhabits; and if it has become a "ruling class," as it seems to be, it is doomed to generate the very instrument of its own destruction.

And yet, as Hough (Hough and Fainsod 1979, pp. 556–76) has cogently pointed out, analysts of the Soviet scene have been particularly unsuccessful in their predictions of the development of Soviet society, and unwilling to recognize the significance of the roles of different leaders (Lenin, Stalin, Khrushchev, Brezhnev) in imparting new directions in that society. Who can tell what Brezhnev's successors have in mind.

REFERENCES

Bialer, Seweryn. 1962. "But Some Are More Equal Than Others." In *Russia Under Khrushchev,* edited by Abraham Brumberg, pp. 240-62. New York: Praeger.

Bloch, Sidney, and Peter Reddaway. 1977. *Psychiatric Terror: How Soviet Psychiatry Is Used to Suppress Dissent.* New York: Basic Books.

Breslauer, George W. 1978. "On the Adaptability of Soviet Welfare-State Authoritarianism." In *Soviet Society and the Communist Party,* edited by Karl W. Ryavec, pp. 3-25. Amherst: University of Massachusetts Press.

Brzezinski, Zbigniew. 1961. "The Nature of the Soviet System." *Slavic Review* 20, no. 3: 351-68.

Campbell, Robert W. 1978. "Economic Reforms and Adaptation of the CPSU." In *Soviet Society and the Communist Party,* edited by Karl W. Ryavec, pp. 26-40. Amherst: University of Massachusetts Press.

The Case of Leonid Pliusch. 1976. Introduction by Peter Reddaway. Boulder, Colo.: Westview Press.

Cocks, Paul. 1978. "Administrative Rationality, Political Change, and the Role of the Party." In *Soviet Society and the Communist Party,* edited by Karl W. Ryavec, pp. 41-59. Amherst: University of Massachusetts Press.

Connor, Walter D. 1972. *Deviance in Soviet Society: Crime, Delinquency and Alcoholism.* New York: Columbia University Press.

"Cultural Détente at Scientific Congresses: The Secret Report of the Czech Sociologists." 1977. Edited and introduced by Lewis S. Feuer. *Orbis* 20 (Spring): 115-27.

Daniels, Robert V. 1962. *The Nature of Communism.* New York: Random House.

Djilas, Milovan. 1957. *The New Class: An Analysis of the Communist System.* New York: Praeger.

Eisenstadt, S. N. 1964. "Social Change, Differentiation and Evolution." *American Sociological Review* 29, no. 3: 375-86.

Field, Mark G. 1972. "Soviet Psychiatry and the Polity: A Study of the Medicalization of Deviance." *Annals of the New York Academy of Medicine* 48, no. 1: 82-92.

Fischer, George. 1961. *Science and Politics: The New Sociology in the Soviet Union.* Ithaca, N.Y.: Cornell University Press.

The Grigorenko Papers. Writings by General P. G. Grigorenko and Documents on His Case. 1976. Introduction by Edward Crankshaw. Boulder, Colo.: Westview Press.

Hough, Jerry F. 1965. "The Soviet Concept of the Relationship Between the Lower Party Organs and the State Administration." *Slavic Review* 24, no. 2: 215-40.

───── . 1969. *The Soviet Prefects: The Local Party Organs in Industrial Decision-Making.* Cambridge, Mass.: Harvard University Press.

Hough, Jerry F., and Merle Fainsod. 1979. *How the Soviet Union Is Governed.* Cambridge, Mass.: Harvard University Press.

Inkeles, Alex, and Raymond A. Bauer. 1959. *The Soviet Citizen.* Cambridge, Mass.: Harvard University Press.

Joravsky, David. 1970. *The Lysenko Affair.* Cambridge, Mass.: Harvard University Press.

Kassof, Allen. 1964. "The Administered Society: Totalitarianism Without Terror." *World Politics* 26 (July): 558-75.

Lipset, Seymour Martin. 1963. *The First New Nation.* New York: Basic Books.

Lowenthal, Richard. 1976. "The Ruling Party in a Mature Society." In *Social Consequences of Modernization in Communist Societies,* edited by Mark G. Field, pp. 81-118. Baltimore: Johns Hopkins University Press.

Medvedev, Zhores A., and Roy A. Medvedev. 1971. *A Case of Madness.* New York: Alfred A. Knopf.

Moore, Barrington, Jr. 1954. *Terror and Progress USSR: Some Sources of Change and Stability in the Soviet Dictatorship.* Cambridge, Mass.: Harvard University Press.

Overstreet, Harry, and Bonaro Overstreet. 1964. *The Strange Tactics of Extremism.* New York: Norton.

Parsons, Talcott. 1977. *The Evolution of Societies.* Englewood Cliffs, N.J.: Prentice-Hall.

Rostow, Walt W. 1960. *The Stages of Economic Growth: A Non-Communist Manifesto.* New York: Cambridge University Press.

Russell, Bertrand. 1920. *Bolshevism: Practice and Theory.* New York: Harcourt, Brace, and Howe.

Shipler, David K. 1979. "Brezhnev and His Colleagues Are Devoted to the Status Quo." *New York Times,* June 24, p. E3.

Skillings, H. Gordon. 1969. "Interest Groups and Communist Politics." In *Communist Studies and the Social Sciences: Essays on Methodology and Empirical Theory,"* edited by Frederick J. Fleron, Jr., pp. 281-97. Chicago: Rand McNally.

Stalin, J. 1940. *Problems of Leninism.* Moscow: Foreign Language Publishing House.

8

RELIGION AND ATHEISM IN THE USSR
Jerry G. Pankhurst

In the late 1960s, common wisdom had it that religion had established a pattern of long-term, perhaps fatal, decline. Right or wrong, religion just did not seem to have the power over people or institutions that it once had, and secularization seemed to be winning the day. More recently there has been a major reevaluation of this thinking in many quarters. While mainstream religions do not appear to be gaining many adherents, there is some indication that at least their decline has moderated or even stopped, and they now occupy a stable position. More important, however, there has been born a spate of cults and sects, and conservative or evangelical religions are flourishing.

Such changes have prompted the prominent sociologist Robert Nisbet (1979) to argue that we are in the midst of historic transition; the allure of the secular political order has faded, leaving room for the religious order to reassert itself and establish a new world predominance similar to that which it enjoyed during the Middle Ages.

Whether such a grandiose prediction will come true, it does seem to be the case that religion has reenlivened itself as a political (or counterpolitical) force in many parts of the world. For example, the 1979 Iranian revolution under the leadership of the Ayatollah Khomeini is one sign of the worldwide Islamic revival that is generally aimed against secularizing political tendencies. In the nations of Latin America, "liberation theology" with a Christian-Marxist orientation has been animating revolutionary movements. And the election of a pope from Poland has brought new international dynamism to Roman Catholicism and has electrified the believers of Communist nations.

Indeed, the election of Pope John Paul II reminded the world that within the "Communist bloc" there was at least one nation that could truly be described as a "religious nation." In Poland antireligious activities, even though constituting evidence of the official atheism of the Polish Communist leadership, are relatively weak and diffuse; the Catholic Church claims the allegiance of over 90 percent of the population, more than half of whom would be found in church on a given Sunday (Chrypinski 1975).

The drama of religious resurgence is being played out in the Soviet Union as elsewhere. While there is no question that the USSR, unlike Poland, is a highly nonreligious society at present, and perhaps the overall trend continues to go against religion there, nevertheless some believers are extremely active and some religious groups are having striking success in obtaining and retaining members. Most significantly, during the 1960s and 1970s believers have gained a political voice that they have not had since the earliest days of the Soviet regime.

This change has not yet manifested itself in any sense of obligation on the part of the state leadership to consult with religious leaders or otherwise elicit the support of believers when some policy that affects them is to be promulgated. This is not the type of political voice that the religious groups in the USSR have gained. However, the Soviet leaders have been led to adopt an approach toward religion that includes some consideration for the religious viewpoint, for otherwise they increase the potential for arousing religious dissent, for antagonizing international opinion, for stimulating criticism of Soviet protection of human rights, or for engendering a spate of internal protests.

MAJOR SOVIET RELIGIOUS GROUPS

The USSR is the first modern nation to have declared the promotion of atheism as an official policy. While the government is statutorily neutral on questions of religion, as required by the clause of the Soviet Constitution that guarantees "freedom of conscience,"* the Communist party (CPSU) claims

---

*Article 52 of the 1977 Soviet Constitution reads as follows:

> USSR citizens are guaranteed freedom of conscience, that is, the right to profess any religion or to profess none, to perform religious worship or to conduct atheistic propaganda. The incitement of hostility and hatred in connection with religious beliefs is prohibited.
>
> In the USSR the church is separate from the state, and the school is separate from the church (English translation found in *Current Digest of the Soviet Press* 29, no. 41).

The "incitement of hostility" clause is new in this constitution, but the rest of the article is only slightly revised from the earlier one. The most noteworthy feature is the guarantee of atheistic propaganda without a similar guarantee for religious propaganda. This is the basis upon which religious missionary or evangelization activities are prohibited in the USSR. In fact, it reflects the essential ban on all notices of even legitimate religious activities, such as worship services, in all legal publications except those few that are directly permitted the churches for internal circulation.

no such neutrality (Timasheff 1960, p. 437). Thus, CPSU's dominance and control of the government organs insures that the state, in fact, is not totally neutral in regard to religion. Through state and party operations, religious institutions are limited in the scope of their activities, and the religious consciousness of the population is combated.

It is a great irony that this "first atheist nation" should nevertheless contain within its borders large and active religious communities, including representatives of four of the world's great religions: Buddhism, Judaism, Christianity, and Islam. While the Soviet Buddhist community is small, numbering perhaps 50,000 followers (Antic 1976), it has some importance because it is located near the strategic border with China. Buddhism has also had an influence upon some Soviet intellectuals. However, it is the other religious groups that require greater attention here.

Identification with Judaism or Islam connotes ethnic ties as well as religious group adherence. (See the essays by Ralph Clem in this volume.) Since the Arab-Israeli conflict is a major problem of international affairs, and the apparent strengthening of religious concern among Muslims all over the world is causing political instability in Muslim nations, the Soviet Jewish and Islamic groups have great international significance.

According to several commentators, the Soviet military incursion into Afghanistan was at least in part motivated by the fear that the conservative religious ideology of the rebels might spread into the Islamic Central Asian region of the USSR. There are approximately 40 million nominal Muslims in the USSR (Feshbach 1979, p. 686), and while not all are active believers, the spread of the Islamic revival into this sector of the Soviet population could have enormous consequences for economic and political development. (See Bennigsen 1975, 1977; also see Ralph Clem, "The Ethnic Dimension, Part II," and David Heer, "Population Policy," in third volume.)

Since the late 1960s the emigration of Jews from the USSR has been a focal concern of the international human rights movement. In fact, until the early 1970s the Soviet Jewish population exceeded even the population of Israel, the U.S. Jewish population being the largest in the world. With emigration and assimilation reducing the Soviet Jewish community—it dropped from 2.15 million to 1.81 million between the census years of 1970 and 1979 (Ts.S.U. 1980, p. 24)—it has now assumed third place in size. Even though the majority of Soviet Jews are highly secularized, they pose a major problem for Soviet domestic and foreign policy, and the world attentively watches how the USSR treats this religious-ethnic minority group. (See Gitelman 1977; Davis 1976.)

Christianity is the traditional faith of the Russian core of the Soviet Union, as well of the Western frontier regions from the Baltic republics through Belorussia and into the Ukraine and Moldavia, and of Georgia and Armenia. Virtually every major variant of Christianity is represented in the USSR, but by far the largest denomination is the Russian Orthodox Church, which numbers more than 40 million adherents, according to an official tally (Bundesinstitut 1976, p. 62). In fact, the Russian Church is the largest Eastern Orthodox Church in the world. (Furthermore, 60 million of the world's 70 million Eastern Orthodox Christians live in Communist nations; see Sapiets 1970.)

Roman Catholicism is concentrated along the western frontier of the Soviet Union, with some 2.25 million Latin-rite Catholics in Lithuania and up to 3.5 million in the entire USSR (Vardys 1977). The Lithuanian Catholics have been at the forefront of religious dissent, and since 1972 have published an underground journal, the *Chronicle of the Catholic Church in Lithuania* (Bociurkiw 1975). Besides the regular Roman Catholics, the USSR also contains large numbers of Eastern Rite Catholics (Uniates), who, although their church was abolished and officially absorbed into the Russian Orthodox Church after World War II, remain active. This group must operate entirely underground, and has become a focus for Ukrainian nationalism (Markus 1975a, 1975b).

With their own national churches, the Georgians and Armenians have been somewhat out of the mainstream of religious deveopments in the USSR. The Georgian Church has experienced a severe decline in recent years, with only 40 churches remaining open and an undetermined but surely small group of faithful (Reddaway 1975). Conversely, the Armenian Apostolic Church—a Monophysite church that went into schism from most of the rest of Christianity after the Council of Chalcedon in 451—has some security and strength, although it is under official pressure. There is a strong relationship between Armenian national identity and the Armenian Church, and this provides support for the church, even among many nonbelievers.

Soviet Protestants are extremely varied in composition. They range from the traditional Lutherans, found primarily in Latvia and Estonia, who number about 850,000 (Antic 1976), to Adventists, to small and scattered groups of Jehovah's Witnesses. The most important and widespread Protestant group in the Soviet Union is the Evangelical Christians and Baptists (often called simply Baptists or ECB). The ECB church is, in fact, a composite of several Protestant strains, including the regular Baptists, the more Methodist-like Evangelical Christians, the Pentecostals—although their union with the others has been particularly precarious—and some groups of Mennonites. All told, ECB probably numbers about 3 million adherents, a number that includes those who are regular participants in ECB activities but who may not have met the stringent requirements for membership (Lane 1978, p. 140). Besides this 3 million, there is an undetermined but large number of ECB believers who are not associated with the official ECB organization in the USSR. Their role is very important, as will be explained below.

Finally, mention should be made of the native Russian religious groups that are scattered throughout the Soviet Union. Largest among these is the

Old Believers, who probably total no more than 5 million adherents today. (This estimate dates from Anderson 1964.) There are also groups of Molokans, True Orthodox Christians, Dukhobors, and some others. (See Lane 1978 for thorough discussions in English of these various groups.) In general, the Russian sectarian groups have not fared well under Soviet rule, and they seem to be dying out rather quickly, their place being taken in part by the evangelical Protestant groups (Klibanov 1969, 1973).

It must be recognized that any count of members or adherents of these religious groups in the USSR is only a very rough estimate based on various official and unofficial statements. There are no government data on religious affiliation available, and it is clear that the churches themselves are partly involved in self-censorship when it comes to describing their own denominations. Nevertheless, these figures indicate that there remains a very large number of believers in the Soviet Union whose denominations represent a broad range of religious persuasions.

SOVIET ATHEISM AND INTEREST-GROUP CONFLICT

As we have had more and more opportunities since the mid-1950s to take a close-up look at the state and society of the USSR, it has become very clear that simplistic notions regarding the Soviet system as fully totalitarian, a dictatorship, or a police state do not adequately serve the purposes of objective comprehension of that nation. However much such ideas may have been appropriate for the era of Josef Stalin's rule, since his death Soviet society has revealed itself as one where various groups vie for influence, prestige, and power. While there is near monopolization of the police power and other political power resources by the state organs and the Communist party, the latter has increasingly revealed its own internal diversity, and other groupings have emerged to declare their legitimacy and their ability to promote special interests both within and outside of official structures (see, for instance, Skilling and Griffiths 1971; Hough 1977). Such groupings may be found in intellectual, nationality, and religious affairs, as well as elsewhere.

While the official acceptance of these movements of diversification and development of semiautonomous areas of influence depends on many factors, the broader political dynamism of the situation calls for a closer look at some of its facets. Even lacking official sponsorship or recognition, some movements may influence Soviet politics through representing popular interests and preferences in the sociopolitical arena (see McCarthy and Zald 1977). Such interests may be quite inchoate or subtle, or they may be explicit and well-developed.

The process whereby group interests become articulated to the degree that we may term the group an "interest group" is of central importance here. The concept "interest group" has many meanings in the sociological and political science literature, but here the usage specified by Ralf Dahrendorf (1959, pp. 237, 289-95) is adopted. According to this approach, latent interests are those that can be identified by an outside observer but are not fully recognized by group members. The opposition of other groups can cause individuals to become activated in pursuit of common interests, and this changes the interests from latent to manifest. Whole categories of people may be drawn together by the emergence of shared manifest interests, and the resulting group is termed an interest group.

For the USSR, an "antireligious group" that has developed clear manifest interests in opposition to religion may be identified. It is called the "state/party" here because it is largely through state and party means that its activities are realized. There are many denominations that may be seen as specific religious interest groups. However, there is only an incipient "religious group" in the sense of an interest group devoted to the pursuit of general religious interests. The following discussion attempts to clarify these designations and the interrelationships between these groups.

From the start it must be noted that the religion-related interests of the state/party are fairly well established insofar as the state/party adheres to the Marxist ideology of atheism. In addition to the ideology, Bociurkiw (1973, pp. 38-40) has pointed out that there are three underlying attitudes of the Soviet elite that tend to motivate it toward more severe antireligious measures. These are the "historical memory," in which the church is associated with the oppressive tsarist state and with the support of counterrevolutionary activities in the early post-Revolution period; the "ideological legacy" of Lenin and his followers, which interpreted Marxist atheism in a militant way under the influence of the Russian anticlerical tradition; and the "authoritarian aspirations" of the leadership, which aimed to integrate all aspects of society under the purview of the party and attempted to transform them into the party's "conveyor belts." The latter was a very difficult task, since religion was a distinctly non-Marxist orientation, and the result of attempts to integrate religion into the party-led institutional framework often was suppression of religious activities.

Since the Revolution of 1917, the state/party has maintained an antireligious campaign, although its virulence and focus have varied from period to period. Furthermore, there has developed a cadre of professional and amateur atheists, perhaps 6-10 million in number (Antic 1977), who are devoted to antireligious activities and represent a clear occupational interest group centered on these activities. They may work in the communications media, in the schools and other educational institutions, in factories and offices, and even in private homes, where they carry out "individual work" among believers to help free them from the allegedly harmful effects of their faith.

While the "antireligious group" advocated opposition to all forms of religiosity, one cannot easily describe a "religious group." Instead, there are many separate religious traditions and organizations, each of which puts forward its own claims to legitimacy and autonomy, aimed not only against the state/party, but also, to a certain extent, against each other. Were these diverse groups to come together in cooperative or ecumenical activities directed at fostering religious interests, they would provide a more viable counterinfluence to the state/party's antireligious campaign. Such a religious interest group might fight for greater publication rights for religious literature or for fewer bureaucratic requirements when a new congregation wishes to be organized, or it might fight for less harassment of religious activists or for the right to proselytize. In addition, it might struggle for a school curriculum in which "scientific atheism" was an optional subject instead of a required one. All of these interests clearly unite the various denominations on a latent level, although they are seldom articulated openly except by dissidents.

Given these shared latent interests, we must immediately ask why they are not made manifest interests. First, of course, are the pressure and restrictions of the state/party. To openly espouse these ends means to jeopardize, to a greater or lesser extent, one's status and way of life. For energetic advocacy in this area, many religious dissidents have found their way to prison on charges of antistate activity (Keston College 1977). Indeed, such activities present a fundamental challenge to accepted ways of Communist party administration. However, there are very significant reasons other than state strictures why (until very recently) there has not developed an ecumenical movement aimed at the protection of religious rights. While we cannot review all of these reasons here, a brief overview may indicate the more important ones.

During the 1930s the state/party attempted to abolish all religious organizations, hoping thereby to end religious influence in Soviet society. This effort was probably doomed to failure in any event, but the invasion by Nazi Germany intervened to require that the state/party reorganize the churches in order to support the war effort. The new organizations, however, were given their lease on life fully at the sufferance of the state/party, and therefore the leadership became in certain regards obliged to fulfill state/party ends. Harvey Fireside (1971) has termed the postwar religious leaders "junior partners" to the state because in many spheres they took on state functions. This has meant that the life-style of the religious leadership has become entangled with its state/party functions and interests, and its members are thus hard-pressed to mount a campaign against the state/party, their benefactor. The seeming co-optation of the official All-Union Council of Evangelical Christians–Baptists (AUCECB) led to a major schism in the 1960s that formed itself into the unofficial Council of Churches of the ECB (CCECB) (see Bourdeaux 1968). Major protests against leadership co-optation are also found among the Orthodox (Bourdeaux 1970). Nevertheless, the leadership's state involvements hinder religious interest-group development (see Murvar 1968).

But we can go even deeper to understand the lack of ecumenical spirit in the Soviet Union and the reluctance to mount a religious civil rights campaign. Historically, the Russian Orthodox Church has not been a compromising church. In its historical isolation it evolved the ethnocentric theology of "Moscow, the Third Rome" and the idea of the Russian Church as the Church Universal. As Vatro Murvar (1971) has shown, Russian sectarian groups further emphasized Orthodox tendencies toward seeing the world as seamless and undifferentiated, with groups designated only as good or evil according to a single measure of worth. In general, Russian Orthodox religious culture fostered a "take it or leave it" attitude, and often forced the taking.

Along with these blockages to ecumenical relations among the churches, the Russian Orthodox Church never fostered an intellectualized faith, but instead stressed the magic of the rite (see Lane 1975). The ritualist orientation tends not to stimulate religious activism, except as directly related to the ability to carry out the rites, and the latter is essentially maintained in the USSR, although with some limitations.

Finally, the established Orthodox were not ready for the disestablishment brought about by the February Revolution in 1917. They had not digested this fact when the October Revolution placed in power a directly antagonistic party of Bolsheviks. A reaction of conservative retrenchment was almost inevitable, in spite of significant earlier strides in a liberal direction. The protracted attack on the church as a counterrevolutionary force further squelched movements for reform within it. It is only since about 1970 that we see the beginning of reformist thinking once again in the Russian Church. In the meantime, the exclusivist orientation has predominated.

With the Russian Orthodox Church as the central religious institution in the Soviet Union, the smaller or more localized religious groups, though varying in their tendency to accept ecumenical or cooperative activities, could not in themselves mount a viable nationwide religious rights movement. (There are important movements for the special rights of various groups, such as the Baptists and Lithuanian Catholics, but they are on a lower level of analysis than the type of movement of concern here.)

Thus, it is clear that there are many sources of lack of unification among the religious groups that are more complex than simple state/party pressure against such unification, however important such pressure has been. Since a major antireligious campaign in 1958-64, there has developed a protest movement of major dimensions in the USSR. Prominent among Soviet dissidents are religious activists, and since approximately 1976 we have seen some clear movements among them toward the sort of cooperation based on common interests that may presage the beginning of a cooperative or ecumenical religious interest group. In part, these developments are undoubtedly the result simply of time—that is, the religious groups have had a long period without war in which they have once again become well organized. (This has perhaps provided the Orthodox in particular the opportunity to begin a reexamination of their position.) It is perhaps inevitable that they should begin to mount protest against the constraints of the Soviet system.

On the other hand, there are clear indications that the cooperative activities of the religious groups that are now emerging are responsive in some ways to international relations. Our understanding of the processes involved here is significant, in order that we may properly evaluate the effects (intended or otherwise) of the human rights campaign of the Carter administration and of the other human rights activities that have become a part of international diplomacy. After some additional material is introduced, this question will be addressed (see also Pankhurst 1978c).

OPTIONS FOR ANTIRELIGIOUS POLICY

What are the options for antireligious policy in the USSR? What organizational options for adaptation to the antireligious program are open to and taken by the religious movements? And what are the effects that the religious movements themselves have upon the state/party? Although complete and final answers cannot be given here, these questions may be examined by a brief review of the situation of the Russian Orthodox Church and the Evangelical Christians and Baptists.

Let us imagine that the antireligious motivations of the regime were unchecked by other contingencies. In such a situation, one would expect that all organized religious activities would be outlawed, and there might be attempts to suppress even individual and private religious observances. Although this would not eliminate many aspects of personal belief in supernatural forces, religious superstitutions, and such, it could succeed to a great extent in removing the influence of religion upon policy formation. With no organization having leadership that could speak for religious group interests, religious considerations would be eliminated. This, in large measure, appears to be the case in Albania (Prifti 1975), so it is a situation not unimaginable. To a comparable, though somewhat less severe, degree, this approach was carried out during the 1930s in the USSR. At that time all religious bureaucracies were eliminated, and the churches were left with only informal and seemingly illegal central leadership. For the Russian Orthodox, on the eve of World War II, only the dioceses of Leningrad and Moscow retained any open co-ordinating activities. The Baptists and Evangelical Christians had no such activities.

One can also imagine a situation where the imperative of Marxist atheism involves for the party only a sort of expansive exemplariness. That is, the party would see itself as the exemplar of the alleged good of atheism and minimize direct suppression of religious activities. The East European Marxist nations also provide examples of this type of approach, as in Poland

(Heneghan 1977), East Germany (Howard-Johnston 1978; Ward 1978; Oestreicher 1978), Hungary (Kovats 1977; Aczel 1977; Cserhati 1977), and perhaps Romania (Hitchins 1975). In these countries the major religious groups have some meaningful input into policy development and there is a church-state dialogue evident. To a certain extent this condition existed in the USSR in the period between the end of World War II and 1958, and in relations with many non-Orthodox groups, it was also the case in the 1920s. (The Orthodox Church in the 1920s did not experience this relatively benign treatment largely because of its association with the prior government and its connection with counterrevolutionary activities both inside and outside the Soviet state.)

Although we have not yet mentioned the most recent periods in Soviet policy, these considerations indicate the variety of responses to the problem of religion taken by the policy makers. In general, the periodization of church-state relationships described by Nicholas Timasheff (1942, 1946), writing during World War II, seems appropriate. Timasheff identified six distinct phases of policy before the war, three aimed at eradication of religion and three in retreat from that aim because of popular resistance. The last retreat, he stated, was also stimulated by the threat of war at the end of the 1930s. Since he treated only policy toward the Orthodox Church, this perhaps oversimplified the dynamics of the 1917–28 period, when the Orthodox Church faced an increase in pressure until 1923 and then a decrease, while the sectarians experienced a fairly consistent low pressure (and even some support) from the state and party. Nevertheless, this indicates, in a very general way, the pattern of relationships through the war years. As mentioned above, the rapprochement with the churches that was begun during the war lasted until 1958.

Contrary to Timasheff these policy variations need not be seen as a "retreat" from Communist principles. As Bociurkiw (1973) has shown, these variations and the ones going on into the 1960s and 1970s (which will be discussed below) are consistent with an overriding principle of "the Leninist formula subordinating the struggle against religion to the 'interests of the class struggle of the proletariat.'" More specifically, Bociurkiw sees these variations as responsive to considerations related to internal and external security, peasant policy, nationality policy, and foreign policy. Sometimes, he finds these considerations require a moderation of the attack upon religion in order not to undermine efforts in these other policy areas. During times when these policy areas are not so crucially related to antireligious activities—that is, when a more "pragmatic" approach to the antireligious struggle is not justifiable in terms of greater ends—then the ideological "fundamentalists" exert a stronger influence upon the topmost leadership that is shaping policy, and stimulate a more repressive approach to religion.

Bociurkiw and other commentators have recognized the importance of the religious believers, their reactions to repressive policy, and their organization upon the policy formation process. Further analysis suggests that there is a direct relationship between the organizational forms of the churches and the policy options adopted by the authorities. In particular, it appears that the stronger the repression of religious practices, the greater the tendency for schisms or variant sects to develop among believers, and thus the greater the difficulty in surveillance of religion as it becomes organizationally fragmented. This is particularly the case when the schisms are illegal in the Soviet context, and are thus forced to carry on their activities clandestinely. Since this sectarian tendency occurs in response to the repressive policies of the regime, it may be called "responsive sectarianism."

Paradoxically, however, if the regime adopts a very benign approach to religion, it also finds itself faced with schisms. This seems to be increasingly the case as the hold of the Orthodox hierarchy upon the faithful becomes weaker through secularization, and as some of the Orthodox believers move to other sectarian faiths (most importantly the Baptists). Related most directly to internal religious evolution, this type of sectarian formation might be called "theological sectarianism."

Figure 8.1 portrays these relationships graphically. Since the curve relating state antireligious pressure to religious organizational differentiation seems to approximate hyperbola, the pattern is labeled the "hyperbolic principle" of church-state relations. (There is no exact calculus possible, so perhaps a parabola or other bowl-shaped curve would be as applicable. Further discussion of the principle is found in Pankhurst 1978b.)

Surveillance of the state of religion is the minimal condition required for a Marxist antireligious program that expects to witness and guide the "withering away" of religion. Therefore, too much organizational differentiation among religious believers is undesirable, because it makes surveillance more complicated and difficult. Optimum antireligious policy should seek to maintain sufficient pressure to safeguard its own "militant atheist" identity, while not exerting so much pressure as to cause extreme organizational fragmentation, which would undermine the surveillance capability.

Though never formulated in this way as a specific principle, the Soviet state/party seems in general to be aware of the problems indicated here by the hyperbolic principle. For example, in a 1936 resolution the Commission on the Affairs of Cults, attached to the Presidium of the Central Ideological Commission, reported that

> ... administrative practices with the violation of laws, as facts and materials of [our] inquiry show ... [are] not forwarding the overcoming of religiosity, frequently lead to activity of sectarianism, its partial growth, the appearance of new religious rites, and to the organization of underground religious sects which provide favorable soil for counter-revolutionary activities of anti-Soviet elements (quoted in Lialina 1977, pp. 118-19).

FIGURE 8.1
The "Hyperbolic Principle" of Church-State Relations in the USSR

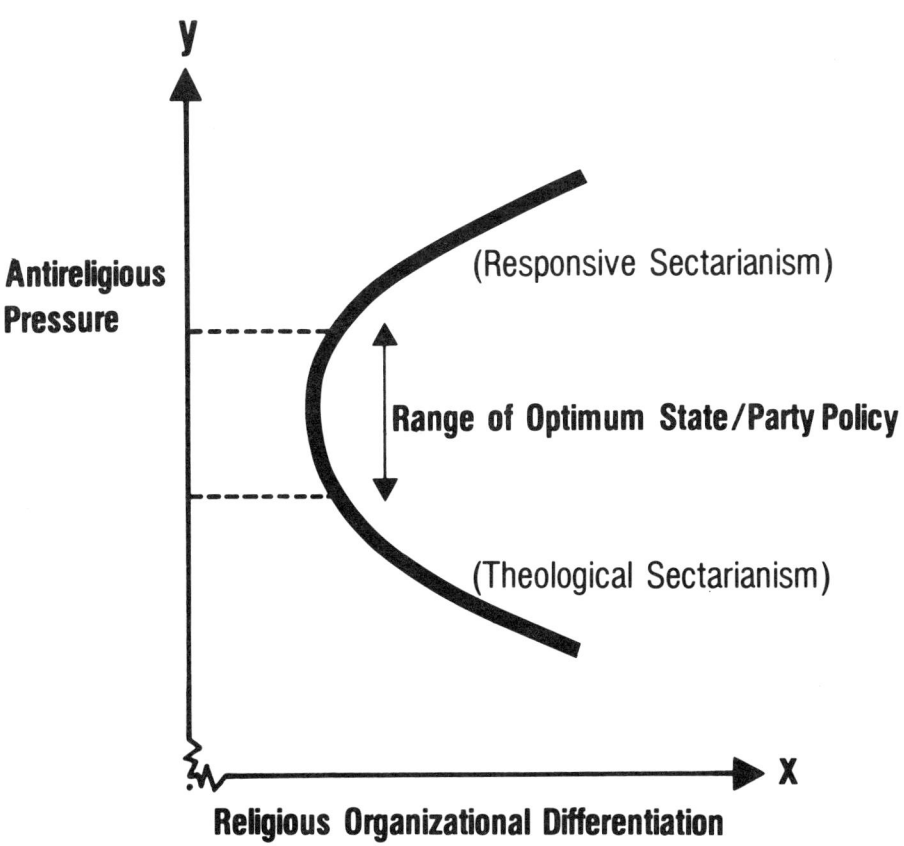

Source. Pankhurst 1978b, Figure 1.

The commission, it appears, was grappling with the problem of responsive sectarianism. The coercive approach had simply driven religion underground toward sectarianism, where there was even "partial growth." Atheist leaders were soon publicly recognizing that at least half of the total population were believers (Anufriev and Kobetskii 1974, p. 17), and this paved the way for a pre-World War II easing of the antireligious campaign (see Fireside 1971, p. 167; Konovalov 1974, pp. 111-13) though there were additional—and certainly more compelling—reasons for the church-state concordat that was established during World War II, these prewar developments indicate the attempt by the state/party to find that optimum level of antireligious pressure that would lessen the sectarian tendency but at the same time maintain the antireligious program in force at a subjectively and ideologically satisfactory level.

The wartime concordat led to a postwar period of accommodation between church and state, but the dynamics of this period give further evidence of the hyperbolic principle. This period came to an abrupt end in 1958, when the so-called Khrushchev campaign was launched. Bociurkiw has attributed the campaign to three elements:

> [I]t was an important political resocialization undertaking in connection with [Khrushchev's] grand design to "build communism" in the "present generation;" it was an aspect of his "destalinization" course—a return of the original "Leninist principles" in the Soviet religious policy; and, possibly, it was a concession to the party "ideologues" disconcerted and demoralized by his ideological innovations and pragmatic experiments in other policy spheres (1973, p. 49).

To these possible motivations for initiating the new policy, it must be added that the churches were consolidating gains made because of the wartime concordat. And in line with the hyperbolic principle, the return of prisoners from the Stalinist prison camps had induced significant unease among the churches, with the apparent growth of some unofficial variants of theological sectarianism (Bourdeaux 1968, 1971). In particular, while the state had hoped for a unified Protestant church under the officially recognized All-Union Council of ECB (AUCECB), major problems of unification of this group had not been solved (Mitrokhin 1974; Lialina 1977; Rowe 1975; Simon 1974, p. 157; compare Klibanov 1969, p. 104).

The Khruschev campaign lasted from 1958 through 1964. During that time more than half of the remaining Orthodox churches were closed, the number of theological seminaries was reduced from eight to three, and the number of monasteries dropped from 69 to 10-15 (Bourdeaux 1971, pp. 29-31; Bociurkiw 1971, p. 135; Conquest 1968, pp. 37-38; Simon 1974, pp. 73, 112, 115). Among the ECB there was evidence of a new push for dissolution of nonregistered congregations (that is, those not affiliated with the

AUCECB) and even of the closing of many of the AUCECB congregations, as well as an attempt to formalize the nondemocratic structure of the AUCECB, which had been hastily established in the war years (Bourdeaux 1968, pp. 20-21; Bociurkiw 1971, p. 135; Conquest 1968, pp. 104-08; Simon 1974, pp. 154-55). Jews and Muslims also suffered severe setbacks, as did other religious groups (see, for instance, Conquest 1968, pp. 67-127).

After the fall of Khrushchev in 1964, there was a reassessment of the campaign (discussed in Bociurkiw 1971; Blane 1974). What has ensued is an anomalous phase in which the official groups have regained some lost privileges and have made advances in some ways, while the pressure on unofficial groups that surfaced with considerable vigor during the campaign has been maintained at a fairly high level. (There may have been some amelioration of this situation in the late 1970s.) This appears to be the most complex stage of church-state relations in the Soviet era.

Detailed accounts of the Khrushchev campaign may be found elsewhere, and it is necessary to review here only a few major events and their consequences. These will form the basis for a clear understanding of the present relationship between church and state in the USSR.

THE KHRUSHCHEV CAMPAIGN AND ITS EFFECTS

As is very evident from *samizdat* (underground literature) documentation, the Khrushchev campaign made clear to many believers the extent of state/party meddling in the affairs of the churches. The authorities mounted the attack on religion in many ways, but the manipulation of the church leadership that took place was the measure that most directly launched the large religious dissent movements of the 1960s and the 1970s. (Documentation of the following may be found in Bourdeaux 1968, 1970.)

For the Orthodox, the major occasion was the convening of an unusual synod of bishops in 1961. The synod was unusual because there was less than 24 hours' notice of its convening. The essential point of the decisions of the irregular synod was to revise the Church Regulations of 1945 by depriving the parish priest of the right to serve on the parish *dvadtsatka* (the founding and general decision-making group) and the executive council, made up of three persons who run the day-to-day affairs of the parish. These resolutions of the synod specifically limited the priest's activities to the spiritual service of the parish, especially the proper fulfilling of the sacramental duties. Thus, for all administrative matters, the priest was at the mercy of the *dvadtsatka*, and especially of the small executive council. He became, in essence, only an employee of the parish, and thus could be much more easily removed, and his influence in administering parish affairs could be minimized. Through the elaboration of the control functions of the Council for Russian Orthodox Church Affairs and the manipulation of the composition of the parish administrative bodies (see Secret Instructions 1973; Sawatsky 1976), the state apparently hoped to control any independent-minded priests who might wish to implement innovative programs or otherwise protect or increase the appeal of the church. In short, these developments created the circumstances by which the state/party could carry out its massive campaign.

In response to these happenings, in the summer of 1965, Archbishop Yermogen led a delegation of eight bishops to visit Patriarch Alexi. They gave him a declaration recounting the problems with the 1961 synod and demanding that a general church council be called to rectify the situation. An open letter also was circulated by the priests Eshliman and Yakunin that further recounted the difficulties of the church with the state and charged the church administration with not fulfilling its duty to protect the church in the face of attack. For their actions Eshliman and Yakunin were banned from all priestly functions and Yermogen was involuntarily "retired" to the Zhirovitsy Monastery. However, the dissent movement that they began continued to grow in scope through the end of the 1960s and into the 1970s. Among the movement's major spokesmen were Anatoli Krasnov-Levitin, Boris Talantov, Aleksandr Solzhenitsyn, Archpriest Vsevolod Shpiller, and others.

The experience of the ECB Church was very similar to that of the Orthodox. For the ECB the precipitating incident comparable with the 1961 synod of bishops came in 1960, when the AUCECB promulgated the New Statutes (constitution) for the denomination, and distributed a Letter of Instructions to the senior presbyters regarding the implementation of the New Statutes. The New Statutes made official a hierarchical order for the ECB bureaucracy, with no democratic checks on its incumbents, a situation that contradicted the orientation of many of the groups within the ECB communion. It also included several stipulations or omissions regarding common activities that were unacceptable to many (see Bourdeaux 1968, pp. 28-31). The Letter of Instructions directed, among other things, that missionary and proselytizing activities were to be restricted and that work with children and youth was to be limited. Overall, the letter tended to limit the prerogatives of local ministers and their congregations, and it strengthened the role of the centralized bureaucracy through a hierarchical organization of presbyters.

Following the promulgation of the New Statutes and the Letter of Instructions, a group led by Alexei Prokofiev and Gennadi Kryuchkov began to meet to consider needed changes in the statutes and to develop an agenda for a proposed national congress of the ECB to revise the statutes and establish a policy for implementation. This group took the name "Action Group" or *Initsiativnaia gruppa*. From this, its members are often referred to as *Initsiativniki*. After failing in their efforts to have a congress called to revise the statutes, and later failing to gain representation at the ECB congresses that did so, the *Initsiativniki* denounced the AUCECB leadership and claimed that they should be the proper heads of the ECB Church. After a very successful mobilization effort, this group in 1965 formed the Council of Churches of

ECB (CCECB), a direct schismatical contender with the AUCECB for the allegiance of the ECB faithful (see Mitrokhin 1974, pp. 82-83). For their efforts, during 1961-64 at least 197 of their number were imprisoned.

The CCECB has remained in existence as an illegal Protestant church in the USSR. Allied with it is the group called the Council of Prisoners' Relatives, which has maintained an information network among the ECB concerning problems of persecution experienced by Soviet Baptists. Both the CCECB and the Council of Prisoners' Relatives have made massive contributions to *samizdat* both for their own edification and for the information of a broader public about the difficulties of religion in the USSR.

Now we may reconsider the hyperbolic principle in light of the developments of the 1960s. According to that principle, the increased state/party pressure of a campaign such as that of 1958-64 should have caused an increase in sectarian movements of the responsive type. This is very clearly what happened for the ECB, where various strands of diffuse differentiation in the movement focused in the formation of the CCECB, a group providing an alternative to the AUCECB for individuals and congregations of evangelical Protestants.

The political importance of this schism became most evident in 1965, when the CCECB directed its attention more toward the authorities, seeking legitimation from them, than toward the AUCECB. Nevertheless, from the very start the schismatic movement was based on an understanding of its problems as rooted in the interference of the state/party, as allegedly sanctioned by the AUCECB.

So far, this supports the hyperbolic principle, but when the developments of the Orthodox Church are considered, the principle becomes less clear, as was found earlier. Certainly, Yermogen, Eshliman, Yakunin, Levitin, and others have not started an Orthodox sect. It is possible that the closing of a church or the removal of a priest has led some believers to shift their allegiance to one of the already existing sects, such as the True Orthodox Church, the True Orthodox Christians, or others, but we do not have any information on this. However, there is strong evidence of a move toward the ECB by some (Pankhurst 1978, ch. 5). In any event, this is not sect creation, but movement among the possible options already in existence.

Although there are ample signs of popular Orthodox dissatisfaction with the church-state relationship in the 1960s, there are few signs of a coalescence of a movement in response, except among the intelligentsia. And this latter is clearly a movement of a "responsive sectarian" type in terms of the hyperbolic principle. It is possible that, should the intelligentsia take a fully schismatic stand, they would find some followers among the larger category of Orthodox adherents.

The leaders of the ECB schism proved themselves to be among the intellectuals of the ECB, not the "fanatics" that were portrayed in the Soviet press. Their writings show them to be promoting arguments very similar to those of the Orthodox dissidents, and Michael Bordeaux (1970) has convincingly argued that the Orthodox were directly influenced in their opening of protest by the activities of the Baptists. It is important to note that the CCECB movement was fully mobilized by the time the first major protests of the Orthodox were made in 1965.

These considerations lead to the conclusion that the state/party pressures have had a different effect upon the Orthodox and the ECB, not because the pressure was experienced in significantly different ways, but because the two groups possessed different resources whereby they could mobilize social movements in response to these pressures, and could develop such mobilization in the form of effective social movement organizations (see McCarthy and Zald 1977).

The hyperbolic principle, as qualified here, describes important dynamics in the interest group conflict involving the Baptists, the Orthodox, and the state/party. The above considerations suggest that the ECB has an advantage in relation to the Orthodox as both groups face the state/party. The ECB has a greater flexibility of response to state/party pressure that is built upon its structural resources, which allow for increased autonomy of action on the part of individual adherents and clergy in contrast to the Orthodox. This autonomy may be exercised in the formation of partially legitimated movements of protest against church policy as it becomes too tied to state/party control.

In turn, this development may lead to revitalization of the religious message of the church and provide a foundation for continued expansion of the number of adherents. Some expansion may come at the expense of the Orthodox because of their comparative weakness on this dimension. The revitalization of the religious message implies that the understanding of the religious interests of the ECB, and the comprehension of the opposition of those interests to the state/party's antireligious interests, are strengthened for ECB adherents. In other words, those interests become more manifest, and the Baptist group as an interest group is thereby strengthened. Thus, it may more directly challenge the state/party or antireligious group.

In large measure these developments became possible only after the World War II change of policy by the state/party that allowed the reconstitution of the religious bureaucracies and the unification of the Evangelical Christians and Baptists. The reasons for that policy change were clearly compelling the state/party, but they nevertheless laid the groundwork for the present organization-based interest group conflict.

For religious groups, schisms or other forms of splintering usually are not seen as desirable. However, these considerations of what I have called the hyperbolic principle suggest that it is not necessarily so undesirable in the context of Soviet society. This is a context characterized by high secularization of the population, and the task of religious groups is to protect themselves from further erosion and grow wherever they can. Clearly, the formation of schisms would not be desirable if there were a larger and stronger religious base in such a society. The example of Poland, where more than 90 percent of the population is counted nominally Catholic, indicates the importance of mere size for a religious group to prosper in the face of an officially atheist controlling elite.

But in the Soviet case, religious organizational differentiation presents policy makers with a dilemma: how do you exert antireligious pressure without decreasing your ability to abet the "withering away" of religion? In the post-Khrushchev era, we see the state/party trying to conquer this dilemma by strengthening the official church organizations in some ways, while maintaining a continuing pressure upon schismatics and dissidents. (This was most recently reflected in legislation changes in 1975; see Steeves 1977.) However, the dissidents and schismatics of the Orthodox and the ECB tradition have been able to continue, often with startling success. As long as that is so, the state/party will continue to be on the horns of this dilemma and religious faith will continue to be a real option in Soviet society.

CURRENT RELIGIOUS CONDITIONS

It was earlier asserted that there is a religious resurgence occurring in the USSR. It is now possible to put such a resurgence in perspective. The events that have been briefly reviewed indicate that one form of that resurgence is the increased amount of religious dissidence since the end of the Khrushchev antireligious campaign. This has been a major component in the diverse dissenting activities that have been witnessed in the USSR since the mid-1960s including literary protests, nationalist protests, and other movements seeking political, social, or economic reorganization of the USSR.

These dissenting movements have arisen at the same time that the government has reached out to other nations, seeking better relations and greater cooperation through the policy of détente. This has allowed much more information to become available about Soviet society, and some of it has aroused protests in the West. Strengthened and emboldened by foreign support and attention and perceiving the Soviet government as constrained by such attention, the protest movements within the USSR have become very sensitive to international relations.

This has clearly contributed to the development among religious dissenters of greater cooperative, ecumenical relationships, often even involving nonbelieving dissenters like Andrei Sakharov. For example, after the Helsinki pact of 1975, there grew up in the USSR groups of dissenters seeking to keep track of the Soviet record on human rights. Called the Helsinki Monitoring Groups, one of their central concerns was the religious situation (Monitoring Group 1977). Also in 1975 the World Council of Churches initiated an investigation of religious conditions in the USSR. In 1976 there was organized in the USSR an ecumenical Christian Committee for the Defense of Believers' Rights, one of whose early protests concerned the refusal of permits for dissidents to go to Geneva for a meeting of the World Council of Churches.

These and other developments dating from the mid-1970s attest to the incipient growth of a true religious group (in the sense outlined above) that could act as a more significant counterbalance to the antireligious group of the state/party. It is clear that such developments have been very responsive to international interest in human rights in the Soviet Union. While most of the major leaders of the ecumenical dissent efforts are now in prison camps or exile, there are others who are just becoming active. As long as the hyperbolic principle constrains antireligious policy and mediates against a return to the conditions of the Khrushchev years, it is unlikely that the policies of the state alone could eliminate these movements. Their continuation depends upon several factors. Most important are continued international attention that support dissent and the induction of additional believers into protest activity.

This last factor that would support the development of a religious group counterbalancing the antireligious group indicates the final issue to be considered in this essay, the state of religious faith in general in the USSR in the face of all the pressures for secularization.

The first and most important fact to consider is that without a doubt there has been a high degree of secularization in the USSR since the 1917 Revolution. Before 1917 atheism was unthinkable except for a few radical intellectuals (although religious faith may have been of little consequence for many people). As noted above, by the late 1930s the official point of view was that about half of the population could still be considered religious believers. This included about one-third of the urban population and two-thirds of the rural population (Anufriev and Kobetskii 1974, p. 17). Current Soviet sociological estimates place the percentage of the population who are believers at 15-20 percent of the adult population, with 10-15 percent of the urban population and 20-30 percent of the rural population in that category (Kobetskii 1978, p. 24; Lane 1978, pp. 223-24). It is probably the case that such estimates, made as they are by professional atheist investigators, underestimate the number of people who hold at least some positive relationship to traditional religious conceptions and religious organizations. However, even taking this into consideration, there has been a great drop in the amount of religious adherence of the population.

Given other major changes in the Soviet Union—for example, massive urbanization, industrialization, and increased educational attainment—and the lack of societal support for religion, perhaps such a decrease in religious involvement is not surprising. Using several indicators of religiosity, Christel Lane (1975) found that Orthodox believers were very similar to members of national or established churches of Europe, such as those in England or Sweden. "The majority of Orthodox are . . . traditional Christians who believe and/or practice because their fathers and forefathers did so for centuries" (p. 136). They scored low on all religiosity indexes except participation in rites of passage such as baptisms, confirmations, weddings, and funerals. Lane concluded that "Religious commitment of Orthodox in its present configuration is thus shaped by the interaction of influences emanating both from the characterisics of a [national] church-type organization and a militantly atheist socialist society." Obviously, the apparent popular decline of the Orthodox Church is not fully attributable to state/party policy.

By comparison, while 86 percent of Americans indicated in a 1976 survey that their religious beliefs were "very" or "fairly important" to them, and 42 percent attended church regularly (Gallup 1977, pp. 17, 24), many would contend that this religious involvement is nevertheless very shallow and represents a generally "pro-religion" situation in the United States. One sociologist has speculated that there may be greater religious faith in the USSR than in the United States because the Soviet Union retains more "features of a traditional peasant society (of which religion is usually a part)" (Hollander 1973, p. 187).

It is important to note that the process of secularization is not inevitable and not unidirectional. Nisbet's views concerning the reassertion of religion in the future were noted at the beginning of this essay. Elsewhere he has explained his ideas of the cyclical nature of secularization processes more fully. (Nisbet 1970). While David Martin (1969) complains of the abuse of the term "secularization" for ideological purposes—it is often identified with "progress"—the concept may be useful if we avoid simplistic formulations. (See the critical review of the debate over secularization by Robertson 1974; compare Berger 1969, pp. 105-07.)

While the long-term trend seems to indicate a decrease of religious involvement in the Soviet Union—and this is supported by much Soviet sociological research—there are significant developments within this pattern of decline. It is possible that they could presage a reversal of the secularization process, although they do not necessarily indicate this at present.

In the face of secularization, the strength of the ECB and other Protestant groups is noteworthy. Their vigor may represent a major readjustment in the religious allegiances of the Soviet population. Over the period of Soviet history, there has been a clear shift among believers toward Protestantism. Table 8.1 provides illustrative data from one region of the USSR.

The shift toward evangelical Protestantism may represent a "normative reaction to normlessness" (Becker 1957, 1960) within the Soviet context of secularization and antireligious activities. Such a reaction does not necessarily imply the incipience of real "normlessness" but, rather, a perception or feeling by some people of severe threat to what they consider sacred values. In response, social movements arise to reassert, perhaps in a modified form, the values at issue through the establishment and dispersal of what they consider a stronger normative system. The particular growth of the Western sects, especially Baptism, in view of the weakening of the Russian Orthodox

Church, seems to fit such a pattern of normative reaction. Stephen and Ethel Dunn (1964) have pointed out the shifting functions of the sects in Russia, and specifically of the shift toward the Western sects, which now seem to represent the most viable platform for protest against the regime in terms of religion.

TABLE 8.1
Religious Organizations and Groups in Rostov Oblast, 1917 and 1972

Religious Organization or Group	Number in 1917	Number in 1972 Registered	Number in 1972 Not Registered
Russian Orthodox churches	401	64	—
Russian Orthodox monasteries	3	—	—
Russian Orthodox ecclesiastical schools	2	—	—
Old Believer churches	16	4	12
Armenian-Gregorian churches	16	2	—
Roman Catholic churches	3	—	—
Jewish synagogues	12	1	—
Muslim mosques	2	1	—
Baptist houses of prayer	2	8	33
Seventh-Day Adventist houses of prayer	—	2	15
Christians of Evangelical Faith prayer houses (*Piatidesiatniki*)[a]	—	—	25
Jehovah's Witnesses groups	—	—	2
True Orthodox Christian societies[b]	—	—	10
"Ioanniti" societies[c]	—	—	5
"Khristovovery" groups (*Khlysty*)	—	—	1
Skoptsi groups	—	—	1
Total	457	82	104

Note: In a footnote to this table, Voroshilov notes that it was "composed from archive materials of the Official Committee for Religious Affairs attached to the Council of Ministers of the USSR for Rostov oblast and from the current archives of the Rostov oblast house of scientific atheism, taking into account changes in the borders of the Don Army oblast."

[a] Pentecostals.

[b] An underground Orthodox group, True Orthodox Christians do not accept the present hierarchy of the Russian Orthodox Church.

[c] The Ioanniti are an Orthodox sect that appeared during the last two decades of the 19th century. They are named for St. John of Kronstadt, whom they especially revere, and operate clandestinely.

Source: Voroshilov 1974, pp. 75-76.

The normative reaction to normlessness is a natural process engendered in situations of social change that dislocate and disorient those involved. The

Soviet leadership and Communist party are embarked on an attempt to build a new society, a communist society, which requires overthrowing present conditions and replacing them with new social forms. Recognizing that new social forms require some normative or ethical anchorage, the state/party promotes "communist morality" and the communist upbringing of the population. In connection with this, there have been established in the 1960s and 1970s socialist rites of passage to commemorate major stages in the life cycle (Lane 1979). These, coupled with the mass political holidays that have been celebrated since the Revolution of 1917, make up a set of rituals and ceremonies in direct opposition to similar religious practices. (See the comments by Mark Field on the "secular faith" of Marxism-Leninism in his essay in this volume.)

Jennifer McDowell (1974) and Christel Lane (1979) find increasing support among the population for the new ceremonies for birth and marriage, although Soviet funeral rites are still quite infrequent. Urban populations have accepted the rites more quickly than have rural populations. However, "There is a possibility that ritual involvement is merely motivated by a desire to mark important events in personal life in an elevated form and that the rhetoric of Marxism-Leninism is no more than an acceptable backcloth" (Lane 1979, p. 275).

Whether this is the case, or whether there is sincere interest in linking the ideological orientation with the life cycle is an important question for the future of religion in the USSR. The state/party would prefer that the population shift its observances to the socialist ceremonies, and though this shift has partially been achieved, it is not clear how far it will go. If these state/party alternatives to religious rites are successful in the long run, they would severely undermine the appeal of religion. Viewed as functional alternatives to religion, their acceptance could also be related to a resurgence in religious interest that is refocused upon these socialist rites.

At present we can discern no certainties about the future of religion and atheism in the Soviet Union. However, we do know enough about the situation to warn against incautious conclusions that are too often heard. One is that religion is dead—or at least is in its death throes—in the USSR. In fact, although reduced in size, the institution of religion is very much alive; many people worship regularly, there is intellectual and spiritual activity evident, and there are signs of significant intellectual and even popular interest in religion. While the Protestant groups seem to be having the greatest success in gaining and retaining members at present, the Orthodox intellectual movement is very strong and influential. In addition, Soviet Muslims and Jews show signs of significant religious interest.

Another incorrect conclusion occasionally heard is that the ideology of Marxism-Leninism is completely dead in the USSR, and that people are turning en masse to religion. There has been much secularization of the Soviet population; and while this has not necessarily meant unqualified acceptance of

Marxism-Leninism, the ideology is certainly not dead, particularly insofar as it orients the major antireligious program of the state/party.

The present stage is one in which the excesses of the Stalin and Khrushchev eras are being reduced. This has meant a moderated, though still militant, atheist program. It has also meant the reinvigoration of certain strands of religious activity. Religious dissent is the clear expression of a renewed interest in religion among intellectuals and some other groups of the population.

In general, since the mid-1960s the question of religion and atheism has become politicized. It has become a problem in the political arena, especially because believers have begun the processes of interest group development, processes that were driven completely underground in the 1930s, began to consolidate after World War II, were submerged during the Khrushchev campaign, and emerged with real impetus in reaction to that campaign. While this interest group development is not a mass movement, it does insure that religion will continue to be a real alternative in Soviet life.

REFERENCES

Aczel, Gyorgy. 1977. "The Socialist State and the Churches in Hungary." *New Hungarian Quarterly* 18, no. 66: 49-62.

Anderson, Paul B. 1964. Testimony before the Subcommittee on Europe, Committee on Foreign Affairs, U.S. House of Representatives, 88th Cong. 2d Sess. In *Recent Developments in the Soviet Bloc,* pt. 1 (Jan. 27-30). Washington, D.C.: U.S. Government Printing Office.

Antic, Oxana. 1976. "Numbers of Religious Persons in the USSR." *Radio Liberty Research* RL 58/76 (Feb. 2).

_____. 1977. "The Promotion of Atheism in the Soviet Union Today." *Radio Liberty Research* RL 258/77 (Nov. 8).

Anufriev, L. A., and V. D. Kobetskii. 1974. *Religioznost' i atiezm (sotsiologicheskie ocherki).* Odessa: Maiak.

Becker, Howard P. 1957. "Current Sacred-Secular Theory and Its Development." In *Modern Sociological Theory in Continuity and Change,* edited by Howard P. Becker and Alvin Boskoff, pp. 133-85. New York: Holt, Rinehart, and Winston.

_____. 1960. "Normative Reactions to Normlessness." *American Sociological Review* 25: 803-10.

Bennigsen, Alexandre A. 1975. "Islam in the Soviet Union: The Religious Factor and Nationality Problem in the Soviet Union." In *Religion and Atheism in the USSR and Eastern Europe,* edited by Bohdan R. Bociurkiw and John W. Strong, pp. 91-100. Toronto: University of Toronto Press.

_____. 1977. "Modernization and Conservation in Soviet Islam." In *Religion and Modernization in the Soviet Union,* edited by Dennis J. Dunn, pp. 239-79. Boulder, Colo.: Westview Press.

Berger, Peter L. 1969. *The Sacred Canopy.* Garden City, N.Y.: Doubleday-Anchor Books.

Blane, Andrew. 1974. "A Year of Drift (Part I)." *Religion in Communist Lands* 2, no. 3: 9-15.

Bociurkiw, Bohdan R. 1971. "Religion in the USSR After Khrushchev." In *The Soviet Union Under Brezhnev and Kosygin,* edited by John W. Strong, pp. 135-55. New York: Van Nostrand.

_____. 1973. "The Shaping of Soviet Religious Policy." *Problems of Communism* 32, no. 2: 37-51.

_____. 1975. "Religious Dissent in the USSR: Lithuanian Catholics." In *Marxism and Religion in Eastern Europe,* edited by Richard T. DeGeorge and James P. Scanlan, pp. 147-75. Boston: D. Reidel.

Bolshakoff, Serge. 1950. *Russian Nonconformity.* Philadelphia: Westminster Press.

Bourdeaux, Michael. 1968. *Religious Ferment in Russia: Protestant Opposition to Soviet Religious Policy.* New York: Macmillan.
———. 1970. *Patriarch and Prophets: Persecution of the Russian Orthodox Church Today.* London: Macmillan.
———. 1971. *Faith on Trial in Russia.* London: Hodder and Stoughton.
Bundesinstitut für ostwissenschaftliche und internationale Studien (Cologne). 1976. *The Soviet Union, 1974-75: Domestic Policy, Economic, Foreign Policy.* London: C. Hurst and Company.
Chrypinski, Vincent C. 1975. "Polish Catholicism and Social Change." In *Religion and Atheism in the USSR and Eastern Europe,* edited by Bohdan R. Bociurkiw and John W. Strong, pp. 241-55. Toronto: University of Toronto Press.
Conquest, Robert, 1968. *Religion in the USSR.* New York: Praeger.
Cserhati, Jozsef. 1977. "Open Gates." *New Hungarian Quarterly* 19, no. 67: 48-62.
Dahrendorf, Ralf. 1959. *Class and Class Conflict in Industrial Society.* Stanford: Stanford University Press.
Davis, Moshe. 1976. "Jewish Spiritual Life in the USSR: Some Personal Impressions." *Religion in Communist Lands* 4 (Winter): 20-23.
Dunn, Stephen, and Ethel Dunn. 1964. "Religion as an Instrument of Culture Change: The Problem of the Sects in the Soviet Union." *Slavic Review* 23: 459-78.
Feshbach, Murray. 1979. "Prospects for Outmigration from Central Asia and Kazakhstan in the Next Decade." In *Soviet Economy in a Time of Change,* vol. 1, pp. 656-709. Washington: Joint Economic Committee of the U.S. Congress.
Fireside, Harvey. 1971. *Icon and Swastika: The Russian Orthodox Church Under Nazi and Soviet Control.* Cambridge, Mass.: Harvard University Press.
Gallup, George. 1977. "Religion in America." *Gallup Opinion Index,* no. 145 (August): 1-120.
Gitelman, Zvi. 1977. "Judaism and Modernization in the Soviet Union." In *Religion and Modernization in the Soviet Union,* edited by Dennis J. Dunn, pp. 280-309. Boulder, Colo.: Westview Press.
Heneghan, Thomas E. 1977. "The Loyal Opposition: Party Programs and Church Response in Poland." In *Eastern Europe's Uncertain Future,* edited by Robert R. King and James F. Brown, pp. 286-300. New York: Praeger.
Hitchins, Keith. 1975. "The Romanian Orthodox Church and the State." In *Religion and Atheism in the USSR and Eastern Europe,* edited by Bohdan R. Bociurkiw and John W. Strong, pp. 314-27. Toronto: University of Toronto Press.
Hollander, Paul. 1973. *Soviet and American Society: A Comparison.* New York: Oxford University Press.
Hough, Jerry F. 1977. *The Soviet Union and Social Science Theory.* Cambridge, Mass.: Harvard University Press.
Howard-Johnston, Xenia. 1978. "Editorial." *Religion in Communist Lands* 6, no. 2: 74-75.
Keston College. 1977. *Christian Prisoners in the USSR 1977.* Keston, England: Keston College.
Klibanov, A. I. 1969. *Religioznoe sektantstvo i sovremennost'.* Moscow: Nauka.
———. 1973. *Religioznoe sektantstvo v proshlom i nastoiashchem.* Moscow: Nauka.
Kobetskii, V. D. 1978. *Sotsiologicheskoe izuchenie religioznosti i ateizma.* Leningrad: Leningrad State University.
Konovalov, B. N. 1974. *K massovomu ateizmu.* Moscow: Nauka.
Kovats, Charles E. 1977. "The Path of Church-State Reconciliation in Hungary." In *Eastern Europe's Uncertain Future,* edited by Robert R. King and James F. Brown, pp. 301-11. New York: Praeger.
Lane, Christel. 1975. "Religious Piety Among Contemporary Russian Orthodox." *Journal for the Scientific Study of Religion* 14: 139-58.
———. 1978. *Christian Religion in the Soviet Union: A Sociological Study.* Albany: State University of New York Press.
———. 1979. "Ritual and Ceremony in Contemporary Soviet Society." *Sociological Review* 27, no. 2: 253-75.

Lialina, G. S. 1977. *Baptizm: illiusii i real'nost'*. Moscow: Politizdat.
Markus, Vasyl. 1975a. "Religion and Nationality: The Uniates of the Ukraine." In *Religion and Atheism in the USSR and Eastern Europe*, edited by Bohdan R. Bociurkiw and John W. Strong, pp. 101-22. Toronto: University of Toronto Press.
———. 1975b. "The Suppressed Church: Ukrainian Catholics in the Soviet Union." In *Marxism and Religion in Eastern Europe*, edited by Richard T. DeGeorge and James P. Scanlan, pp. 119-32. Boston: D. Reidel.
Martin, David. 1969. *The Religious and the Secular: Studies in Secularization*. New York: Schocken.
McCarthy, John D., and Mayer N. Zald. 1977. "Resource Mobilization and Social Movements: A Partial Theory." *American Journal of Sociology* 82: 1212-41.
McDowell, Jennifer. 1974. "Soviet Civil Ceremonies." *Journal for the Scientific Study of Religion* 14: 266-79.
Mitrokhin, L. N. 1974. *Baptizm*. 2d ed. Moscow: Politizdat.
Monitoring Group. 1977. "Monitoring Group Reports on Religious Discrimination." *Religion in Communist Lands* 5, no. 2: 126-27.
Murvar, Vatro. 1968. "Russian Religious Structures: A Study in Persistent Church Subservience." *Journal for the Scientific Study of Religion* 7, no. 1: 1-22.
———. 1971. "Messianism in Russia: Religious and Revolutionary." *Journal for the Scientific Study of Religion* 10, no. 4: 277-388.
Nisbet, Robert. 1970. *The Social Bond*. New York: Knopf.
———. 1979. "Progress and Providence." *Society* 17, no. 1: 4-7.
Oestreicher, Paul. 1978. "Postscript." *Religion in Communist Lands* 6, no. 2: 95-96.
Pankhurst, Jerry G. 1978a. "The Orthodox and the Baptists in the USSR: Resources for the Survival of Ideologically Defined Deviance." Ph.D. dissertation, University of Michigan.
———. 1978b. "The 'Hyperbolic Principle' in Church-State Relations in the USSR: Natural Restraints on Soviet Antireligious Policy." Paper presented at the annual convention of the American Association for the Advancement of Slavic Studies, Columbus, Ohio, Oct., 12-15.
———. 1978c. "Human Rights Diplomacy and Religious Dissidence in the Soviet Union." Paper presented at the annual meeting of the Society for the Scientific Study of Religion, Hartford, Conn., Oct., 27-29.
Powell, David E. 1975. *Antireligious Propaganda in the Soviet Union: A Study in Mass Persuasion*. Cambridge, Mass.: M.I.T. Press.
Prifti, Peter. 1975. "Albania—Towards an Atheist Society." In *Religion and Atheism in the USSR and Eastern Europe*, edited by Bohdan R. Bociurkiw and John W. Strong, pp. 338-404. Toronto: University of Toronto Press.
Reddaway, Peter. 1975. "The Georgian Orthodox Church: Corruption and Renewal." *Religion in Communist Lands* 3 (July-Oct.): 14-23.
Robertson, Roland. 1974. "Religious and Sociological Factors in the Analysis of Secularization." In *Changing Perspectives in the Scientific Study of Religion*, edited by Allen W. Eister, pp. 41-60. New York: Wiley.
Rowe, Michael. 1975. "Pentecostal Documents from the USSR." *Religion in Communist Lands* 3, nos. 1-3: 16-18.
Sapiets, Janis. 1970. "The Orthodox Church in the Soviet Union and Eastern Europe." In *The Soviet Union and Eastern Europe: A Handbook*, edited by George Schöpflin, pp. 467-71. New York: Praeger.
Sawatsky, Walter. 1976. "The New Soviet Law on Religion." *Religion in Communist Lands* 4, no. 2: 4-10.
Secret Instructions. 1973. "Secret Instructions on the Supervision of Parish Life" (directed to local authorities regarding the surveillance and supervision of religious activities in their area). English text in *Religion in Communist Lands* 1, no. 1: 30-33.
Simon, Gerhard. 1974. *Church, State and Opposition in the USSR*, translated by Kathleen Matchett. Berkeley: University of California Press.

Skilling, H. Gordon, and Franklyn Griffiths, eds. 1971. *Interest Groups in Soviet Politics.* Princeton: Princeton University Press.
Steeves, Paul D. 1977. "Amendment of Soviet Law Concerning Religious Groups." *Journal of Church and State* 19: 37-52.
Timasheff, Nicholas S. 1942. *Religion in Soviet Russia, 1917-1942.* New York: Sheed and Ward.
———. 1946. *The Great Retreat.* New York: Dutton.
———. 1960. "The Inner Life of the Russian Orthodox Church." In *The Transformation of Russian Society,* edited by Cyril Black, pp. 425-37. Cambridge, Mass.: Harvard University Press.
Tsentral'noe Statisticheskoe Upravlenie pri Sovete Ministrov SSSR (Ts.S.U.). 1980. *Naselenie SSSR.* Moscow: Izdatel'stvo politicheskoi literatury.
Vardys, V. Stanley. 1977. "Modernization and Latin Rite Catholics in the Soviet Union." In *Religion and Modernization in the Soviet Union,* edited by Dennis J. Dunn, pp. 348-81. Boulder, Colo.: Westview Press.
Voroshilov, A. S. 1974. "Religioznost' kak predmet sotsiologicheskogo issledovaniia (opyt konkretno-sotsiologicheskogo issledovaniia v Rostovskoi oblasti)." Candidate dissertation, Rostov-on-Don University.
Ward, Caroline. 1978. "Church and State in East Germany." *Religion in Communist Lands* 6, no. 2: 89-95.

9

CRIME AND DELINQUENCY IN THE SOVIET UNION
Louise Shelley

    Articles in specialized journals by Soviet legal scholars and criminologists leave no doubt that there is a crime problem on a mass scale in the Soviet Union. Moreover, contrary to the theorizing in these journals, this problem is sustained by contemporary conditions and cannot be explained simply as a holdover from the tsarist period.

    Western scholars must rely almost exclusively upon Soviet scholarly publications to ascertain the extent and causation of criminality, for the subject is otherwise deeply shrouded in government secrecy. As a result not even Soviet citizens are in a position to evaluate fully the nature of the problem. No crime statistics are made public, penal institutions are closed to foreign visitors, and newspapers and popular publications, instead of printing crime rates, proclaim consistently that crime is withering away under socialism. The infrequent descriptions in the press of acts that violate the law are meant to strengthen and direct appropriate moral outrage. The contrast with the sensational accounts that commonly headline Western news is most striking.

    Nevertheless, a careful reading of the Soviet literature, when combined with information obtained from Soviet émigrés and from interviews with Soviet criminologists in and outside the USSR, does provide a firm basis for evaluating the similarities and differences between Soviet and Western patterns of crime.

CONTEMPORARY SOVIET CRIMINOLOGY

The early Soviet concern about crime was manifested by the initiation of criminological research very soon after the 1917 Revolution. The 1920s were innovative years that saw, for example, the opening of experimental penitentiaries. Studies were conducted on the personality of the criminal and the effect of social forces on crime (Shelley 1979a). This work ended abruptly in 1936 with the political repression initiated under Stalin. It was only in the mid-1950s, after Stalin's death, that the study of crime resumed under the direction of the criminologists surviving from the 1920s (Solomon 1974). Following the traditions of much of Western Europe, criminology is considered a part of law, and training for research in this field is conducted at law schools throughout the country. Since the reappearance of government-sanctioned criminology, scores of increasingly sophisticated researchers have been trained to study the cause, prevention, and characteristics of Soviet crime and delinquency.

The members of the Soviet criminological community carry out their research under many different auspices. Trained in law and with supplementary education in the social sciences, they conduct studies that provide decision makers in government with information required to formulate criminal and general social policy (Solomon 1978, pp. 33–41.)

Though criminologists are accorded considerable respect and influence in the USSR they often do not have the research opportunities or data necessary for comprehensive analyses. Older and established scholars are sometimes allowed direct access to the data in the procurator's office* or in police files. They also can assemble data from labor camps and other sites. Young researchers and graduate students are less trusted and thus have far more limited access to crime data and classified research.

Because of the limitations placed on its scholars, Soviet criminology cannot compete intellectually with many of the more sophisticated Western criminologies, but this does not reduce its influence within the Soviet Union. In contrast with the United States, the research of criminologists is used extensively by policy makers responsible for changes in the administration of law and police practice in urban centers. For example, research on the "parasite" law resulted in reducing its use, and studies of crime in Moscow have resulted in increased vigilance in regard to offenders not registered in the city.

A further difference from the situation in the United States is the fact that many of the influential criminologists are not employed by universities but are on the staffs of research institutes affiliated with the Academy of Sciences, the procuracy, and the Ministry of Internal Affairs (MVD), the primary police organ.

---

*The procurator is responsible for the proper execution of the law from the stage of police investigation through review of the sentence.

The preeminent criminological research institute in the Soviet Union for much of the period since the mid-1960s was the All-Union Institute for the study of Crime and the Elaboration of Preventive Measures, under the auspices of the USSR Procuracy and Supreme Court (Solomon 1978, p. 57). Much of the research referred to in this essay was conducted by staff members at the institute who published their results in its journal, *Problems in the Fight Against Crime*, and in other professional journals and edited collections. The once revealing publications of this institute are no longer as informative, because a change in leadership has resulted in stricter ideological controls over the research topics and writings of its staff of criminologists. In private conversations with the author, Soviet scholars have stated that its former place in criminological research has been increasingly assumed by the MVD institute, where personnel have the access to data and the intellectual freedom necessary to make intelligent policy recommendations.

The limited data revealed in journal articles preclude a thorough evaluation of Soviet research. The lack of quantitative sophistication is readily apparent, yet conclusions seem to be well supported by empirical findings. Also clear is the fact that Soviet scholars could benefit immensely from greater access to the international body of criminological scholarship and further training in the social sciences. (Conversely, international criminology could profit greatly from increased input of competent Soviet scholarship on crime.)

Despite such shortcomings, Soviet criminology has produced studies that provide Western scholars with significant insight into crime and delinquency in the USSR. It is important to note that the authoritativeness of the research is often greater than is suggested by the often primitive methodology, for Soviet criminologists are able to use their positions as members of the criminal justice apparatus to supplement the information obtained from officially collected data with that from informal contacts with police and court personnel.

The police and court statistics (obtained by trusted researchers at the central, and some local, offices of the police and procuracy) have some of the same problems as the comparable data from sources in the United States that are compiled in the FBI's Uniform Crime Reports. No independent body is responsible for collecting Soviet crime statistics. Instead, the local authorities forward crime figures to the central office (Juviler 1976, p. 133). Most jurisdictions underreport crime in an effort to favorably impress the central party bureaucracy. For this reason Soviet criminologists, like their colleagues in the United States, cautiously use crime data from these sources as indicators of trends over time or for comparing regions. They are not viewed as trustworthy measures of the actual incidence of crime.

THE SOVIET THEORY OF CRIME

Most Western criminological theory builds upon the writings of Émile Durkheim, who saw crime as a "normal" and even necessary part of society.

According to Durkheim, it is through the processes of identification, accusation, and punishment of criminals that a group or society establishes for itself the bounds of proper behavior. Indeed, Durkheim contended that without such processes there would be no means for the moral cohesion of societies. Thus, few scholars in the West seriously entertain the possibility that crime (or at least "deviance") can be totally eliminated from society, since the environment of human action, society itself, demands it (compare Erikson 1962).

Starting from a totally different premise, Soviet criminology is in this respect far more optimistic. It is argued that crime can be eliminated, because it is possible to eradicate its primary sources—"vestiges from the past" and susceptibility to the influence of capitalist societies. Following the writings of Karl Marx, it is asserted that this will occur when the society moves from the current socialist stage of development to the ultimate achievement of Communism. This progressive change to Communism is seen as the way in which the social environment is corrected so as to eliminate the causes of crime.

It is significant to note that Soviet theory differs also from the Marxist criminology that has emerged in Continental Europe, England, and the United States. According to the latter, crime can be reduced, but this occurs through the movement toward a classless society different from that envisioned in Soviet writings. Contemporary Western Marxist criminology is also more concerned with crime causation among specific social categories, such as juvenile delinquents or the underemployed; this is not of central theoretical interest to Soviet criminologists.

Some Western criminologists have investigated biological factors related to crime, but in the USSR, since the only acceptable causal explanations are those allowing for the complete eradication of crime, biological factors have no place. In the Soviet view, "If biology determines crime then criminal law and punishment are unnecessary, and it is only necessary to cure the individual" (Karpets 1966, p. 52). The few Soviet criminologists who consider biological factors are severely criticized by their colleagues.

While the Soviet criminologist may make the claim that there is "nothing in the nature of Soviet society which could give rise to crime" (Gertsenzon 1960, p. 17), crime in capitalist society is, of course, viewed in a very different light. The theory predicts that it will continue to grow and is rooted in exploitation, unemployment, and poverty—features inherent in the structure of capitalism (Karpets 1966, p. 56). These economic and social shortcomings were supposedly overcome in the USSR in the 1930s. The program of the Communist party of the Soviet Union states: "The rise in the material wellbeing, cultural level and consciousness of the working people creates all the necessary conditions for uprooting crime" (ibid.).

If so many years have passed since the elimination of the economic and social shortcomings, how do the Soviet criminologists account for the fact that the Soviet Union has not yet achieved its goal of total liquidation of all crime?

I. I. Karpets quotes Lenin in answering this question:

> Under socialism, the material and technical base is less developed than under communism, and the growth of material security, the cultural level and the consciousness of the members of society have not yet reached sufficiently high levels. . . .Consequently in our society, which is building communism, the conditions for eliminating crime and the reasons giving rise to it have not yet been fully established (1966, p. 55).

In private conversations many Soviet scholars reject the publicly espoused view that crime is withering away under socialism and will disappear with the achievement of communism. However, they still show fundamental agreement with the following dominant beliefs found in officially published crime studies: bourgeois influences from the past and from abroad are the only causes of crime in contemporary Soviet society; the citizenry plays a vital role in the prevention of criminality—that is, this is not simply a job for the government's criminal justice system; and the control of crime is most effectively achieved when offenders are subjected to a treatment that serves both to punish and to rehabilitate.

Soviet criminologists include a great deal under the rubric of bourgeois vestiges of the past: the traditions and habits of certain groups in the population; individual characteristics such as cupidity, cynicism, coarseness, despotism, selfishness, philistine attitudes, egoism, lack of human dignity, and indifference to the fate of others; and conditions elsewhere commonly viewed as social problems, such as alcoholism, one-parent families, and low educational attainment. It is contended that vestiges remain significant even though presocialist conditions no longer exist, in part because of "lags of consciousness"—that is, because under certain circumstances motivations may change more slowly than social conditions.

Along with vestiges of the past, the other primary Soviet explanation for the existence of crime in Soviet society is the harmful influence of Western bourgeois society. But this explanation of criminality has become acceptable only since Stalin's death. The doctrine of "socialism in one country" was Stalin's primary contribution to Soviet Marxism, and according to this conception, "internal contradictions could be solved by the Soviet state while the external contradictions continue to prevail" (Marcuse 1961, p. 82). It had, thus, been unacceptable to assert that hostile bourgeois influences could cause crime or prevent its eradication in the USSR.

This brief overview cannot do justice to the many nuances found within Soviet theorizing on crime, but it does provide an indication of the primary focus of such theory. Obviously, most Western scholars would view the general Soviet orientation as overly simplistic and seriously flawed. Attributing the cause of crime to hostile bourgeois influences might have had appeal in the ideologically charged atmosphere of the 1950s, when the explanation was first adopted; but it seems to have little relevance, let alone explanatory power, in the present, when Soviet authorities are encouraging cultural and economic exchange with capitalist countries.

Similarly, the great importance given to "vestiges of the past" is unfounded. The criminal habits and traditions of some people can account for only a tiny fraction of the total crime in the USSR, and the idea that negative individual characteristics can be eliminated seems utopian even to recent Soviet thinkers. As M. D. Shargorodskii writes, "Individual excesses may occur even when there is a classless society" (cited in Gertsenzon 1960, p. 27). This Soviet statement acknowledges that there are human limitations.

Finally, while the third group of vestiges (alcohol abuse, low educational level, broken homes, and the like) may contribute to crime commission, it is doubtful that these factors will disappear under the existing social system. They have all been affected directly or indirectly by Soviet social policy, and not always in ways that would reduce their potential for crime causation.

Furthermore, despite Soviet protestations, Western criminological theory may be applied to the Soviet context. The most relevant of the Western theories are those pertaining to the conditions of modern society and the causation of juvenile delinquency. Such theories illuminate processes that go on in the context of any human society. While it is impossible to adequately consider the potential of such theoretical approaches here, there seems no reason why one might not profitably consider crime causation in the Soviet Union in terms of Robert K. Merton's (1967, pp. 131-40) anomie theory, Thorsten Sellin's (1971) theory of culture conflict, Edwin Sutherland's theory of differential association (Sutherland and Cressey 1955, pp. 77-80), the opportunity theory of Cloward and Ohlin (1960), various radical theories (such as Gordon 1973; or Spitzer 1975), or any of the other major theoretical approaches found in the international criminological tradition.

Western criminological theory is not capable of explaining all of Soviet criminality, just as it is incapable of explaining all of criminality in capitalist societies; but it does provide significant insights into the complex crime problems of a modern society. It also indicates that in many fundamental aspects the impact of urbanization and industrialization on crime is similar in all societies, regardless of the form of economic development they have chosen to pursue.

Under Soviet rule the authorities in the USSR have not succeeded in abolishing crime, instead they have transformed it under the unique conditions of Soviet society. The following description of Soviet criminality will attempt to demonstrate those crime characteristics that are distinctive to the USSR and those that resemble internationally observed patterns of criminal behavior. The analysis will focus on the extent of change in the distribution of crime and the nature of offenders that has occurred since the 1917 Revolution.

THE GEOGRAPHY OF SOVIET CRIME

Data from other societies show a close relationship between the level of crime and economic development. The limited data on geographic variation in crime patterns in the Soviet Union are consistent with this research. High crime rates and a large proportion of crime involving property offenses are characteristics of more developed nations. In the USSR this pattern is found in the industrialized western regions. Lower crime rates and a higher proportion of crimes against persons are common to nations with a low level of development, and this second crime pattern exists in the Soviet republics where agriculture still has a particularly dominant role in the economy.

These generalizations apply more readily to the universally recognized crimes against property or persons, as opposed to the distinctly Soviet crimes of speculation (the purchase and resale of goods at a profit), parasitism (the refusal to work at meaningful labor), and political crimes against the state. However, the latter represent only a small proportion of all crimes committed.

It has been reported that the number of crimes per capita in urban areas of the USSR is 40 percent higher than in rural areas (Connor 1972, p. 174). This, again, is perfectly consistent with other nations of the world. In rural areas family and neighbors usually exercise greater social control over individual behavior. Also important is the far more limited variation in the level of economic wellbeing of rural residents. The anonymity of cities and more widespread feelings of relative deprivation may foster the higher incidence of crime there.

While Soviet urban-rural differences in criminality resemble those of other societies, the usual correlation between urbanization and higher levels of criminality does not exist in the USSR. The highest rates of criminality are not found in the largest cities, such as Moscow, Leningrad, and Kiev, but are recorded in the new medium-size cities of the North, Siberia, and the Far East.

The current distribution of crime in the USSR (and also in Bulgaria, which follows Soviet demographic policies) is so different from that of most industrialized and industrializing countries because the regime restricts the internal mobility of its population to achieve the goals of a centralized planned economy. These population controls include the internal passport and registration system, the removal from major cities of convicted offenders, and the closure of major urban centers to new residents. As a result of these administrative orders that restrict personal mobility, the major cities are closed to new inhabitants, and individuals authorized to live in those centers may lose this privilege if convicted of other than petty crimes.

The result of these measures is that the crime-prone youthful male work force is effectively denied entry to major cities, and criminals and recidivists who would threaten the urban order are effectively removed from these areas. Thus, whereas crime in other industrialized and industrializing countries is concentrated primarily in the older large urban centers, in the Soviet Union the highest crime rates are in the new industrializing communities where the population is composed of the crime-prone groups of youthful male urban migrants, released convicts, and other less desirable individuals excluded from attractive urban areas.

This aspect of the geography of crime has evolved only during the Soviet period. Directly after the 1917 Revolution the major cities of the Soviet Union suffered from high crime rates. The youth left homeless after years of war were responsible for a significant amount of violent crime. Other categories of offenders, such as prostitutes and those displaced by the revolution, also contributed to the high homicide and theft rates. The crime rates of many large Soviet cities have declined since the 1920s as economic, social, and political policies have favored the major urban centers. Rapidly developing towns that have received large numbers of migrants have, in contrast, experienced a consistent growth in crime.

The dynamics of Soviet criminality are closely associated with the degree of internal migration of the Soviet population. Between 4 and 6 percent of all Soviet citizens move annually (Babaev 1974). Migrants from rural areas go either to heavily populated regions or to sparsely populated areas that Soviet authorities believe would benefit from an increase in population (Babaev 1968, pp. 86–87). The destination of rural Russian migrants is frequently other republics or areas of the Russian Republic with non-Slavic inhabitants of totally different cultural, linguistic, and ethnic backgrounds. Serious adjustment problems of the migrants often result in criminality. Those arriving in already settled communities may feel alienated from the indigenous population, thereby increasing the migrants' propensity to commit criminal acts. In accordance with opportunity theory, the same result can be expected in newly settled urban areas because of the weak institutional and community structure.

These conclusions are based on large-scale studies of criminal behavior conducted primarily in the late 1960s and early 1970s by the Institute for the Study of Crime and the Elaboration of Preventive Measures and on interviews with scholars engaged in this research. Official data and survey methods were used to examine national crime patterns. Although the raw data have not been made available, the author's discussions with Soviet scholars suggest that the research was conducted with some sophistication and attention to quantitative research methods. The following analysis of the geography of crime is based almost entirely on articles in journals available to the public.

One finding from crime research conducted in the RSFSR (Russian Republic) is that the highest crime rates exist in the regions where migrants constitute an especially large proportion of the population. Studies conducted in 1963, 1965, and 1968 suggest that this relationship is due to the crime among migrants, and show that regions experiencing population decline due to out-migration are less crime-prone (Babaev 1968).

Rural areas have traditionally had lower crime rates than urban areas, and this is explained by the general physical inaccessibility and the economic homogeneity of the rural population. Urban areas in the Soviet Union have traditionally had higher rates of property crime and lower rates of violent crime than rural areas. Since the 1917 Revolution, the rates of property crime and crime against persons have both been higher in the urban environment.

Theft of state or communal property and livestock, violent crimes, and making and selling *samogon* (home brew) have traditionally been the characteristic forms of crime in the rural parts of the Soviet Union (Criminal Personality 1971 pp. 96-97). For a number of reasons, peasants commit an especially large proportion of the crimes against state property. First, the access of state and collective farm workers to government property makes theft feasible. Second, peasants working on these farms have an acute need for grain for their privately owned animals. Because they frequently cannot acquire such food legally, they resort to theft of government crops. And third, peasants have failed to internalize the socialist precept that state property serves the community as a whole rather than the needs of individuals. The state has always been intolerant of this form of criminal behavior, and in the late 1930s this easily detectable offense was extensively prosecuted. The number of prosecutions for this offense has declined only in proportion to the decrease in the peasant population.

Violent crime in Russia in the 19th century was disproportionately a rural phenomenon, a pattern of criminal behavior common to almost all preindustrialized societies. With the advent of industrialization and urbanization at the turn of the 20th century, the location of violent crime shifted in Russia, following the crime patterns observed earlier in England, France, and Germany during their industrial revolutions (Tobias 1967; Zehr 1976). Therefore, by the 1920s the Soviet rate of violent crime was higher in urban than in rural areas (Criminal Personality 1971, p. 114). With the continued exodus of young males from rural areas to the developing cities, there has been a further reduction in the level of rural violence. While violent crime is still more common in rural areas than crimes against personal property, the traditional rural propensity toward violent crime is not so marked.

Bootlegging is the only traditionally rural crime that continues on a mass scale. This offense, usually the domain of older women, has been the most common female offense since the pre-Revolutionary period (Gernet 1924, pp. 185-86). Women with limited financial resources, the result of low monthly salaries or even lower retirement pensions (sometimes as little as $30 a month), turn to this form of criminality as an easy means of increasing their income.

Urban criminality is characterized by violent offenses against property and persons. The property crimes of theft, *grabezh* (open stealing), and *razboi* (armed robbery) are overwhelmingly urban offenses. This is explained by the concentration of wealth in cities and the paucity of material possessions in the countryside. Violent crime is higher in the city even though firearms used for hunting are more readily available in the countryside. Crime is not evenly dispersed within Soviet cities. Recent studies have shown that it is concentrated in older areas of cities that traditionally have had high crime rates and in the new city regions that house workers who have recently moved in from the countryside.

A large proportion of youthful offenders come from the residential areas surrounding Soviet cities. The communities surrounding major cities, in contrast with the United States and Western Europe, are not the privileged retreats of the prosperous, but are the homes of young workers and their families who could not obtain permits to live in major cities. These workers, forced to commute long hours under unfavorable conditions to their schools and jobs, are a source of much urban criminality (Derviz 1971, p. 70).

OFFENDERS AND THEIR OFFENSES

The offense patterns of the Soviet Union are not noticeably different from those observed in societies that are not fully industrialized. The reason is that even though the western parts of Russia and the Baltic republics are quite developed, many of the other parts of the country have not acquired the social patterns associated with industrialization.

TABLE 9.1
Percentage Distribution of Convictions in the USSR, by Category of Offense, Circa 1960 and 1976

		1976	
Offense	Circa 1960	Number	Percent
Hooliganism	24.0	235,215	24.1
Crimes against the person	17.0	168,013	17.2
Crimes against the state and public property	17.0	156,451	16.0
Crimes against personal property	16.0	151,934	15.6
Vehicular crimes	5.0	97,388	10.0
Economic crimes	5.0	43,653	4.5
Crimes against the system of administration	4.0	38,445	3.9
Official crimes	4.0	37,669	3.9
Crimes against justice	1.5	13,892	1.4
Others	6.5	33,430	3.4
Total	100.0	976,090	100.0

Source: Gertsenzon and Authors' Collective 1968, pp. 118-19; Neznansky 1979, p. 211.

Important evidence on convictions for major crimes is shown in Table 9.1. The data come from a Soviet textbook of the late 1960s that gave the percentage distribution in about 1960 and a Soviet émigré who was able to supply the actual number of convictions for 1976. The distribution of offenses during this period remained remarkably constant, with the exception of vehicular crimes, whose proportional representation doubled.

The Soviet crime statistics reveal that a significant share of the crimes committed involve attacks against the person. As development of a nation proceeds, crimes against the person become relatively less frequent in comparison with crimes against property. For that reason, developed countries as a whole indicate that only 10 percent of the crimes committed are against the person, while in developing countries a comparable figure is 43 percent (United Nations 1977, pp. 12-14). The relatively constant Soviet figure of 17 percent places the Soviet Union in the intermediate stage between developing and developed countries.

The crime rate in the Soviet Union presently fluctuates among republics and even within republics. Regional variations are explained by ethnic differences, population composition, level of urbanization, and the extent of police surveillance.

From conversations with Soviet criminologists, it has been learned that in the Baltics republics, one of the most urbanized regions of the Soviet Union, the crime rate has risen dramatically since World War II. While the crime rate there exceeds that of the large cities, like Moscow and Leningrad, and the developing regions of the country, it is still considerably below the comparable American rate. However, the number of cases reported there, as in the United States, represents only a fraction of the total number of crimes committed.

In a Baltic city of 100,000, a survey of the population revealed that there were 10 crimes (including those unreported to police) against property and the person for every 100 residents. By comparison, American residents of a city of the same size would be victimized about twice as often. Similarly, the reported victimization rate for the total population of the Baltic republics is approximately half the rate reported for the United States (U.S. Department of Justice 1978).

Using selected crime rates and national data on the distribution of convictions by type of offense, Louise Shelley (1978) has estimated that Moscow has 442 convictions a year per 100,000 residents. For the Baltic city referred to above, the comparable figure is 500. The discrepancy between the conviction rates in the two cities may be even larger than is at first apparent, because the high degree of police surveillance in Moscow can be expected to result in a closer correspondence between the conviction rate and the crime rate.

The Moscow crime rate, while less than that of a small city in a highly urbanized region, seems to exceed that of most cities in an economically developing region like Georgia. A selection of seven Soviet Georgian police blotters for 1976 revealed a total of 471 crimes under investigation by the police (see Shelley 1979b). The 471 crimes cited in the blotters, while representing only a portion of the crimes known to the police, appear to be among the most serious cases under investigation. The most common offenses were economic (bribery, embezzlement, speculation) rather than the more usual crimes against property and the individual. These indicators of the amount and nature of Georgian criminality combine to suggest that though the actual commission rate for the Georgian Republic and its cities considerably exceeds the number of cases described in the blotter, it still has relatively less crime against the person and private property than do the more urbanized regions of the Soviet Union. It can, however, be expected that as Georgia becomes more urbanized, its crime rate will more closely resemble that of the presently more economically developed regions of the USSR.

Criminality in the USSR despite the unique conditions of Soviet society, does not differ significantly in terms of its rates or distribution from that observed in other countries. Similarly, the Soviet criminal population is also reminiscent of that found in other nations.

The following analysis of the personality of the Soviet offenders and the nature of their offenses is based on reports of 20 years of classified criminological and social-psychological research conducted in the USSR since the death of Stalin. While the political and economic structure of the USSR differ significantly from that of Western societies, the Soviet Union has failed to produce a criminal whose social and demographic characteristics are distinctly different. Though no age nor social group is devoid of criminality, the Soviet offenders, like their counterparts in the West, are typically young males of poor working-class background residing in a large town or city.

THE SEX OF OFFENDERS

Male and female offenders, in the Soviet Union as in both developing and developed countries, have strikingly different patterns of criminal behavior. Women commit only 12-18 percent of all offenses (Criminal Personality 1971, p. 57). Men participate more significantly in violent offenses and hooliganism (disorderly conduct) while the crimes of women are primarily property offenses. Only in homicide and embezzlement is there some convergence between the proportional contributions of male and female offenders.

In addition, while the criminality of men is concentrated in a small range of offenses that frequently involve the use of force, the criminality of women is more diversified. Though women commit a wide range of property offenses, their crimes are primarily those of opportunity and not of violence. The violent forms of property theft continue to be almost exclusively the domain of men; 98.4 percent of all open stealing and armed robbery offenses are committed by male assailants (Criminal Personality 1971, p. 93).

The large number of women in the Soviet labor force has provided them with the opportunity to committ job-related offenses. Approximately 50 percent of women in Soviet labor camps are reportedly there for crimes related to their work as salespersons. The large-scale employment of women in business enterprises has been associated with an increased number of women involved in the theft of state and public property. Although they constitute only 14–17 percent of persons convicted of crime, women are 36 percent of those convicted for the theft of state and public property (Criminal Personality 1971, p. 85). This is more than double the figure for the immediate post-Revolutionary period (Gernet 1931, p. 141).

SOCIAL CHARACTERISTICS OF OFFENDERS

Juvenile delinquents are the future criminal population, for most mature offenders have records as youthful offenders. Therefore, the higher the proportion of crimes committed by youthful offenders, the worse the prognosis for the future crime patterns of a country. In this light, one of the most alarming crime trends in the Soviet Union today is the increasing percentage of offenses committed by juvenile offenders. In private conversations with the author, a Soviet criminologist stated that persons under age 18 are responsible for more than half the crime in the highly urbanized Baltic region. Furthermore, it was suggested that these youthful offenders, almost evenly divided between males and females (a surprising development), are committing increasingly violent crimes, many of them senseless acts, as well as the usual property crimes.

The evidence regarding the social class and family background of Soviet criminals reveals a familiar picture. While the offenders in a few categories of crime, such as theft of socialist property, have comparatively better financial and social positions than the average Soviet citizen (Criminal Personality 1971, p. 89), most offenders have had a disadvantaged home life. Criminals in the USSR, as in many other societies, are frequently the product of broken homes, alcoholic parents, and family incomes below the Soviet-determined poverty level.

The average educational level of offenders lags behind that of the general population. Murderers, hooligans, and recidivists have an even lower level of educational attainment than the average Soviet offender. In the 1960s, 67.8 percent of murderers had only a seventh-grade education, while the comparable figure for the general population was 59.5 percent in 1959 (Criminal Personality 1971, pp. 65, 115).

Unemployment is not officially recognized in the Soviet Union, and all able-bodied adult males and unmarried females who are without jobs are defined as criminals under the parasite laws. Although peasants and members of the intelligentsia are sometimes convicted of crimes, the majority of Soviet offenders are workers and unemployed individuals. Unemployed offenders are most heavily represented in property offenses; 20 to 30 percent of all property convictions involve unemployed individuals (Criminal Personality 1971, p. 100). Most of the offenders, however, are workers of limited skill level and frequently hold jobs that rely on physical strength rather than specialized training.

PATTERNS OF CRIME COMMISSION

Criminals rarely operate in organized gangs, yet in the period from 1963 to 1968, between 21 and 28 percent of all crimes were committed by groups (Criminal Personality 1971, p. 83). Fraud, embezzlement, and other financial manipulations involving large amounts of state capital are more frequently committed by groups than offenses involving small amounts of money. Violent crimes against property are almost always committed by more than one offender, while this is the case in less than one-fifth of all thefts of personal property. Crimes against the person often take this form. For example, one quarter of all homicides are perpetrated by more than one assailant.

Russia and the Soviet Union have consistently had a higher rate of group rape than Western societies. Recent data indicate that between 28 and 37 percent of all rapes are committed by multiple assailants, and this is down from a figure of over 50 percent for the pre-Revolutionary period (Criminal Personality 1971, p. 84). At present rape is an increasing problem among juvenile offenders (Criminal Personality 1971, pp. 122-23).

Alcoholism, a very serious and possibly growing problem in the Soviet Union today, is directly related to criminal behavior. Alcohol use is particularly associated with hooliganism and the commission of violent crimes against the person (murder, rape, and assault). Intoxication is also highly correlated with arrest for crimes against property (Connor 1972, p. 46). In Moscow, half of the offenders recently convicted of property offenses and 70 percent of those convicted of homicide committed their crimes while drunk (Kuznetsova 1971, p. 29). Other regions of the USSR show even higher correlations between drunkenness and criminality (Connor 1972, pp. 47-48).

POLITICAL CRIME

The analysis of offenders and their offenses does not apply to the category of political crimes (state crimes) as they are defined under the Soviet legal codes. Soviet authorities claim that there is no political criminality in the USSR, and there is no particular criminal code concerned with this form of behavior. Instead, crimes against the state and the system of administration are subsumed under the standard criminal code, and encompass such acts as anti-Soviet agitation and propaganda, attempts to exit illegally from the Soviet Union, libel and slander against the Soviet state, and insulting representatives of Soviet authority. These crimes are not only separated in the criminal code from other acts of illegal behavior, but they are also treated differently by the judiciary. Political defendants require special defense attorneys, and courtrooms are often closed during these proceedings.

Political crimes represent only a small fraction of total Soviet offenses. An analysis of Soviet crime statistics in the late 1960s revealed that less than 10 percent of all offenses committed could possibly be classified as political (Ostroumov 1970, p. 248). Part of the reason that political cases are so rare may be that this category of offender is harshly treated by the Soviet justice system. Acquittals in political cases are almost unknown, and offenders are often sentenced to lengthy terms of imprisonment or exile.

The absence of Soviet research makes it difficult to construct a picture of the typical political offender. The celebrated political defendants have primarily been educated individuals, often from distinguished families. However, as these political dissenters have pointed out, they are not representative of the entire criminal population tried under the political articles of the criminal code. Their writings on their experiences in labor camps reveal that many of their fellow inmates in special prisons for political criminals were simple workers who naively told anti-Soviet anecdotes in public or attempted to cross the Soviet border without permission (Marchenko 1969; Bukovsky 1978).

It is this group of political offenders and the Soviet response to their behavior that most clearly distinguishes the Soviet crime problem from that of Western Europe and the United States. While the United States has draft resisters and civil rights protesters, their behavior is never viewed as such a threat that the government will resort to serious violations of its usual criminal procedure to insure convictions in all cases brought to trial.

RECIDIVISM

The problem of recidivism has engendered much debate in the Soviet Union (see Solomon 1978, ch. 7). In the United States, recidivism is extremely difficult to gauge because of the multiplicity of jurisdictions in which a criminal may be convicted and incarcerated, and because of the high and uncontrolled mobility of the population. In the USSR, with one's place of residence—including a prison or camp—always recorded on one's internal passport, and with a unified criminal justice system, it is much easier to get reliable data on recidivism of criminals. Thus, while recidivism rates for the United States range from 30 to 70 percent, depending on the particular study, for the Soviet Union the proportion of recidivists among the population of convicted offenders is about 30-35 percent. (Since the 1950s the Soviet recidivism rate has been standardized to reflect the proportion of the criminal population that has incurred new criminal penalties within three years of the last conviction.) Among Soviet property offenders, the recidivism rate has consistently remained at 33 percent. Although these rates of recidivism are not necessarily high relative to those elsewhere, they are a disappointment in light of the intense efforts to reduce the level of Soviet crime.

Soviet men are more frequently recidivists than women. In 1963-67, only 5.7 percent of the women in labor camps were returnees to institutional confinement, while the corresponding figure for men was 30-50 percent (Criminal Personality 1971, p. 59). (While women consistently receive milder punishments than men, this disparity in sentencing does not account for all the variation observed in the percentage of males and females incarcerated.)

Soviet recidivism patterns for murder (see Table 9.2) are unusual when compared with those of other societies. In most societies, homicide has one of the lowest rates of recidivism of any offense. It could be expected that the recidivism rate for murder would have declined with the elimination of the Soviet criminal underworld and its professional "hit men" (see Chalidze 1977), but instead it has nearly tripled since the immediate post-Revolutionary period. The lengthy sentences imposed for homicide—up to 15 years of institutional confinement—make it possible to repeat murder only after long periods of incarceration. Why there is such a recidivism pattern for murderers, then, requires additional investigation.

TABLE 9.2
Rates of Recidivism for Murderers and Rapists, 1926-66

		Recidivism Rate	
Source	Year	Murderers	Rapists
Survey of convicts	1926	12.8	—
Analysis of sex crime in RSFSR	1920's	—	6.0 to 9.1
Figures from 1 oblast, RSFSR	1954-57	39.3	36.7
Material from 4 oblasts, RSFSR	1953-59	36.8	—
Research among inmates	1958-60	34.2	—
Research of All-Union Criminalistics	1957		23.3
Research institutes in various republics	1960	36.5	
Controlled research of 3 oblasts in RSFSR	1963	40.0	
Research statistics of various republics	1964	30.2	25.2
Research statistics of 15 oblasts, RSFSR	1966	—	22.4

Note: The exact basis for figuring the recidivism rates varies, but beginning with the studies of the 1950s, it has been standardized to indicate the percentage of convicted offenders who had another conviction within the three years prior to the offense for which the criminal penalty is currently being served.

Source: Criminal Personality 1971, p. 124.

An increase in the rate of recidivism for rapists is also observed during the Soviet period. The four most recent studies cited in Table 9.2 demonstrate that recidivism among rapists has approximately tripled since the 1920s. This phenomenon has occurred despite harsh sentences and the heightened police controls for such crimes.

CONCLUSION

Crime and delinquency are not major threats to social order in the Soviet Union. The Soviet Union is not, however, eliminating its crime problem, as its ideology predicts. Instead, it is facing an increasing problem from its juvenile offenders and its youthful migrants and recidivists located in remote, urbanizing regions of the country.

Soviet authorities have developed a sophisticated set of theories to explain the persistence of illegal behavior long after its scheduled disappearance. These theories attempt to explain crime causation in terms of vestiges of the past and pernicious Western influences, both forces beyond the control of the Soviet state. These explanations are inherently flawed because many of the causative factors described as vestiges are direct results of Soviet policies, and the influence of bourgeois vestiges on Soviet society is not convincing as an explanation of crime so long after the Revolution of 1917.

Regardless of the means by which Soviet criminologists attempt to explain the endurance of crime within their society, they must contend with a situation that is partly of their own creation. Not only have Soviet laws created new categories of criminals, such as speculators and parasites, but they have also produced a distinctive geography of criminality. The unique distribution of Soviet criminality that has resulted in the relocation of crime from major urban centers and rural areas to the developing cities of the Far East and Far North is a direct consequence of Soviet police and demographic policies. This dispersion of criminality, while eliminating some of the tensions of urban life in major cities, has made regions in desperate need of increased manpower increasingly undesirable places to live.

The Soviet system is ideologically committed to fostering the development of the "new Soviet person," and the criminal justice system is viewed as a fundamental institution for achieving this end through its capacity to educate and coerce. But not all citizens yet (or probably ever will) conform to this model of the "new Soviet person" and crime persists. While the methods of control used in the Soviet Union have reduced crime in some regions, they have failed to confirm the Marxist prediction that "crime will wither away under socialism." Indeed, the evidence presented here supports Durkheim's view of the normalcy of crime, its inevitability within society.

REFERENCES

Babaev, M. M. 1968. "Kriminologicheskie issledovaniia problem migratsiia naseleniia." *Sovetskoe gosudarstvo i pravo* 3:86-89.
_____. 1974. "Demograficheskie protsessy i problemy territorial'nykh razlichii prestupnosti." *Voprosy bor'by s prestupnost'iu* 21:9
Bukovsky, Vladimir. 1978. *To Build a Castle,* London: Andre Deutsch.
Chalidze, Valery. 1977. *Criminal Russia.* New York: Random House.
Cloward, R. A., and L. E. Ohlin. 1960. *Delinquency and Opportunity.* Glencoe, Ill.: Free Press.
Connor, Walter D. 1972. *Deviance in Soviet Society: Crime, Delinquency and Alcoholism.* New York: Columbia University Press.
Criminal Personality. 1971. *Lichnost' prestupnika.* Moscow.
Deriviz, O. V. 1971. "Rabota ili ucheba vne mesta postoiannovo zhitel'stva—odin iz faktorov prestupnosti nesovershennoletnikh." *Prestupnost' i ee preduprezhdenie.* Leningrad.
Erikson, Kai T. 1962. "Notes on the Sociology of Deviance." *Social Problems* 9 (Spring): 307-14.
Gernet, M. N. 1924. *Prestupnyi mir Moskvy.* Moscow.
_____. 1931. *Prestupnost' za granitsei i v SSSR.* Moscow: Sovetskoe zakono datel'stvo.
Gertsenzon, A. A. 1960. "The Community's Role in the Prevention and Study of Crime." *Soviet Review* 2, no. 1: 14-27.
Gertsenzon, A. A., and Authors' Collective. 1968. *Kriminologiia.* Moscow: Iuridicheskaia literatura.
Gordon, David M. 1973. "Capitalism, Class and Crime in America." *Crime and Delinquency* 19 (Apr.): 163-86.
Juviler, Peter H. 1976. *Revolutionary Law and Order.* New York: Free Press.
Karpets, I. I. 1966. "On the Nature and Cause of Crime in the USSR." *Soviet Law and Government* 5 (Summer): 52-60.
Kuznetsova, N. F., ed. 1971. *Sravnitel'noe kriminologicheskoe issledovanie prestupnosti v Moskve v 1923 i 1968-69 gg.* Moscow: Izdatel'stvo Moskovskogo universiteta.
Marchenko, A. 1969. *My Testimony* Oxford: Pall Mall Press.
Marcuse, Herbert. 1961. *Soviet Marxism.* New York: Vintage Books.
Merton, Robert K. 1967. *Social Theory and Social Structure.* Rev. ed. New York: Free Press.
Neznansky, Fridrikh. 1979. "New Information on Soviet Criminal Statistics." *Soviet Union* 6, no. 2: 208-11.
Ostroumov, S. S. 1970. *Sovetskaia sudebnaia statistika.* Moscow: Izdatel'stvo Moskovskogo universiteta.
Sellin, Thorsten. 1971 "Conflicting Norms." In *The Criminal in Society*, edited by L. Radzinowicz and M. E. Wolfgang, pp 395-99. New York: Basic Books.
Shelley, Louise. 1978. "Crime in Moscow in 1923 and 1968-69." Paper presented at the International Criminological Symposium, Stockholm.
_____. 1979a. "Soviet Criminology After the Revolution." *Journal of Criminal Law and Criminology* 70 (Fall):391-96.
_____. 1979b. "Criminality in Soviet Georgia in 1976." *Papers on Soviet Law* 3 (Fall): (in press).
Solomon, Peter H., Jr. 1974. "Soviet Criminology: Its Demise and Rebirth." *Soviet Union* 1, no. 2:122-40.
_____. 1978. *Soviet Criminologists and Criminal Policy.* New York: Columbia University Press.
Spitzer, Steven. 1975. "Toward a Marxian Theory of Deviance." *Social Problems* 22, no. 5: 638-51.
Sutherland, E. H., and D. R. Cressey. 1955. *Principles of Criminology.* 5th ed. New York: Lippincott.
Tobias, J. J. 1967. *Crime and Industrial Society in the 19th Century.* New York: Schocken Books.

United Nations. 1977. *Crime Prevention and Control.* Report of the Secretary-General. New York: United Nations.

U.S. Department of Justice. 1978. *Sourcebook of Criminal Justice Statistics 1977.* Washington, D.C.: U.S. Department of Justice.

Zehr, Howard. 1976. *Crime and Development of Modern Society: Patterns of Criminality in 19th Century Germany and France.* Totowa, N.J.: Rowman and Littlefield.

10

THE PLACE OF WOMEN
Michael Paul Sacks

The term "culture" can be defined as a "community of communications, consisting of socially stereotyped patterns of behavior, including habits of language and thought" (Deutsch 1966, p. 37). Individuals immersed within a culture tend to confuse what is prevalent with what is possible. This is what Peter Berger and Thomas Luckman have called the "reification of social reality":

> Reification is the apprehension of human phenomena as if they were things, that is, in non-human or possibly suprahuman terms. Another way of saying this is that reification is the apprehension of the products of human activity *as if* they were something else than human products—such as facts of nature, results of cosmic laws or manifestations of divine will (1966, pp. 88–89).

The distinct boundaries of male and female behavior are a central facet of any culture. Yet the recent resurgence of the women's movement in the United States (now evident on an international scale) shows the growing recognition that these boundaries have limited rather than defined human potential.

The change in women's work role in the United States since 1940 has bolstered attempts to rewrite cultural scripts. At the turn of the century the highest proportion of women working—about one out of three—was in the age group 20 to 24. Marriage and family responsibilities were viewed as incompatible with female employment. Just prior to World War II, 45 percent of young women had jobs, but the pattern of sharp decline in older age groups persisted. By 1950, however, it was clear that married women were entering the work force in growing numbers. In 1960, well before the women's movement emerged as a significant force in the United States, the proportion employed was still high among young women but reached a second and even higher peak (47.4 percent) among women who had completed their child rearing—that is, those aged 45 to 49. Today, with nearly half of all married women bringing home a paycheck, the presence of even very young children does not prevent women from combining employment with domestic chores: more than one-third of women with children under age three are working (Oppenheimer 1970, pp. 3-8; Hayghe 1978, p. 53).

Appreciating this change in the United States is essential, but when it is examined in a comparative perspective, it can provide a far more stringent palliative to "reification." The Soviet Union (USSR) is striking in this regard. Except in urban areas during the 1920s and early 1930s, the working-age woman engaged solely in housework has been a rarity. Today nine out of ten women aged 20 to 49 are employed—a figure higher than any other industrialized nation (Sacks 1977, p. 199). Whereas in the United States nearly one in three women works part-time, this is true of 0.5 percent of Soviet women.

This essay shows that there are also important similarities in the roles of women in the United States and the USSR. However, the primary objective is not to juxtapose the cultures, but to explore the extent to which change and continuity in the work done by women in the course of industrialization is due to conceptions of behavior deemed appropriate for females as opposed to the economy and constraints within the family that shape the obligations and opportunities of women. In essence, what is considered is an issue fundamental to the social sciences: the impact and interrelationship between ideas and material conditions. Finally, the essay stresses the way in which the process of change varies among regions within the Soviet Union due to the historical context within which the early stages of economic development take place.

THEORETICAL PERSPECTIVES

William J. Goode (1963) contends that female employment outside the home is a product of a change in values that is associated with industrialization. In their hiring practices employers come to place less emphasis on gender and greater stress on ability to perform work tasks. He argues that the egalitarianism is also manifested in the family. Rights and responsibilities previously allocated according to sex and age become increasingly based on "the uniqueness of each individual . . . the 'human' qualities of warmth, emotionality, character and so on . . ." (1963, p. 21).

Marxist writings also stress the close association between female employment and progress toward sexual equality. However, it is the change in work activity of women that is the critical factor, and the diffusion of altered values is viewed as result rather than a cause of employment. In *The Development of Capitalism in Russia*, Lenin (1964, pp. 545-46) states that large-scale industry draws women into the work force and out of the stifling isolation of their patriarchal households. It "stimulates their development and increases their independence" despite the harsh work conditions that prevail under capitalism. In considering the tasks to be achieved after the 1917 Revolution, Lenin later wrote: "As long as women are engaged in housework, their position is still a restricted one. In order to achieve the complete emancipation of women and to make them really equal with men, we must have social economy, and the participation of women in general productive labor" (*The Woman Question* 1951, p. 52).

A third position, one that I argue is best supported by evidence pertaining to Soviet women, is that of Louise A. Tilly and Joan W. Scott (1975, 1978). They contend that historical developments in England and France refute both Goode and the Marxists. The early employment of women neither resulted immediately in women's liberation nor derived from what Goode called the "gradual, logical, philosophical extension to women of originally Protestant notions about the rights and responsibilities of the individual" (Goode 1963, p. 56). To the contrary, women's early employment in factories involved work that was directly related to their traditional domestic activities and was at least initially marked by continuity in women's status. Women's work was "less the product of new ideas than of the effects of old ideas operating in new or changing contexts" (Tilly and Scott 1975, p. 42). The survival of the household depended upon economic contributions from every member, and the demand for female labor in industry made it possible for women to fulfill traditional obligations in a novel work setting. This was merely an extension of the common pattern in which mothers combined bearing and raising children with production for family consumption or for exchange, while both daughters and sons made an economic contribution from a very early age and, depending on the family's needs, would later either work at home or "be sent off to seek jobs as servants and apprentices" (Tilly and Scott 1978, p. 34).

Tilly and Scott (1978, pp. 230-31) concede that values did change, but only gradually; and this appears to be associated with developments that reduced women's productive activities. By separating the household from the place of work, industrialization increased the difficulty of combining motherhood and wage labor. Married women's employment declined further as a consequence of a sex-based division of labor, which limited the types of work available to women; the rise in male wages, which reduced the necessity for women to work; and the "new emphasis on the needs of children," which increased women's domestic responsibilities.

The distinct employment pattern of Soviet women can to an important extent be explained by a difference in the timing and presence of these factors.

The values that emerged, however, appear to be surprisingly similar to those of other industrialized nations. Tracing the change in the supply of and demand for female labor in the nonagrarian sector reveals the unique aspects of Soviet development.

THE CASE OF SOVIET RUSSIA

Comprising three-quarters of the territory and over half the population of the USSR, the Russian Republic is by far the largest of the 15 republics and contains the most important centers of political and economic activity. I focus initially on this area, for it is here that one would expect the most direct impact of the Communist ideology, the drive for industrialization, and the devastation and rapid recovery from World War II. (In some cases, however, the absence of data for the Russian Republic has necessitated substituting figures for the USSR as a whole. This does not appreciably distort the general picture.)

Employment in Tsarist Russia

Women had worked in tsarist factories since at least the 18th century, though they primarily earned wages as agrarian laborers, servants, and charwomen (Kharchev 1964, p. 18). The 1897 census revealed that in European Russia nearly 40 percent of adult female industrial workers were married (Troinitskii 1906, Table 2, pp. 2-6). They constituted about a fifth of all workers in industry but were heavily concentrated in textile and clothing manufacturing. Because women were less active in politics and accepted lower wages than men, it was not surprising that they were hired in growing numbers in the 1890s and became even more desirable employees after the Revolution of 1905 (Glickman 1977). The substantial increase in the demand for women during World War I resulted in their being represented in nearly every type of industry. By 1917 women constituted about 40 percent of factory workers (Sacks 1976, pp. 25-26).

Thus, the Soviet era began with a well-established heritage of female employment in the nonagrarian sector. As shown below, the rise in male wages and the restrictive sex-typing of occupations—factors that reduced the proportion of women combining work and family responsibilities in Western Europe—were lacking or of a very different nature in the Soviet Union. The type of work done by Soviet women changed substantially, but the proportion of women working showed only a slight and temporary decline in the course of economic development, and the prospects are that this will change little in the foreseeable future.

Female Labor: Supply and Demand

The shift of women from agriculture to employment in the urban industrial economy can best be appreciated in terms of a supply-and-demand model. This directly parallels the analysis of the U.S. labor force by Valerie K. Oppenheimer (1970), and the contrast with her findings is enlightening. The sharp rise in female employment in the United States between 1940 and 1960 was the result of a surge in the demand for workers in the clerical and service sector, much of which was labeled as appropriate only for females. Unable to substitute male labor and facing a declining pool of young women (due to a lower age at marriage and a longer period of schooling) employers were forced to hire older and married women in growing numbers.

The demand for labor in the Soviet Union was far more extreme and more general. Thus, it contributed to the employment of women in a much broader range of occupations. Furthermore, some of the same dire conditions that fostered this demand also produced a massive supply of women seeking work in the nonagrarian sector. Except perhaps during World War II, there were no comparable factors influencing the supply of American women.

In 1910 the population within the territory of what is now Soviet Russia was approximately equal to that of the United States, but in the next half-century the two had dramatically different patterns of mortality. By 1970 the United States contained 205 million people, compared with only 130 million in Soviet Russia. According to estimates for the USSR as a whole, the population declined by 2.8 million each year during the Revolution and the Civil War (1917-21). During the forced collectivization of agriculture (1929-35), about 5.5 million perished. Political purges and widespread famine in these decades also took a heavy toll, but even these tragedies were dwarfed by the population loss of 20-25 million during World War II (Dodge 1966, p. 20; Matthews 1972, ch. 1).

During the early 1920s the heavy migration to cities and the disruption of the economy resulted in widespread unemployment. Fears were expressed that women, especially, would suffer under the planned stress on heavy industry, where traditionally few females were employed. Norton Dodge (1966, pp. 175-76) argues that during this period "agitation for an increase in the employment of women was motivated by a desire to relieve unemployment and to secure the economic independence of women rather than to mobilize unused manpower reserves" for production purposes. However, the rapid industrial growth of the late 1920s and early 1930s created a major labor shortage. Housewives in the city, unlike migrant families from rural areas, constituted a source of workers that would not further aggravate the problems of providing food and housing. Thus, it is surely the fit between the ideology relating women's work to their liberation and the needs of the economy that fostered even greater efforts to provide occupational opportunities to women.

Between 1932 and 1937 industry expanded by over 4 million workers; 82 percent were women. In the decades that followed, the priority placed on rapid economic development, plus the population decimation of World War II, assured that the demand for female labor would never again slacken. Moreover, the use of female labor would itself fuel industrial growth, for it made possible the heavy allocation of production to investment rather than consumption. Not only were there more workers per urban family, but employed women served their nation doubly by also providing household services that, if supplied by the market, might have diverted considerable investment from other sectors of the economy (compare Ofer 1973, ch. 9).

The heavy investment in education (see essay by Dobson in this volume) greatly benefited women and assured that they would be qualified for the emerging positions in the economy. In 1897, 85 percent of the women were illiterate, compared to 56 percent of the men. By 1939 the gap between males and females in the employed population was already small and was further reduced as achievement levels rose rapidly (see Table 10.1). The increased attendance at school and the expanding readership of the press also must have provided the state with improved channels for influencing women's choice of employment.

TABLE 10.1
Employed Persons in the Russian Republic with a Higher and with a Secondary Education, by Sex: 1939, 1959, 1970 (per 1,000 persons)

	Higher Education		Secondary, Complete and Incomplete	
	Males	*Females*	*Males*	*Females*
1939	16	10	119	99
1959	36	35	392	417
1970	68	65	578	602

Source: Ts.S.U. RSFSR, 1971, p. 25.

The supply of females was most strongly influenced by the very demographic conditions that had resulted in the labor shortage, for the fatalities of war and political conflicts were far greater among males than females. Enormous numbers of women were left to support their families. There were several decades during which countless others lived with the prospect that such a situation could easily befall them. In Soviet Russia as early as 1926, the sex ratio (the number of males per 100 females) was 91. In 1959 this was ten points lower, and in the group aged 35 to 59 there were only six men to every ten women (Ts.S.U. 1930, Table 1, p. 3; 1972a, p. 5).

But even if a male wage earner were present in the household, economic necessity required that women work outside the home. A husband's salary was simply insufficient to support a family, and this remains the norm today. When questioned about their motives for working, Soviet women are quick to note their financial need (Mikhailyuk 1970, p. 4; Kharchev and Golod 1969, p. 448; Slesarev and Yankova 1969, p. 421).

With a pace of urbanization that "has probably been the most rapid in the history of mankind" (Lewis and Rowland 1979, p. 158), females had increasingly to pursue wage labor outside of agriculture. The forced collectivization launched in 1928-29 provoked substantial out-migration from rural areas; the perception of growing employment opportunities in cities was a persisting attraction. Between 1926 and 1939 the urban population of Soviet Russia had more than doubled and nearly doubled again by 1959. The proportion of the population that was urban burgeoned from 18 to 52 percent in just over three decades. Presently the figure is 60 percent (Ts.S.U. 1963, p. 11; *Vestnik statistiki* 1979, p. 69). Furthermore, the urban population became more concentrated in large cities, where work in agriculture was surely very limited. Thus, the number of Soviet Russian workers in agriculture (excluding those engaged in work on private plots of land [see the essay by Roy Laird and Ronald Francisco in this volume]) dropped from 46 million in 1926 to 20 million in 1939 and only 14 million by 1959 (Ts.S.U. 1963, pp. 39, 280, 290; 1972a, p. 77).

Child care and domestic responsibilities make employment especially difficult for women unless there are other family members to share these chores or unless they can be reduced through a network of service institutions. In 1919, Lenin wrote:

> Notwithstanding all the liberating laws that have been passed, woman continues to be a *domestic slave*, because *petty housework* crushes, strangles, stultifies and degrades her, chains her to the kitchen and to the nursery, wastes her labor on barbarously unproductive, petty, nerve-racking, stultifying and crushing drudgery. The *real emancipation of women* . . . will begin only when . . . this petty domestic economy . . . is transformed on a mass scale into large-scale socialist economy (The Woman Question 1951, p. 6; emphasis in the original).

Except, perhaps, since about the mid-1960s, it is clear that such change did not occur. The increase in the supply of women seeking nonagrarian employment cannot be attributed to a decline in housework. Severely overcrowded urban apartments have lacked hot water, and as late as 1956 only one-third had any form of plumbing. Modern appliances have been in short supply and of poor quality. There are endless complaints about cafeterias and the whole range of service institutions. In 1970 it was reported that laundries handled only 3 percent of the nation's requirements and that the combination of all the service institutions reduced the time spent on housework by a mere 5 percent. Child-care facilities have never met the demand; in 1960 only 13 percent of the children aged one through six could be accommodated in preschool institutions (Sacks 1976, pp. 43-53). Bernice Madison (1977, p. 322) notes that even today the facilities are sufficiently limited to encourage "women to take additional unpaid maternity leave despite the loss of earnings and job opportunities involved."

Soviet men, like their counterparts the world over, devote little time to housework. A comparison of studies of time use from the 1920s and the 1960s shows no change in this highly unequal division of domestic labor (Sacks 1977a). Furthermore, while there is evidence that the extended family has been uncommon among workers during the entire Soviet period, it is clear that in recent decades married women have received very little help from their mothers. Young couples prefer to live apart from their parents, and this is confirmed by census data (Sacks 1976, p. 41).

The number of children that women bear has declined, but this has been accompanied by a sharp reduction in infant deaths. The result is that there has not been a substantial change in the number of children who survive in each family (Mazur 1967). However, since women can now have the children they desire over a far shorter period, it is unlikely that there is a child old enough to care for young siblings. Furthermore, the urban nuclear family is relatively isolated, making it difficult to share child care with other women or to combine such tasks with productive labor, as mothers might do in a rural setting.

In sum, women had to combine arduous family responsibilities with nonagrarian employment. There was a change in the type of work women did, not in the fact that they were engaged in productive labor. Utilizing women in industry and even substituting them for men in a wide variety of occupations when there was a labor shortage was not a cultural innovation of the Soviet era. It was, therefore, predictable that with the difficult financial conditions—a product of low male income levels and broken or vulnerable households—plus the acute demand for all types of workers, women responded by seeking to take advantage of expanding occupational opportunities. The national investment in education enhanced their employment prospects and facilitated the spread of an ideology supportive of women working outside the family. Work was portrayed not only as a means of contributing to national strength, but also as a source of personal development and even as a prerequisite for a woman to be an appropriate role model for her children (Danilova 1968, pp. 38-40). A Soviet commentator remarked, "In families in which women do not work, the youngsters are inculcated with a scornful attitude toward women and their work" (Labzin 1965, p. 102).

This work ideology fit well not only with women's traditional obligations to contribute to the household but also with the new demands upon the family and the leadership's goal of rapid economic development. As such, the ideology has come to be widely accepted. But it is not possible to determine the extent to which adherence to such beliefs had an influence on women's seeking employment independent of the other factors compelling them to alter their behavior.

The 1926 census shows that among those aged 16 to 54, nearly 90 percent of women were working, but in cities this fell off to only 40 percent (Gruzdeva 1978). Work rates of these urban women appear to have risen steadily with the onset of the First Five-Year Plan in 1928 (Dodge 1966, p. 33). Subsequently the only decline in employment occurred among those aged 14 to 19—a result of increased school attendance—and among women in their fifties due to retirement.

The birth rate dropped quite steadily during the Soviet period, with no appreciable baby boom following World War II. This meant that the surge of labor force entrants in the 1960s and early 1970s seen in the United States and Western Europe was absent in the USSR. Consequently, there were increased efforts to recruit the remaining pool of young women who were engaged solely in homemaking and tending private gardens, and to raise the work rates of older women. Qualification for increased pensions provided the incentive for the latter to return to work. Since this reserve of labor consisted of many with low education and limited work skills who would receive low wages, the rise in the minimum wage also proved effective as an incentive. Day-care centers expanded and could accommodate a fifth of preschoolers by 1965 and nearly a third by the early 1970s (Sacks 1976, p. 43).

A full two-thirds of those recruited to the Soviet work force between 1961 and 1970 were formerly housewives or engaged only in private agriculture. Work rates reached such a high level that future entrants could come only from among the youth (Litvyakov 1969, pp. 106-07, 192-93). In the 1970s such conditions promoted experiments with part-time work and even cottage industry (Feshbach and Rapawy 1973, p. 494; Radko 1979) in an effort to maintain the high work-force participation of women and also to increase the birth rate. Small birth cohorts in the past assure little slackening in the demand for female labor.

THE CONSEQUENCES OF NONAGRARIAN EMPLOYMENT

Just before World War II, nearly two-thirds of female workers in Soviet Russia were engaged in agriculture (including the private sector). By 1959 this had fallen to 40 percent, and by 1970 was only 17 percent (Ts.S.U. 1963, pp. 156, 286; 1973b, p. 165; 1973c, p. 171). How did the combination of high labor-force participation rates and rapid shift out of agriculture influence the relative status of men and women both at work and in the family?

The double burden of the working woman has already been mentioned: full-time employment is combined with many hours of housework and child care, and this appears unaltered over the Soviet era. (Such continuity in the face of technological advancement is consistent with an extensive cross-national study conducted in 1965 [Robinson et al. 1973] and time-budget data for the United States over the period from the 1930s to the 1960s [Vanek 1973]). A working woman's career is deeply affected by the heavy demands of her domestic obligations. She has less time to devote to study and other activities that could promote her occupational advancement. Indeed, her total work burden adversely affects the general quality of her life by reducing recreation and even sleep, relative to men. In urban areas Soviet men have about as much free time as women have housework (Sacks 1977). Men benefit directly from the domestic division of labor:

> By freeing males from the performance of routine household maintenance and child care, which would otherwise divert time and energy from educational and professional activities, Soviet women in effect advance the professional mobility of males at the sacrifice of their own (Lapidus 1978, p. 278).

A second indicator of sexual inequality is the disparity in the paychecks of men and women. This results in part from the fact that women are concentrated in sectors of the labor force where the wages are low. However, in a sophisticated secondary analysis of Soviet data from the capital city of the Armenian Republic, Michael Swafford (1978) concludes that even if there were no differences between men and women in their educational background, their level of skill, and the industries in which they were employed, women would still earn only about 72 percent as much as men. While there are problems with this analysis and with generalizing the results to the USSR as a whole, the finding is consistent with a number of studies indicating the female earnings are between two-thirds and three-quarters those of men (Chapman 1977; Lapidus 1978, pp. 192-94). Again, the finding is hardly unique to the USSR: Women in the United States who work full-time earn about 60 percent as much as men—a figure that has remained unchanged since the 1970s. Among professionals the figure rises to only 70 percent (Norwood and Waldman 1979, p. 7; compare Suter and Miller 1973).

Differences in earnings are a reflection of the vertical structure of occupations: the higher the prestige and authority of the position, the smaller the percentage of women among the personnel. This appears to be true in virtually every field. Textile manufacturing is a particularly vivid example, for it is an industry long dominated by women. In Soviet Russia in 1959, women constituted 85 percent of textile workers, but they accounted for a mere 15 percent of the assistant foremen. While the category was omitted from the 1970 census publications, we can assume that time alone will not alter this inequity.

Female underrepresentation is particularly blatant in the professional occupations, for it is here that there is greater detail in the published census categories (Sacks, forthcoming A). Women constitute 90 percent of persons in the field of medicine; this falls to about 60 percent of chief doctors and heads of hospitals. While women predominate in education, they account for only a quarter of the directors of secondary schools. Fewer than one in ten enterprise directors are female (Dodge 1977). At the upper levels of the state and party, women are even more scarce (Moses 1978, p. 15; Lapidus 1978, ch. 6).

The bottom of the status hierarchy also reveals important sex differences. A recent study of machine-construction workers aged 25-29 showed that the least skilled work categories contained 70 percent of the women, as compared with only 17 percent of the men (Kotlyar and Turchaninova 1975, p. 73). Other evidence reveals that in many industries, women constitute the great majority of workers performing tedious and physically demanding unmechanized tasks (Mikhailyuk 1970, p. 66), and that a woman spends three times as long as a man in the lowest job categories before she receives a promotion (Shteiner and Karpukhin 1978, p. 8). In the Soviet census the number of women among manual workers lacking any specialized skill (*raznorabochie*) is conspicuously omitted (Sacks, forthcoming A).

It is possible to summarize the overall extent to which women are under- and overrepresented in a series of occupations by using a commonly applied measure of segregation. This may be interpreted as the proportion of men or women who would have to change occupations in order for women to have the same representation in all occupations. It is similar to measures of racial segregation that show the proportion of pupils who would have to be bussed to integrate a school system. (Because we are interested in comparisons over time and between regions, a standardized measure is used. This controls for variation in the structure of the total labor force. The procedure entails assuming simply that there is the same number of workers in each of the nearly 100 nonagrarian occupational categories for which appropriate data were available in the Soviet census (Sacks 1976, pp. 79-87). Unfortunately, because of differing occupational classifications, the measure cannot be used to compare the Soviet Union with other nations.)

The finding for Soviet Russia over the period for which we have comparable data—1939 through 1970—is quite surprising. Despite the societal disruption engendered by World War II, the pace of industrialization, and women's gains in educational achievement, there was no change in the overall extent to which occupations were either male- or female-dominated. Neither the extreme demand for women nor their increasing skills had altered the sex labeling of occupations. Thus, for example, females continued to predominate among food, garment, postal, textile, and public dining workers, as well as among doctors, typists, telephone operators, secretaries, and teachers. Males remained well over the majority of those in the field of law, among composers, painters, radio-telegraphers, plumbers, woodworkers, those in transportation, machine construction, and metallurgy. There were many small changes in female representation that tended to cancel out each other.

Comparable research has been done on the work force in the United States. This suggests that while change is slow and even absent in some decades of the 20th century, World War II appears definitely to have reduced occupational sex differences (Williams 1976). Though it may be that change is better detected because of the much more detailed occupational categories available in the U.S. census, I will return to this unexpected finding for Soviet Russia and consider the conditions that might have produced it.

The meaning of this trend in overall sex differences must be interpreted with caution. While different has often meant unequal, this is not always the case. The greater access of Soviet women to professional employment is an important example. Census data show that while the percentage of females in the total work force of Soviet Russia rose by five points (from 49 to 54) between 1939 and 1959, the percentage point increase among professional and semiprofessional personnel was four times as great (from 34 to 54). The number of women in these occupations grew by over 3.5 million, while the number of men actually declined by 300,000. Women's rapidly rising educational attainment—a significant achievement in itself—was of fundamental importance in opening opportunities to them. Between 1959 and 1970, despite the more balanced sex ratio, women continued to enter professional and semiprofessional occupations in disproportionate numbers: They constituted nearly three-quarters of the additional personnel (Sacks 1976). In 1970 women constituted a larger proportion of those in the semiprofessional categories, yet they still were more than half of all professionals (Dodge 1977, p. 208).

Although the number of women is relatively low in the higher professional ranks, they remain far better represented than their counterparts in Western Europe or the United States. Consider, for example, the fact that in the Russian Republic women account for about 40 percent of the engineers, more than 25 percent of both the judges and the neurosurgeons, over 50 percent of the specialists working in research institutes, 45 percent of the teachers in schools of higher education, 38 percent of the principals of secondary schools, and 86 percent of all economists and planners (Ts.S.U. 1973c, pp. 170-74; Dodge 1977; Ts.S.U. RSFSR 1977, p. 303).

The segregation of women from men in the work sphere may be positive for women if it results in interaction and broader awareness that in turn may promote women's organization and greater political effectiveness. Particularly relevant here are observations of Colette Shulman, based on her discussion with Russian women:

> If I had to select the one satisfaction most widely felt by the working woman at all levels of society, I would say that it is the work-collective as a source of community and communication and of mutual support in coping with daily problems of life. And here I mean not the official formal collectives, but the intangible organic ones that women themselves create, with their own leaders and norms of conduct and laws of friendship (1977, p. 376).

The segregation of the young and highly educated professional women may have especially constructive ramifications. Women's isolation within the confines of the family appears to have been a significant obstacle to their recognizing common grievances and perceiving their problems as rooted in the structure and priorities of the broader society.

There is an interesting parallel to the emergence of a subculture and social protest among the young. Schools segregate the young from adult society and may promote an independent and critical perspective on that society as well as the organization required to manifest opposition:

> Youth that are in close and continual contact with adults are often in close and continual supervision by them. This and close contact itself, leads youth to be near replicas of these adults and less free to bring about social change. A degree of segregation from adults increases the change that a new generation can bring about. Adults often regard youth-initiated change with some fear, but it is one of the major means by which societies change to meet new conditions (Coleman et al. 1974, p. 132).

There is also signficant sex segregation within the educational system. In Soviet Russia women constitute about nine of every ten students in specialized secondary education programs in the fields of health, of economics and law, and of education, art, and cinematography, and about two-thirds of the college-level students in these areas (Ts.S.U. RSFSR 1977, p. 317). Thus, associations and perspectives nurtured at work may build upon the school experience of female professional and semiprofessional personnel.

There is also evidence of women acting as an interest group:

> A special "commission on women" was established at the national and local levels of all trade unions in 1969, whose charge included eliminating serious health and safety hazards for working women. . . . In factories and farms throughout the Soviet Union, dormant "women's councils," an auxilliary arm of local Party committees, have apparently been reactivated in recent years. . . . In most collective farms, five to nine women will form the local women's council; their influence has also been enhanced by the support of the deputy chairman for cultural affairs on collective farms, an elected position first instituted in 1960 and typically held by a female doctor or teacher with broadly defined responsibilities for defending women's interest on the farms (Moses 1978, pp. 21-22).

Women are nearly absent from the pinnacle of political power (only one woman has ever been a member of the Politburo and the percentage of females on the Central Committee peaked at 4.2). However, Jerry Hough (1977, pp. 141-48) argues that they are afforded significant input as a result of their substantial representation at lower levels and their predominance among "professionals normally involved in policy advocacy and analysis as part of their vocation." To the extent that occupational segregation promotes awareness of their mutual interests, it may act to enhance the importance of these channels of influence for women.

Finally, the movement of women out of agriculture is itself an indicator of the improvement in their status. There is a peasant proverb cited as a symbol of women's position within 19th-century rural Russia: "A hen is not a bird, and a woman is not a person" (Glickman 1977, p. 63). Unquestionably, there has been change during the Soviet era. Collectivization gave peasant women greater control over their own earnings, and may have secured their allegiance to the Soviet state (Dodge 1966, pp. 65–66). However, women's opportunities for advancement in agriculture remain exceedingly narrow; significant upward mobility necessitates migration to the cities. Remaining behind is clearly more costly to women than to men. Most females are engaged in difficult manual labor with very low remuneration and long hours. Operators of farm machinery are almost exclusively male. Housework is made more arduous by the far greater lack of services and household amenities than in urban areas. It is, thus, a positive sign that while men initially were more readily able to take advantage of urban opportunities, in recent decades in Soviet Russia women have ceased to be overrepresented among agricultural workers (excluding private agriculture) (Sacks 1976, ch. 6; see also the essay by Laird and Francisco in this volume).

THE CHANGE IN BELIEFS ABOUT WOMEN

Has the change in women's work roles been associated with the diffusion of an egalitarian ideology? Is there now less emphasis on sex differences as women have come to prove themselves capable of succeeding in such diverse work spheres? The lack of public opinion surveys prevents a definitive answer to these questions, but there is intriguing evidence that developments that Tilly and Scott saw in Western Europe may have close parallels to those in the Soviet Union.

They argue that it is the growing middle class that was associated both with a change in values and with a decline in married women's work. Rising prosperity—largely a product of high male income and reduced job instability—altered relations between both parents and children and men and women; it fostered an ideology supportive of women's confinement to the domestic sphere.

> Goode assumes that the idea of "woman's proper place" with its connotations of complete dependency and idealized femininity is a traditional value. In fact, it is a rather recently accepted middle-class value not at all inconsistent with notions of "rights and responsibilities of the individual." The division of labor within the family which assigned the husband the role of breadwinner and the wife the role of domestic manager and moral

guardian emerged clearly only in the nineteenth century and was associated with the growth of the middle class and the diffusion of its value (Tilly and Scott 1975, p. 41).

Unlike Western Europe, in Soviet Russia there was not a decline in married women's employment outside the home. However, other conditions may have been conducive to the diffusion of similar values. In recent years there has been a rise in the standard of living; the deficit of males has been reduced, allowing for more "normal" nuclear family relations; the population is far more concentrated in urban areas and has achieved substantial educational attainment. While couples are having fewer children, the sharp decline in infant mortality, especially in the post-World War II period, has assured the survival of nearly all to adulthood. The investment of love, attention, and material resources in children is further enhanced by the opportunities for social advancement via the educational system and job market. This, again, increases the possible rewards of such investment, as parents' aspirations for their children rise in response to such opportunities (Tilly and Scott 1978, ch. 8). The Soviet state's emphasis on the critical importance of caring for children has also had a positive impact on parents' sense of responsibility (Bronfenbrenner 1970; Liegle 1975). Finally, the population has had increasing exposure to the values of Western societies regarding women and children.

Vera Dunham (1976) has analyzed the themes in the fiction of the Stalinist period as an indicator of the changing values and role models that the regime chose to extol. She convincingly demonstrates that the censors permitted stories to be published in which bourgeois ideals were viewed favorably. The state, Dunham concludes, gave legitimacy to these ideals in a deliberate attempt to broaden political support, especially in the critical years following World War II. Such support was deemed essential not only because of widespread popular discontent but also because of the necessity to elicit further sacrifice to recover from the vast destruction. Coercion alone was inadequate; the demands could be met only by the "search for new and reliable allies in the population":

> The Soviet political leadership had chosen and nurtured certain allies in the past. It had relied in those earlier days on the workers. It had appealed too to the intelligensia, but this time it looked for a new force, sturdy and pliable. And it was the middle class which offered itself as the best possible partner in the rebuilding of the country. The middle class had the great advantage of being "our own people": Totally Stalinist, born out of Stalin's push for the industrialization, reeducation, and bureaucratization of the country, flesh of the flesh of Stalin's revolution from above in the thirties, and ready to fill the vacuum created by Stalin's Great Purge and by the liquidation of the Leninist generation of activists (Dunham 1976, p. 13)

While it was unacceptable to advocate that women devote themselves solely to household tasks, the stories show that they still had primary responsibilities for creating "domestic bliss." The ideal wife would "comfort her shellshocked husband and . . . support his aspirations." To demand equality at work and at home would surely have been viewed as a selfish act in the fiction of the period.

Sexist values are widely evident today. Letters to the press illustrate how extreme this may be among men: "Free a woman from the kitchen and you give her freedom to be a silly hen. Who needs such a woman? A woman is supposed to adorn the family hearth, just as flowers adorn the meadows" (quoted in Kuznetsova 1967, p. 7). A male graduate student writes:

> Girls for all your equality with us men, stay feminine, gentle and weak (in the best, Marxist sense of this concept), stay beautiful not only internally but also in your manners (Kurgansky 1967).

There are many professionals who stress women's natural propensity for raising children and the importance of making changes in employment to allow women to devote more time to this. A well-known demographer argues that "nurseries were a necessity in their own time, but now we are wealthy enough not to have to deprive a child of its mother's affection" (Urlanis 1971).

There is evidence of a sharp clash between men and women over these issues. There are many female adherents to the "feminist" population policy position that opposes measures designed to encourage childbearing in a way that they see as directly competing with women's occupational advancement (Yanowitch 1977, pp. 179-80). In recent years there has been increasing discussion of the importance of altering the early socialization of males and pressuring adult men to insure that they assume a more equal share of housework (see, for example, Yankova 1975, pp. 48-49). And women are responding with their own letters to the press:

> As for what you call beauty, let the philistines be moved by it. We have equal rights, after all, so we won't need any philosophizing about whether a girl ought to be feminine. Our time is a time of strong personalities. There is a struggle ahead of us for a place in life (Novikova 1978).

Yet there does appear to be a consensus about fundamental sex differences. Drawing upon his conversations with leading women intellectuals in the Soviet Union, Jerry Hough observes:

> Several spoke of lower rates of political participation as the result of a natural and not particularly worrisome division of labor: both men and women have regular jobs, and the man combines his with political activities (really duties) and the woman hers with household responsibilities.

Few Soviet women with whom I have spoken would have any quarrel with the female vice-president of the Academy of Pedagogical Sciences and a member of the Presidium of the Committee of Soviet Women who asserted in a published interview that "woman by her biological essence is a mother—a teacher trainer (*vospitatel 'nitsa*)" and that she has "an inborn ability to deal with small children, an instinctive pedagogical approach" (1977, pp. 150-51).

Without longitudinal data on public opinion, it is impossible to ascertain either the class origin or the time at which these views on sex differences emerged and spread. While Tilly and Scott's argument is plausible, it is also possible that contemporary values are a direct extension of traditional perspectives. In any case, the transformation of women's work role outside the family is clearly compatible with views that stress the distinctions between males and females. To the extent that this bolstered the unequal division of labor in the home and attitudes that women are less capable in leadership positions, such distinctions have detracted from women's attainment of status and opportunity equal to those of men.

EXPLAINING THE CONTINUITY IN OCCUPATIONAL SEX DIFFERENCES

Persisting employment differences surely bolster beliefs regarding differences in male and female capabilities. As noted above, this persistence is particularly surprising in light of the acute social dislocation. In this section some possible explanations for the occupational segregation are considered and Soviet Russia is compared with the other republics in a partial test of the hypothesized sources of continuity and change.

The measurement of sex differences in the nonagrarian occupations is based on the period between 1939 and 1970. One possiblity is that this misses the critical period when women were first drawn into the Soviet labor force. Both the initiative of the state and the high demand for labor beginning in the late 1920s may have compelled employers to place less emphasis on sex than on ability. By 1939 sex differences may have reached such a low level that further decline could not easily be achieved. In other nations the decline in the under- and overrepresentation of women may be observed simply because segregation was initially at such a high level (compare Cooney 1975).

Alternatively, there are compelling reasons to expect that a comparison between the 1926 and 1939 Soviet censuses—a complex task that remains to be undertaken—will also show continuity. First, the high proportion of women in tsarist industry meant that Soviet Russia inherited a well-established sexual division of labor in the nonagrarian sector. Second, the acute shortage of facilities to relieve the burdens of child care and housework during the first decades after the 1917 Revolution seriously impeded women's ability to compete with men. And finally, industrialization during the early Soviet period involved the recruitment of a rural, conservative, and largely illiterate peasantry—a group neither receptive to innovation nor readily accessible due to the undeveloped state of both the communications network and the evolving political structure. These factors may not only have prevented a radical change in women's occupational roles in the nonagrarian sector, but may also have reinforced early patterns so that subsequent change was far more difficult. There is an inertia built into social structures; present forms are to a large extent a product of the conditions prevalent at the time they first came into existence (see Stinchcombe 1965).

The substantial differences between republics within the Soviet Union (see the essays by Heer and Clem in this volume) with respect to both cultural heritage and the timing of economic development make it possible to test the importance of some of the factors in the above explanation with data from the 1939, 1959, and 1970 censuses.

Most significant is the comparison of Soviet Russia with the Central Asian republics. While there is considerable controversy over the exact ranking of socioeconomic development of the republics, those in Central Asia—Kirgizia, Tadzhikistan, Uzbekistan, and Turkmenistan—are all consistently placed at or bordering on the bottom (Silver 1974; Divilov 1976; Dellenbrant 1977; Wagener 1971). Russian peasant women lived in a highly patriarchal society, but the Muslim culture of the indigenous population of Central Asia restricted women's activities to an even greater extent. Gregory Massell's study of Soviet efforts to alter the subordinate status of these women before 1930 (1974) shows the fierce resistance to change. The absence of development meant that there was no class of industrial workers to foment the destruction of the pre-Revolutionary power structure. Massell's interpretation is that there was a deliberate strategy to use women as a "surrogate proletariat" and to exacerbate sexual and generational tensions as a substitute for class struggle. The explosion of violent opposition actually resulted in an uncontrollable situation for Soviet authorities and necessitated a retreat from this direct attack on male privilege.

The very strength of this traditional culture may have provided especially deficient guidelines for allocating male and female labor in the modern economy, which emerged rapidly and at a later stage than in Soviet Russia. World War II provided a substantial boost to this economic development. As a consequence of the Nazi invasion of June 1941, the Soviet government was compelled to relocate major enterprises and their personnel to Central Asia and other regions away from the anticipated war zone (Lewis, Rowland, and Clem 1976, p. 76).

While this sharp discontinuity with the traditional society may have enhanced the potential for innovation, there also existed a political apparatus and a communications and transportation network that probably made it far more possible to take advantage of this potential than was true in Soviet

Russia in the 1920s. At this later stage the state may have had the resources necessary to direct change in the economically developing cities. But perhaps the most significant asset was that those recruited were likely to be receptive to change. As Ralph Clem discusses at length in his essays in this volume, Russians predominated among the population taking advantage of opportunities in Central Asia. They had the requisite skills, education, and work discipline. Their migrant status meant that they were likely to be young and relatively free of family responsibilities.

It may be hypothesized that under these conditions, the impact of World War II reduced occupational sex differences in Central Asia. Moreover, if the nationality composition of the population is important, demographic changes during the 1960s should stem such a reduction. Specifically, the indigenous nationality groups were likely to enter the labor force in growing numbers because of the rise in their educational attainment; the growth in the proportion of young persons in the population as a consequence of the high rate of natural increase (a low death rate combined with a high birth rate); their increased presence in cities; and their access to the more extensive communications and transportation network. These developments generate a higher level of what Karl Deutsch terms "social mobilization": "the process in which major clusters of old social, economic and psychological commitments are eroded or broken and people become available for new patterns of socialization and behavior" (quoted in Dellenbrant 1977, p. 12).

Important here is the interrelated sex and nationality hierarchy of mobilization: males before females and Russians before indigenous Muslim nationality groups. The indigenous males are likely to be recruited at a time that overlaps with Russian females. It may have been only in the 1960s that large numbers of indigenous females entered the nonagrarian work force—and this, I argue, is the critical change. Compared with women of Slavic nationality within Central Asia, Muslim women are at a distinct disadvantage in competing with men because of their larger family size, lower educational attainment, lesser work experience, and, possibly, their early socialization to be more submissive.

The paucity of Soviet data on the nationality composition of the labor force makes it difficult to test the arguments sketched above. For example, lacking are any figures even on the number of women working outside of agriculture by nationality. One is compelled to resort to occupational data available only for the population of the republics as a whole. The data exist for 11 republics that consituted the Soviet Union in 1939 and for all 15 for 1959 and 1970. The measure of occupational sex differences in the nonagrarian occupations shows that it is indeed in the Central Asian republics that there was a decline between 1939 and 1959 in the extent to which females were either over- or underrepresented (see column 3 of Table 10.2) It would appear that the years of war, rapid industrial growth, and an accompanying heavy influx of Russians reduced the measure in these republics from a level that was considerably above that of Russia to an equal or a lower level, as in the case of Uzbekistan. Yet it is interesting to note that the variation between republics is small and that the sex differences in Soviet Russia may actually have been at or near a very low threshold.

TABLE 10.2
The Standardized Measure of Occupational Differentiation by Sex: 1939, 1958, 1970

	Data from 1959 Census			Data from 1970 Census		
Republic	1939	1959	1959 Minus 1939	1959	1970	1970 Minus 1959
Russia	55.7	54.6	-1.1	53.5	54.8	1.4
Ukraine	56.9	54.2	-2.7	53.8	54.0	0.2
Belorussia	58.4	55.8	-2.6	54.2	55.7	1.5
Lithuania	a	b	b	54.0	54.3	0.3
Latvia	a	b	b	54.6	51.5	-3.1
Estonia	a	b	b	55.0	56.4	1.4
Moldavia	a	b	b	53.3	50.3	-2.7
Georgia	57.8	54.8	-3.0	53.6	52.2	-1.4
Azerbaydzhan	56.4	52.1	-4.3	50.9	51.8	0.9
Armenia	61.9	57.1	-4.8	55.0	54.5	0.5
Kazakhstan	59.0	56.5	-2.5	54.6	57.3	2.9
Uzbekistan	57.5	50.9	-6.6	50.5	48.6	-1.9
Kirgizia	61.0	55.6	-5.5	52.6	54.2	1.6
Tadzhikistan	63.0	54.1	-8.9	50.3	50.8	0.5
Turkmenistan	60.5	53.3	-7.2	52.1	53.9	1.8
Mean						
11 republics[c]	58.9	54.5	4.5	52.8	53.4	1.3
15 republics	—	—	—	53.2	53.4	1.5
Std. deviation						
11 republics[c]	2.38	1.85	2.38	1.67	2.42	0.73
15 republics	—	—	—	1.59	2.42	0.89

Note: The categories upon which the measure is based exclude agriculture and forestry. There were 96 occupational categories used from the 1959 census and 93 from the 1970 census. The formula for calculating the measure is as follows (Williams 1976, p. 38):

$$\text{Std. measure} = \sum \left| \frac{\left[\frac{\left[\frac{M}{T}\right] 1000}{\sum \left[\frac{M}{T}\right]}\right] - \left[\frac{\left[\frac{F}{T}\right]}{\sum \left[\frac{F}{T}\right]}\right]}{2} \right| (100)$$

M = The number of males in a given category.
F = The number of females in a given category.
T = All persons in a given category.   [a]Data not available.
[b]Data available but not relevant.
[c]These are the republics that constituted the USSR at the time of the 1939 census.
Source: Based on volumes of the 1959 and 1970 censuses of the USSR.

Occupational categories published in the 1970 census differed from those of prior censuses. Fortunately, data for 1959 were also in the 1970 census volumes, making possible exact comparisons between the two points in time (see columns 5 and 6 of Table 10.2). As expected, this decade of relative social stability and of both a more balanced sex ratio and increased mobilization of the native population brought no significant change in the overall level of sex differences.

There is an interesting paradox in the change during recent decades. Native Central Asian women appear to be entering the nonagrarian labor force in growing numbers and experiencing an improvement in their status. However, women overall may be less able to compete with men in the nonagrarian occupations. This appears to be due to the change in nationality composition: a decreasing proportion of the women are Russian or of other nonindigenous nationality.

Data on educational attainment of employed persons show this rather clearly. The last two columns of Table 10.3 show that between 1959 and 1970 women of the indigenous nationality groups have made often substantial gains relative to Russian women residing in the republic (a ratio of 100 means the groups are equal; figures over 100 in this case indicate a Russian advantage).

While comparisons can be made between employed males and employed females from as early as 1939, such data by nationality were omitted from Soviet publications. The male/female comparison shows the definite progress for women between 1939 and 1959. The ratio declines markedly when we compare columns 1 and 2 and also columns 4 and 5. However, between 1959 and 1970 there are striking reverses in Kirgizia, Tadzhikistan, Turkmenistan, and Kazakhstan—all republics where a substantial proportion of the population is Muslim. The proportion of employed men with higher education increased far more than the comparable figure for women (see the ratios in columns 5 and 6). Native women are better off, relative to Russian women, but the increasing numbers of native women among the employed results in employed women overall comparing less favorably with men.

Males of the indigenous nationality groups in Central Asia were also at a disadvantage in competing with the Russian in-migrants. While the issue requires further investigation, there is some evidence suggesting that these men were more likely to enter "women's work"—occupations in which women predominated at least within the Slavic republics—than were their Russian counterparts (see Sacks, forthcoming b). A number of factors may have contributed to this. First, the indigenous male population was competing largely with women if they chose such employment. Even if these were Russian women, as men they were at less of a disadvantage than were indigenous females. Second, Russian women may have had particularly wide opportunities and have been drawn into the higher-status or better-paying jobs, and even into those where Russian males were heavily concentrated. Third, the

TABLE 10.3
The Educational Attainment of Men Compared with Women and of Russian Women Compared with Women of the Indigenous Nationality, by Republic: 1939, 1959, 1970

	Ratio of Males to Females[a]						For Women, the Ratio of Russians to Titular Republic Nationality[b]	
	At Least Some Secondary Education			Higher Education				
Republic	1939	1959	1970	1939	1959	1970	1959	1970
Russia	115	95	97	160	103	105	100	100
Ukraine	122	110	105	170	111	114	160	128
Belorussia	182	113	107	200	121	117	227	156
Lithuania	—	92	96	—	96	95	222	146
Latvia	—	96	96	—	86	97	103	99
Estonia	—	92	95	—	106	97	131	108
Moldavia	—	126	110	—	119	118	330	194
Georgia	129	111	104	165	119	111	108	96
Azerbaidzhan	166	128	120	190	134	138	176	145
Armenia	190	108	104	155	109	113	120	113
Kazakhstan	151	98	102	150	93	113	195	125
Uzbekistan	152	111	112	175	128	93	170	131
Kirgizia	149	111	107	150	107	120	193	134
Tadzhikistan	183	110	112	167	124	152	191	152
Turkmenistan	153	101	109	160	122	156	134	122

Note: The data are based on the employed population only.

[a]The percentage of males with the specified educational level is divided by the comparable figure for females and then multiplied by 100.
[b]For the population residing within the republic, the percentage of employed women of Russian nationality is divided by the comparable figure for employed females of the titular republic nationality. This is then multiplied by 100.

Source: Ts.S.U. 1972b, Table 7; Ts.S.U. 1973a, Table 56.

initially very limited work rates of indigenous women outside of agriculture may have created an acute demand for workers in occupations elsewhere filled by women. Finally, these males may have felt less compromised in doing "women's work" both because of their early socialization within a culture that provided no clear guidelines for the sexual division of labor in this sphere of employment and because movement even into low-status jobs in the modern economy represented significant social mobility for them. This may be analogous to the attraction of lower-middle-class males in the United States to public-school teaching as an alternative to the blue-collar employment common to their social stratum.

Thus, overall decline in occupational sex differences in many republics between 1939 and 1959 may have been due not to women entering men's occupations, but to men of lower-status nationality groups entering occupations the Russians label "women's work." This points to the necessity of examining disaggregated data—the trends within specific occupations by sex and nationality—to discern fully the nature of change and who benefits from it.

CONCLUSION

Data omitted from published sources and the lack of public opinion surveys complicate the analysis of sex differences in the Soviet Union. But the problems go beyond this because change and continuity are often combined in complex ways. A distorted picture can easily result from an overreliance on aggregate measures, through failing to examine the Soviet case in historical and comparative perspective, or from too narrow comparisons between occupations or social groups. Unfortunately, the critical determinant of a scholar's findings is often his or her initial bias toward the USSR.

There is little disagreement that sex differences have been remarkably resistant to change. Time use in the family and the pattern of over- and underrepresentation of women throughout the occupations are convincing evidence that neither the fact of women working outside the home nor the process of industrialization itself will eliminate the labels "women's work" and "men's work." But when does different mean unequal? When does different mean less political power or influence for women? Can there be persisting differences, and yet change that increases women's input into significant decisions or increases their access to social rewards?

I have no complete answer to these questions. There is a definite need here for the further development of theory and empirical measures. This is not to deny that Soviet women today have profound grievances. The sharp disparity in the pay of males and females, the inordinate number of women among those in arduous unskilled labor, their underrepresentation at the upper end of the status hierarchy, and their having to assume most household chores even after a workday as long as that of their husbands, all point to the need for an effective Soviet women's movement. Such a movement cannot take the same form as that in the United States because of differences in permissible forms of manifesting discontent and differences in the available channels for shaping change. The 1980s will reveal the political significance of Soviet women's occupational segregation, of their high level of educational attainment, of their predominance in many professional occupations that afford them input into policy decisions, and of their growing activity in such groups as women's councils.

Yet the potential for change in sex differences may have its historical moment, which once past, may leave social structures too rigid to permit further change, particularly in the absence of social crisis. The 1920s may have been a time of great potential for Soviet Russia. The spread of industry to less-developed regions in later decades may have been a second auspicious period. To realize the potential may have required resources and social stability lacking in the 1920s. During the later development in Central Asia there was, possibly, a lack of adequate commitment to the goal of sexual equality. Another limiting factor may have been the influx of migrant workers and employees from the already advanced regions. They would initially benefit from occupational opportunities arising from relative backwardness. Their educational attainment, youth, and considerable freedom from family responsibilities may have made them receptive to change, particularly under the demanding conditions of World War II. However, these migrants were already influenced by the sex structure existing in their place of origin. The population that might have experienced the sharpest break with the past—females of the indigenous nationality groups—was insulated from change that largely occurred in cities and was mobilized only at a later historical stage.

This, of course, has direct implications for nations that are now beginning to industrialize. Their potential for developing social structures that are distinct from those in the industrialized nations will surely depend upon the ideological commitment of the elites, the resources available as new structures are created, and their ability to resist the encroachments of the more developed nations. From the study of regions where such conditions prevail or were present for even a brief time, we may learn much about the constraints upon human potential imposed by gender distinctions.

REFERENCES

Berger, Peter L., and Thomas Luckman. 1966. *The Social Construction of Reality*. New York: Anchor Books.

Bronfenbrenner, Urie. 1970. *Two Worlds of Childhood: U.S. and U.S.S.R.* New York: Russell Sage Foundation.

Chapman, Janet G. 1977. "Equal Pay for Equal Work?" In *Women in Russia*, edited by Dorothy Atkinson, Alexander Dallin, and Gail W. Lapidus, pp. 225–39. Stanford: Stanford University Press.

Coleman, James S., et al. 1974. *Youth: Transition to Adulthood.* Chicago: University of Chicago Press. The Coleman work is the report of the Panel on Youth of the President's Science Advisory Committee. Coleman is the chairman and the report is generally associated with him. Others on the panel and listed on the book's cover are Robert H. Bremmer, Burton R. Clark, John B. Davis, Dorothy H. Eichorn, Zvi Griliches, Joseph F. Kett, Norman B. Ryder, Zahava Blum Doering, John M. Mays.

Cooney, Rosemary Santana. 1975. "Female Professional Work Opportunities: A Cross-National Study." *Demography* 12:107-20.

Danilova, E. Z. 1968. *Sotsial'nye problemy truda zhenshchiny-rabotnitsy.* Moscow: Nauka.

Dellenbrant, Jan Ake. 1977. "Regional Differences in the Soviet Union: A Quantitative Inquiry into the Development of the Soviet Republics." *Bidrag til Ostatsforskningen*, vol. 5. Sweden: Research Center for Soviet and East European Studies, Uppsala University.

Deutsch, Karl. 1966. *Nationalism and Social Communication.* 2nd ed. Cambridge, Mass.: M.I.T. Press.

Divilov, S. I. 1976. *Chislennost' i struktura zanyatykh v narodnom khozyaistve: metodika perspektivnykh raschetov.* Moscow: Ekonomika.

Dodge, Norton T. 1966. *Women in the Soviet Economy.* Baltimore: Johns Hopkins University Press.

———. 1977. "Women in the Profession." In *Women in Russia*, edited by Dorothy Atkinson, Alexander Dallin, and Gail W. Lapidus, pp. 205-24. Stanford: Stanford University Press.

Dunham, Vera S. 1976. *In Stalin's Time: Middle Values in Soviet Fiction.* Cambridge: Cambridge University Press.

Feshbach, Murray, and Stephen Rapawy. 1973. "Labor Constraints in the Five Year Plan." In *Soviet Economic Prospects for the Seventies*, pp. 485-563. Washington, D.C.: U.S. Government Printing Office.

Glilkmann, Rose L. 1977. "The Russian Factory Woman, 1880-1914. In *Women in Russia* edited by Dorothy Atkinson, Alexander Dallin, and Gail W. Lapidus, pp. 63-84. Stanford: Stanford University Press.

Goode, William J. 1963. *World Revolution and Family Patterns.* New York: Free Press.

Gruzdeva, Ye. V. 1978. "Vocations and Qualifications: Statistics on Work Done by Women." *Ekonomika i organizatsia promyshlennovo proizvodstva* no. 3; 47-53, condensed in *Current Digest of the Soviet Press* 30, no. 31:9.

Hayghe, Howard. 1978. "Marital and Family Characteristics of Workers, March 1977." Special Labor Force Report no. 216. Washington, D.C.: U.S. Department of Labor, Bureau of Labor Statistics.

Hough, Jerry F. 1977. *The Soviet Union and Social Science Theory.* Cambridge, Mass.: Harvard University Press.

Kharchev, Anatoly G. 1964. *Brak i sem'ya v SSSR.* Moscow: Mysl'.

Kharchev, Anatoly G., and S. I. Golod. 1969. "Proizvodstvennaya rabota zhenshchin i sem'ya." In *Sotsial'nye problemy truda i proizvodstva*, edited by G. V. Osipov and Ya. Shchepan'sky, pp. 439-56. Moscow: Mysl'.

Kotlyar, A. E., and S. Ya. Turchaninova. 1975. *Zanyatost' zhenshchin v proizvodstve.* Moscow: Statistika.

Kurgansky, V. 1967. Letter written to *Komsomolskaya pravda*, Dec. 15, 1966, translated in *Current Digest of the Soviet Press* 19, no. 11:2.

Kuznetsova, Larisa. 1967. "Whose Job Is the Kitchen?" *Literaturnaya gazeta.* July 12, p. 12, translated in *Current Digest of the Soviet Press* 19, no. 33:7-8.

Labzin, A. L. 1965. "Stroitel'stvo kommunizma i ustranenie ostatkov neravenstva v polozhenii zhenshchiny." *Filosofskie nauki* no. 1:98-106.

Lapidus, Gail W. 1978. *Women in Soviet Society: Equality, Development, and Social Change.* Berkeley: University of California Press.

Lenin, V. I. 1964. *The Development of Capitalism in Russia* Moscow: Progress.

Lewis, Robert A., and Richard H. Rowland. 1979. *Population Redistribution in the USSR: Its Impact on Society, 1897-1977.* New York: Praeger.

Lewis, Robert A., Richard H. Rowland, and Ralph S. Clem. 1976. *Nationality and Population Change in Russia and the USSR: An Evaluation of Census Data, 1897-1970*. New York: Praeger.
Liegle, Ludwig. 1975. *The Family's Role in Soviet Education*. New York: Springer.
Litvyakov, P. P. 1969. *Demograficheskie problemy zanyatosti*. Moscow: Ekonomika.
Madison, Bernice. 1977. "Social Services for Women: Problems and Priorities." In *Women in Russia*, edited by Dorothy Atkinson, Alexander Dallin, and Gail W. Lapidus. Stanford: Stanford University Press.
Massell, Gregory J. 1974. *The Surrogate Proletariat: Moslem Women and Revolutionary Strategies in Soviet Central Asia: 1919-1929*. Princeton: Princeton University Press.
Matthews, Mervyn. 1972. *Class and Society in Soviet Russia*. New York: Walker.
Mazur, Peter D. 1967. "Reconstruction of Fertility Trends for the Female Population of the U.S.S.R." *Population Studies* 21, no. 1:33-52.
Mikhailyuk, V. B. 1970. *Ispol'zovanie zhenskovo truda v narodnom khozyaistve*. Moscow: Ekonomika.
Moses, Joel C. 1978. "The Politics of Female Labor in the Soviet Union." *Western Societies Program Occasional Paper no. 10*. Ithaca, N.Y.: Western Societies Program, Cornell University.
Norwood, Janet L., and Elizabeth Waldman. 1979. "Women in the Labor Force: Some New Data Series." Report 575. Washington, D.C.: U.S. Department of Labor, Bureau of Labor Statistics.
Novikova, S. 1978. "Is Beauty Philistine?" *Komsomolskaya pravda*, Aug. 30, p. 4, condensed in *Current Digest of the Soviet Press* 30, no. 42:7.
Ofer, Gur. 1973. *The Service Sector in Soviet Economic Growth: A Comparative Study*. Cambridge, Mass.: Harvard University Press.
Oppenheimer, Valerie Kincade. 1970. *The Female Labor Force in the United States: Demographic and Economic Factors Governing Its Growth and Changing Composition*. Berkeley: Institute for International Studies, University of California.
Radko, N. 1979. "Mama Works at Home." *Literaturnaya gazeta*, May 16, p. 13, condensed in *Current Digest of the Soviet Press* 31, no. 22:15.
Robinson, John P., Philip E. Converse, and Alexander Szalai. 1973. "Everyday Life in Twelve Countries." In *The Use of Time: Daily Activities of the Urban and Suburban Population in Twelve Countries*, edited by Alexander Szalai, pp. 17-86. New York: Russell Sage Foundation.
Sacks, Michael Paul. 1976. *Women's Work in Soviet Russia: Continuity in the Midst of Change*. New York: Praeger.
―――. 1977a. "Unchanging Times: A Comparison of the Everyday Life of Soviet Working Men and Women Between 1923 and 1966." *Journal of Marriage and the Family* 39 (Nov.): 793-805.
―――. 1977b. "Women in the Industrial Labor Force." In *Women in Russia*, edited by Dorothy Atkinson, Alexander Dallin, and Gail W. Lapidus, pp. 189-204. Stanford: Stanford University Press.
―――. "Missing Female Occupational Categories in the Soviet Censuses." *Slavic Review*, forthcoming *a*.
―――. *Work and Equality: The Division of Labor in Soviet Society*. New York: Praeger, forthcoming *b*.
Shteiner, A. B., and D. N. Karpukhin. 1978. "Women's Work and Work by Women." *Ekonomika i organizatsia promyshlennovo proizvodstva* no. 3:36-47, condensed in *Current Digest of the Soviet Press* 30, no. 31:8-9.
Shulman, Colette. 1977. "The Individual and the Collective." In *Women in Russia*, edited by Dorothy Atkinson, Alexander Dallin, and Gail W. Lapidus, pp. 375-84. Stanford: Stanford University Press.
Silver, Brian. 1974. "Levels of Sociocultural Development Among Soviet Nationalities: A Partial Test of the Equalization Hypothesis." *American Political Science Review* 68 (Dec.):1618-37.
Slesarev, G. A., and Z. A. Yankova. 1969. "Zhenshchina po promyshlennom predpriyatii i v sem'e." In *Sotsial'nye problemy truda i proizvodstva*, edited by G. V. Osipov and Ya. Shchepan'sky, pp. 416-38. Moscow: Mysl'.

Stinchcombe, Arthur L. 1965. "Social Structure and Organizations." In *Handbook of Organizations*, edited by James G. March, pp. 142-93. Chicago: Rand McNally.
Suter, Larry E., and Herman P. Miller. 1973. "Income Differences Between Men and Career Women." *American Journal of Sociology* 78 (Jan.): 962-74.
Swafford, Michael. 1978. "Sex Differences in Soviet Earnings." *American Sociological Review* 43 (Oct.): 657-73.
Tilly, Louise A., and Joan W. Scott. 1975. "Women's Work and Family in Nineteenth Century Europe." *Comparative Studies in Society and History* 17 (Jan.): 36-64.
———. 1978. *Women, Work and Family*. New York: Holt, Rinehart, and Winston.
Troinitskii, N. A., ed. 1906. *Chislennost' i sostav rabochikh v rossii na osnovanii dannykh vseobshchie perepisie Rossiiskoi Imperii 1897*. Moscow: Gosudarstvennii ministr vnutrennikh delenji.
Tsentral'noe statisticheskoe upravlenie pri sovete ministrov RSFSR (Ts.S.U. RSFSR). 1971. *Narodnoe khozyaistvo RSFSR v 1971 g.: statisticheskii ezhegodnik*. Moscow: Statistika.
———. 1977. *Narodnoe khozyaistvo RSFSR za 60 let: statisticheskii ezhegodnik*. Moscow: Statistika.
Tsentral'noe statisticheskoe upravlenie pri sovete ministrov SSSR (Ts.S.U.) 1930. *Vsesoyuznoi perepis' naseleniya 1926 goda*. Vol. 26:*Rossiiskaya Sotsialisticheskaya Federativnaya Sovetskaya Respublika, otdel 2: zanyatiya*. Moscow: Izdanie TsSU Souza SSSR.
———. 1963. *Itogi vsesoyuznoi perepisi naseleniya 1959 goda: RSFSR*. Moscow: Gosstatizdat.
———. 1972a. *Itogi vsesoyuznoi perepisi naseleniya 1970 goda*. Vol. 2: *pol. vozrast i sostanyanie v brake naseleniya SSSR*. Moscow: Statistika.
———. 1972b. *Itogi vsesoyuznoi perepisi naseleniya 1970 goda*. Vol. 3: *uroven' obrazovaniya naselenya SSSR*. Moscow: Statistika.
———. 1973a. *Itogi Vsesoyuznoi perepisi naseleniya 1970 goda*. Vol. 4: *natsional'nyi sostav naseleniya SSSR*. Moscow: Statistika.
———. 1973b. *Itogi vsesoyuznoi perepisi naseleniya 1970 goda*. Vol. 5: *raspredelenie naseleniya SSSR po obshchestvennym gruppam*. Moscow: Statistika.
———. 1973c. *Itogi vsesoyuznoi perepisi naseleniya 1970 goda*. Vol. 6: *raspredelenie naseleniya SSSR po zanyatiyam*. Moscow: Statistika.
Urlanis, B. 1971. "Babushka v sem'e." *Literaturnaya gazeta*. Mar. 3, p. 11.
Vanek, Joann. 1973. "Keeping Busy: Time Spent in Housework, United States, 1920-1970." Ph.D. dissertation, University of Michigan.
Vestnik statistiki. 1979. "O predvaritel'nykh itogakh vsesuyuznoi perepisi naseleniya 1979 goda." No. 5: 67-79.
Wagener, Hans-Juergen. 1971. "Regional Output Levels in the Soviet Union." *Radio Liberty Research Paper*, no. 41.
Williams, Gregory. 1976. "Trends in Occupational Differentiation by Sex." *Sociology of Work and Occupations* 3 (Feb.): 38-62.
The Woman Question: Selections from the Writings of Karl Marx, Frederick Engels, V. I. Lenin and Joseph Stalin. 1951. New York: International Publishers.
Yankova, Z. A. 1975. "Razvitie lichnosti zhenshchiny v sovetskom obshchestve." *Sotsiologicheskie issledovaniya*, No. 4: 42-51.
Yanowitch, Murray. 1977. *Social and Economic Inequality in the USSR: Six Studies*. New York: Sharpe.

SUGGESTED READINGS

CHAPTER 1: THE ETHNIC DIMENSION OF THE SOVIET UNION, PART I

Conquest, Robert, ed. *Soviet Nationalities Policy in Practice.* New York: Praeger, 1967.
Goldhagen, Erich, ed. *Ethnic Minorities in the Soviet Union.* New York: Praeger, 1968.
Katz, Zev. Rosmarie Rogers, and Frederick Harned, eds. *Handbook of Major Soviet Nationalities.* New York: Free Press, 1975.
Low, Alfred D. *Lenin on the Question of Nationality.* New York: Bookman, 1958.
Pipes, Richard. *The Formation of the Soviet Union.* Rev. ed. New York: Atheneum, 1968.
_____. "Reflections on the Nationality Problems in the Soviet Union." In *Ethnicity: Theory and Experience,* edited by Nathan Glazer and Daniel P. Moynihan, pp. 453-65. Cambridge, Mass.: Harvard University Press, 1975.
Silver, Brian, "Levels of Socio-Cultural Development Among Soviet Nationalities: A Partial Test of the Equalization Hypothesis." *American Political Science Review* 68, no. 4 (1974): 1618-37.

CHAPTER 2: THE ETHNIC DIMENSION, PART II

Allworth, Edward, ed. *Soviet Nationality Problems.* New York: Columbia University Press, 1971.
_____, ed. *The Nationality Question in Soviet Central Asia.* New York: Praeger, 1973.
Azreal, Jeremy. "Emergent Nationality Problems in the USSR." Rand Corporation Report R-2172-AF. Sept. 1977.
Bennigsen, Alexandre, and Chantel Lemercier-Quelquejay. *Islam in the Soviet Union.* London: Pall Mall Press, 1967.
Clem, Ralph S., ed. *The Soviet West: Interplay Between Nationality and Social Organization.* New York: Praeger, 1975.
Hodnett, Grey. "The Debate over Soviet Federalism." *Soviet Studies* 28, no. 4 (1967): 458-81.
Lewis, Robert A., Richard H. Rowland, and Ralph S. Clem. *Nationality and Population Change in Russia and the USSR: An Evaluation of Census Data, 1897-1970.* New York: Praeger, 1976.
Rakowska-Harmstone, Teresa. "The Dialectics of Nationalism in the USSR." *Problems of Communism* 23, no. 3 (1974): 1-22.
Shibutani, Tamotsu, and Kian M. Kwan. *Ethnic Stratification: A Comparative Approach.* New York: Macmillan, 1965.
Simmonds, George W., ed. *Nationalism in the USSR and Eastern Europe.* Detroit: University of Detroit Press, 1977.
Van Dyke, Vernon. "The Individual, the State, and Ethnic Communities in Political Theory." *World Politics* 29, no. 3 (1977): 343-67.

CHAPTER 3: POPULATION POLICY

Cohn, Helen DesFosses. "Population Policy in the USSR." *Problems of Communism* 22, no. 4 (July-Aug. 1973): 41-55.
Feshbach, Murray, and Stephen Rapawy. "Soviet Population and Manpower Trends and Policies." In Joint Economic Committee, Congress of the United States, *Soviet Economy in a New Perspective*, pp. 113-154. Washington, D.C.: Government Printing Office, 1976.
Heer, David M. "The Demographic Transition in the Russian Empire and the Soviet Union." *Journal of Social History* 1 (Spring 1968): 193-240.
_____. "Recent Developments in Soviet Population Policy." *Studies in Family Planning* 3, no. 11 (Nov. 1972): 257-64.
_____. "Three Issues in Soviet Population Policy." *Population and Development Review* 3, no. 3 (Sept. 1972): 229-52.
Leedy, Frederick A. "Demographic Trends in the USSR." In Joint Economic Committee, Congress of the United States, *Soviet Economic Prospects for the Seventies*, pp. 428-84. Washington, D.C.: Government Printing Office, 1973.
Lewis, Robert A., Richard H. Rowland, and Ralph S. Clem. *Nationality and Population Change in Russia and the USSR: An Evaluation of Census Data, 1897-1970*. New York: Praeger, 1976.
Lorimer, Frank. *The Population of the Soviet Union: History and Prospects*. Geneva: League of Nations, 1946.
Macura, M. "Population Policies in Socialist Countries of Europe." *Population Studies* 28, no. 3 (Nov. 1974): 369-79.
Meek, Ronald L., ed. *Marx and Engels on the Population Bomb*. Berkeley: Ramparts Press, 1971.

CHAPTER 4: SOCIALISM AND SOCIAL STRATIFICATION

Connor, Walter D. *Socialism, Politics, and Equality: Hierarchy and Change in Eastern Europe and the USSR*. New York: Columbia University Press, 1979.
Inkeles, Alex, and Raymond A. Bauer. *The Soviet Citizen: Daily Life in a Totalitarian Society*. Cambridge, Mass.: Harvard University Press, 1959.
Lane, David. *The End of Inequality? Stratification Under State Socialism*. Baltimore: Penguin, 1971.
Lenski, Gerhard. "Marxist Experiments in Destratification: An Appraisal." *Social Forces* 57 (Dec. 1978): 364-83.
Lipset, Seymour Martin, and Richard B. Dobson. "Social Stratification and Sociology in the Soviet Union." *Survey* 19 (Summer 1973): 114-85.
McAuley, Alastair. *Economic Welfare in the Soviet Union: Poverty, Living Standards, and Inequality*. Madison: University of Wisconsin Press, 1979.
Matthews, Mervyn. *Class and Society in Soviet Russia*. New York: Walker, 1972.
Smith, Hedrick. *The Russians*. New York: Quadrangle, 1976.
Yanowitch, Murray. *Social and Economic Inequality in the USSR: Six Studies*. White Plains, N.Y.: Sharpe, 1977.
Yanowitch, Murray, and Wesley A. Fisher, eds. and trans. *Social Stratification and Mobility in the USSR*. Commentary by S. M. Lipset. White Plains, N.Y.: International Arts and Sciences Press, 1973.

CHAPTER 5: EDUCATION AND OPPORTUNITY

Dobson, Richard B. "Educational Policies and Attainment." In *Women in Russia,* edited by Dorothy Atkinson, Alexander Dallin, and Gail Warshofsky Lapidus, pp. 267-92. Stanford: Stanford University Press, 1977.
Dobson, Richard B., and Michael Swafford. "The Educational Attainment Process in the Soviet Union: A Case Study." *Comparative Education Review* 24 (June 1980): 252-69.
Fitzpatrick, Sheila. *Education and Social Mobility in the Soviet Union 1921-1934.* Cambridge University Press, 1979.
_____, ed. *Cultural Revolution in Russia, 1928-1931.* Bloomington: Indiana University Press, 1978.
Inkeles, Alex, and Raymond A. Bauer. *The Soviet Citizen: Daily Life in a Totalitarian Society.* Cambridge, Mass.: Harvard University Press, 1959.
Jacoby, Susan. *Inside Soviet Schools.* New York: Hill and Wang, 1974.
Liss, L. F. "The Social Conditioning of Occupational Choice." In *Social Stratification and Mobility in the USSR,* edited by Murray Yanowitch and Wesley A. Fisher, pp. 275-88. White Plains, N.Y.: International Arts and Sciences Press, 1973.
Rutkevich, M. N., ed. *The Career Plans of Young,* edited and translated by Murray Yanowitch. White Plains, N.Y.: International Arts and Sciences Press, 1969.
Swafford, Michael. "The Socialization and Training of Soviet Industrial Workers." In *Industrial Labor in the U.S.S.R.,* edited by Arcadius Kahan and Blair Ruble, pp. 19-41. New York: Pergamon, 1979.
Vasil'eva, E. K. *The Young People of Leningrad: School and Work Options and Attitudes,* translated by Arlo Schultz and Andrew J. Smith. Introduction by Richard B. Dobson. White Plains, N.Y.: International Arts and Sciences Press, 1976.

CHAPTER 6: OBSERVATIONS ON RURAL LIFE IN SOVIET RUSSIA

Adams, Arthur E., and Jan Steckelberg Adams. *Agriculture in the USSR, Poland, and Czechoslovakia.* New York: Free Press, 1971.
Belov, Fedor. *The History of a Soviet Collective Farm.* New York: Praeger, 1955.
Dunn, Stephen P., and Ethel Dunn. *The Peasants of Central Russia.* New York: Holt, Rinehart, and Winston, 1967.
Laird, Roy D. *Collective Farming in Russia.* Lawrence: University of Kansas Press, 1958.
Laird, Roy D., and Betty A. Laird. *Soviet Communism and Agrarian Revolution.* Harmondsworth, England: Penguin, 1970.
Maynard, Sir John. *Russia in Flux.* New York: Macmillan, 1948.
Millar, James R., ed. *The Soviet Rural Community.* Urbana: University of Illinois Press, 1971.
Mitrany, David. *Marx Against the Peasant.* London: George Weidenfeld and Nicolson, Ltd, 1951.
Volin, Lazar. *A Century of Russian Agriculture from Alexander II to Khrushchev.* Cambridge, Mass.: Harvard University Press, 1970.

CHAPTER 7: SOVIET SOCIETY AND COMMUNIST PARTY CONTROLS

Bloch, Sidney, and Peter Reddaway. *Psychiatric Terror: How Soviet Psychiatry Is Used to Suppress Dissent.* New York: Basic Books, 1977.
Connor, Walter D. *Socialism, Politics and Equality: Hierarchy and Change in Eastern Europe and the USSR.* New York: Columbia University Press, 1979.

Djilas, Milovan. *The New Class.* New York: Praeger, 1957.
Field, Mark G., ed. *Social Consequences of Modernization in Communist Societies.* Baltimore: Johns Hopkins University Press, 1976.
Fleron, Frederick J., Jr., ed. *Communist Studies and the Social Sciences: Essays on Methodology and Empirical Theory.* Chicago: Rand McNally, 1969.
Hough, Jerry F. *The Local Party Organs in Industrial Decision-Making.* Cambridge, Mass.: Harvard University Press, 1969.
Hough, Jerry F., and Merle Fainsod. *How the Soviet Union Is Governed.* Cambridge, Mass.: Harvard University Press, 1979.
Ryawac, Karl W., ed. *Soviet Society and the Communist Party.* Amherst: University of Massachusetts Press, 1978.

CHAPTER 8: RELIGION AND ATHEISM IN THE USSR

Bociurkiw, Bohdan R. "The Shaping of Soviet Religious Policy." *Problems of Communism* 32 (May-June 1973): 37-51.
Bociurkiw, Bohdan R., and John W. Strong, eds. *Religion and Atheism in the USSR and Eastern Europe.* Toronto: University of Toronto Press, 1975.
Dunn, Dennis J., ed. *Religion and Modernization in the Soviet Union,* Boulder, Colo.: Westview Press, 1977.
Dunn, Ethel. "The Importance of Religion in the Soviet Rural Community. In *The Soviet Rural Community,* edited by James R. Millar, pp. 346-75. Urbana: University of Illinois Press, 1971.
Klibanov, A. I. "Fifty Years of Scientific Study of Religious Sectarianism." *Soviet Sociology* 8 (1970): 239-78.
Lane, Christel. *Christian Religion in the Soviet Union: A Sociological Study.* Albany: State University of New York Press, 1978.
Marshall, Richard H., Jr., ed. *Aspects of Religion in the Soviet Union, 1917-1967.* Chicago: University of Chicago Press, 1971.
Powell, David. *Antireligious Propaganda in the Soviet Union: A Study of Mass Persuasion.* Cambridge, Mass.: M.I.T. Press.
Religion in Communist Lands. The journal of England's Keston College, every issue contains articles and documents related to the Soviet religious situation.
Simon, Gerhard. *Church, State and Opposition in the USSR,* translated by Kathleen Matchett. Berkeley: University of California Press, 1974.

CHAPTER 9: CRIME AND DELINQUENCY IN THE SOVIET UNION

Chalidze, Valery. *Criminal Russia.* New York: Random House, 1977.
Connor, Walter D. *Deviance in Soviet Society: Crime, Delinquency and Alcoholism.* New York: Columbia University Press, 1972.
_____. "Criminal Homicide, USSR/USA: Reflections on Soviet Data in a Comparative Framework." *Journal of Criminal Law and Criminology* 64, no. 1 (1973): 111-17.
Juviler, Peter H. *Revolutionary Law and Order: Politics and Social Change in the USSR.* New York: Free Press, 1976.
Shelley, Louise. "Soviet Criminology After the Revolution." *Journal of Criminal Law and Criminology* 70, no. 3 (1979): 391-96.
_____. "The Geography of Soviet Criminality." *American Sociological Review* 45, no. 1 (1980): 111-22.
Solomon, Peter H., Jr. *Soviet Criminologists and Criminal Policy.* New York: Columbia University Press, 1978.

CHAPTER 10: THE PLACE OF WOMEN

Atkinson, Dorothy, Alexander Dallin, and Gail W. Lapidus, eds. *Women in Russia.* Stanford: Stanford University Press, 1977.
Dodge, Norton T. *Women in the Soviet Economy.* Baltimore: Johns Hopkins University Press, 1966.
Fisher, Wesley. *The Soviet Marriage Market: Mate Selection in Russia and the USSR.* New York: Praeger, 1980.
Geiger, H. Kent. *The Family in Soviet Russia.* Cambridge, Mass.: Harvard University Press, 1968.
Lapidus, Gail W. *Women in Soviet Society: Equality, Development, Social Change.* Berkeley: University of California Press, 1978.
Massell, Gregory H. *The Surrogate Proletariat: Moslem Women and Revolutionary Strategies in Soviet Central Asia: 1919-1929.* Princeton: Princeton University Press, 1974.
Sacks, Michael Paul. *Women's Work in Soviet Russia: Continuity in the Midst of Change.* New York: Praeger, 1976.

AUTHOR INDEX

Adams, Arthur E., 146
Adams, Jan Steckelberg, 146
Aitov, N. A., 111, 121, 128, 133
Arutiunian, Iurii V., 94-95, 102, 103, 104-05

Bauer, Raymond, 116
Bauman, Zygmunt, 90
Bell, Daniel, 35, 38, 57, 58
Bell, Wendell, 38
Belova, V.A., 78
Berger, Peter L., 227
Bialer, Seweryn, 166
Bociurkiw, Bohdan R., 187, 191
Bourdeaux, Michael, 198
Bryden, Judith G., 81
Brzezinski, Zbigniew, 110
Bukharin, Nikolai, 91-92

Campbell, Robert W., 177
Chapman, Janet, 98
Chuiko, L.V., 52
Chulanov, Iu. G., 111
Churbanov, V., 104
Clem, Ralph, 4, 184, 245
Cloward, Richard A., 213
Connor, Walker, 11, 34
Coser, Lewis, 5

Dahrendorf, Ralf, 187
Daniels, Robert V., 163
Deutsch, Karl, 37, 139, 245
Dienes, Leslie, 26, 56
Djilas, Milovan, 166, 173
Dobson, Richard B., 134, 172
Dodge, Norton T., 231
Dunham, Vera, 241
Dunn, Ethel, 202
Dunn, Stephen P., 202
Durkheim, Emile, 163

Eisenstadt, S. N., 162
Engels, Friedrich, 63-64, 66
Enloe, Cynthia, 39, 46

Field, Mark, 6
Filippov, F. R., 93-94, 109, 133
Fisher, Wesley, 52
Foltz, William, 11, 38, 59
Francisco, Ronald A., 4

Gendel', V. G., 121, 124, 128
Glazer, Nathan, 37, 47, 58
Goldthorpe, John H., 89-90
Goode, William J., 228, 240
Gordon, L. A., 102
Gurr, Ted Robert, 35-36, 59

Hechter, Michael, 39
Heer, David M., 70, 81
Holubnychy, Vsevolod, 22
Hough, Jerry F., 173, 180, 239, 242
Huntington, Samuel, 110

Inkeles, Alex, 97, 103, 116
Iovchuk, M. T., 106

Karpets, I. I., 212
Kassof, Allen, 5, 173
Klopov, E. V., 102
Kogan, L. N., 106
Koropeckyj, Iwan, 26
Kulagin, G., 130
Kvasha, A. Ya., 75, 76, 77-78, 79
Kwan, Kian M., 41, 42

Laird, Roy D., 4
Lane, Christel, 200, 203
Lenin, Vladimir Ilich, 18, 19, 20, 21, 22, 43, 229, 233
Lenski, Gerhard, 112
Luckmann, Thomas, 227

Madison, Bernice, 234
Malthus, Thomas, 63
Mannheim, Karl, 5
Martin, David, 201
Marx, Karl, 163
Massell, Gregory H., 244
Maynard, Sir John, 140
McDowell, Jennifer, 203
Mehlan, K. H., 70
Merton, Robert K., 213
Miller, John H., 46
Moynihan, Daniel P., 37, 47, 58
Murvar, Vatro, 189

Nechaeva, G. A., 110
Nisbet, Robert, 182, 201

Ohlin, Lloyd E., 213
Oppenheimer, Valerie K., 231
Ossowski, Stanislaw, 92-93

Pankhurst, Jerry G., 12
Parsons, Talcott, 161
Perevedentsev, V. I., 44, 72, 74, 75, 76-77, 78, 149, 153
Pipes, Richard, 17
Piskunov, V. P., 75, 77

Raeff, Marc, 41
Rakowska-Harmstone, Teresa, 46, 57, 59
Rodgers, Allan, 26
Rossi, Peter, 97
Rostow, Walt W., 168
Russell, Bertrand, 166
Rutkevich, M. N., 93-94, 106, 109, 127-28, 131

Sacks, Michael Paul, 66

Schroeder, Gertrude, 26
Scott, Joan W., 229, 240-241, 243
Sellin, Thorsten, 213
Sennikova, L. I., 110
Shargorodskii, M. D., 213
Shelley, Louise, 4
Shibutani, Tamotsu, 41, 42
Shipler, David K., 175
Shkaratan, O. I., 94, 103
Shubkin, V. N., 95
Shulman, Colette, 238
Silver, Brian, 28, 50, 53
Slesarev, L. A., 110
Stalin, Joseph, 19, 98, 168
Steshenko, Valentina S., 75, 77
Sutherland, Edwin, 213
Swafford, Michael, 134, 236
Szporluk, Roman, 49

Tilly, Louise A., 229, 240-41, 243
Timasheff, Nicholas, 191
Treiman, Donald, 97
Trotsky, Leon, 91
Turgenev, Ivan, 154

U.S. Central Intelligence Agency, 85
Urlanis, Boris Ts., 66, 75-76

Vershlovskii, S. G., 124
Vodzinskaia, V. V., 95, 97

Weber, Max, 165
Wolfe, Bertram, 167

Yanowitch, Murray, 106

Zemtsov, L. G., 120
Zwick, Peter, 27

SUBJECT INDEX

abortions, 81, 83-84; data on, 83; first legalization of, 66; policy questioned, 68; relegalization of, in 1955, 70-71, 75
Academy of Sciences, 209
acculturation, 34, 40, 52
achiever groups, 37-38, 40, 42, 47
Adventists, 185
affirmative action, 36, 38, 58, 133
Afghanistan, 85, 184
agricultural development of Central Asia 79
agricultural labor force, 233, 235
agricultural production, 85, 177
agrogorady, 142
Aid to Families with Dependent Children program, 81-82
Albania, 190
alcoholism: and crime, 220, 221; increase with industrialization, 171; as vestige of the past, 212, 213
Alexander II, Tsar, 17
Alexander III, Tsar, 17
All-Union Council of ECB, 188, 194, 196-97
All-Union Institute for the Prevention of Crime and the Elaboration of Preventive Measures, 210, 215
Alma-Ata, 45
Altays, 17
American Council of Learned Societies (ACLS), 1
anomie theory, 213
anti-clerical tradition in Russia, 188-89
antireligious campaign: of 1930s, 188, 190; of 1958-64, 189, 194-95, 197, 199, 200, 204
antireligious policy: options for, 189-96; subordinated to class struggle, 191

Arab-Israeli conflict, 184
Armenia: Christianity in, 184; forged academic documents in, 133; women's wages in, 236
Armenian Apostolic Church, 185
Armenians, 13, 16-17, 28, 53; as an achiever group, 37, 42-43, 47; national identity and Armenian Church, 185
arts, policy in the, 169, 175-76; and ethnic awareness, 50
Asia, (Soviet), 16, 17 (*see also* Central Asia)
assimilation, 34, 40, 47-53
Astrakhan, 16
atheism: before 1917, 200; in Poland, 183; in USSR, 183, 187 (*see also* antireligious campaign, antireligious policy)
authority, political (*see* legitimacy, political, power, political)
Azerbaydzhan, 27, 74
Azeri, 12, 16-17, 53

Baku, fertility and abortions in, 68
Balkars, 16
ballet, 103
Baltic language group, 13
Baltic republics, 26, 27, 53, 56-57, 74, 216, 218, 220 (*see also* Estonia, Latvia, Lithuania)
Baltic Sea, 16, 17
Baptists (*see* Evangelical Christians and Baptists)
Bashkirs, 12, 16, 20, 53
Basque region, 39; separatist movement in, 33
Bavaria, 167
Belgium, 33
Belorussia, 17, 19, 56, 184; and Belorussian language use in, 49

Belorussian nationality, 12, 16, 51; fertility rate for, 53
Bessarabia, 16, 19
biology in USSR, 174
birth rate (*see* fertility)
Bolsheviks (*see* Communist Party of the Soviet Union, Social Democrats)
books: reading of, 102-03; control over, 169
Brezhnev, Leonid I., 180; and cult of personality, 160; on private agriculture, 149; and Soviet political structure, 169, 173
bribery for education admissions, 131
brigades on collective or state farms, 147
Buddhism in USSR, 184
Bukharin, Nikolai, 91-92
Bulgaria, 98, 214
bureaucracy, 5
Buryats, 16, 17

Canada: crisis of federal order in, 33; inequality in, 99
capital stock, accumulation of, 6, 40, 173
capitalism: and class structure, 89-93; and crime, 211; and education, 133-34; and female employment, 229-31; and population problems, 63; Soviet images of, 7, 47-48
Caspian Sea, 16
Caucasus region, 16-17, 19, 79; fertility rates in, 53-54, 74; labor force in, 54-55
censors, 7, 176
census, Soviet, 23, 12, 184, 237, 238; and ethnicity, 50-51; of 1897, 230; of 1926, 235, 186-87; of 1939, 243, 244; of 1959, 244; of 1970, 236, 244, 247; of 1979, 12
census, U.S., 238
Central Asia, 16-17, 19, 20, 27, 44, 184; fertility and population growth in, 53-54, 74, 77-80, 85-86, 168; labor force in, 55; women in, 244-49, 250 (*see also* Kirgizia, Tadzhikistan, Turkmenistan, Uzbekistan, Muslims in USSR)
Central Ideological Commission, 192

Central Statistical Administration (Ts.S.U.), 82
Chalcedon, Council of, 185
Chechens, 16, 53
child allowance program, 68-70, 74, 81, 83-84; current debate over, 74-77, 78-79; data on, 83; Soviet, compared to other programs, 80-82; supplemented in 1974, 72-73
childcare (*see* preschool childcare and education)
China, People's Republic of, 12, 85, 161; population of, 84
Chinese, 37
cholera epidemic, 153
Christian Committee for the Defense of Believers' Rights, 199-200
Christianity, 163, 184, 185-86; and Marxism, 182 (*see also the names of specific groups*)
church: as analogue for party, 164; as counter-revolutionary force, 187, 189, 191; and dialogue with state, 191; as focal point of traditional village, 140; pre-Revolutionary landholding and, 141 (*see also* religion)
Chuvash, 13, 16, 20, 51, 53
Civil War (1917-1923), 19, 231
class conflict, 89
class, social, 35, 94; defined by Lenin, 88-89; structure in U.S., 92-93; structure in USSR, 89-93, 171-72 (*see also* working class, peasantry, white-collar stratum in USSR)
class war, 88
clergy: deprived seat on parish council, 195-96; Orthodox and ECB contrasted, 198; pastoral mission shift, 159; role restricted, 196
cold war, 2
collective farms, 89, 98, 141, 142-44, 145-46; and *agrogorady*, 142; chairman of, 141, 145-46; and Model Charter of 1935, 146; pension system on, 68 (*see also* peasantry)
collectivization of agriculture, 88, 115, 138, 139, 142, 144, 146-47; and female employment, 66, 240; and population processes, 231, 232

communist morality, 164, 166-67, 203
Communist Party of the Soviet Union (CPSU), 2, 97; and antireligious policy, 183-84, 187-88, 189-95, 199, 203, 204; congresses of, 165; and control of economy, 176-78; and control over specialists, 171; and "cult of the Party," 160; early (Bolshevik) nationality policy of, 19-20, 22; educational attainment of members, 106; on farms, 142, 152; Fifteenth Congress (1927), 22; functions in Soviet society, 156-59, 180; as overseer of social change, 89, 115, 203; and population policy, 74-75; and promotion of equality, 111-12; and Russian dominance, 45-46; as a secular church, 160-61, 163-67, 203; in Smolensk, 20; worker participation in, 105-06 (*see also* Social Democrats)
communist stage of development, 89, 211
communist upbringing, 203
comparative approach, 2, 8, 249; in ethnic studies, 33-34, 41
comrades' courts as successor to *mir*, 144
conflict, class (*see* class conflict)
conflict, interethnic, 37-38, 39-40, 41
conquest, 36
Constitution of the USSR, 165, 169; and federal form, 20; and religion, 183-84
cooptation: of minority elites, 42; of religious leadership, 188
Council of Churches of ECB, 188, 196-97
Council of Prisoners' Relatives, 197
Council for Russian Orthodox Church Affairs, 195
crime, 208; and city structure, 217; and employment, 220-21; forms of, for intellectuals, 176; increase with industrialization, 171, 214, 216; new Soviet forms of, 224; no biological causes seen, 211; organized, 221, 223; and societal development, 218-19; Soviet theory of, 210-13; in rural areas, 216; and women, 216, 219-20, 223; and youth, 217 (*see also* crimes against the person, political crime,

prison camps, property crimes, rape, recidivism, violent crime)
crimes against the person, 216, 218, 219, 220-21
crimes against the state (*see* political crime)
criminal offender: characterization of, 219-21; political, 222
criminology: Soviet, 208-10; Western, 209; Western Marxist, 211, 213; world, 8, 210, 213
Croatia, 39
cult of personality, 159-60
cultural consumption and stratification, 102-03
cultural facilities, access to, 27, 128
culture conflict, theory of, 213
culture defined, 227
Czechoslovakia, 98, 175

Dagestan, peoples of, 53
death rate (*see* mortality)
delinquency: increase with industrialization, 171; and rape, 221; theoretical causes of, 213; trends in USSR, 220, 224
demographic transition, 64, 74
deprivation, relative (*see* relative deprivation)
detente in international relations, 199
developed nations: crime pattern in, 218; population policy in, 81-82
developing nations: crime pattern in, 218; population policy in, 80-81
deviance increase with industrialization, 171
dictatorship of the proletariat, 19-20, 23, 91
differential association, theory of, 213
differentiation, organizational, in religious sphere, 191-94, 197, 198-99
differentiation, societal, 161-67; and CPSU controls, 172-74; and Orthodox culture, 188-89
diffusion of ideas of Western-style sociology, 5-6
dissidence in USSR, 12, 164-65, 168, 176, 199; religious, 183, 185, 188, 189-90, 195-97, 198, 199-200, 204
division of labor, 161

Dnepr River, 16
drunkenness, 144 (*see also* alcoholism)
druzhinniki, 105
Dukhobors, 186
Durkheim, Emile, 210-11, 224
dvadtsatka, 195
dvor, 140, 144, 147-49
Dzyuba, Ivan, 56

East Africa, 37
Eastern Orthodox Church (*see* Orthodox Church)
ECB Church (*see* Evangelical Christians and Baptists)
econometric models in agriculture, 151
economic development of USSR, and development of Soviet sociology, 5-6
economic geography of USSR, 26 (*see also* regional development in USSR)
ecumenical activities, 188-89; and dissent, 199-200
education: access to, 23, 27, 127-32; and antireligious program, 187-88; attainment among nationalities, 28, 54, 59, 247; Bukharin's views on, 91; in Central Asia and Caucasus region, 79-80; and crime, 220-21; and cultural consumption, 102; and equal opportunity, 131-34; ethnic quotas in, 58; and fertility decline, 67-68; and finances, 123-24; and industrialization, 172; and job satisfaction, 104; Khrushchev's reforms of, 49, 117-18; main features of Soviet system of, 118-20; and mobility; 111, 116-17; and party membership, 106; and pro-natalist policies, 84-85; and public participation, 105; and rising expectations, 36; and rural youth, 150; and Russian language usage, 44, 48-49, 79-80; and secularization, 200; and socio-economic background, 120-22, 124-27; special schools, 130; subsidization of, 99; and women, 231-32, 239, 247 (*see also* tuition fees, stipends, educational)
Egypt, ancient, 161
elderly, 68
electrification of the countryside, 147-48

elite, Soviet political, 89-92, 109, 166, 170; and antireligious program, 189
elites, non-Russian, 17
endogamy, (*see* intermarriage)
energy resources (*see* natural resources)
Engels, Friedrich, 7; and ethnicity questions, 21-22; on population policy, 63-64
England (*see* United Kingdom)
environment, societal, 160, 161
equality: cross-national comparisons of, 98; ideal of, 92-93, 98; of opportunity and education, 131-32; of sexes, 228, 229, 235-43, 249-50; and structured social inequality, 111-12
Eritrean secession struggle, 33
Eshliman, Fr. Nikolai, 196, 197
Estonia, 17, 19; Lutherans in, 185 (*see also* Baltic republics)
Estonians, 13, 16, 28, 43, 47
Ethiopia, 33
ethnic group (*see* ethnicity)
ethnic stratification, 36-38; and internal colonialism, 39; and population growth rates, 54; in Tsarist Russia, 41-42; in USSR, 43-47
ethnicity, 32-34, 40-41; and assimilation 47-53; and conflict, 38-39; defined, 11, 22; and differential population growth, 53-55; and group mixing, 40, 50; and group size estimates, 50-51; and modernization, 34-36; and policy in academia, 50; and political change, 33, 57-60; and Soviet future, 53-59; and stratification of groups, 36-38 (*see also* ethnoterritories, ethnic stratification)
ethnoterritories, 23, 26, 27, 28, 38-40, 41, 44-45, 54, 55-57 (*see also* federalism)
Evangelical Christians and Baptists, 185, 189, 192, 194; autonomy of action among, 197-98; leadership manipulation in, 196-97; leadership of schism, 196, 197-98; move from Orthodox Church to, 192, 197, 198; schism among, 188, 190, 197-98; and secularization, 201-02 (*see also* All-Union Council of ECB, Council of Churches of ECB)

evolution, societal, 161-62
exogamy (*see* intermarriage)

family planning, 80-81
Far North region of USSR, 20, 224
federalism, 20; and ethnoterritoriality, 38-40, 46, 49-50, 55-57; and Russian dominance, 46
feminist views on family and population policy, 77, 242-43
fertility in USSR: and abortion policy, 68, 70-71; data concerning, 82-83, 234, 235; and demographic transition, 64-66; and educational attainment, 67-68; among ethnic groups, 53-54; and health care, 67-68; and housing shortage, 67; policy shifts concerning, 83-84; and policy toward women, 66, 235-36; and post-World War II age and sex structure, 71-72; in rural areas, 66-67; and social security, 68; and urbanization, 66-67
Finland, 19
Finnic language group, 13
Finns, 21, 51
firearms, 216-17
France, 156; child allowance program in, 81; crime patterns in, 216; educational attainment in, 134; lycée in, 119; women's role in, 229
friendship choice, 103
functions of organizations, 158-59

Gelbakhiani, P., 131
genetics in USSR, 174-75
Georgia, Soviet: Christianity in, 184, crime in, 218-19; demonstrations in, 32
Georgians, 13, 16-17, 28, 43, 47, 53
Germans in USSR, 13, 51
Germany, 19, 20, 68, 157, 172, 173, 188, 244; antireligious policy in GDR, 190-91; gymnasium in, 119; FRG, 81
Gorky, 129
gossip in kolkhoz markets, 152-53
governmental structure, differentiation of, 162
Greece, 161, 162
Greeks, 37

Grigorenko, Petr, 164
guns (*see* firearms)

health care, 23, 27, 99, 101, 174-75; and mortality and fertility, 67-68, 81
Helsinki monitoring groups, 199
Helsinki Pact of 1975, 199
higher education (*see* education, *VUZy*)
holidays, mass political, 203
homicide (*see* violent crime, crime against the person)
hooliganism, 219, 220
housework: compared to men's free time, 235-36; employment needs added to, 233-34; Lenin's views on, 233; men's participation in, 242; and women's education, 102
housing, 27, 99, 169; and fertility in USSR, 67, 85; rural, 142, 147-50, 233; state distribution of, 101-02
human rights, 183, 184, 190, 199-200
Hungary: antireligious policy in, 190-91; inequality in, 98; population policy in, 75; revolution in, 167
hyperbolic principle of church-state relations, 192, 197-98

icon corner, 149
ideology: decline in appeal of, 35, 58-59; and rising expectations, 36, 59
immigration, by ethnic groups, 36, 39,
India, 12, 161; population of, 84
Indians, 37
industrialism as a model of Soviet society, 170-72
industrialization in USSR, 23, 26, 52, 54, 66, 115, 141, 168, 172; of Central Asia, 79, 86; and crime, 213-16; and occupational structure, 92; and secularization, 200; of Siberia, 86; and women's role, 228-31, 232, 243, 249-50
inequality (*see* equality, class, social, occupational stratification, standard of living)
infant mortality rates, 83, 234, 241
Ingush, 16, 53
Initsiativniki, 196-97

265

integration, societal, of differentiated spheres of action, 162-63
intelligentsia, 109, 110-11, 115, 121, 129-30, 171, 178, 197, 203, 241
interest groups, 35, 41, 58, 90, 158, 169, 170, 179, 186-87; within the CPSU, 159, 165-66, 178; and religion, 186-87, 198-99, 200, 204; of women, 239-40
intermarriage: ethnic, 34, 40, 52-53; socio-occupational, 103
internal colonialism, 39
International Research and Exchanges Board (IREX), 1, 3
International Sociological Association, 5
investment, economic, 232
Iran, 139, 182
irredentist situations, 17
Irtysh River, 86
Islam, 16; revival in, 182, 184 (*see also* Muslims in USSR)
Israel, 161, 176, 184
Ivan IV (the Terrible), Tsar, 16

Japan, 177
Jehovah's Witnesses, 185
Jews, 12, 13, 16, 27, 28, 51; as an achiever group, 37-38, 42-43, 47, 58; and dissent, 58, 59; emigration from USSR, 32, 176, 184 (*see also* Judaism in USSR)
job satisfaction, 103-04
journalistic accounts of the USSR, 4
Judaism in USSR, 184, 194-95 (*see also* Jews)

Kabardinians, 16
Kalinin Province, 94
Karelians, 51
Kazakhs, 12, 16-17, 45, 53
Kazakhstan, 17, 26, 45, 247
Kazan', 16, 21, 108
KGB and control of intellectuals, 175
Khakas, 17
Khomeini, Ayatollah, 182
Khrushchev, Nikita, 180; agricultural policy of, 142; and antireligious campaign, 194-95; and cult of personality 159-60, 167; educational reforms of,

117-18; and pro-natalism, 71; and Soviet political structure, 169
Kiev, 45, 97, 214
kindergarten (*see* preschool childcare and education)
kinship system, 161-62; and ties under industrialism, 170-71
Kirgiz, 12, 13, 16-17, 45, 53
Kirgizia, 45, 74, 244, 247 (*see also* Central Asia)
kolkhoz (*see* collective farms)
kolkhoz markets, 151-52
Komi, 53
Krasnodar, 94, 148
Krasnov-Levitin, Anatoli, 196-97
Kryuchkov, Gennadi, 196
kulaks, 88

labor camps (*see* prison camps)
labor force: in Central Asia, 54-55, 79-80, 245-49; national shortage, 231-33, 235; shortage in Siberia, 55, 79 (*see also* agricultural labor force)
lags of consciousness, 212
land ownership in USSR, 144-45
land reform in Iran, 139
language shift, 34, 40, 43-44, 50, 52; and assimilation policy, 48-49
languages, non-Russian: use in education, 48-49
Latin America and "liberation theology," 182
Latvia, 17, 19; Lutherans in, 185; population growth in, 74 (*see also* Baltic republics)
Latvians, 13, 16, 28, 43, 47
law: Soviet, 224; as training for criminologists, 209
Lebanese, 37
legitimacy, political, of Party, 165, 169
Lenin, Vladimir Ilich, 7, 180; and antireligious program, 187; as charismatic figure, 165; and class analysis, 88-89, 94; on crime, 212; and nationality policy, 18-22; and population policy, 66; and Soviet political structure, 169, 172; on superiority of industrial organization, 138, 147; on women's role, 229

Leningrad: crime in, 214, 218; fertility and abortions in, 68-69; special schools in, 130; stratification studies in, 95, 111, 122-23, 124
liberation theology, 182
Lithuania, 17, 19, 32, 185 (*see also* Baltic republics)
Lithuanians, 13, 16, 189
Lutheran Church, 13, 185
Lysenkoism, 174

machine-tractor stations (MTS), 139, 142, 152
Mao Tse Tung, 163
March of Dimes, 159
Mari, 16, 51
marriage: religious, 201, 203; socialist, 203; and women's roles, 227-28 (*see also* intermarriage)
Marx, Karl, 7; and nationality question, 21; on population policy, 63-64
Marxist-Leninist theory and ideology: and antireligious program, 187, 203-04; on crime, 210-13; and development of Soviet sociology, 4-6; and family policy, 75-76; and female employment, 228-29, 232; and nationality policy, 18, 21-22, 47; and peasant policy, 146; as secular faith in USSR, 163-67, 203-04; and Soviet economic policy, 176-77
McCarthyism, 164
mechanization of agriculture, 78, 141, 150-51
media: access to, 23; and antireligious program, 187-88; and language use, 49-50; tight controls over, 152-53, 169
medicine, 175
Mediterranean region, 37
melting pot, 34
Mennonites in USSR, 185
mental health (*see* psychiatric treatment)
Mesopotamia, 161
Michels, Robert, views addressed by Bukharin, 91
middle class values and women's role, 240-42

Middle East, 33, 37
migration, 45, 50, 55, 39, 64; and Central Asia, 78, 79-80, 85, 103, 110; and crime patterns, 214-15; rural to urban, 140-41, 150-51, 231, 233, 240 (*see also* immigration)
military intervention, foreign, 19
military, Soviet, 157
military-strategic policy: and antireligious program, 191; and ethnic group factors, 55; and investment patterns, 158; and location of industry, 26; and population policy, 82-83, 84-85; and pre-World War II birth rate, 68
mineral reserves (*see* natural resources)
minimum wage in USSR, 99, 100, 144, 235
ministers, religious (*see* clergy, religion, church)
Ministry of Internal Affairs (MVD), 209; institute of, 210
Minsk: fertility and abortions in, 68-69; conference in, 151
mobility (*see* occupational mobility)
mobilization (*see* social mobilization, social movement mobilization)
models of Soviet society, 2, 170 (*see also* theories of Soviet society)
modernization: and ethnicity, 34-36, 37, 41, 52, 59-60; evolutionary pattern of, 161, 170-71; and internal colonialism, 39; and peasantry, 154; and social mobilization, 139
Moldavia, 17, 19, 26, 27, 184
Moldavians, 13, 16
Molokans, 186
monasteries, 194
monocracy, 169-70
Mordvinians, 13, 16, 20, 51, 53
mortality in USSR: data on, 82-83; and Demographic Transition, 64-66; among ethnic groups, 53-54; and post-World War II age and sex structure, 71-72 (*see also* infant mortality)
Moscow, 94; crime in, 209, 214-15, 218-19; fertility and abortions in, 66, 68-69; peat bogs burning near, 152-53; stu-

nurseries (see preschool childcare and education)
Novosibirsk, 95-97
nomenklatura, 145
normative reactions to normlessness, 201-02
Nigerian civil war, 33
Nizhnii Tagil, 109
169; readership of, 102-03, 232
formation on crime, 208; policy for,
newspapers: content of, 105, 242; and information on crime, 208; policy for, 169; readership of, 102-03, 232
new Soviet person, 224
New Economic Policy (NEP), 88-97
neo-Slavophilism, 58, 168
natural resources, 85
nation-state, 35
nationality (see ethnicity)
17, 18; in USSR, 19-20
nationalist movements: in tsarist Russia, 17, 18; in USSR, 19-20
National Defense Foreign Language (NDFL) Fellowships, 1, 3
national-communism, 167-69
nation building, 17; and ethnicity, 34, 35, 38, 41
Napoleon, 156

Muscovite state, 16
Muslims in USSR, 12, 140, 184, 195; child allowance program among, 78-79, 84; high fertility among, 73-75; population policy debate over, 77-80, 85-86; women among, 244-49 (see also Central Asia)
"Mother Russia" tradition, 153
murder (see violent crime; crime against the person)
Moslems (see Islam; Muslims in USSR)
Moscow State University, 131
Rome," 189
dents in, 117, 128-29, as "Third Rome," 189

occupational variation among nationalities, 28, 44-45; and Russian language usage, 44
Old Believers, 186
opportunity theory, 213, 215
Orthodox Church: Eastern, 12, 13, 150, 168, 185; Georgian, 185; Russian, 184-85, 189, 190-91, 192, 197, 198, 199, 200-01, 202, 203
Ossetians, 16, 28

Palestinian problem, 33
parasitism, 209, 214, 220, 224
passport, internal: and crime control, 214, 222; and ethnic/nationality labeling, 50; for peasants, 141
Patriarch Alexi, 196
peasantry, Soviet: classes within, 150; and control over production, 177-78; crime among, 216; earnings on collective farm, 140; in higher education, 116; emancipation of, 140; in higher education, 116; income of, 152; and public participation, 106, 138, 141; quality of life for, 153-54; and religion, 200-01; and Slavophiles, 168; under socialism, 89; stability and patriotism of, 139; and women, 240, 244-45 (see also collective farms)
pedology, 116
pensions, 68, 76, 99, 100, 101-02, 235
Pentecostals in USSR, 185
Persian language group, 12-13
Peter I (the Great), Tsar, 16
petroleum production in USSR, 85
physical sciences, 171, 174
planning: in education, 119-20, as Party function, 174; of wages and salaries, 89-90
Pliushch, Leonid, 165
pluralism, political, 165, 170, 173
Poland, 16, 19, 182; antireligious policy in, 191, 199; inequality in, 98
Poles in USSR, 13, 21, 51
police, Soviet, 209, 210 (see also Ministry of Internal Affairs [MVD], KGB)
Polish sociologists, 6
political crime, 214, 221

Ob River, 86
occupational differentiation by sex, 237-38, 243-49
occupational mobility, 106-11; in Central Asia, 249; men's vs. women's, 235-36; occupational stratification in USSR, 93-97; 171; and female employment, 236-38

269

Pope John Paul II, 182-83
popular press, Soviet, 7
population policy: and international prestige, 72; Marxian theory on, 63-64; and Soviet legislation, 64-73, 83; two major goals in, 82; and World War II losses, 69
poverty in USSR, 99-100; and crime, 220
power, decision-making; worker sense of, 104-05
power, political, 5, 19, 35; and CPSU, 166, 167, 177-78, 186; and ethnic groups, 35, 36, 57-60; and promotion of equality, 111-12; and Soviet class structure, 90-91, 105-06; and wealth in U.S., 91; and women, 239-40, 244, 249-50; (see also legitimacy, political)
preschool childcare and education, 76-77, 85, 120-21, 235, 241; and changing women's roles, 228, 229, 233-34, 242
press (see books, newspapers, popular press, Soviet)
priests (see clergy)
prison camps, 200, 209, 220, 222, 223; Stalinist, 194
private plots, 144-45, 149, 152, 177, 233
procurators, 209
productivity of workers, 6
professionals (see specialists)
Prokofiev, Alexei, 196
proletarian dictatorship (see dictatorship of the proletariat)
property crime, 216, 218, 219, 220, 221
prostitutes, 215
Protestants in USSR, 185, 197, 203; illegal group of, 197; shift of believers toward, 201; state sought unified church for, 194 (see also Adventists, Evangelical Christians and Baptists, Jehovah's Witnesses, Lutherans, Mennonites, Pentecostals)
Provisional Government, 18
psychiatric treatment, of dissidents, 176

rabfaki, 115
radical theories of crime, 213
radio: listeners, 102; policy for, 169
rape, 221, 224
recidivism, 214, 220, 222-24
redemption payments for land, 140
Reds (in Civil War), 19
reference group: change with industrialism, 170-71; for peasantry, 153
Reformation, 161, 167
regional development in USSR, 23-28, 40
relative deprivation: and crime, 214; and ethnic group conflict, 35-36, 59; and Soviet peasantry, 139, 153, 154
religion: and dissent (see dissidence in USSR, religious); and de-differentiation, 162-63; forms in USSR, 183-86, and interest group formation, 187-90; as model for Soviet Party and ideology, 160-61, 163-67; and normative reactions to normlessness, 201-03; political voice of, 183, 191; politicization of, 204; in rural areas, 150, 153; and ties under industrialism, 171 (see also Buddhism, Christianity, church, clergy, Islam, Judaism)
religious leadership, 188, 197; manipulation by state, 195-97
Renaissance, 161, 166
research visits to the USSR, 1-2
residential segregation, 40, 39
resources for social movements, 198
revolution: for February 1917, 18-19, 189; Iranian (1979), 139, 182; and Marxist politics, 2, 182; of November 1917, 8, 58, 68, 88, 97, 138, 144, 187, 189, 200, 202-03, 215, 231; and social mobilization, 139; U.S. and USSR, 92
rites of passage: religious, 201; socialist, 203
ritualist orientation among Russian Orthodox, 189
Roman Catholic Church, 12, 182; in Poland, 183, 199, in USSR, 185, 189 (see also Lithuania, Uniates)
Romania, 19; antireligious policy in, 191
Romanians, 13, 16
Rostov, 127
RSFSR, 20, 140, 230; Christianity in, 184; crime in, 215, 216, migration from, 215; number of abortions in, 66; population growth in, 74; research

270

samogon, 216
scholarships (see stipends, educational)
scientific atheism, 188
sects in USSR, 185-86, 189, 191, 192-94, 197, 201-02
secularization, 182-83, 192, 198, 200-03
seminaries, 194
serfs in Russia, 41-42, 140, 147
Seventh-Day Adventists (see Adventists)
sex ratio, 232, 238, 247
Shpiller, Archpriest Vsevolod, 196
Siberia, 16, 19, 20, 55, 56, 79-80, 85-86, 214
Slavophiles, 168
Slovenia, 39
Smolensk archive, 20
Social Democrats, and nationality policy, 17-18
social mobilization, 35, 50, 169, 178-79, 180, 245, 247; and Soviet peasantry, 139, 152, 154
social movement mobilization, 198
social security system, 68
social sciences in USSR, 171
Social Science Research Council (SSRC), 1
socialism: alleged progress under, 153; and crime, 208, 211-13, 216, 224; and education, 133-34; and equality, 92; and ethnicity, 33, 47, 59-60; and family policy, 75-76; Michels' views on, 91; and mobility, 106, 110; and poverty, 63; and pro-natalism, 71; Soviet imagine of, triumph of, 7, 8; proclaimed in 1936, 88 (see also Marxist-Leninist theory and ideology)
sociology: Bukharin on, 91; Soviet, development of, 4-7, 118, 171, 175; Soviet research on religion, 200, 201; Soviet, and the study of stratification, 91-92, 94-95, 116, and the study of the USSR, 2-4, 7-9; world, 8-9
Solzhenitsyn, Alexander, 153, 168, 196
Southeast Asia, 37
Soviet area studies, 3-4
Soviet Russia (see RSFSR)
Sovietization, 51-52
Soviets (i.e., councils), 178
sovkhoz (see state farms)
space projects, 169
Spain, 33, 39
specialists, in USSR, 171, 174-76, 178; women as, 237, 238
speculation, criminal, 214, 224
Sri Lanka, 33
Stalin, Joseph, 180; agriculture policy of, 142, 144, 147, 152; and collectivization, 138, 142; and criminology, 209; and cult of personality, 159-60, 167; and dictatorship, 169, 186; and education, 116; and inequality, 98, 112, and Lysenkoism, 174-75; and middle-class values, 241; and modernization, 172; and nationality policy, 19, 20, 47; and population policy, 66; and "socialism in one country," 167-70, 212; and sociology, 5
standard of living, 97-101; and population policy, 82 (see also ethnic stratification)

Russian Republic (see RSFSR)
Russian Social Democratic Labor Party (see Social Democrats)
Russianization, 52
Russification, 52

in, 94-95, 215; success of preparatory faculties in, 132; women's work in, 229-40, 245
Russian Empire, 16-17, 19, 21, 41-42, 64
Russian language: as general language of USSR, 43-44, 51-52, 78; lack of fluency in Central Asia, 79, 85; usage in education, 48-49; 79-80; usage in the media, 49
Russian nationality or ethnicity, 12-13, 16, 17, 23-26, 27, 28, 42, 43-44, 45-46, 51-52, 59; in Central Asian labor force, 245; dominance of military by, 55; fertility rate for, 53-54; and "Great Russian chauvinism," 42-43, 168; and national-communism, 167-68; and neo-Slavophilism, 58-59; 168; and penetration into non-Russian ethnoterritories, 44-45, 56-57

Udmurts, 16, 51, 53
Ufa, 111, 120, 121
Ukraine, 16, 17, 19, 26, 45, 56, 151, 153, 184; population growth in, 74; and Ukrainian language use in, 49
Ukrainian nationality, 12, 16, 45; and assimilation, 51; fertility rate of, 53; and nationalism, 56, 185
Uniform Crime Reports, 210
unions, trade: in Tsarist Russia, 42; and women's welfare, 239
United Kingdom: crime patterns in, 216-17
United States: affirmative action in, 38; crime in, 218, 222; criminology in, 209, 210; education in, 119-11, 133; grain imports from, 85; labor force in, 235; no child allowance program in, 81, 82; population patterns of, 84, 231; receives Smolensk archive, 138, 146, 150, 154; stratification in, 90-91, 92, 97, 98, 247-49; support of Jewish emigration, 32; women in, 227-28, 231, 236, 238, 250
Urals region, 16, 53, 106
urbanization in USSR, 23-26; and crime, 213-16, 218; of ethnic groups, 27, 45, 54; and language shift, 50; and mobility, 110; and population growth, 66-67; and secularization, 200; and women's employment, 232-33, 236
Uzbekistan, 45, 74, 244, 246 (see also Central Asia)
Uzbeks, 12, 16-17, 45, 53

vestiges, crime as, 211, 212-13, 224
victimization, 218
village (see mir, peasantry)
violent crime, 216-17, 219, 221; and recidivism, 223-24
Volga-Kama region, 16, 53, 108, 153
VUZy: admission criteria for, 127-28; preparatory faculties at, 132, 134; "proletarianized," 115; social composition of students, 131-32

starosta, 140, 146
state crime (see political crime)
state farms, 141, 142-44
statistical handbook, Soviet, 4, 6, 82-83
stipends, educational, 120, 128
Supreme Court, Soviet, 210
Sverdlovsk, 110, 123
Sweden, 99, 200
Swedes, 16
Synod of Bishops, 195-96
Syzran, 121, 124, 134

Tadzhikistan, 44, 46, 74, 244, 247 (see also Central Asia)
Tadzhiks, 12, 17, 44, 53
Talantov, Boris, 196
Tashkent, 45
Tatar ASSR, 94
Tatars, 12, 16, 20, 28, 43, 47, 53
Tbilisi, 32
television, 169
textile workers: pension plan established for, 68; women as, 230, 236
theatre, 103
theories of Soviet society, 167-72
totalitarian model: and change after Stalin, 169-70, 186; in ethnic studies of USSR, 33; and Party controls, 173
Transcaucasus (see Caucasus region)
Trotsky, Leon, 92, 165
True Orthodox Christians, 186, 197
True Orthodox Church, 197
Tsars: and alliance with church, 187; and Russian Empire expansion, 16-17, 19, 41-42
tuition fees, 116, 120
Turgenev, Ivan, 154
Turkey, 16
Turkic language group, 13
Turkmen, 12, 16-17, 53, 74
Turkmenistan, 74, 244, 247 (see also Central Asia)
tutors for entrance examinations, 128-29
Tuvinians, 17

West, Soviet and Russian antagonism toward, 168
white-collar stratum in USSR, 89
Whites (in Civil War), 19
women: and abortion policy, 71; beliefs about, 240-50; change in status of, in USSR, 54, 247; and childcare responsibilities, 228, 229, 233-34; and crime, 216, 219-20, 223; in education, 239, and labor force, 66, 71, 76, 77, 97, 228, 230-33; Lenin on, 229; Lenin's views and USSR population, 150; Muslem, 245-47; and occupational segregation, 237-38, 243-47; and participation in collective, 146, 238, political role of, 239, 242-43; and population policy, 74; in professional occupations, 237, 238-39, 240; treatment in Iran, 139; wage differences with men, 236; work ideology, 234; work role of, 227-30
women's movement, 227, 228, 249-50
workers' faculties (*see rabfaki*)
working class: as allies for leaders, 241;

World Council of Churches, 199-200
World War II: and CPSU, 173; impact on Central Asia, 244-45, 250, and world population growth, 84

xenophobia, 168

Yakunin, Fr. Gleb, 196, 197
Yakuts, 16
Yermogen, Archbishop, 196, 197
Yugoslavia: decentralization in, 33, ethnic animosity in, 33; inequality in, 98

Zhirovitsy Monastery, 196
zveno, 147

educational forms after 1917 Revolution, 115-16; under socialism, 89

ABOUT THE EDITORS AND CONTRIBUTORS

MICHAEL PAUL SACKS is associate professor of Sociology at Trinity College, Hartford, Connecticut. He is currently on leave at Queens College, CUNY, and a resident scholar at the Russian Institute, Columbia University. He is author of *Women's Work in Soviet Russia: Continuity in the Midst of Change* (Praeger 1976) and *Work and Equality: The Division of Labor in Soviet Society* (Praeger, forthcoming). Dr. Sacks' present research interest is in the relationship between economic development and the age, sex, and nationality composition of the work force based on the 1926 Soviet census. He received his Ph.D. in sociology from the University of Michigan.

JERRY G. PANKHURST is assistant professor of Sociology and associate of the Center for Slavic and East European Studies at Ohio State University. He is also a member of the Board of Directors of the Society for the Study of Religion under Communism. With a dissertation concerning the Orthodox and the Baptists in the USSR, he was awarded a Ph.D. from the University of Michigan. Dr. Pankhurst has been on several study visits to the USSR, including a research exchange supported by the International Research and Exchanges Board (IREX). Current research interests include a comparative examination of the political impact of religion in the USSR and Eastern Europe.

RALPH S. CLEM is associate professor of International Relations at Florida International University, Miami. He received his Ph.D. in geography from Columbia University and is the author, co-author, or editor of several books and articles on social geography of the Soviet Union and the ethnic situation in that country.

WALTER D. CONNOR is chairman of East Europe/USSR Studies at the Foreign Service Institute, U.S. Department of State. He has published numerous analyses of Soviet and East European topics, including *Socialism, Politics, and Equality: Hierarchy and Change in Eastern Europe and the USSR* and *Deviance in Soviet Society: Crime, Delinquency and Alcoholism*. His Ph.D. in Sociology is from Princeton University.

RICHARD B. DOBSON is a national fellow at the Hoover Institution at Stanford University. Dr. Dobson has published numerous articles and chapters in books on education and status attainment in the Soviet Union and is currently completing a book on this subject. He received his Ph.D. in sociology from Harvard University.

MARK G. FIELD is professor of Sociology at Boston University. He is also an associate in the Russian Research Center at Harvard, visiting lecturer at the Harvard School of Public Health, and assistant sociologist at the Department of Psychiatry, Massachusetts General Hospital. His extensive publications deal primarily with medical sociology and the Soviet Union. He was awarded a Ph.D. from Harvard University.

RONALD A. FRANCISCO is associate professor of Political Science and Soviet and East European Area Studies at the University of Kansas. He is the author of "The SPD in East Berlin, 1945-1961," "The Future of East German Agriculture," and a coeditor of Agricultural Policies in the USSR and Eastern Europe. He earned a Ph.D. from the University of Illinois, Urbana-Champaign.

DAVID M. HEER is professor of Sociology and associate director of the Population Research Laboratory at the University of Southern California. Having received a Ph.D. from Harvard, he has previously held positions at the Population Division of the U.S. Bureau of the Census, University of California at Berkeley, and Harvard University. His many publications include After Nuclear Attack: A Demographic Inquiry and Society and Population.

ROY D. LAIRD is professor of Political Science and Soviet and East European Studies at the University of Kansas and founder of the ongoing Conference on Soviet and East European Agricultural and Peasant Affairs. He is a coauthor of The Future of Agriculture in the Soviet Union and Eastern Europe and To Live Long Enough: The Memoirs of Naum Jasny, Scientific Analyst. Laird has written The Soviet Paradigm: An Experiment in Creating a Monohierarchical Polity. He was awarded a Ph.D. from the University of Washington.

LOUISE SHELLEY is an assistant professor at the School of Justice, American University. She received an M.A. in criminology and a Ph.D. in sociology from the University of Pennsylvania. Having studied at the Law Faculty of Moscow State University while on IREX and Fulbright-Hayes Fellowships, Dr. Shelley has written Modernization and Crime and a number of articles on crime and criminology in the USSR. She has also edited Readings in Comparative Criminology.

DATE DUE

APR 1 2 1988			
DEC 1 3 1988			
APR 2 2 1989			
DEC 3 1 1989			
NOV 1 5 1990			
NOV 1 3 199			
DEC 1 1 1992